BOFFO!

BOFFO!

[
How I Learned to Love the Blockbuster and Fear the Bomb
]

PETER BART

EDITOR-IN-CHIEF

miramax books

HYPERION

NEW YORK

PHOTO CREDITS

CSI: Corbis
Lord of the Flies: Photofest
Blair Witch Project: Photofest
Real World: Time & Life Pictures/Getty Images
Mama Mia: Photofest
Batman: Photofest
Baywatch: Courtesy of Baywatch
Oprah: Time & Life Pictures/Getty Images
Cats: Time & Life Pictures/Getty Images
Godfather: MPTV
Snow White: Hulton Archive/Getty Images
All in the Family: Courtesy of CBS
American Grafitti: Photofest
Hair: Time & Life Pictures/Getty Images
Sound of Music: Corbis
I Love Lucy: Courtesy of CBS
Gunsmoke: Hulton Archive/Getty Images
Psycho: Hulton Archive/Getty Images
Casablanca: Hulton Archive/Getty Images
Life With Father: Photofest
The Best Years of Our Lives: Corbis
Modern Times: Corbis
The Birth of a Nation: Corbis (2)
The Big Parade: Corbis (2)
Ben Hur: Photofest
Easy Rider: Hulton Archive/Getty Images
King Kong: Corbis

ISBN 1-4013-5216-2

First Edition
10 9 8 7 6 5 4 3 2 1

CONTENTS

Acknowledgments

The depth and breadth of research required in writing this book would have been insurmountable if not for the help and encouragement provided by the staff of *Variety*. Special thanks to the following stalwart writers and researchers:

Josef Adalian
Justin Chang
Ann M. Donohue
Jill Feiwell
Lisa Horowitz
Nicole LaPorte
Denise Martin
Katherine Morfoot
Zachary Pincus-Roth
Patricia Saperstein
Michael Schneider

I owe a major debt of gratitude to Tad Smith, CEO of Reed Business, and Charles Koones, Publisher of *Variety*, for their support and encouragement in many areas involving not only this book but also the documentary *BOFFO!*, financed by HBO, which was prepared concurrently and which dealt cinematically with similar themes of pop culture.

I could not have had more superb mentoring in the art of documentaries than from Sheila Nevins, President of HBO Documentaries, her talented supervising producer John Hoffman, and Bill Couturier, who brilliantly directed the piece.

Special thanks, too, to J. C. Suares, my long-term friend, whose drawings and designs have contributed so much over the years to the success of *Variety* and who inspired many of the ideas and hypotheses advanced in this book.

And a special and unique contribution was made by Timothy M. Gray, the gifted editor of *Variety* and *Daily Variety*, without whose guidance, intelligence, and literary skills this book could never have been completed.

Apart from the help provided by present-day members of the *Variety* staff, I also owe a debt to several former "muggs" whose advice and anecdotes were immensely valuable. Two books about Sime Silverman, *Variety*'s founder, were especially helpful—*Lord Broadway* by Dayton Stoddart, published by Wilfred Funk in 1941, and *Inside Variety* by Peter Besas, former bureau chief for *Variety* in Madrid, privately published in 2000.

My assistant, Bashirah Muttalib, was also enormously helpful in marshalling facts, pages, interviews, and otherwise dealing with the daily chaos of the book, TV shows, newspaper deadlines, and other exigencies. And a special acknowledgment, to Phyllis Fredette, who stood by me and prodded me onward through it all.

Introduction

How I Learned to Love the Blockbuster and Fear the Bomb

The writing may seem chaotic. The kaleido-scope of news stories may seem jarring or even occasionally contradictory. The lexicon may range from the whimsical to the illiterate.

Despite all this, the pages of *Variety* over the course of one hundred years play out as a vivid (if not lunatic) diary of our pop culture. Indeed, it's more an opera than a diary—the unrelenting interplay of vision and greed, the strivings of the artists versus the hustle of the promoters. There are heroes, villains, and abundant Red Carpet histrionics.

On one level, *Variety* chronicles the obsessive search for the Holy Grail of show business: the mega–hits christened by the paper as blockbusters. Time and again those showmen who managed to capture the moment and conquer the audience somehow persuaded themselves that they'd discovered the magic formula for success—one that could be replicated on de-mand—only to find that their recipe, which worked to such perfection on first try, inevitably imploded on the next.

Thus D. W. Griffith, whose outrageous gamble with *The Birth of a Nation* resulted in history's most profitable film, doubled his bet with *Intolerance* and gave birth to a debacle. Walt Disney felt he'd found the Holy Grail with *Snow White and the Seven Dwarfs*, the first feature-length animated blockbuster. His next effort, *Fantasia*, all but capsized his promising em-pire. George Lucas felt quite vindicated when *American Graffiti* became the miracle hit at Universal after the studio had scorned his film; then *Howard the Duck* brought him back to Earth with a loud thud. Lucas's

Introduction

friend, Francis Coppola, following *Godfather I* and *II*, rediscovered reality in the form of *One from the Heart* and *The Cotton Club*.

A history of one hundred years of our pop culture unfolds as the saga of vast success followed by abject humiliation. It is a vibrant and lurid account of explorers smugly wandering the wilderness of the pop arts, hitting the mother lode and then self-destructing, never again repeating their success.

The story of these adventurers is as colorful as the tales they sought to tell. They managed to overcome their doubters, and the disdain of critics, to capture their prize, only to discover that the same hubris which carried them to victory, would send them spiraling to defeat.

They fit no set profile. The driving forces behind the blockbusters have been filmmakers, ranging from Griffith to Coppola; or actors, from Chaplin to Warren Beatty; or maverick producers, from Merian C. Cooper to Samuel Goldwyn; or writers, from Anne Nichols to Norman Lear. The principal trait they shared was their complete, unequivocal, uncompromising commitment to their vision.

The neophyte playwrights who devised two of the biggest hits in Broadway history—Anne Nichols and Jack Kirkland—believed so deeply in their work that they invested their meager savings in their shows; Nichols even borrowed money from the mob. The disdain of the critics was as irrelevant to them as it was to the creators of popular television who faced critical scorn with *All in the Family* or *Baywatch*. These "trail blazers" felt that they uniquely knew what the public wanted—and they prevailed.

Hollywood has always believed itself to be firmly at the center of the filmmaking universe; yet total outsiders have consistently been able to steal center stage. When Universal agreed to fund the nerdy San Francisco filmmakers who devised *American Graffiti*, it was more an inadvertency than an executive mandate. The studio didn't "get" George Lucas. No one at the studio was plugged into the youthful car fanciers cruising Main Street in Modesto, California. Indeed, no one quite understood why Lucas, or his friends like Francis Coppola, were so adamant about basing their lives and careers in or around San Francisco rather than networking at the studio hothouse.

In the same vein, Broadway wasn't hospitable to *Cats*. The power players of the theater world felt Andrew Lloyd Webber to be a rather oleaginous Brit whose music sounded more faux Puccini than pop. Surely he'd been foolish to mortgage his home in London to finance an over-budgeted musical about felines, whose lyrics evoked the poems of T. S. Eliot. Even after London audiences responded ecstatically to the show, Broadway was standoffish. Finally a Hollywood music producer, David Geffen, wrote the big check necessary to find *Cats* a Broadway home. After *Cats* became a runaway hit in New York, a veritable fusillade of Brit musicals migrated to Broadway, many of which failed to find an audience across "the pond."

Whenever and wherever a hit materialized, of course, promoters have poured money and energy into an effort to replicate it. Indeed, the history of show business is steeped in stories of sequels, remakes, and blatant rip offs that tanked upon delivery. Though the magic recipes were lavishly pursued, the soufflés consistently sank. *Life with Father* filled theaters for nine years on Broadway, but *Life with Mother* played to empty seats. Dennis Hopper thought he could recapture the magic of *Easy Rider* in *The Last Movie*, but his effort was stillborn. The twenty-somethings who appeared out of nowhere to create a mythic hit in *The Blair Witch Project* couldn't get a follow-up off the ground. *Casablanca*, to everyone's surprise, represented the perfect blend of jeopardy and romance, yet neither the studio (Warner Bros.) nor the filmmaker (Hal Wallis) could come close to re-creating it in film or TV. Richard Zanuck became the hottest young studio chief in Hollywood for backing *The Sound of Music*, but the success of the syrupy show ultimately reined in his career as an executive, when he sought to emulate the formula in *Doctor Doolittle* and *Hello Dolly*.

What all this demonstrates is that show business, in the end, represents the ultimate leveler. No matter how self-important the impresario, or how vast his financial commitment, failure is always lurking around the corner. Irrespective of how much wealth had been accumulated, or how many awards collected, every test will be just as severe, every performance just as demanding.

If power players and billionaires have found themselves frustrated by the whims of the marketplace, so have the self-styled arbiters of good taste. Time and again, the shows destined to change the tastes and tempos of our pop culture offended the prevailing critical and cultural establishment. These culture clashes have been ablaze in *Variety*, whose pages over the years have tracked "the numbers" as well as charted the reactions of the cultural arbiters. The upshot is that commerce and culture usually seem headed on a collision course.

On Broadway, the ability of *Abie's Irish Rose* in 1922, and *Tobacco Road* in 1933, to find fiercely loyal audiences for decade-long runs was an affront to the theater sophisticates, triggering gloom-and-doom assessments of the future of Broadway. Yet today, both plays would fit effortlessly into the prime time television schedules—a cross-cultural sitcom à la *All in the Family* and a switch on *The Beverly Hillbillies*. Similarly, the record run of *Life with Father* annoyed serious playgoers in the '40s, but it, too, was a precursor to *Dallas*.

The mind-bending success of *Mamma Mia!* in the '90s also prompted outcries about the future of the musical, but its ability to transplant itself to some thirty-three locations around the world (including Las Vegas) served as a clear signal that a new genre of cabaret-style songbook musicals had emerged and that pop music—in this case Abba tunes—which so appalls the cognoscenti lent an emotional underpinning to the format.

The same forces were in evidence in the early '50s when *I Love Lucy* was to change the face of a new medium. The early reception to the show was far from loving. For one thing, neither the network nor advertisers shared Lucille Ball's enthusiasm for casting her Cuban-born husband, Desi Arnaz, nor did they appreciate his business demands. Lucy and Desi finally took their act on the road, vaudeville-style, to prove to the "suits" that audiences would respond to them as a couple. The basic notion of filming a weekly sitcom before a live studio audience in Los Angeles (TV at the time was a New York-based industry) appalled TV insiders. In becoming a mega-hit, *I Love Lucy* demonstrated that the box in the living room couldn't sell tickets, but it could move products. And Lucy's clowning would prove a boon to advertisers.

Indeed, in the realm of film, the initial pitch of the basic storylines of most blockbusters proved unpalatable to financiers and distributors. *The Godfather* was deemed a bad risk because Mafia movies weren't "good box office" and because Francis Coppola's dynastic approach was thought to be too cerebral. The original *King Kong* was problematic because audiences would not empathize with a giant ape. *Snow White and the Seven Dwarfs* was a preposterous gamble because animated cartoons ran no longer than twenty minutes at most, and audiences would not sit still for feature-length cartoons. *The Best Years of Our Lives* didn't make sense because World War II was just ending and filmgoers didn't want to think about combat anymore. *Modern Times* was bad news because silents were fading out, and *The Blair Witch Project* was a documentary in search of a movie. That was the "first buzz," anyway.

The vital connection of story to zeitgeist has always been a pivotal issue for Hollywood. While studios traditionally have been eager to anticipate changes in audience tastes, they tend to be very bad in reacting to these changes. In the '60s and '70s when a large segment of the audience was caught up in the mythology of sex, drugs, and rock 'n' roll, studios were still offering staid period pieces like *Darling Lili*. A film like *Easy Rider*, from today's perspective, plays like a bad acid trip, but it magically captured the tempo of the moment. In the theater, *Hair* had audiences dancing in the aisles (and tossing off clothing) but the studios were releasing weary musicals like *Paint Your Wagon*, in which Lee Marvin and Clint Eastwood serenaded one another.

Hollywood, too, was confounded by the growing disconnect between budgets and box office. The orthodox thinking of old-line production mavens through the '40s and '50s was to lavish money on production values and star names. Yet, suddenly, glittering sets and wardrobes didn't seem to matter. Films shot on location, on minuscule budgets, started stealing the thunder. By the '60s, audiences were rallying behind renegade films like *Bonnie and Clyde* or *Midnight Cowboy*, which were made on relatively short schedules in remote locations. Even more puzzling, the success of these films stemmed from word of mouth, not the blasts of pricey ad campaigns.

There has been an abundance of examples in theater, TV, and film where the absence of money actually spurred creativity rather than inhibited it. *American Graffiti* and *The Graduate* are classic examples of filmmakers scampering for each shot and settling for two "takes" where others would have demanded twenty. The on-the-fly scenes created an energy and spontaneity that might not have been present after numbing repetition from different angles and against different backgrounds. The actors in "renegade" stage hits like *Tobacco Road* seemed energized knowing that their playwrights had invested their own money in the shows and even volunteered to take pay cuts to survive.

In television, one of the truly innovative series of the '90s owed its origins to an absence of money. The still-youthful MTV was eager to diversify its menu of music videos and felt viewers would welcome an idiosyncratic teen soap opera. Budgets for a scripted show of this sort, however, far surpassed what the network was willing to spend so producers "settled" for an entirely new kind of production, which became *The Real World*. A diverse group of attractive and exhibitionistic young people was planted in a house for cameras to record their every conversation and movement. The resulting confrontations, though occasionally stilted and tedious, nonetheless enticed a surprisingly wide audience, which clearly preferred spontaneity to script. The lack of budget worked to MTV's advantage (the show is still on the air after over a decade).

Given these and other inhibitions, the underlying reality about blockbusters is this: With few exceptions, they weren't conceived of as blockbusters. Rather, they represented (however misguided) their creator's notion of art. They often turned out to be tasteless, even vulgar, but they did not become legendary because committees of corporate "suits" sat down to conjure up a surefire mega-hit.

Not that they didn't try. In the period between *Jaws* and the *Indiana Jones* films, studio executives came to believe that so-called tentpole pictures (the studios' major films) could effectively be put on an assembly line. The feeling was that the Coppola–Lucas, hot-shot auteur era was phasing out. The vast new ancillary market of video was starting to open up. Overseas revenues were on the rise. Further, the maverick studio chiefs of the '60s and '70s—the Evans–Calley–Picker school—were losing power as their projects fizzled; they were replaced by television-trained executives like Michael Eisner and Barry Diller. Their corporate experience dictated that projects should not originate with writers or directors but rather with the network development apparatchiks, who supervised new projects and hired writers to implement their formulae. The Paramount of Diller, Eisner, and Katzenberg was especially active in this transfer of power. Tentpole movies like *Top Gun* or *Beverly Hills Cop* were nurtured by the studio or by producers very close to the studio. These were "high concept" movies that, to studio eyes, would be surefire commercial hits. Films like *Flashdance* were nurtured under satellite companies with the understanding that Paramount could pick them up if they looked promising. (After seeing the first cut of *Flashdance*, Diller and Eisner foolishly opted to sell off half their interest to reduce the studio's financial exposure.)

The concept of studio as creative czar never quite worked out. The studio hierarchs made as many bad calls as did their outside suppliers. Expensive script write-offs became commonplace. Further, the objective of replicating every success with a sequel showed ever-increasing futility. *Speed* was a big hit. *Speed 2* tumbled off the assembly line. *Jaws 2* was less than a thrill ride and *More American Graffiti* failed to get noticed. The studios were now amply staffed with eager young business school graduates raring to develop business models to emulate the success of tentpole hits, but finding talented filmmakers to implement these "success recipes," proved extraordinarily difficult. Though studios still excelled at marketing and distributing, they stumbled in the process of innovation.

Over the decades, to be sure, the hits have kept rolling in from unexpected sources. *Casablanca* struck Warner Bros. hierarchs as the wrong picture at the wrong time. Its script seemed sternly anti-Nazi, but the Germans weren't yet officially our foes. It was also a steamy romance, but its stars, Ingrid Bergman and Humphrey Bogart, disliked both the story and one another.

George Lucas never pictured *Star Wars* as the start of an empire. It was, for him, a personal film that probably would reach a relatively small audience. Indeed, when he showed his first cut to friends, all of them, except one, warned him that the film didn't work. The one exception was Steven Spielberg, who, upon seeing the raw film without effects, predicted matter-of-factly that it would gross $100 million. His forecast was low.

Francis Coppola backed into *The Godfather* full of doubts and reservations, knowing Marlon Brando was box office poison and Al Pacino was an unknown. In Coppola's mind, this would probably be an art picture; even the cinematography, like the casting, was aimed more at cinephiles than at the mass audience. Since he didn't want to shoot it to begin with, at least he would have the satisfaction of shooting it his way.

As Peter Guber, the studio chief turned producer, has remarked, "There are no rules, and you break them at your peril." All too often the breakage entails the loss of fortunes and the smashing of egos.

There's a certain delicious irony in the fact that it would fall to *Variety* to chronicle the games of the superstars and the mega-companies. The sensibility of *Variety*, since its establishment a century ago, was that of a workingman's journal. Its focus was on the ordinary hoofer, the comic, the working actor, even the working stagehand. Its basic vocabulary was a sort of self-invented "slanguage," a patois created by its reporters to reflect their sense of the street as well as to mask their marginal literacy.

The patron saint of *Variety* was neither a journalist nor an entertainer, but rather a tough kid from Syracuse, who, at thirty-two, had wearied of working in his father's "banking" business (i.e., as a pawnbroker) and felt a strong lure to show business. The lure must have been powerful, because when his weekly was launched with a $2,500 loan, there were already seventeen daily newspapers in New York and five established entertainment journals. Though his connections were as lean as his writing skills, Sime Silverman was determined to be his own man. He zealously resisted pressures from advertisers and fought periodic wars with the power players of his day, such as the Shuberts, B. F. Keith, and Edward Franklin Albee—theater owners and producers who did their best to put him out of business. Sime's stubborn independence sustained him through strikes, boycotts, betrayal, and endless litigation.

Given his street-fighter mind-set, it was no surprise that Sime tended to hire "street characters" (they called themselves "muggs") to do his reporting rather than literary stylists. His loyalties resided with characters like Jack Pulaski, who looked like a battered prizefighter, and liked to hold forth at the old Roxy Bar & Grill, attacking ticket gouging and other foibles of the rich and powerful. But his ultimate writing star was a onetime trolley car conductor named Jack Conway, whose review of Eugene O'Neill's *The Hairy Ape* began: "Coming out of the theater, all the peasants had a different version of what it was all about." Conway, who favored words like "palooka," "bimbo," and "gams," explained his literary approach in a *Variety* column as follows: "Slang has saved me from night school and made it possible to get my pennies without making weight for the erudite word slingers who are big leaguers in the three-syllable racket."

Variety's slanguage colored its headlines as well as its reporting. Among its most famous: "Wall Street Lays an Egg," about the 1929 crash; "Hip Nip in Hub," about a Japanese pianist succeeding in his Boston club debut; "Blitz Boffs Buff," about the impact of a snowstorm in Buffalo; and "Ruffled Hare Airs Rich Bitch," about irate complaints by playwright David Hare against Frank Rich, the critic of the *New York Times*. In researching the origins of *Variety*'s most famous headlines, Peter Besas, himself a onetime "mugg," found that "Wall Street Lays an Egg" was written by Claude Binyon, who later became a Hollywood director, while "Sticks Nix Hick Pix" was framed on July 17, 1935, by *Variety*'s esteemed editor, Abel Green.

While Sime Silverman staunchly stood behind his ragtag band of journalists, he never paid them well and rarely displayed special business acumen in running his company. In 1915, he took out ads in his own paper trying to sell shares of stock; he didn't sell a single share. He once bought a rival weekly, the *Clipper*, and tried to put *Billboard* out of business, but *Billboard* survived and the *Clipper* folded. A daily called the *Times Square Daily* started by Sime also folded.

In better times, however, Sime lived in style and relished the high life on Broadway, even starting an antique automobile collection. He dressed expensively, favoring dark brown suits and custom-made shoes. He conducted himself like a man of importance, making sure he was seen at key industry functions. At the same time he continued his occasional stints as a critic, favoring vaudeville, but occasionally reviewing a new movie, his writing always reflecting his just-the-facts mandate. He filed a review of a comedy titled *An Exciting Honeymoon*, commenting "The fun is amusing, the picture well-worked-out and the audience remained in its seats until the close." The movie was seven minutes long.

Throughout its early years, of course, advertising had been a key to *Variety*'s survival. Initially, the ads were basically pushing performers as diverse as jugglers, high-wire walkers, minstrels, animal acts, singers, and random freaks. Theaters bought space to proclaim the virtues of their particular venues. Booking agents trumpeted their clients, ranging from Major Bowes to Houdini.

Ads for silent films began to populate *Variety* by the mid-'20s, such as for *The Phantom of the Opera* starring Lon Chaney. Distributors realized they could use *Variety* to spread the word about the success of their films in specific markets, hoping to expand the contagion nationally and even internationally. This was, of course, long before the era of multiscreen release schedules. But it all meant valuable revenue for the newspaper.

By the late '20s and '30s, *Variety* had begun to earn wider respect for both its integrity and its stylistic idiosyncrasies. H. L. Mencken saluted *Variety* for being "one of the most fecund makers of American Slang." The *American Mercury* ran a piece facetiously praising Sime Silverman for setting "a world's record for bad English." Hugh Kent, the author, suggested that *Variety* writers drew their vocabulary "from the brothel, the race track and from bootlegging." Kent added: "*Variety*'s assaults on sound English are used with perfect naïveté."

It was in this period that the *Variety* glossary was expanded to embrace words like soap (daytime serial), ozoner (drive-in theater), oater (Western), kudo (award), blockbuster (big hit), boffo (terrific), tub thumper (press agent), praisery (a PR firm), legit (theater), and so forth.

Though macho in its attitudes, *Variety* occasionally displayed a curious prissiness toward pop culture. When the Shubert brothers opened a racy show in the '20s called *Artists and Models*, *Variety* responded with editorials attacking displays of nudity. The Shuberts filed a $100,000 libel suit against the newspaper, thus setting the pattern for a series of legal assaults lasting until the mid '50s.

As the entertainment business continued to evolve, *Variety* tried to readjust its news menu. By the '40s, the weekly that once covered minstrel shows now billed itself as the journal of "screen, radio, bands and stage." And as its critics fanned out to review the widening spectrum of entertainment, they always signed their reviews with the four-letter code that came to be enshrined as "sigs." The "sigs" sometimes were traceable—editor Abel Green signed his reviews "Abel"—but other "sigs" like "Ibee" (Pulaski) or "Rush" (Al Greason) bore no clue to the writer's identity. There was never any official explanation of this code, which dated back to a reviewer named "Skig," who, in fact, was Sime's seven-year-old son, Sidne. If the code worked for a seven year old, it could work for the rest of the staff.

Though *Variety* built remarkable reader loyalty over the decades, it nonetheless fell victim to the problems inherent in family ownership. After

Sime's death at sixty in September 1933, his company was left rudderless at a difficult economic time. Sime's son, Sidne, was frail and distanced from the business, ultimately dying of tuberculosis. The business side of *Variety* fell under the command of number crunchers like Harold Erichs, whose philosophy was to cut costs, not invest in the business.

It was the feisty editor Abel Green who energized the paper during this time and sustained it throughout his lengthy reign, spanning five decades, until his death in 1973. Green was a *Variety* "lifer," joining the paper as a hustling young reporter, ultimately taking over as editor when Sime's health began to falter. While Sime avoided publicity, Green loved the spotlight, regularly hitting the show biz "watering holes" like Lindy's and Dinty Moore's as well as the night club circuit. He dressed smartly, always sporting a bow tie. In true *Variety* tradition, he was notoriously cheap, rarely picking up the tab. He also zealously avoided dispensing either gifts or pay raises.

Colleagues found Green remarkably productive, generating story assignments while also turning out a considerable volume of copy, ranging from short news pieces to reviews. Through it all, Green maintained his reputation as a friend to the stars, his relationships ranging from Sophie Tucker to Groucho Marx, from Joe E. Lewis to Georgie Jessel. Jimmy Durante would drop by the office to chat with Green, and plug a new show, leaving with, "See you later at the Stork Club." Green used these contacts to insert plugs for *Variety* in films and radio shows, thus becoming a pioneer in product placement. Hence Judy Garland was reading a copy of *Variety* on the train in *For Me and My Gal*, and *Variety* was clutched by dancers through a key number in *Give a Girl a Break* with Debbie Reynolds and Marge Champion.

As a writer and editor, Green resolutely adhered to the precepts of the Sime school of journalism. The front pages of *Variety* were gray and packed with short pieces—as many as sixteen on page one alone, most a mere paragraph in length. "Fancy" writing was discouraged and reporters were warned to avoid "human interest" or other "puff pieces." Reviews, too, were written in a consistent monotone laced with slanguage, with the emphasis on commerce over art. When Green reviewed *Saratoga Trunk*, starring Gary Cooper and Ingrid Bergman, he noted that the movie "packs plenty of b.o. shekels for everybody. A cinch for the exhibitors, it's made-to-order film fare at a time when pure escapism is worth it's weight in marquees."

Abel Green apparently spoke in slanguage, as well as wrote it. If he didn't understand a reporter he would say, "You're talking in Braille." His sentences burst forth in fragments, reflecting both his nervous energy and short attention span.

When he died in 1973, the obituaries embraced vivid reminiscences from those who had worked for him. Vincent Canby, a onetime *Variety* reporter who became a film critic with the *New York Times*, described Green as "a man whose style was his total content." He continued: "Under Abel Green's editorship, reading *Variety* was always like browsing through an elegant flea market of information. You were as likely to learn the name of the next president of CBS as you were to learn that Walter Winchell, then in NY for a testimonial dinner, was having a dreadful time with his teeth or, as Abel called them, his 'chompers' . . ."

By 1956, the third Silverman, Syd, age twenty-four, had been anointed president of *Variety*. A tall, gracious man with a soft face and a quick smile, Syd presented a stunning contrast to his fiercely ambitious grandfather. Where Sime was "street," Syd was pure Princeton. Syd favored Dewar's scotch and was a committed family man who went home to his wife and kids every night in White Plains. Where Sime loved Broadway, Syd showed little interest in show business. He surely would have preferred the family business to have focused on golf or foreign cars (both of which interested him), rather than entertainment. But *Variety* was thriving in the '50s and Syd knew he'd do well to leave it alone. *Daily Variety*, which had been started in Los Angeles in 1933, was a solid enterprise, regularly turning a profit of between $2 million and $6 million a year. Its editor, Tom Pryor, was a stolid, humorless man who had channeled many of Sime's journalistic precepts—keep the stories concise, the salaries low, and the advertisers in their place. The newspaper was autonomous and colorless as well.

And Syd didn't want to change any of it, even when potential threats loomed. By the '80s, *Variety* had lost its clout in the area of TV coverage due to staff defections and the rise of competitive publications, such as *Electronic Media*. The weekly's gray pages that left ink on the hands of readers began to lose their relevance. Revenues from special reports were dwindling. Reporters and copy editors continued to hammer away on their Remington typewriters, but their office on West Forty-sixth Street looked increasingly like a Dickensian workhouse.

Clearly change was mandated—a new building, computers, a sharper design. Syd resisted them all. He even vetoed minor innovations, such as the start-up of dailies at the Cannes Film Festival (which post-Syd became hugely profitable).

Syd felt further pressure because three of his children were now working at *Variety* and *Daily Variety* and there was tension as to the emerging pecking order. Two sons, Michael and Mark, were diligent workers, but neither showed a flair for leadership to match their attitude of entitlement. A daughter, Marie, showed no interest in taking the reins.

Syd's decision to sell *Variety* in July 1987 came as a shock to the staff and even to Syd's children, but it shouldn't have. Though Syd never articulated the reasons for his decision, there were abundant clues: The weekly, by then, was losing a few million dollars a year, undercutting *Daily Variety*'s profits. New capital was needed to bring the newsroom and production into the twentieth century.

The most aggressive bidder, Reed Elsevier, an Anglo-Dutch company, seemed benign, and its executives, all straight-talking types, promised the family continued autonomy and offered them five-year contracts to prove it. The purchase price of $56 million exceeded the offers that had come from other potential buyers.

By selling *Variety*, Syd, a man who hated making decisions, further distanced himself from that responsibility. His kids would be serving a new corporate master and it would be up to them to prove themselves.

Of course, events didn't proceed as planned. Though the corporate executives from Cahner's Publishing Co., the American subsidiary of Reed Elsevier, were sincere in their commitments to the Silvermans, none was around long enough to follow through. Ron Segel, the president, died of a heart attack a year after the acquisition. Other executives involved in the discussions drifted away to other companies. Cahners itself changed its name to Reed Business and a succession of new executives arrived to oversee the affairs of *Variety*. The Silvermans found themselves confused and alienated.

I was brought in as editor of *Variety* by Robert Krakoff, a sharp, tough-minded publishing executive who succeeded Segel, and by a mercurial young deal-maker named Stephen Pond, who had been put in charge of resuscitating *Variety*. In 1989, Gerry Byrne, the founding publisher of *Electronic Media*, which had become a *Variety* nemesis, was named publisher of *Variety* and he and Pond promptly dismissed most of the advertising staff. New ad representatives were hired with the mandate to get out in the field and compete, not sit in the office and take orders. The habits of the past were to be banished.

On the editorial side, the Reed hierarchs made their expectations clear: They wanted a sharp new *Variety*, more expansive in its coverage and more accessible in its writing. Though I had moved back to New York to oversee the weekly, implicit in my mission was to consolidate the overlapping (and competing) staffs of weekly and *Daily* with the aim, not simply of cutting costs, but of expanding coverage and utilizing the staff more effectively.

The issues confronting *Variety* were not hard to identify: The newspaper's constituency had changed radically. Its readers were no longer the hoofers, but rather a vastly more sophisticated community of artists and artisans, both corporate and creative. The median income of a reader of *Daily Variety* was now $350,000 a year. The task, then, was to reinvent a *Variety* that would be at once a knowledgeable resource, but also, at times, a witty one. *Variety* had to become smarter, without losing its attitude and its slanguage.

It also had to deliver its information and insights more promptly and with greater efficiency. This meant building Variety.com, creating *Daily Variety Gotham* for New York readers, extending the reach of *Weekly Variety* overseas, starting a Chinese-language edition published in Beijing, and reaching further into the still-wider audience that radio and television provided.

Syd Silverman liked to keep an old framed cover of the *Saturday Evening Post*, depicting two ragtag vaudevillians; a folded *Variety* protruding from one of their pockets. The cover meant a lot to Syd and to his grandfather, Sime. But alas, the vaudevillians were no more; nor was the *Saturday Evening Post*; nor was the *Variety* that they knew and nurtured.

New era. New newspaper. But still a boffo show.

What follows, herein, are behind-the-scenes glimpses at the biggest hits of the past hundred years in theater, television, and film as seen through the lens of *Variety*. The voyage from present-to-past reveals recurring themes and also recurrent crises. The traumas of creating *The Godfather* were evident fifty years earlier on the set of *The Big Parade*. The "it can't be done" chorus that almost blocked *Lord of the Rings* was omnipresent sixty-four years earlier on *Snow White and the Seven Dwarfs*.

Many worthy academic tomes have analyzed the impact of the pop arts on our society. Virtually all agree that movies in particular infiltrate our psyche in remarkable and even insidious ways.

"Movies carry some sort of psychic charge that no other art form, perhaps no other spectacle, can quite match," observes Rutgers professor Colin McGinn in his book, *The Power of Movies*. McGinn makes a worthy effort to analyze "the metaphysics of the movie image."

BOFFO! However, has a far more visceral purpose. It examines how and why these projects got made to begin with, the various strands of popular taste (or vulgarity) they tapped into and how the unique visions of the artists (or perpetrators) were enhanced (or distorted) during the tortuous trek from the moment of "eureka" to the ultimate release. In short, this is a book about the down-and-dirty of the pop arts.

The process of selecting which "mythic hits" to focus on is obviously a subjective one. The aim is to spotlight the true milestones—the projects often underrated and overlooked that affected how the public thinks about entertainment—but, at the same time, to steer away from those shows that have been overanalyzed. Hence *The Best Years of Our Lives* is scrutinized, but not *Gone with the Wind*; *Life with Father*, but not *Death of a Salesman*. This book is not intended as an all-inclusive history, but rather as an entertaining micro-view. Hence, we apologize for the omissions . . . but not really.

BOFFO!

1 | Heroes in Capes
Batman (1989)

The experience of seeing *Batman Begins* in 2005 reminded me of the degree to which all superhero movies tend to blend together. Here was a movie that combined elements of *Spider-Man, Superman, Kill Bill*, the old *Shadow* radio series, the old *Batman* TV series and even a bit of *Doc Savage*. It was as if random pages had come flying out of old comic books to create an absurd pastiche of plots and scenes and random mayhem. Batman or Bruce Wayne, his true name, could scale buildings as skillfully as Spider-Man, change costumes as adeptly as Clark Kent, and disappear as instantly as The Shadow. He could even learn the arcane skills of Asian masters as deftly as Uma Thurman in Quentin Tarantino's *Kill Bill* mock-epics.

Whereas the classic superheroes were presented to us fully formed, Christopher Nolan, the director of *Batman Begins*, opted to present his audience with a bonus serving of pop psychology to explain the origins of the Batman myth—one that has extended through sixty-plus years of comic books, two TV series, and now six movies. This process involved a major conceit: Namely, that a little bit of backstory would reasonably explain why a man would choose to put on bat clothing, invest in a "Batmobile," build a "Batcave," and dedicate his energies to defeat the forces of evil, all because of a few childhood traumas. Having been dispensed all of this psychological insight, the audience is still left with the overriding reality that this is about a comic book character: Don't we have too much information?

The heavy helping of backstory also dances around another supposed distinction between *Batman* and *Superman*: Namely, while both favor Speedo-and-spandex wardrobes, *Superman* supposedly possesses supernatural powers while poor *Batman* is grounded by mortal limitations. While this is laid in rather heavily in *Batman Begins*, it does not restrict our hero from performing acrobatics of Olympian proportions.

When I was a kid, it was my assumption that comic books were kid stuff. My own involvement was rather peripheral. I vaguely remember picking up an occasional *Batman* comic and plowing through it, but the stories struck me as, well, comic-bookish. My need for wish fulfillment was apparently subnormal, or at least manifested itself in other ways, like walking girls home from school.

Those assumptions were incorrect, of course. At that time comics were being read avidly (but furtively) not only by teenagers, but by many adults, for whom supernatural powers and capes posed an exciting escape. This phenomenon persists into the present, but much more openly. Indeed, when curiosity took me to a vast ingathering called Comic-Con in 2005, I encountered a convention hall in San Diego packed with nearly 100,000 comic book "fanboys" (and girls), some of them well into their thirties, who relished sharing their avid loyalty to a range of comic book heroes. They were self-professed geeks—*Variety* called the four-day session "A Big, Fat Geek Wedding."

And an abundance of suppliers and vendors were on hand to exploit these odd passions. Some 1,000 booths peddled everything from masks to inflatable swords, from sabers to life-size "Darth Vader" statues. Also on hand were representatives from Hollywood studios touting mainstream movies, like the next *Superman*, as well as offbeat fare with titles like *Aeon Flux* and *Tenacious D in: The Pick of Destiny*.

The world of comic books clearly had morphed into a vast international multilayered business involving video games, DVDs, movies, TV shows, and all manner of gear. After all, imaginations had to be stimulated, wishes fulfilled, and wallets invaded—that was the overwhelming message of Comic-Con.

"What does the perennial popularity of superheroes tell us about our own society's needs and values?" asks Stan Lee, who as the head of Marvel Comics and the creator of some of comics' most enduring superheroes, including Spider-Man, is the Homer of the comicbook world. "Superhero writers and artists, like all creative people in every medium, have always, with surprising accuracy, reflected our society and the times we live in."

Talk to comic book creators and, as good storytellers, they'll start tracing their heroes back to biblical times. They'll tell you Sherlock Holmes clearly took to detection as a protest against the bland monotony of his existence and the need for—what else—wish fulfillment.

The birth of *Batman* in 1939 was more mundane. A company called Detective Comics (which later became DC) needed a new character to help sell comic books and hired a man named Bob Kane (later joined by Bill Finger) to invent him. They acknowledged that they wanted their character to be a bit on the weird side—"a weird menace to all crime," is the way they rationalized it.

From the outset, *Batman* seemed a bit odd and androgynous, but in crossing into television in January 1966, the character became more accessible, even user-friendly. It also became clear that he would never age. As if to emphasize the kinder-and-gentler *Batman*, the actors in the TV series conspired to create a campy movie version, which is still available in DVD.

The campy *Batman* was soon to fade, however, before the onslaught of film auteurs who were to create increasingly noirish versions of the legend on increasingly enormous budgets using increasingly intricate effects. Indeed, if there were indications of early neurosis in the *Batman* character induced by childhood traumas, this subtext was to become stranger in subsequent techno-dramas.

Batman, the movie, like most important properties, did not emerge magically from the studio development machine. Rather it was more like a sinister stew, simmering on some back burner but never quite achieving the focus of anyone's attention. It was as though somewhere in the studio's collective subconscious there was an instinctual recognition that *Batman* was not so much an inspiration as an inevitability. Hence no one was willing to put a halt to the seemingly endless succession of scripts and treatments that writers kept hammering out.

It was finally the team of Peter Guber and Jon Peters who determined to bring some focus to the *Batman* franchise. Having scored with films like *Rain Man* and *The Color Purple*, the producing team had "heat" at the studios. They also became alert to an interesting business opportunity: DC Comics, then a subsidiary of Warner Bros., had allowed the rights to the

Batman comic books to slip away; they'd fallen into the hands of a couple of journeyman attorneys who had not been able to do anything with the property. Guber and Peters, then operating under the name of Casablanca, wrote a check for $150,000 to tie up rights.

Breathlessly reporting this deal to friends at the studios, the producers encountered a surprising absence of interest. Universal, with whom Casablanca then had a deal, yawned and said, "We pass." Meanwhile, Guber got a surprise call. Frank Wells, the chief of business affairs at Warner Bros., wanted the project. In fact, he insisted on making a deal. Guber couldn't quite figure out why: Wells, who later became second in command at Disney, was not in any way involved with the production side of Warner Bros. A deal was nonetheless closed and Guber later learned that Wells's initiative did not reflect his own passion; rather he'd gotten an angry bawling out from Steve Ross, his überboss at Warner Bros.'s parent company, then called Warner Communications. Ross, it turned out, was furious that the rights to many properties owned by Warner Bros. affiliates had been allowed to drift away. Ross believed these various titles and logos, however obscure, would ultimately have a significant business value—even *Batman*.

The Warner Bros. deal, however, by no means translated into a quick production green light. Indeed, still further screenplays were developed at the studio with little progress. Clearly, the studio still didn't get it. Was it a kid picture, and, if so, why was its budget so lofty? Was it a horror picture, and, if so, why did its characters defy credibility?

Guber was an insistent and vocal advocate who brought superb salesmanship to every meeting. What *Batman* represented, he argued, was a business—a terrific business. The way to "sell" it to the studio, he concluded, was not through normal production channels, but through the anonymous bureaucrats at the back lot who had bottom-line responsibilities. He started to pay regular visits to the merchandising troops, who rarely saw a live producer. *Batman* merchandise could be a big winner, he pointed out. He dropped by the music department; *Batman* music could also yield big bucks. As Guber later recalled: "What I wanted to do was to motivate the circle of department heads around Warner Bros. to keep reminding the production team that *Batman* could be a hot commodity."

Guber knew full well, of course, that he would never get his green light unless he could bring some serious "elements" to the table. The term "elements" is a studio euphemism for name directors and stars, and Guber had some interesting targets in his sights. His first call: Tim Burton, who had just scored with *Beetlejuice* and, as Guber knew, was a long-term comic book fanboy. Also in Burton's favor was that he had just worked with Michael

Keaton, who, in Guber's mind, would make an interesting, if offbeat, Batman. Keaton had both energy and quirkiness. He was at once amusing and combustible.

Neither Burton nor Keaton gave their assent to Guber's entreaties, however. Both felt *Batman*, the movie, was a stretch—an expensive one at that. Their ambivalence was shared by Mark Canton, then head of production at Warner Bros., who served under Bob Daly and Terry Semel. By no means an intellectual, Canton liked the idea of a comic book movie. The possible Burton–Keaton combination, however, worried him, as did the prospective budget. (Canton was later recruited by Guber to be his production chief at Sony Pictures when Guber became CEO of that company.)

A final piece of theatrical casting was clearly needed, and Guber thought he could produce that component: Jack Nicholson would play the Joker. The studio had suggested other names for the "heavy"—Robin Williams and Tim Curry among them. Nicholson had much more weight than those actors, however. The problem was to lure him to the role. This would require face time with the director and, equally important, some creative dealmaking.

Guber and Nicholson were not close, but they shared a keen enthusiasm for the town of Aspen, Colorado, where both owned expansive properties. Learning that Nicholson was planning a hiatus in Aspen, Guber called the still-undecided Burton and said: "We're going to see Jack. We'll go horseback riding with him. I'll fly you there. Don't worry about a thing." Burton's response was quick: He had never been on a horse. Further, he didn't like Aspen.

Guber's recollection of subsequent events is as follows: "I persuaded Tim to sit on a horse. We went riding with Jack. We talked about *Batman* and Jack became more and more interested in playing the Joker. Tim later told me the horseback ride was more traumatic than directing the movie."

To secure Nicholson's commitment, two maneuvers were required. First, assurances would be given that his presence at the London location would be limited to three weeks. Second, he would receive a substantial gross participation in the film. As it turned out, both provisions would later be substantially revised.

Robin Williams indicated that he, too, had become a pawn in the Nicholson negotiation. When Nicholson declined to give a quick "yes" to the offer, Williams says he was approached to play the Joker. Nicholson was then told of Williams's interest and he finally acquiesced. Williams was bitter about "being used," as he put it, while acknowledging that this sort of leverage is not uncommon in the care and feeding of stars.

While Warner Bros. was treading ever closer to a green light, the Burton–Keaton combination was still being scrutinized warily. Raised in working-class Burbank, California, Burton's initial two films, *Pee-wee's Big Adventure* and *Beetlejuice*, had reflected his flaky, idiosyncratic personality. A movie geek, Burton admired the work of Vincent Price and director Roger Corman. After attending the California Institute of the Arts, Burton worked in Disney's animation department making short films and soaking up the studio atmosphere. These influences were revealed in his first film when Pee-wee Herman finds his lost bicycle and rides from soundstage to soundstage at a movie studio, passing through a hallucinogenic array of sets ranging from a Japanese monster film to a "Beach Blanket Bingo" movie.

Hence a Tim Burton movie, Warner Bros. knew, would be splashy, comic-booky, and probably a bit dark. Casting Keaton perhaps could ameliorate the "dark" element. Keaton had brightened up such films as *Mr. Mom* and *Night Shift*. His ego, however, was badly bruised when Woody Allen fired him during the first week of shooting on *The Purple Rose of Cairo*. Thinking about *Batman* now, Keaton was nervous that, if he tried to strike a superhero pose, the audience might laugh.

Keaton kept wobbling, even after Nicholson finally signed on. "I always wanted to do a movie with Jack, but I didn't know if I wanted to blow it on this one," he later said. "We didn't even have that many scenes together."

In the end, the lure of the superhero won out and Keaton signed his deal.

The studio was still nervous about the budget, however, which had edged toward $47 million as the start date drew near (it was ultimately to blow past $55 million). Studio executives were also uneasy about the dark look of the designs by Anton Furst, whose vision of Gotham was bleak in the extreme. Furst and Burton both were influenced by Frank Miller, the graphic novelist and designer whose *Sin City* series was later to develop a considerable cult following. Miller had done his version of a *Batman* piece and it was at once grim and claustrophobic. The character of the Joker was even more ghoulish.

Tim Burton didn't help things with his personal rhetoric. A man who enjoyed tweaking "studio suits," Burton during one meeting told Canton that he saw *Batman* as "a kind of Grand Guignol opera with Gotham City as an oppressive metropolis, crammed with urban decay and decadence, besieged by crime—what 'hell' would look like if it were a city." Neither thoughtful nor well read, Canton did not react with enthusiasm to "Grand Guignol" intimations—indeed, it's doubtful he knew what Burton was talking about. He nonetheless again phoned Guber to report that the drift of the project made him uneasy.

The several writers who had taken a turn at *Batman* also were cognizant of the studio's ambivalence. At one point, Sam Hamm, the writer of the moment, was instructed by a top studio executive: "Make it real!" This advice was conveyed with great urgency, which led Hamm to wonder, "Here's millionaire Bruce Wayne, whose only source of pleasure in life is putting on his mask, cape, and leather boots and going out to look for rough trade. That's an inherently absurd comic premise. So, 'make it real!'"

Long before Hamm, Tom Mankiewicz, who was a cowriter on *Superman*, had also prepared a *Batman* draft. Burton and his then girlfriend, Julie Hickson, had conceived a thirty-page treatment, which led to a further succession of writers including Hamm and Warren Skaaren. Commented Hamm: "Nobody could quite figure out what to do with *Batman*. The basic story is about a guy in the process of realizing what a fucked-up cat he is. It's the first script I've written in which the lead character is an overt psychopath."

The fact that *Batman* finally got a green light from Warner Bros. represented a triumph of salesmanship on the part of the producers, who convinced the studio that, artistic issues aside, the project was a smart business proposition. Ancillary rights would be sold, merchandise would be peddled, foreign audiences would be cajoled, the comic-book community would be supportive, and the money would roll in.

In the end, the studio shrewdly sensed that a new epoch of filmmaking was dawning—one in which studios would rely more and more on sequels and so-called tentpole pictures that would help support an entire program of films. Studios could not depend on sleeper hits emerging from the forest of development projects. They needed franchises, and *Batman*, if they got lucky, could represent just that sort of windfall.

The production in London was arduous. Tim Burton, while inventive, was not a natural leader who could resolutely move his company from scene to scene. Unlike Alfred Hitchcock, who could cut a picture in his head so that the number of "takes" he demanded was never excessive, Burton liked to shoot many, many takes, even if it meant falling behind schedule.

Keaton was all right with this sort of program. He knew his director's modus operandi. Kim Basinger, who was cast as Vicki Vale, also proved a collaborative performer. Besides, she was spending her free time in the company of the ever-volatile Jon Peters. That relationship, some felt, resulted in some added scenes for the actress. She had campaigned to be present in the final showdown in the tower, for example, and also kept telling Peters the film needed to focus more on the love story between Vicki and Bruce Wayne. Her suggestions proved to be persuasive.

As filming fell behind schedule, however, Nicholson became upset. Corralling the two producers in his dressing room one night, he shouted expletives at them for two hours, complaining about the hours required to apply his makeup, the sluggish pace of shooting, the lousy London weather, the fact that there were no basketball games to attend in London, etc. He said he had a solution to his dilemma: He was going home.

Guber remembers the scene: "Here was Jack, his face already distorted by the grotesque smile of the Joker, yelling his head off, the smile never leaving his face. It was surreal. It was noisy."

Despite his petulance, Nicholson managed to remain the consummate pro. He was not one to walk off a movie. However, he did win promises from his producers. Efforts would be made to speed things along. Further, his back-end deal would be improved to increase his gross participation. The upshot: Once the revenues were counted up, Nicholson's cut resulted in a $60 million payday, the richest any actor had received from a movie up to that time. (Tom Cruise's paydays on subsequent films were even higher, thanks to his first dollar-gross participations, as were Keanu Reeves's on *The Matrix* pictures.)

With *Batman* finally in the can, Warner Bros. mounted a ferocious ad campaign to support its hoped-for franchise. An iconographic logo was featured— an abstract bat that was emblazoned on all marketing materials. TV ads and trailers were ubiquitous, as though *Batman* were being injected into all the arteries of our pop culture.

The fans seemed to get it. Long lines greeted the first showing. The critics, not surprisingly, were less exuberant. Roger Ebert said *Batman* was "a great looking movie with a plot you don't care too much about." Vincent Canby, writing in the *New York Times*, commented that the filmmakers "have elected to avoid the camp style that made the *Batman* television series so popular twenty years ago. Instead they treat the material with a kind of Langian intensity that has no point. It's just there." *Variety* liked the film's commercial possibilities, singling out Nicholson for "stealing every scene that he appears in . . . a masterpiece of sinister comic acting."

Some critics took note of the profusion of merchandise that had accompanied the release of *Batman*: a *Batman* watch priced at $34.95, a baseball cap for $7.95, and so forth. There was also a *Batman* emblem that was sent free with any order of $50 or more. The *Washington Post* noted that "this is going to be the 'batblast' of the summer thanks to Warner Bros.'s jillion dollar TV campaign."

If the sheer intensity of the *Batman* foray bothered some, the basic tone of the film distressed a few loyalists. The *Los Angeles Times* ran a letter from one such fan complaining, "By casting a clown in the lead role, Warner Bros. and Tim Burton have defecated on the history of *Batman*." When the studio dispatched its representatives to the Comic-Con comic book convention that summer, their presentation was greeted with scattered boos. A front-page story in the *Wall Street Journal* challenged the entire marketing effort as an example of Hollywood overreach.

Despite all this, revenue kept adding up. The United States grosses rose to $251 million with overseas grosses totaling around $162 million. The merchandise was selling briskly and other potential sources, including video, seemed bountiful. "When you total up all the various revenue streams, *Batman* turned out to be a billion-dollar enterprise," Guber says. In the end, as the studio had hoped, it was indeed a superb business proposition.

Artistically, however, the *Batman* legend prompted mixed messages. Film historian David Thomson summarizes it this way: "The picture business has elected to regard Burton as a genius who brings children and teenagers into the movie theaters. Yet his two biggest pictures, the *Batman* pair, are strangely dark and slyly adult. They are not content with the comic books or the TV *Batman* of the 1960s. They can be read as very disturbing films—or might be, if they were better organized."

Christopher Nolan's *Batman Begins* seems to fortify Thomson's analysis. It tried at once for flair and action to please the kids, but layered in the "dark and slyly adult" strands to satisfy the mature audience.

And the attitudes of the studio seemed equally ambivalent. On the one hand, Warner Bros. yearned to protect its franchise by holding true to the *Batman* legend. That meant mandating thrilling "Batmobile" chases, acts of derring-do, and even a smidgeon of love interest. But Joel Schumacher, the talented filmmaker who directed *Batman Forever* in 1995 and *Batman and Robin* in 1997, remembers the many phone calls during production from his bosses. Their frequent interventions did not concern story or performance; rather they reminded the director to continue insinuating as many product placements as possible so that the studio could reap the benefit of tie-in advertising and other random promotions. In their minds, *Batman* was first and foremost an industry.

That was what Hollywood franchises were all about. The artistic stuff—well, it was sort of peripheral.

Stan Lee had a point when he said that our superheroes "tell us about our own society's needs and values." Except that he probably should have amended it to reflect "our studio's needs and values."

2 Abba Strikes Gold

Mamma Mia! (1999)

In January 2003, I decided that I had postponed the inevitable long enough. As *Variety*'s editor-in-chief it was my responsibility to stay abreast of pop culture. Yet the Abba musical, *Mamma Mia!* had been playing to sold-out houses on Broadway for a year and a half, and in London for over four years, and I had cowered at the thought of sitting through it. This was not so much a hit as an aberration, I told myself. And it was all about Abba music! The Swedes loved Abba, maybe even the Brits—OK, they were popular with the Aussies, too. But surely their oddly harmonized soft rock would not forever resonate on Broadway.

I admit to treating myself to a martini before the performance. I walked into the Winter Garden Theater feeling like someone who'd agreed to a blind date and knew it wasn't going to work out. I slumped into my seat, and buried my face in the program, not wanting to be recognized at this distinctly downmarket event. A stupid reaction, I told myself. A couple behind me was chatting it up, obviously delighted to be there. Two middle American, middle-aged ladies in front of me said this was the high point of their visit to New York. The theater was packed; the mood ebullient.

And now the show started. The relationship of performers-to-audience at most shows initially represents a curious standoff, especially on Broadway and especially with shows that have been running for some time. It's as though the audience says, "Strut your stuff! Show me!" Not this night at *Mamma Mia!* From the first appearance of the principals, the audience was applauding. From the first tune, it was singing. And by the second act, a few couples were dancing in the aisles.

For a moment I felt I'd wandered into the wrong place. This wasn't Broadway, this was Las Vegas! We'd all sing a little, dance a little, and then head for the slots.

Worse still, the exhilaration was contagious. My toe was tapping. I was laughing at jokes that were blatantly obvious. By God, I even liked the Abba melodies (although they all sounded alike to me).

Still pondering this the next morning, I noticed a press release from the Mandalay Bay Resort & Casino in Las Vegas. They had booked a $7 million *Mamma Mia!* production to play Vegas starting in February 2003. "Given that the content of the show is light and brisk, it has every feature that would spell success for the Las Vegas Strip," was the quote attributed to Glenn Schaeffer, the Mandalay president.

Finally Broadway and Vegas had found a happy convergence. It wasn't quite about theater, in the conventional sense. It was about a melding of the stage musical and cabaret. And it was going to work, big time.

In the succeeding years, *Mamma Mia!* would continue to fill theaters on Broadway and to pack the Mandalay ballroom, too. By the start of 2005, there were fourteen productions of the musical playing around the world to some 18,000 customers a night, generating $8 million a week in ticket sales. International companies were visiting places like South Africa, Estonia, Osaka, and—the ultimate triumph—were even planning to open in stolid Stockholm, with the Abba lyrics, originally written in English, finally translated into Swedish.

Mamma Mia! had broken all the rules of conventional wisdom in the theater. Primarily, it had revived a long-extinct genre of "songbook" shows, thus sending producers scurrying back to the works of John Lennon, Bob Dylan, and the Doors. (Ironically, *Buddy*, stemming from the songs of Buddy Holly, had been a hit in London starting in 1989 but hadn't made it to the United States.) It reminded everyone that the great divide between Europe and the United States in film and music may melt away in theater. Finally, it underscored the fact that a musical did not have to be somber in theme to achieve success on Broadway. In mood and tone

Mamma Mia! was the mirror opposite of *Les Misérables*, *The Phantom of the Opera* or *Miss Saigon*. There was no pretense—just show tunes.

The phenomenal success of *Mamma Mia!* also came to represent an almost operatic turn of fortune for the two women who conceived of and produced the show. By all standards, Judy Craymer and Catherine Johnson were losers at the high-stakes game of legitimate theater. Expelled from school at sixteen, Johnson was married and divorced by the time she was twenty-four. By thirty she was living on welfare with two young children and working part-time cleaning pubs. Then she won a playwriting contest that changed her life. She started picking up TV writing jobs and ultimately met Judy Craymer, who was struggling desperately to get *Mamma Mia!* off the ground.

Craymer, who was then working as an assistant to a theater producer, had recklessly incurred personal debts of $35,000 in her fruitless *Mamma Mia!* quest. Friends and colleagues repeatedly told her she was crazy, that Abba was passé. Craymer herself, who had grown up in middle class surroundings, never was a fan of the music. She was convinced, however, that the songs, woven together, would provide the framework for a poignant musical. Her problem was that no one agreed with her—not even the members of Abba.

The union of Craymer and Johnson was not one of winners. Craymer was not in a position to pay a prestigious writer to help her construct a play script. Johnson was not about to get hired to craft a musical.

Both women, to be sure, had the last laugh. No one knows the precise figures on their take, but Craymer pulls in roughly $4 million a year from the shows and has a 50 percent share of Littlestar, the company that produces *Mamma Mia!* companies around the world. Her fortune is in the tens of millions. She is now forty-seven.

Johnson pulls in roughly the same annual earnings from the show. Also forty-seven, she ranks up there with J. K. Rowling, who also was once on welfare, as the two wealthiest women writers in England. Speaking of Rowling, Johnson says, "At least she could afford to go to a café to work on her writing. I couldn't even afford that."

Love 'em or hate 'em, Abba songs are the motor that has driven the phenomenon to a worldwide gross of more than $1 billion, making it the world's number one musical.

Abba—a pop quartet whose name was formed from the first-name initials of members Agnetha Fältskog, Benny Andersson, Björn Ulvaeus, and Anni-Frid (a.k.a. Frida) Lyngstad—burst onto the international music scene when its song "Waterloo" won the Eurovision Song Contest in April 1974. They soon became megastars, not only in Europe but also in Australia; in 1975, Australia's Top Ten singles included five songs by Abba, and a year later, an Abba TV special scored more viewers than the first moon landing. "Dancing Queen" became number one everywhere, including the United States, and a 1977 world tour sold out in Europe and Australia.

Abba's popularity continued into the early '80s, but there were tensions within the group. The four were actually two married couples: Faltskog and Ulvaeus, and Andersson and Lyngstad. The marriages, however, weren't as smooth as the harmonies. Both couples ended up divorcing, the former in 1979, and the latter in 1981.

After the breakup of the band in 1982, the women returned to their solo careers. Benny and Björn collaborated with lyricist Tim Rice and book writer Richard Nelson on the musical *Chess*, which had a three-year run in the West End; a Broadway production, however, lasted only sixty-eight performances (and seventeen previews) at the Imperial Theater in 1988.

Judy Craymer, who still was working at Rice's production company, met Benny and Björn when she was an executive producer of *Chess* in London. And although she was more of a punk-rock fan in the 1970s and '80s, the idea of an entertainment built around Abba songs started to percolate. "I just knew those Abba songs had a story to tell. I was kind of fixated on it," she said.

When Craymer joined forces with writer Catherine Johnson, the two initially focused on a television movie. Craymer first pitched the idea to Ulvaeus and Andersson at the end of the '80s—but they were underwhelmed. "At that time, Abba was something in the past to me, something I thought would be completely finished and not remembered at all," says Björn Ulvaeus.

Craymer recalls, "I don't think if I'd approached Björn and Benny to use their songs in a stage musical in the first place, rather than in a film, I would have won them 'round. It took ten years to get this project going."

Strong sales for the *Abba Gold* album released in 1992 helped the cause (it sold 26 million copies), as did movies such as *Muriel's Wedding* and *The Adventures of Priscilla, Queen of the Desert*, both of which placed Abba songs to great effect.

"Several film treatments had been written by now, but Björn and Benny still hadn't said yes, so nothing had gone beyond its start as film or television," Craymer said. "I'd meet occasionally with Björn and Benny and say I was still keen on doing it. And they'd say, 'If you can find the right writer . . .' Which was their way of putting me off another year."

The breakthrough stemmed from an accident of timing.

Ulvaeus happened to catch a production of *Grease* in London's West End.

He immediately saw how a musical with Abba music would fly. "The show wasn't very good, but from it I could see the potential in an Abba musical: something fun, uplifting and above all, a lot of songs that people know," Ulvaeus said. "After all, the Abba music was far better than that of *Grease*."

In late 1996, Björn and Benny finally granted Craymer the rights to use the Abba songs and she set up a production company, Littlestar Services, with them and Australian producer Richard East. The two Abba women, Agnetha and Frida, took no interest in the show or in the women who fronted it. By 1997, Craymer had quit her day job to focus full-time on her musical. She persuaded Abba's record label, Universal Music, to put up about half of the £2.5 million capitalization for the West End production; Björn and Benny persuaded a Swedish bank to put up the rest—after all, they still represented two of Sweden's major resources.

"By that time, I had studied Abba songs forensically, and knew they fell into two generations—I knew it had to be holidays, it had to be weddings," said Craymer. "The story had to go with what those songs conjured up in one's imagination. I set out with [the idea that] these songs told a story, they took us on an emotional journey. Not in a pretentious way, but they made you feel good."

To be sure, Johnson freely admitted she, too, was not an Abba fan; growing up, her tastes ran to glam rock or punk—groups like The Clash and The Buzzcocks.

Craymer was discussing the project with Johnson over drinks one day when Johnson said, "What about a mother–daughter story?" And that was it. "It was kind of a steamroller after that," says Craymer.

"We wanted to make it very universal," says Johnson. "Abba songs cover two phases of relationships. There's upbeat, happy songs like 'Honey Honey' and 'Lay All Your Love on Me.' Those are very much about falling in love, what we call the 'young songs.' Then we've got the songs about disillusionment and the end of romance, songs like 'The Winner Takes It All' and 'Knowing Me, Knowing You.' Rather than telling a linear story from 'Honey Honey' to 'The Winner Takes It All,' we thought it would be more interesting to have an older generation and a younger generation. And, of course, you also hope then to be able to get a younger audience and an older audience."

The plot was simplicity itself: Donna, a single mother, lives on a Greek island with her twenty-year-old daughter, who's about to get married. The daughter reads her mother's diary and discovers that her absent father could be one of three men. Without telling her mother, she invites them all to the wedding in order to try to figure out which is her real dad. When they return to the island they last saw twenty years earlier, along with Donna's two best friends from her carefree younger days—with whom Donna was part of Abba-like singing group "Donna & the Dynamos"—the party begins.

Some media critics suggested that Johnson stole the plot from an obscure movie, 1968's *Buona Sera, Mrs. Campbell*, but Johnson denies that. Indeed, the movie involves American service men and, while it starts with a similar setup, veers off in quite divergent directions. The mother–daughter theme is conspicuously absent.

"None of us had a clue that it was going to be the success that it was," Craymer said. "[Catherine] didn't have a track record in musicals—she was regarded as a fringe playwright and had written for several TV shows—but that didn't matter. I just knew she knew what had to be achieved. And it was the same with Phyllida [Lloyd, the director]. I thought it amazing that Phyllida wanted to take a meeting about doing a musical. She's very well known for her opera direction and legitimate theater work. But it really appealed to her, partly because it's not particularly traditional—it is a play with music, it's not sung through—and she felt that it had theatrical themes to it, in the sense of lost parents, unrequited love, a *Comedy of Errors* set on an island."

In its own unpretentious way, Craymer believes, "*Mamma Mia!* is a landmark. It was the first major musical in years to break out of the doom and gloom, suboperatic mold of *Phantom* and *Les Misérables* and rediscover the joys of musical comedy."

Audiences apparently were ready for some sunshine. Within a month of its April 6, 1999, opening at London's Prince Edward Theatre, the advance booking period had been extended a year into the future, and by September 12, 1999, the box-office advance reached £8 million!

While the critics' response was mixed, insiders quickly sensed this was one show that was critic-proof. "Word of mouth got out that it was a fun show," Craymer notes.

In fact, there were a few "money" reviews: "It is funny and feel-good and keeps its tongue firmly in its cheek. The hits come thick and fast," said the *Daily Mirror* when the production opened.

The *Express* wrote: "What makes the musical—a tacky but ridiculously enjoyable wallow in some of the most mind-bending songs ever recorded—is the cheek with which each number is cued up. . . . The songs never stop. . . . It works and Abba fans will go berserk for it. So take a chance on me and go for a laugh."

The *Independent* declared that "Phyllida Lloyd's handsome production generates a terrific mood of airborne silliness. Abba is pop's pithiest palindrome and, whichever way you read it, *Mamma Mia!* looks like a hit."

The show went on to experience months of sold-out performances in London. "Actually, we weren't even meant to open in a theater as big as the Prince Edward," Craymer said. "Björn kept saying it should be smaller. But there wasn't a smaller theater available, and Cameron Mackintosh, who owns the Prince Edward, offered us the Prince Edward. I think people did think it wasn't going to be around that long. I remember Cameron saying around the opening, 'You'll be here for five years, dear.' And, of course, we were there five years before moving to the renovated Prince of Wales, which is gorgeous" in May 2004.

In London, *Mamma Mia!* recouped its entire investment in twenty-seven weeks. But still there was uncertainty at Littlestar about how it would play elsewhere. Abba had been huge in Europe and Australia, but less so in the United States. "Björn and Benny were like, 'You'll never take this to Broadway, you can never do this outside London,'" Craymer said.

The journey to the States and Broadway was almost inadvertent, Craymer explains: "There wasn't a kind of master plan to it."

The producers were offered Toronto by the group that controlled the Royal Alexandra Theatre. It wasn't Broadway, but the stakes wouldn't be so high and the audiences there are famously polite. "We were going to play six months and then tour into the States, starting in San Francisco, then L.A., Boston, and Washington," says Craymer. "About three weeks before we opened in Toronto, we had a discussion about staying longer. So we suddenly had two productions—we had the tour scheduled as normal, and we created a company that stayed in Toronto where it ran for five years. Then the tour went into the States, and Broadway still wasn't on the horizon, although discussions had taken place, and the Shubert Organization's Gerry Schoenfeld had talked to us about various theaters. So by the time we got into Broadway, we had an advance of about $20 million. *Mamma Mia!* just created great word of mouth."

Mamma Mia! thus rode into New York on an ocean of good buzz. Two weeks after it opened, it had already chalked up ticket sales second only to the mega hit *The Producers*. "It was an unusual road that we went on, and I wouldn't have changed it, really," says Craymer.

One thing that might have changed, looking back, was the date they opened in New York: October 18, 2001, over a month after the terrorist attacks. "It was a very difficult time. Another challenge or another mountain, in hindsight, that one should be opening a show at such a terrible time, a tragic time. But you had to go on. People had been employed, they would lose their jobs if we didn't. Everything was about carrying on, trying to get back to normality," Craymer says. "There was something restorative in its own small way that *Mamma Mia!* had that effect. People needed something kind of foolish and fun. I know the cast, everyone, was like, 'What are we doing?' Phyllida was very strong at the helm and saw people through that. It actually did help in the sense that Broadway is there to entertain people."

"It seemed inconceivable that we should even be rehearsing," says Lloyd. "It felt almost obscene that we should be getting our minds to engage with this show that seemed so far away and lightweight at such a terrible time. But when we opened, it was one of the first things that people who had been feeling very alienated actually felt like going out to see."

Or, as Craymer puts it: "I think it just says a lot about people getting up and getting back to normal. *Mamma Mia!* does completely take your mind away from possible distractions."

The critics agreed: The October 18 Broadway premiere was embraced as theatrical comfort food in the wake of Sept. 11. "A giant singing Hostess cupcake opened at the winter Garden Theater last night," said the *New York Times*. "*Mamma Mia!*, which weaves a few threads of romantic comedy around a bumper crop of old Abba tunes, is a thoroughly preposterous show, but it's also a giddy, guilty pleasure," said *Variety*'s Charles Isherwood.

The show's immediate success on Broadway led some to predict that it might run as long as its predecessor in the Winter Garden Theater, *Cats*. And *Cats*, which closed in New York in 2000, grossed more than $2 billion.

Now a proven hit in the United States, *Mamma Mia!* found itself wooed by a city notorious for its willingness to gamble on something new. "The other unusual path *Mamma Mia!* took," Craymer says, "was to be the first full-length West End show to open on the Strip in Vegas. Mandalay Bay wanted the full Broadway show, but we went out of our way to make clear that we weren't going to Las Vegas-ify it. It had no special effects. And it couldn't be shortened in any way," she explains. "It's not a particularly long show, but it did have two acts and an intermission, and it did have the curtain call at the end. And of course they're not used to that in Vegas."

It was something of a surprise hit in Sin City. The shows that become Vegas staples—think Siegfried & Roy and Cirque du Soleil—dazzle guests, then dump them at the blackjack tables. Stalwarts like *Fiddler on the Roof* and *Rent* had failed in Vegas; *Chicago* was a modest success, but with locals, not visitors. Says producer Rick Garman, "Vegas is not a place where you want to pay attention to plot." But *Mamma Mia!*'s plot was easy to ignore, which is why Mandalay felt it would be a hit.

And *Mamma Mia!* was rolling out around the world as well. As of December 2004, there were seven non-English-language productions running, including ones in Spanish, Korean, German, and Japanese. Johnson changed the script to reflect the country in which it is playing—so that the characters become German, Japanese, or American.

"The Germans and the Dutch were saying: 'You can't change these songs, we know them in English, translating them will ruin it,' says Lloyd. "But we felt that unless the songs and the dramatic scenes were in the same language, the whole thing would fall apart at the seams. And we wanted local audiences to feel the show was expressly written for them, so that they felt they owned it."

The success worldwide of *Mamma Mia!* has placed the two women who fostered it in a unique position. Sitting on income streams of $2 million a week, with no immediate reason to expect a downturn, Craymer and Johnson have an enormous business to manage and considerable fortunes to invest. "*Mamma Mia!* is my life," says Craymer, who now runs a company with 1,400 employees. "My ambition was that I would never have to work for anyone else again. I wanted the freedom to create projects on my own and not have to go cap-in-hand and that is what I have now done." Thus far, *Mamma Mia!* has not led to another major production, but the distraction of its many companies has kept Craymer more than occupied.

Catherine Johnson continues to write plays, has a TV series, *Playmates*, on Granada/ITV, and remains eternally grateful that she is not, nor ever has been, an Abba fan. "But when I sat down and read the lyrics, they led to the story," she reflects. "I didn't want to get hung up on the music. I wanted to feel the characters coming out of the lyrics. The music would have distracted me."

Her idiosyncratic approach somehow led her to find the strand that held the various songs and characters together. And that in turn led to her mega-hit.

All big hits leave their impact, but it's difficult

to assess whether or not *Mamma Mia!* will be regarded long-term as merely a freak of nature. The show clearly encouraged the development of a spate of so-called songbook or catalog productions, most of which did not light up Broadway. Producers went looking at Bruce Springsteen, Fleetwood Mac, Bob Dylan, and many others as possible sources. A show called *The Education of Randy Newman* made the rounds of regional theaters and the Queen musical, *We Will Rock You*, followed *Mamma Mia!* to Las Vegas with mixed reactions.

Even Craymer acknowledges the limitations of the catalog genre, though representatives of Neil Diamond, The Carpenters, and Dolly Parton have approached her. "It's far more interesting to find a pop composer who will write you a new musical than to go the catalog route," she says. The key to a catalog show is first to reach beyond the group's traditional devotees. "The fans will give you an instant audience," she points out, "but getting beyond those first few months is the real test. It's hard to get it right. There's no such thing as fast forward theater."

3 *Rashômon* in Mafia Land

The Godfather (1972)

The first time I heard of *The Godfather*, it was traveling under another name. A sixty-page manuscript called *Mafia* by Mario Puzo had been acquired by Putnam publishing, from a book scout named George Weiser, and he wanted to be sure I knew about it. Mind you, no special importance was attached to this advisory. *Mafia* wasn't a hot property. Moreover, Puzo was hardly a hot writer in 1969. His two previous novels had been accorded respectful reviews but sold few copies. Puzo felt himself caught in a literary no-man's-land: He had not gained recognition as a serious writer, though his novels were serious in theme, yet he also had not developed a Harold Robbins aura as a commercial storyteller. He had never even tried to tell a commercial story.

And that's where *Mafia* came in, Weiser told me. A tall, genial man who didn't take himself or his work very seriously, Weiser also occupied a no-man's-land. Having once worked for *Publishers Weekly*, he had managed to hot-wire himself into that arcane fraternity of subeditors, rights-peddlers, agents, and readers who made it their business to know the gossip of the book world. Each found his own use for this intelligence: In Weiser's case, he elicited retainers from producers eager to get a first look at promising film subjects. An alert producer who snared the right book could magically transform his meager option into a fat production deal at a studio. The book "buzz" was exchanged at bars and cocktail parties—this was well before the era of the Internet so there were no on-line buzzmeisters to short-circuit the intelligence work.

To be sure, most of the books Weiser recommended were scuzzy romantic novels or thrillers, but a couple of years earlier he had come up with a winner called *The Detective* for a young producer named Robert Evans. Written in 1966 by an obscure novelist named Roderick Thorp, *The Detective* was a genre cop story with vivid characters, and Evans knew exactly how to market it. Then thirty-six, Evans had made a few million dollars in the high-end women's garment business, and also had flirted with stardom in some Hollywood films, so he had both the savvy and the resources to make good on his investment. Having interested Frank Sinatra in the lead role, he marched on Twentieth Century Fox to demand a production deal covering several pictures. This was announced in *Variety* along with a photo showing Evans standing next to Richard Zanuck, then production chief at the studio, thus legitimizing Evans as a new player in the Hollywood establishment.

While Hollywood now recognized Evans as a "comer," the town still wasn't ready one year later for his surprise appointment as chief of production for Paramount Pictures; nor for his decision to hire me as his right-hand man. At the time, I was a West Coast correspondent for the *New York Times* covering racial unrest, politics, and the fast-changing landscape of pop culture— not exactly the résumé of a future film executive. I had gotten to know Evans through a mutual friend, Abby Mann, a screenwriter whose work included *Judgment at Nuremberg* and *Ship of Fools*. Indeed, I had even written a rather snarky piece about Evans in the *New York Times*, which had described the process through which Evans managed to leverage *The Detective* into a production deal. Years later this story took on a different connotation in the Evans legend; supposedly it had figured in the decision by Charles Bluhdorn, chairman of Paramount's parent company, to hire Evans for the top studio job. This version always struck me as amusing, if not apocryphal—no one had ever landed the job of studio chief because of a newspaper story, especially a snarky one, and Evans had by this time already ingratiated himself with Bluhdorn.

Given my new role at Paramount, *Mafia* landed on my desk first, but it didn't make its way immediately to the top of the pile. For one thing, Paramount had just released a movie on a Mafia theme, a turgid piece called *The Brotherhood*, directed by Martin Ritt and starring Kirk Douglas. The film served as a vivid reminder of why Hollywood Mafia movies had consistently failed at the box office. The story involved an abundance of surreptitious plotting in dark rooms, but there was nothing especially menacing or, indeed, especially Italian about the movie.

I had never heard of Mario Puzo but was impressed that his distinguished editor, William Targ, took the trouble to call and fill me in on some background. Puzo, it seemed, had only been able to complete sixty pages of what was to be a lengthy tome: a heavy gambler, Puzo had a wife and three children and had simply run out of money. The sixty pages represented more of a treatment than a novel; attenuated incidents were packed into the chapters that would ultimately be fleshed out in the full-blown manuscript. But Puzo wanted a deal; more specifically, he needed a deal, in order to feed his family while he finished what Targ promised would be a major commercial novel.

When I picked up the sixty pages that weekend, I remember that I urgently wanted to like them. After all, I felt myself to be a fellow writer who had suddenly become a Hollywood functionary, and here was a writer in need. So then came the relief: Puzo's work was riveting. Sure, some of it seemed disjointed, with scenes packed upon scenes, but the characters and the milieu were fascinating. I phoned Evans who, as was his custom, was entertaining a lissome model for the weekend. "You've got to read the Puzo material," I urged. "Don't be put off by the title."

It took a modest sum of money to option the book, but in doing so, it never occurred to Evans, or to me, that this decision would plunge us into intrigues almost as convoluted as those described in Puzo's novel. Before *The Godfather* was to run its course, the lives of everyone involved would be disrupted, their careers would be in serious jeopardy, and the president of Paramount would be fired. Indeed, in the end, it would be the Mafia itself who had the last laugh. Though "the boys" first opposed the movie and issued threats to Paramount for proceeding with production, by the end of the project they would briefly find themselves business partners of the very company they had threatened.

The mythic success of *The Godfather* has inspired many accounts of its troubled creation, and contradictions have inevitably emerged. Success has many fathers, as the cliché goes, and successful people (especially Hollywood people) are prone to exaggeration and self-congratulation. I have talked to key players involved in the various crises on the film only to come away with completely divergent versions of what transpired. This is true even of meetings I personally attended or presided over.

Hence in trying to reconstruct incidents surrounding the production of *The Godfather*, I have opted to let every participant have his say. Mind you, the specific words that follow are not intended to represent precise quotes—too many years have passed to attempt that. Rather, the intent here is to recapture the attitudes and cadences of key participants at that moment in time.

What follows, therefore, is a re-creation—with all the admitted flaws and confusions that a re-creation inevitably entails. In short, *Rashômon* revisited.

The featured players: Mario Puzo, the author; Francis Coppola, the director; Al Ruddy, the producer; Robert Evans, the studio production chief; Stanley Jaffe, the president; Charles Bluhdorn, the chairman of the parent company, Gulf and Western; James Caan, the actor; Dino De Laurentiis, the distinguished Italian producer; and me. At the time I was vice president for production, serving under Evans.

MARIO PUZO: Most of the people involved in the making of *The Godfather* were basically nice people, but they all tried to kill one another. I never understood why. Maybe it was the influence of the story, in that all my characters acted like criminals. Mind you, I never actually did firsthand research into the Mafia, even though everyone assumed I did. I relied on books and on my own imagination. I grew up in Hell's Kitchen, in New York, but the Italian people I knew weren't colorful or criminal or even particularly interesting. Maybe that's why the first books I wrote also weren't interesting. One character in my novel, *The Fortunate Pilgrim*, was tempted by a life of crime, but he didn't do much about it—so no one bought the book. One day I woke up and realized I owed $20,000 to relatives and was sick and tired of telling people, "I'm an artist." My wife was also sick and tired of hearing that. So I found myself writing a book that people might actually want to read. Francis Coppola later called it "a story about a king and his three sons," but I never thought about royalty—I thought about the down and dirty. I wanted this book to have sex and murders and all the stuff readers wanted to wallow in. I wanted to make some money. I never thought it would lead to all the craziness—to Frank Sinatra yelling threats at me across a restaurant, to Francis Coppola getting his butt kicked, or the real Mafia threatening to put me in cement if the word "Mafia" appeared in the screenplay (which was a laugh because it only appeared once, so it was easy to take out).

FRANCIS COPPOLA: I didn't want to direct *The Godfather*. When Peter Bart asked me to read it, I explained that a big commercial novel was not what I was looking to do. I saw myself as a writer and my aim was to direct my own material, not work off someone else's. But here was a major studio offering me a job; or at least it seemed to be offering me a job—when I met Al Ruddy and Bob Evans I could not figure out where they stood. The book hadn't been published as yet, but Ruddy felt it would be a best seller. He'd just produced a picture with Robert Redford and I knew the studio liked him. Evans made it clear he wasn't a fan of *Finian's Rainbow*, my last movie, which I'd just finished at Warner Bros., and that was not a surprise. I spoke with my friends around San Francisco—George Lucas and Walter Murch and all of them—they weren't in favor of my doing *The Godfather*, but they reminded me that I could use the money. In fact, I was broke, which was not unusual. So we kept talking and I met Mario Puzo. Who could not love Mario Puzo? Over time I met with the other people at Paramount and realized this was not a cohesive group. There was Charlie Bluhdorn, an Austrian who was brilliant but was always screaming; Stanley Jaffe, his uptight young president who liked to scream, too; and, of course, Evans, who kept reminding me that an Italian guy should direct *The Godfather*. Bart and I kept talking about the movie and it was becoming clearer that this could be not just a crime movie, but a family odyssey. This was a story of a father and his sons trying to transplant their family traditions and even their business structures, all within the context of American capitalism. Something resonated here. Something got under my skin.

AL RUDDY: When Bart gave me the novel and we began talks with Francis, I could see the movie coming together. But then the book got published and the landscape changed. Here was a novel by an obscure writer that was destined to stay on the best-seller list for sixty-seven weeks, selling a million copies in hardcover and 12 million in paperback before the movie even came out. And that's why Paramount went crazy. A small project that we were quietly putting together suddenly became a cause célèbre and everyone in the company had his own idea of how it should be done. Bluhdorn and Jaffe sent it out to every director they'd ever heard of—Arthur Penn, Franklin Schaffner, and Lewis Gilbert. Dino De Laurentiis and Carlo Ponti, who were great Italian producers, wanted to buy the rights—I think each of them wanted to play the Godfather, not just produce the movie. Burt Lancaster was pushing to take it over. And when Paramount's New York big shots learned that Francis wanted Brando and a young actor named Al Pacino to star in the movie, they went crazy. Here was the biggest novel in the world, and it would star a box-office loser like Brando and an unknown named Pacino. But this was where we all got lucky: The top directors miraculously were turning it down. They said the novel glamorized the Mafia and it was immoral. And Bluhdorn and Jaffe suddenly had run out of ideas, so Ruddy and Coppola didn't sound too bad to them after all, and Evans and Bart were still behind us.

That is, until the casting began. Jaffe, who was barely thirty, said "the Pacino kid" would never get the role of Michael as long as he was president of Paramount. We didn't realize that was an empty threat because Jaffe himself was soon to be fired. Bluhdorn ranted and raved about Brando being box-office poison. Evans wanted Jimmy Caan to play Michael, and suddenly every actor in the world was being tested for every role. Laurence Olivier was even being considered for Don Corleone, and Bluhdorn proposed Charles Bronson. Evans wanted to test Dean Stockwell and Martin Sheen for Michael. Even Ryan O'Neal! Coppola secretly tested his key choices again and liked what he saw. I was called to an eleventh-hour meeting at the Polo Lounge in the Beverly Hills Hotel to settle the casting issue. Evans got so angry he yelled that Pacino was nothing but an "Italian midget." Then he realized that Johnny, the real midget who worked at the Polo Lounge for years giving out messages, was standing right next to him and that he was offended. Evans slipped him a $20 and continued his rant.

ROBERT EVANS: When the novel itself became a celebrity, everything changed for *The Godfather*. I supported Bart's initiative on Coppola, and I liked the fact that Coppola understood the flavor of the piece—finally a Mafia movie that would seem really Italian. But now the whole world was watching *The Godfather* develop and I didn't want to do a little art film— even one that smelled of spaghetti. Al Pacino didn't seem to have the strength to bring Michael to life and the grosses of Brando's last movie, *Burn!*, wouldn't cover our tab for craft services. Francis is the sort of talker who could sell ice to Eskimos, but as a director he had zero experience on high profile pictures. I could have delivered the biggest stars in the world to *The Godfather*—Olivier, Dustin, Jill Clayburgh or Michelle Phillips for Kay (they all tested), and Coppola still wanted Brando and Pacino. When Pacino tested with Diane Keaton, it seemed lifeless. Francis was hiding in San Francisco and had no idea what was at stake here. The tests were going on and on and our movie was beginning to drift away. Olivier became ill, so that ended that possibility. A test was done at Brando's house—it was a cockamamie test really, with Brando standing there, looking a bit confused, and suddenly Francis says, "Let's tape it," and Brando, who was only forty-seven at the time, does something with his jaw and transforms himself into this aging Mafia chief and he's convincing. Now, we have to get this movie together, but Al Pacino isn't even available any more—he's about to start a movie at MGM called *The Gang That Couldn't Shoot Straight*. So I call my personal Godfather, Sidney Korshak, for help. Korshak calls Kirk Kerkorian and they have a conversation about a new hotel Kirk is building in Vegas and Kirk gets the idea that construction will go much more smoothly if his studio, MGM, releases Pacino for our picture. Suddenly Pacino is available for *The Godfather* and who gets the role in the MGM picture? Bobby DeNiro, who had also tested for the role of Michael.

The good news is that our movie is now together. The bad news is that Francis has spent so much time testing actors that he hasn't had time to prep the movie and scout all his locations. Bluhdorn and Jaffe are still yelling about the cast and I have a thirty-two-year-old director who's unprepared, starting a movie based on the most celebrated property in the world.

JIMMY CAAN: There was this craziness and confusion surrounding *The Godfather*. Every actor in America seemed to be reading for every part. I was going to play Michael, which was a good call. Then suddenly I was Sonny. The casting guy told me that, if I had tits, he would have let me read for Kay. The suits in New York didn't want Pacino and didn't want Brando and I couldn't tell whether they wanted Jimmy Caan, or who would decide or when. I thought the movie would never be made. Or maybe it would be produced with a weird cast, like with Redford as Michael and some real life capo playing Don Corleone.

One day I get the call from Coppola. There would be a sort of secret rehearsal in San Francisco and Pacino and Bobby Duvall among others would be there. He wanted me to come and read for both Michael and Sonny. I didn't give a shit, so I went up there and Francis's wife, Ellie, serves corned beef sandwiches and we're all together—all except Brando—and we're all getting along. I am comfortable as Sonny, or as Michael, and most important, I get a feeling that this is a real movie and a real cast. Francis is terrific. But as soon as I get back to Los Angeles, I hear that the suits had heard about the readings and were pissed off about them and that maybe the movie would be called off after all. I tell you, there was more melodrama in the preproduction than there was in the novel.

STANLEY JAFFE: From the moment I started at Paramount I realized that the atmosphere was one of nonstop turmoil. I also realized that, while I was up to the job intellectually, I was not prepared for it emotionally;

The Godfather

27

I'm not sure anybody would have been, and I was only twenty-nine years old at the time.

Charlie Bluhdorn was a brilliant deal maker, but his instincts about film were disastrous. In my first week he showed me a terrible, over-long potboiler called *The Adventurers* directed by a Brit named Lewis Gilbert. I hated the movie, but Bluhdorn loved it—he even told me his chauffeur, Owen, liked it, too, and that Owen had great commercial instincts. Bluhdorn insisted Gilbert be assigned to direct *The Godfather*. I was shocked; I offered him 'scale' (Directors Guild minimum) and fortunately he turned it down. I had been won over by the idea of Coppola and, fortunately, Richard Brooks and Larry Peerce, among others, had turned it down so Coppola had a fighting chance.

When it came to the casting process, however, I found out that I was being made the "heavy." When Coppola delivered his script, my understanding was that we were going with a cast of unknowns. Francis was not considered a top-rung director at that time. The first screen test I saw from him was of Al Pacino, who was an unknown. The test was flat. Jimmy Caan wanted to be Michael, and he was terrific, but Francis favored Pacino. The role of Don Corleone was up for grabs. Even the human resources guy at the company asked to test for it.

I was supportive of Coppola through casting and preproduction. Despite all the noise and frenzy, I saw dailies from time to time and liked what I saw. There was a bad patch early into the shoot when there seemed to be a plot afoot to make Francis look bad. Key elements were missing in the dailies. The editor, Aram Avakian, and the head of physical production for the studio, Jack Ballard, had turned against Francis. Avakian was fired and I yelled at Ballard to clear away the conspiracy stuff.

But then all the noise and anger on *The Godfather* took a back seat to my own problems with Charlie Bluhdorn. He was insisting that a particular actress be cast in the lead of another film, and I'm afraid my response was less than restrained. In fact, I probably yelled something about sticking the idea up his ass. We'd been having troubles, and that was the last straw. So Charlie asked me to give up the presidency and become executive producer of *The Godfather*. I told him I wouldn't assume that role—I had not been an intrinsic part of the film. So the irony of the story was that Brando stayed, Coppola stayed, Evans stayed, and I left. Years later, of course, I returned as CEO of Paramount and its parent company.

DINO DE LAURENTIIS: Charlie Bluhdorn and I had become friendly by the time *The Godfather* was coming together. I had delivered a big movie,

Waterloo, to Bluhdorn, which Paramount was distributing in North America, and Charlie was worried whether an American audience would take an interest in a period picture—even one on such a grand scale. Since I am Italian, Charlie talked endlessly with me about *The Godfather*. He was worried because many important directors had turned it down. I told him that, if he was that worried, I would be glad to produce the movie for him. It would surely be a hit in Italy. One day Charlie turns to me and says, "Dino, you should play Don Corleone." I took it as a joke—I am not an actor, though friends sometimes say I play a lot of roles in putting together my movies. But several of Charlie's executives heard his remark and took it seriously. Years later I still heard people saying, "Charlie offered Dino the role of Don Corleone and he turned it down." But that was never a serious discussion; in fact, I told Charlie that Brando should play the role. This somehow was reversed in the telling. I was quoted as saying Brando would hurt *The Godfather*. But no, Dino De Laurentiis was never intended to play *The Godfather* and never opposed Brando.

ROBERT EVANS: It was Dino who said that if Brando got the role of Don Corleone the movie would be dead in Italy. He was box office poison and he wasn't even Italian. As for Dino playing the part, in some ways he was the Godfather. He was a larger-than-life character in his prime.

STANLEY JAFFE: It was Bob Evans who said he would quit his job if Brando got the role. The line was attributed to me, but I heard Evans say it. I was there.

PETER BART: It was some form of predestination that Brando would get the role. All the threats and speech making about him was irrelevant. I have no idea who said what to whom—all I know is that it was set in Coppola's head and nothing could shake him. It was simply a given. It had also been set in Mario Puzo's head. It was simply a fact of life, so whenever the subject came up in meetings, I would tune it out. The movie god had anointed Brando for this role and nothing would change it.

AL RUDDY: Only a completely dysfunctional company would put a young director through an ordeal like Francis experienced. A director needs to know his studio is behind him when he starts a movie. He should have time to get his thoughts together. But Francis starts shooting and immediately things start going crazy again. He's got a shooting script that's 163 pages long or about forty pages longer than a normal script. In my opinion, 85 percent of the script is pure Mario Puzo. In later years, a myth developed that Francis Coppola reinvented the script, but, trust me, this script was mostly Mario. The first full day of shooting was officially March 29, 1971—the scene in the car that takes Michael and Sollozzo to the Bronx. We had actually shot one day the previous week in front of Best & Co. on Fifth Avenue to take advantage of snow flurries, but the snow naturally didn't materialize. Certain things became instantly clear. First, Coppola had not thought out his setups. Second, Gordon Willis, his director of photography, was so hostile toward him and just about everyone else, that he starts dropping lines like "You're misusing your actors" or "You don't know how to do anything right." That's in front of cast and crew. Francis and Willis had earlier decided that they wanted to shoot a dark, moody movie, but Willis's idea of dark is, like, midnight dark. When Evans and Bart and their production guy, Jack Ballard, saw dailies at the studio they thought they were still wearing their sunglasses—they couldn't make out the actors. Evans said he could neither see nor hear—Brando was mumbling his lines and no one could understand him.

Meanwhile, we're still casting our Mafia types while the real "boys" were making their voices heard. A group that professes it was protecting the image of Italian–Americans was telling us that we cannot shoot in New York. Apparently, they'd even raised money at a rally to stop production of *The Godfather*. At Bluhdorn's request, I met with their representatives and they were typecast perfectly for our movie, down to pinky rings and bulges under the arm. What it all came down to is they wanted the word "Mafia" removed from the script. Apparently, the Justice Department under John Mitchell had even ordered the word removed from official documents—it's all about defending their heritage. Now this organization had some class names associated with it—Colombo, Gambino, Profaci, and so forth—so they're making noise and Paramount was quaking. I met with four of the "boys" and even gave them the script to read. There's only one reference to Mafia in the entire script, which, of course, was once called *Mafia*. The lead guy took about ten minutes to read the first page and asked questions like, "What does 'fade in' mean?" Then he tossed it aside and says to his pals, "This looks good to me, right boys?"

I thought we were in the clear until I got a phone call summoning me to another meeting. I thought it would be with the same guys but it turns out there's a press conference going on and the group was making an announcement that a deal had been made with the studio allowing *The Godfather* to shoot in New York and the script had been sanitized accordingly. The next day Bluhdorn summoned me to another meeting—he was apoplectic that

Paramount had apparently caved to the "boys." "We should disavow the deal and fire you," said Martin Davis, a sour-looking guy who was Bluhdorn's number two. I'd already been taking heat from Bluhdorn because he felt costs were out of control—some of the tests for actors had been scheduled on double golden time over the Thanksgiving holidays, for example. But when Bluhdorn told Francis that I'd be fired, Francis saved my ass. He told Bluhdorn, "Al must stay on the picture. He can get it done."

Here's the rub: At the same time Bluhdorn was denouncing my deal with the Italian group, he was secretly in talks with Michele Sindona and some other miscellaneous hoods who wanted to purchase controlling interest in the Paramount lot. Bluhdorn was dealing with the top of the mob while I was holding the grunts at bay. It was all getting bizarre, but the picture was still shooting and I was still its producer.

FRANCIS COPPOLA: We shot some scenes that were too dark—that was an easy fix. Gordon Willis was difficult, but I learned to adjust to him, too. I'm not a yeller, but I guess I slammed a few doors and stuff. Brando was adjusting to his role and I felt he was brilliant. All this notwithstanding, it became increasingly clear that the studio wanted me out. Sure, I was working twenty-hour days and maybe I was a little paranoid, but I noticed that Aram Avakian, who was originally brought on as my editor, was now following me around and looking furtive about it, like he was tracking me, studying my movements. What this said was that Paramount wanted to fire me and Avakian was an easy and cheap substitute. He even told some guys on the crew as much. I figured, "OK, if that's the game, I keep shooting, I keep my head down and let them make the first move."

CHARLES BLUHDORN: I had made a mistake with Stanley Jaffe. He'd seemed like a very bright kid and I took a chance on him, but he couldn't maintain self-control. Whenever he'd start yelling, he'd get intense nosebleeds and it was ugly to watch. Marty Davis told me that he saw Jaffe staring at himself in the bathroom mirror early in the morning, chanting to himself "You're tough . . . You're tough." I don't know whether he really was tough, but I was beginning to doubt it. I called Al Ruddy into my office one day and I told him Jaffe was being let go and that I wanted Jaffe to become executive producer of *The Godfather*. Now, Ruddy's tough. Not only did he glare at me and say he'd walk off the picture, but he grabbed a fistful of Cuban cigars from my desk and left, slamming the door. I figure this picture is in enough trouble without destabilizing it further. We're getting a little art picture instead of a blockbuster, but, at least, I hope we can release it. And why does Evans keep defending this project? He had promised me a new kind of movie to change the image of Paramount. I knew I'd made mistakes at the beginning. I wanted the studio to make big musicals like *Darling Lili*, for example. I thought that Julie Andrews and Blake Edwards would give us a new *Sound of Music* and that Lerner and Loewe would give us a hit in *Paint Your Wagon*. I had to resort to some accounting magic to make the losses from those pictures disappear, shifting numbers to shell companies. Evans was right in telling me they were yesterday's movies, but at least they became yesterday's losses, even though the SEC didn't like the way I managed it. Fuck the SEC!

PETER BART: I couldn't believe it when I first learned that Francis was in serious jeopardy. The studio had messed with his head throughout the casting process and now, finally, he had some momentum. And who the hell was Avakian? An editor, not a filmmaker! Evans said he's sticking with Francis, but now there were new names coming out of New York. Elia Kazan might take over from Francis. I couldn't figure out who's generating this stuff—Jaffe? Davis? I'd thought of myself as a good newspaper reporter, but I was stumped this time tracing this story. Rumors like this tend to be self-fulfilling. Richard Sylbert, the art director, dropped by my office and he's a friend of Kazan's. I asked him about the rumor and he said he'd heard it, too—it was making its way around New York, and that was not good for the morale on the set. "The idea of bringing him in is ridiculous," Sylbert told me. "Kazan is too old to take over in the middle of a movie." I stared at him and said, "Richard, would you mind repeating that one more time?" I grabbed him by the arm and walked him down to Evans's office. As usual, Evans was on the phone, but I barged in with Sylbert and signaled that it was important. "What's going on?" Evans asked. "Listen to what Dick Sylbert has to say about Kazan," I said. Sylbert repeated what he said to me and Evans nodded gravely. "That's important to know."

After Sylbert left, I returned to Evans's office and asked again. "Is Francis going to get canned?"

"Let's just say there's some discussion," Evans said.

"You're being too subtle for me."

"I think Avakian or someone tied to him has been sabotaging the dailies," Evans said. "The way they're assembled—it's been rigged so that the scenes don't play."

"This sounds like a Mafia plot," I put in.

"Let's just say it's all very suspicious. Let's also say that I've got it handled now."

"Then let me say I'm very grateful. Francis can deliver. I know he can."

"And I know he can, too. I know it now."

So Francis wasn't fired. He fully expected to be. Everyone around him was certain he would not survive. But as things turned out it was Stanley Jaffe who would not survive.

AL RUDDY: Once there was an end to the Coppola-is-out rumors, Francis really hit his stride on the movie and the dailies got better and everyone who saw them knew this was going to be an amazing film. Not that there still weren't problems. Marlon was always a piece of work, but he was bonding with Bobby Duvall, who also was a piece of work. Pacino was getting it done, and Jimmy Caan was an excellent Sonny, though he resented the fact that he didn't have a bigger part. Even at the premiere he grabbed me and said, "My best work has been cut out of the film." That's Jimmy. My own relations with Francis were all right, but, as good a talker as he is, he never really tells you what he's thinking. Turns out he was angry at me over a couple of deal points. He wanted me to give up my "presentation" credit so he could have it, but I declined to do so. I'd been in this from the start—why should I surrender credit? He also wanted me to hire his dad to do the score, but I refused to lock him in. Nonetheless, Francis brought him to the Italian location along with the rest of the family.

When I dissolved my personal company, which was called Alfran (named for me and my then wife, Françoise; we were in the midst of a divorce), Francis learned about it and assumed, to my amazement, that the "Fran" in the company was him and that he would share in my points. He was not happy when I told him this wasn't the case. On the other hand, Francis knew I'd been loyal to him through the difficult times and vice versa, so when we reached the traumas of postproduction, our bond still held firm.

Francis wanted to edit the movie in San Francisco—that was very important to him—but Evans wanted him in Los Angeles. Evans finally let Francis go home, but on the condition that he turn in a cut of roughly two hours, fifty minutes. Frank Yablans, the head of distribution, who was soon to take Jaffe's job as president under Bluhdorn, went crazy. He insisted the picture would never play over two hours and twenty minutes. Still, Evans liked the longer cut. We struck a secret print of that cut, then Francis painfully created a shorter cut of two hours and twenty minutes. Evans ran this cut with Bart and then observed, "This shorter version plays longer than the longer version." He wanted to return to the longer cut and was gutsy enough to demand the release date be delayed from Christmas to March so the editing could be completed without pressure. He caught shit for that but he saved the movie.

Now there was still another round of melodrama about the final nips and tucks. Evans's back was giving him so much pain that he had a hospital bed installed in the editing room and spent day after day going over the movie, frame by frame. A gossip columnist described the scene—the stricken studio chief rescuing his movie. That column totally pissed off Coppola, who felt he had delivered a damn good movie that didn't need a rescue.

ROBERT EVANS: I knew there was greatness in this movie, but I also felt too many great moments had been shortchanged. I admit I'm a perfectionist, but I didn't want to edit this movie from a hospital bed. Yet, I became obsessed with the task of setting it all right, of wringing every nuance from the film. It became an eighteen-hour-day, seven-day-a-week obsession. I was never home. I knew this was hurting my relationship with Ali, [MacGraw, his wife] but too much sweat and blood had been invested in this film to surrender now. I was living a nightmare, but I felt something absolutely amazing was emerging from it.

FRANCIS COPPOLA: I'd given all I had to this movie and suddenly friends were telling me about these column items describing how Evans had locked himself away, recutting my movie—rescuing my movie. Did it upset me? Sure it did. And it went on for years. I finally sent Evans a letter—I sort of regret it now—but it was an instinctual reaction to the bullshit. "Your stupid blabbing about cutting *The Godfather* comes back to me and angers me for its ridiculous pomposity. I've been a real gentleman regarding your claims of involvement," the letter said. I guess it read like a cease and desist order, but this much was true: Evans was a big defender of the picture in its longer version. Another studio chief would have chopped it back to two hours and twenty minutes and it would not have been the film it turned out to be. Evans brought out the best in the movie.

PETER BART: There will never be any way of settling the disagreements over whose contributions were more important to the screenplay—Puzo's or Coppola's—or whose were more important to the final cut—Coppola's or Evans. There were other important players in the screening room as well—the superb editors Peter Zinner and William Reynolds. I was not in a position to judge the process because, even as Evans was focusing on *The*

Godfather, my job was to mobilize next year's movies. *Love Story* and *The Godfather* had given the company a new momentum, and I was determined to keep it going. Among the films in preparation were *Paper Moon, Don't Look Now, Lady Sings the Blues, The Longest Yard, The Parallax View,* and *The Great Gatsby*. There was plenty to look after.

I would drop by the cutting room from time to time, however, and Evans would be sprawled on his back running scene after scene. Now and then he would stop and rerun a scene for me. "This is where it was cut," he would exclaim. "Now here's how it plays out." There would be an added reaction shot, or a fleeting image of an actor delivering some further dialogue. The scenes seemed stronger and Evans was ecstatic. This was what he most loved to do.

True, I'd witnessed this process on other movies. *Love Story* required a major restructuring in postproduction; the entire story was reworked so that it was told as a flashback in the final version. Awkward dialogue scenes between Ali MacGraw and Ryan O'Neal had brought the film to a thudding halt, but they'd been re-edited to play, not on the actors' faces, but on falling snow or on the streets of Cambridge, Massachusetts. All these tricks helped mask the weak performances. Evans had obsessed about the cut on *Love Story*, and between his efforts and those of Arthur Hiller, the director, a crushing bore had been turned into a major hit. So, I knew Evans loved the editing process and I also knew he believed *The Godfather*, with proper nurturing—even perhaps overnurturing—could turn out to be a great movie.

Others in the company did not share that vision. When the finished picture was shown to Paramount's advertising and distribution chiefs, their reaction was dour. "Too talky," the foreign distribution guy told me. "Not enough action. It won't do much business in Europe." Said another, "It's way too long. Needs half an hour taken out of it."

Yablans, then head of distribution (and shortly to become president) knew what he had, however. His plan was bold: Instead of the usual limited release—the accepted approach at the time—*The Godfather* was put out in 400 theaters. And while some exhibitors wanted an intermission because of the film's length, Yablans's mandate was that the film had to play all the way through. Bookings at sixty theaters were cancelled because theater owners had insisted on an intermission. All this caused a considerable stir in the exhibition community.

Now that the film was in the can, Yablans, who had not been much help along the way, suddenly saw a way to capitalize on *The Godfather* to further his own career. The movie that initially had been a blight on everyone's future, suddenly had become a silver cloud, and Yablans, too, was riding sublimely on it.

MARIO PUZO: *The Godfather* created a new life for me. I was no longer a deadbeat starving artist. I was rich. I was a celebrity. I could get free suites in Vegas and gamble. I could rent a house in Malibu for the summer. My kids loved me again. Everyone wanted my next book and everyone wanted *Godfather II, III*, and *IV*.

AL RUDDY: Nightmares don't often have happy endings. Making *The Godfather* was all about a clash of egos. It was a hideous experience. But at the end everyone looked like a genius. Things like that don't happen in the real world. Just in Hollywood.

FRANCIS COPPOLA: I wasn't prepared for what happened when the movie opened. This was, after all, a movie I sort of backed into. I never thought, in my wildest dreams, that it would become the focal point of my life's work. That when I died, the obit would start, "Francis Coppola, who directed *The Godfather* . . ." It was weeks after the release of the movie before I came to realize *The Godfather* would forever distort my life. It would embellish and almost destroy my film career. It would make me a hero and a prisoner of my own mythology.

ROBERT EVANS: The premiere of *The Godfather* was the high-point and low-point of my life. My friend Henry Kissinger flew in from Washington through a blinding snowstorm. My wife, Ali, flew in from her location in San Antonio, Texas. Charlie Bluhdorn was aglow as never before. This was the movie that would give birth to a new Paramount. His dream of being a mogul had come true. But even as I danced with Ali, and I knew all eyes were on us, I also knew that my personal life was about to be shaken to the core and that the good times were now over.

PETER BART: Ali had been bugging me about *The Getaway*. It was a movie I'd been developing for Peter Bogdanovich and Cybill Shepherd. Then McQueen became interested in it. And Ali became interested in McQueen.

She wanted to get to work again. Evans had been less than an attentive husband. She didn't want to become an ornament to a studio chief. The premiere of *The Godfather* seemed like a bizarre ballet. Bob and Ali were dancing amid the glare of flashbulbs. They were the hottest couple in the world for that fleeting moment. They had it all—the looks, the money, the careers. He was going to glory in the success of *The Godfather* and she was going back to her location and to McQueen.

I looked around the room. Did anyone else pick up the subtext? Did real life always have lurid subplots, like movies? And couldn't these damaged lives be salvaged with one more rewrite, or one more week in the editing room?

4 Crime Gets Prime Time

CSI (2000)

Hit shows are the product of conflict—on the screen, and off. Often the conflict is at once intense, yet impersonal. The arguments brought to bear are emotional, not intellectual; after all, the end product, which lawyers like to call "intellectual property," is singularly nonintellectual. And all involved recognize that a mere shadow line separates success from failure—a line that is impossible to define or measure.

In the case of the massively successful television franchise, *CSI*, Michael Eisner, a man who'd always trusted his "gut" to predict audience response, did all he could to kill *CSI*. That put him in direct conflict with Jerry Bruckheimer, his most prolific film producer, for whom *CSI* represented an entry into the world of TV programming. On Eisner's side were several key executives he would soon fire. Opposing him within the Disney empire—but utterly smothered—was the key man who would become president of entertainment of Disney-owned ABC and who would turn it into the number-one network.

The conflict reached the point where Eisner broke a cardinal law of television: He withdrew financial support from *CSI*, even though the show had already landed a preferred slot on the CBS network schedule. Only some eleventh-hour shuffling kept the show aloft. And in the meantime, Eisner gave the green light to two of the most expensive movies in Disney history, which would be produced by none other than Jerry Bruckheimer.

If all this seems confusing, it's nonetheless reflective of the political cross-currents of studios and networks. Ever-shifting relationships each day affect decisionmaking in the areas of script development, casting, production, etc. In the case of *CSI*, however, the stakes were especially high. The key players sat atop the pinnacle of the power hierarchy. There were big chips on the table, both in terms of money and ego.

The uneasy alliance between Eisner and Bruckheimer was in itself a study in contrasts. Eisner is the prototypical Hollywood boss, loudly aggressive, often rude, a bully in meetings who can become smoothly ingratiating when it fits his needs. Bruckheimer by contrast is taut and controlled, a spare man who speaks in calm, clipped sentences, who rarely loses his temper and prefers walking away from confrontation. Where Eisner is gregarious, Bruckheimer is reserved; where Eisner is liberal, Bruckheimer is politically conservative. The two men have little in common except for the willingness to make accommodations when business dictates. Big business, that is.

Bruckheimer's biggest piece of business at Disney are the two sequels to *Pirates of the Caribbean*—two movies being shot back-to-back at a cost well north of $500 million. Bruckheimer is the overseer of these tentpole pictures and is supremely qualified. He possesses both the creative smarts and the online production savvy to create these pricey "tentpoles"—potential blockbusters that hopefully will prop up the studio's overall lineup of films. Eisner's film studio hasn't had a great run lately; the Disney CEO desperately needs a big infusion of revenue from these franchise movies.

Bruckheimer, to be sure, has also proven his talent at coexisting with difficult power players. For twelve years, his partner had been Don Simpson, a bombastic Alaskan-born misanthrope who was a brilliant pitchman-producer. Together they produced hits like *Top Gun* and *Beverly Hills Cop* at Paramount, with Simpson always presenting himself as the creative "idea man," as he put it, and Bruckheimer as the solid numbers guy and line producer. Simpson's presence was at once inspiring and bizarre. Often strung out on drugs, Simpson could be boldly innovative in his approach to filmmaking, yet also incoherent. Bruckheimer, a former ad man from Detroit, knew when to let his partner ramble and when to inject rationality into the discussion. But he never contradicted their carefully delineated job descriptions, content to put himself forward as the trusted numbers guy.

In 1996, however, Bruckheimer had finally had enough of Simpson and launched his own production label. Sadly, Simpson was to self-destruct nine months later, having lived and died by his own definition of the high-life. Bruckheimer's career was soon to burgeon as both an idea man *and* a numbers guy. And by 2002, it was clear that he would establish himself as a formidable force both in film and TV, matching, if not exceeding, the remarkable career of Brian Grazer, also a multimedia whiz.

It was in 1997 that Bruckheimer, having conquered the feature film world, hired Jonathan Littman, a skilled Fox programmer. Littman, who had worked on hits such as *The X-Files* and *Melrose Place*, would serve as head of the new Bruckheimer TV division. Bruckheimer had earlier made a deal at Touchstone, a Disney TV division, but met with meager results. An adaptation of *Dangerous Minds* for ABC drew warm critical response but didn't get viewers excited. A syndicated skein dubbed *Soldier of Fortune, Inc.* also did only fair.

In his new job, Littman initially set out to shrink Bruckheimer's feature hits into small-screen size, only to find it didn't work. "We tried too hard to take what we did in features and make it work on TV," Littman says. "The two genres are separate and distinct."

During his third development season, in 1999, Littman settled on the notion of doing a "murder mystery that skewed young."

Littman had read a script by a feature writer named Anthony Zuiker. A wildly exuberant and uninhibited denizen of Las Vegas, Zuiker had been paying the bills by driving a tourist tram at the Mirage Hotel. "I was going through coverage and I took home this script [by Zuiker]," Littman remembers. It was called *The Runner*. "It was extraordinary. It had characters that were fresh and it was written so well," he says.

In the fall of 1999, Zuiker and Littman finally met up. Littman says the meeting was "very funny"; Zuiker was animated but not that eager to do TV. His burning drive was to become a hot feature writer. "I'm still a frustrated feature writer who's having an affair with TV," Zuiker says. "On the small screen, you're getting your ass kicked every day."

Zuiker remembers being called into Bruckheimer's office. "I talked to him and Jonathan Littman. I said something stupid like, 'I wanted to do something forensic.'" Littman recalls: "Anthony started talking about how his wife's favorite TV show was *The New Detectives*. He wanted to do a scripted take on *New Detectives* set in his hometown of Las Vegas. I said, 'Great.' I don't think he realized that I had bought it in the room."

Before pitching the show to the networks, Littman and Zuiker first took it to Steve McPherson, the spirited young executive who was running Touchstone TV at the time. "It was a clean and easy show to understand," McPherson recalls. "There wasn't a high concept. Zuiker knew Vegas, and he had spent time researching the show. And he's a very animated pitcher, very engaging."

Zuiker returned to Las Vegas to bulk up a formal pitch to the networks.

"He did a two-night ride-along with the real Las Vegas CSI team that turned into a two-week ride-along," McPherson says. Now Zuiker, too, was mastering his forensics.

This further research, while invaluable, also caused *CSI* to come together late in the development process. The pitch meetings to the networks weren't set until November. By then they'd ordered almost all of their drama scripts for the next season.

Zuiker remembers flying into Los Angeles for meetings with Fox and NBC. "I got off the plane and Littman says, 'NBC and Fox have both cancelled because it's too late in the season.'" It didn't seem different enough to them." ABC finally found time to hear the pitch, because Bruckheimer had a deal with the net's sister studio, Touchstone. But Zuiker's pitch didn't go well. ABC said no.

Though CBS was also officially closed to new drama pitches, Littman had a good relationship with Nina Tassler, who at the time was head of drama development there. He decided to give it one more try.

Tassler remembers: "I was driving home on Laurel Canyon and Ventura Boulevard. Jonathan Littman and I were both on our cell phones. He said, 'Even if you don't buy it, I guarantee it'll be one of the most entertaining pitches you've heard.'"

Tassler decided to take time for one more meeting. "It was the last pilot pitched," she recalls. "We have between three hundred and four hundred pitches each year, and by the end, you hit the wall. Still, Zuiker was in perfect form. He spoke a mile a minute, gesticulating all over the place. He clearly had done an extensive amount of research. He was literally bouncing off the couch during the pitch."

Zuiker recalls being disappointed that his audience consisted only of Tassler and that more CBS brass weren't present. "I closed my eyes, and I told myself 'I've never pitched a show like this.' I was so mad that nobody, except this woman, would see me, so I kept my eyes closed the entire time. I opened my eyes only when she said, 'I love it. Go write it.'"

CSI, the thinking man's crime show, was a "go." But not quite yet. Zuiker's first draft of the script turned out not to be ready for primetime. "It was a very dense first draft," Tassler says. "And you had the science aspect, which was over complicated. We had learned from *ER* that the science shouldn't intrude on the storytelling." Tassler had been at Warner Bros. TV during the development of *ER* and recalled, "We had to go through a number of passes to make sure there was clarity."

Leslie Moonves, then president of CBS, had become aware of *CSI* by now. He knew Bruckheimer was trying to break into television and they'd had a couple of lunches to discuss it. Still, Moonves was concerned that Zuiker, Bruckheimer's writer, hadn't done anything of significance up to that point.

"Nina Tassler had said to me, 'Zuiker has a real interesting voice,'" Moonves recalled. Once Zuiker turned in his first draft, "I read the script and I liked it. I didn't love it. I thought it was interesting."

To Littman, the whole process was an example of "intelligent, but harried development." "This was a project that had no time and no money," he says. "But Anthony really listens to people and executes notes well. We turned everything around fast."

To be sure, whatever problems CBS had with the early draft seemed to melt away after actor William Petersen expressed an interest in *CSI*. Petersen's feature credits—including *Manhunter* and *Young Guns II*—had hardly made him a star. But Moonves liked Petersen and had been trying to interest him in a TV show for ten years. CBS had even closed a talent holding deal with Petersen to develop a project for him to star in.

Tassler had a hunch Petersen might cotton to *CSI*, so she called his agent and said the actor should hear Zuiker's idea. A meeting between Petersen, Zuiker, and Littman was set up in the tearoom of the Beverly Wilshire. It was spirited. "We were asked to leave at one point because Anthony was being Anthony," Littman says. Zuiker's animated style "didn't go over well with the maître'd at the tearoom." The meeting lasted four hours. By the end, Petersen was attached.

Petersen's early support proved to be crucial. When Moonves was mulling whether to green light *CSI* from script to pilot, a persuasive call from Petersen made a big difference.

Says Moonves, "Billy's call pushed me over the edge. He was very eloquent explaining why he wanted to do the show. He said to me, 'The reason I've been reluctant to do TV is because I like things that are a little bit off the beaten path.'" Moonves gave *CSI* the green light to pilot. It was the network's last drama pilot order of the year.

With Petersen on board and a green light to shoot, the next big obstacle was finding a director. The director is always key for drama shows because the style set forth in the pilot is generally copied in every subsequent episode. It was an even more important decision in the case of *CSI* because the show was trying to make murder mysteries hip and to attract an audience of young adults. Zuiker felt the visuals should literally take viewers into the evidence explored by crime scene investigators.

"We had a tough time finding a director," Tassler says. "We were holding out for Tony Scott, but he wasn't available."

Bruckheimer had a pick that predictably was more unconventional. The producer wanted to hire a thirty-one-year-old Brit named Danny Cannon. "Jerry said, 'I'd like to go with Danny,' and honestly, we had a bit of hesitancy," Tassler says. "He was new to TV and also to American audiences."

"We had to fight for him," Littman says. "This show wasn't a concept CBS was used to. Jerry wanted someone who hadn't worked much in TV, who would be energized."

Cannon's record in features had been spotty. Bruckheimer had liked a little film shot in 1993 called *Young Americans*. Cannon's second movie, however, was a flop starring Sylvester Stallone, the forgettable *Judge Dredd*. But, like Zuiker, Cannon brought an enthusiasm and fresh perspective to television. And CBS, though apprehensive, decided to take the shot. Cannon got the go-ahead.

Also keeping a nervous eye on the show was Steve McPherson at Touchstone. His company had been all but merged into ABC by this time, which meant an erosion of McPherson's power. But the young executive was committed to deficit financing (covering budget overages beyond a set limit) the show, if it got on the air. In fact, the CBS involvement was a sort of validation—it proved that even his corporate rivals liked his work.

"We were fighting for our lives as a studio," McPherson recalls. "To get some solid business outside of ABC confirmed we were really legitimate." To be sure, he had not yet elicited a reaction from his top executives at Disney, Michael Eisner or Robert Iger (himself a former president of ABC) to his cross-corporate involvement.

All this became moot, however, when the principals finally saw the finished pilot. They didn't like it. The problem, Bruckheimer acknowledges, was "we had simply made it too graphic. It was very strong stuff, but, frankly, it was also a bit disgusting." Compounding the problem was that Moonves had opted to view the pilot over lunch. At one juncture, he put down his knife and fork upon seeing a shot of maggots crawling out of a bullet hole. "They asked us to tone it down," Zuiker says. "There was no ambiguity about their orders."

Tassler, too, had some issues. "There was story confusion that had to be dealt with," she says. And early audience testing confirmed that what she called "the maggot factor" was a big turnoff. "I remember trying to determine how many maggots was the right number of maggots," she said.

Recalls McPherson: "In the first version, you had stuff that had never been on TV before, which was both good and bad. Everybody rolled up their sleeves, and between the first rough cut and the show getting picked up, there was a ton of development."

After several cuts, and many conversations between the network and producers, *CSI* was deemed to be in better shape. Audience testing had turned positive.

It was finally time for the most important screenings of all: the ones in May, just days before the networks set their fall schedules. And again, it was late.

"*CSI* was the last one we screened," says Tassler. "We were under the cone of silence." The "cone of silence" meant Zuiker, Littman, McPherson, and the rest had to wait to see whether their baby would be stillborn.

"We didn't have a sense of where it would fall," McPherson says. "It wasn't on the 'hot list' of buzz-worthy pilots. It was on the bubble."

McPherson remembers flying to New York the week before CBS made its decision. "On Saturday, I got an initial, off-the-record wink that the show was looking good." Then, the good news. "It was the day before CBS was going to make their announcement," McPherson says. "I got a call from Nancy Tellem (then president of CBS Entertainment). She told us it was on the schedule. We were flipping out."

Not only was *CSI* on the schedule but it was getting an almost perfect time slot: Fridays at 9 PM. CBS had been doing badly on that night, so expectations would be low. What's more, *CSI* had what was thought to be a strong lead-in. The show scheduled to air before it, at 8 PM, was the highly anticipated remake of *The Fugitive*. At the time, most insiders figured *Fugitive* would be a major hit.

McPherson was exhilarated—but what he didn't know was that his bosses didn't share his enthusiasm. CBS and Touchstone were officially paired up as coproducers of *CSI*, which meant Touchstone—i.e., Disney—shared production costs.

Now Touchstone's parent, Disney, decided to do something virtually unheard of: It told CBS it wanted out of *CSI*—a show that was already on the schedule. Michael Eisner claimed it couldn't make money on *CSI*, that the proposed budget was too high. Besides, dramas weren't performing well in syndication and international revenue was drying up.

Littman remembers a call from Moonves, "He was ballistic. He said to me, 'Do you know what your studio is doing?' I'm dumbfounded."

Nina Tassler agreed: "I was shocked. Something like this had never happened before in my experience. We were already on the schedule. I didn't understand it. I intellectually could respect the fact that it didn't fit their business model, but we were already so invested in the production."

Said McPherson: "I was stunned and embarrassed."

Few people know precisely what took place behind the scenes, but the now-accepted scenario runs something like this: Lloyd Braun, copresident of television at ABC, marched into Michael Eisner's office and argued that it was absurd that ABC was now effectively a business partner with CBS. The alliance would send the wrong competitive signals, he argued, plus the numbers didn't make sense. By the end of the meeting neither Braun nor Eisner believed *CSI* would prove to be a profitable series or find an audience.

Moonves, however, had come to the opposite conclusion. Indeed, his competitive nature was being put to a test. Following the Disney rejection, he set about offering it to different studios in town, including Paramount. He was pitching it with determination. Yet everyone turned him down. He began to consider the possibility of putting CBS itself in a position of deficit financing the series—an unusual step—when an unlikely ally turned up. A Canadian company called Alliance Atlantis had produced several television movies for CBS and was eager to get into the series business. *CSI* created an interesting opportunity: Not only was the show appealing, but the company would glean some favorable publicity from stepping in, including a banner headline in *Variety*'s MIPCOM issue (MIPCOM is a leading international television trade show).

Moonves liked the affiliation because, as he explains, "This gave us full control of the production." The friendly Canadians, it seemed, had agreed to become silent partners, leaving creative and business decisions to CBS and the producers. This posed a delicious situation for the network, since *CSI* was both expensive and intent on trying new ideas.

Thus, after all the turmoil, the show was set. The moment of truth was at hand.

CSI premiered on CBS on Friday, October 6, 2000, with very little fanfare. All of the media hype was focused on *The Fugitive*, the 8 PM show deemed a sure thing by most of the powerful ad agencies on Madison Avenue.

Critics were mixed in their reactions to *CSI*. Some were put off by the level of gore in the first episode. "*Murder, She Wrote*, this was not," said Laura Fries in her *Variety* review. "Just when police shows are going for bigger and bolder, action moviemaker Jerry Bruckheimer, master of the big bang theory, decides to get small. We're talking hair follicles and fingerprints; *CSI: Crime Scene Investigation* is a painstakingly detailed and sometimes stomach-turning look at the minutiae of evidence that the crack squad of the Las Vegas Criminalistics Department uses to track down bad guys. *Dateline NBC* and Fox's *Police Videos* might seem like a viable alternative to watching people crawl around a toilet bowl in search of toenail clippings."

Other reviews were kinder, but clearly, not many people had much faith in *CSI*—at least not in Hollywood. "They told us if we retained 85 percent of what *The Fugitive* did, we'd be a hit," Zuiker recalls. On the morning of Saturday, October 7, the key players on *CSI* did what everyone in TV does the morning after a big premiere. They called one of the networks' ratings hotlines to see what the Nielsen numbers were.

"I was at the Beverly Hills Hotel with my wife," Zuiker remembers. "We called the NBC hotline. We put it on speakerphone. We were in disbelief."

Littman also called the NBC hotline. "I called it, hung up and called it again. I said to my wife, 'We beat *The Fugitive*. And I called again an hour later to see if there were revised numbers." Not only had *CSI* held on to all of its much-hyped lead-in. It had actually bettered the 8 PM show.

According to *Variety*, *CSI* was the story of the night, building on its *Fugitive* lead-in by 54 percent among adults 18–49 and by 52 percent among adults 25–54.

While disappointed by the performance of *The Fugitive*, Moonves was pleased overall. "The good news was that in *CSI* we had a monster," he said. "We had something important."

If the executives at CBS and Alliance Atlantis were overjoyed, things were less exuberant on the Disney lot. Steve McPherson, who had been so supportive of *CSI* in its infancy, now could do nothing but look on in admiration as someone else held his baby. He remembers also calling the ratings hotline. "At first, I assumed that CBS had put on a two-hour *Fugitive* pilot," he recalled. "Then I realized I'd heard it wrong. The second hour ratings were for *CSI*. I was confounded but I sent those guys champagne."

Having established its beachhead, *CSI* rolled on to establish two other iterations. At age sixty, the taciturn Bruckheimer was to find himself the hottest producer on television, with nine shows on the air—all the while still maintaining his momentum in features.

For McPherson, meanwhile, who had been frustrated with his *CSI* experience, the story would end happily. He became president of the ABC Network at a golden moment. The extraordinary success of *Desperate Housewives* and *Lost* in fall 2004 ultimately lifted his network to the number one position—a turnaround that stunned the television industry.

Thus, even though McPherson didn't have *CSI*, he had the last laugh. And he also had the satisfaction of knowing that, amid all the fierce infighting of the TV programming game, his instincts on *CSI* had been correct.

In a business where you're always flying on your instincts, such validation is a rare and delicious reward.

J Bruckheimer and I were having lunch at The Grill in Beverly Hills, a fraternal Beverly Hills restaurant catering to top agents and producers. A good table at The Grill is considered a badge of recognition and Bruckheimer commands an excellent one. During the course of our lunch, a succession of major players drifted to the table to pay homage to Bruckheimer and to banter about his superb TV ratings. He received them with a certain forced conviviality. Though still reserved and cryptic in his small talk, success has softened his style. After twenty years in Hollywood, the sixty-year-old Bruckheimer has finally learned how to "schmooze."

Our conversation covered many topics. We talked about his one-time production partner, Don Simpson, who ten years earlier had died of a drug overdose. Despite their sharply contrasting lifestyles, and Simpson's swaggering ego, Bruckheimer had stayed loyal until the final six months of his life. At that point, Bruckheimer acknowledged, he'd simply "lost it"—Simpson's self-destructive ways had finally destroyed their partnership. And Bruckheimer had defied the expectations of many studio executives who has assumed that Simpson was the driving creative force and that his partner would never be able to sustain their company without him.

Though Bruckheimer had now reached the high point in his life, his tension was palpable. He had proved himself right on *CSI*, as well as another series, *Cold Case*, but two new shows were on the cusp and he was nervous about whether the networks would again flash the green light or shoot him down. He also knew that Disney's newly appointed President, Robert Iger, was nervous about the soaring production costs of the two sequels to *Pirates of the Caribbean*, which were shooting back-to-back. The decision to make these films represented a $500 million bet on one director, Gore Verbinski, as well as on Bruckheimer. Verbinski's previous film, *The Weather Man*, had just been released by Paramount to devastating reviews and meager box office results. It was a downbeat movie starring Nicolas Cage dealing with middle-age angst, and Disney's middle-aged studio executives were suffering acute angst as they realized that the fortunes of their studio rested on this filmmaker (Verbinski had directed the first *Pirates of the Caribbean*, which was anything but downbeat and grossed $653 million worldwide).

When I asked him about all this, Bruckheimer flashed his steely smile—the purposefully confident look of a combat pilot in those old Hollywood

World War II movies. Indeed, Bruckheimer gave every indication of believing in his own invincibility. He had just doubled the size of his production facility in Santa Monica, a structure he funded so that he could focus his activities near his home and away from the distractions (and supervision) of the Disney studio. He'd also just purchased a new private jet to ease the burden of his incessant travels to locations around the world. He also purchased most of a small town in Kentucky as a gift to his wife, who was born in Kentucky and spent much of her time there. Linda Bruckheimer is an accomplished novelist, and her books are set in her home state.

If Bruckheimer had been on a spending spree, this was dwarfed by the vast amounts of money literally pouring in from his film and television ventures. Indeed, his income exceeded $50 million a year.

"What are you going to do with all your money?" I couldn't resist asking him.

He seemed unfazed by the question. "I don't have to think about that yet," he said. "The big money from syndication doesn't happen for a few years."

"Get real, Jerry," I persisted. "Think philanthropy. Think palaces in exotic foreign lands."

Bruckheimer wouldn't bite. "I'm thinking network pickups," he said. "I'm thinking about bringing in *Pirates* on schedule."

"Don't you ever see it ending?" I asked. "Look at Michael Eisner. He pulled the rug out from under you on *CSI* and now he's in forced retirement. He's in exile from the very company that he built."

"He'll find something else to do," Bruckheimer snapped, as though closing that area of inquiry.

When the check arrived I tried to pay the bill. He yanked the check from my hand and plunked my credit card back on the table. "I'll take it," he said. "You just told me I had too much money."

5 The Hobbit's Big Payday

The Lord of the Rings (2001)

It's a debate that has long raged in cinephile circles: What was the bravest gamble in the history of filmmaking?

Gone with the Wind was an extravagant risk, but at least it was based on the most important best seller of the moment. *Cleopatra* essentially sank a studio, but it didn't start off as a gamble—it just went out of control. *Heaven's Gate*, in retrospect, seems high-risk, but its original (albeit bogus) budget was modest and its director, Michael Cimino, had just come off of one of the best-reviewed movies of the decade, *The Deer Hunter*.

Arguably, the biggest gamble was not a film, but a trilogy—*The Lord of the Rings*. Its director, Peter Jackson, was a relative novice; the financier committed to make all three films even if the first was a bust; the initial budget of $130 million was intimidating enough, but the trilogy ended up costing north of $330 million; the production entity, New Line, earmarked virtually its entire production budget to support the effort; and, finally, the original narrative was so intricate that it had previously scared away such formidable individuals as Spielberg, Kubrick, Harvey Weinstein, Saul Zaentz, and the Beatles, all of whom had dabbled with the project only to become intimidated by its magnitude.

The unlikely individual who was central to this exercise, Peter Jackson, hadn't had anything resembling a box-office hit. Nor had he directed any film of this scope. A pudgy, bearded, usually shoeless filmmaker, Jackson's guileless manner and New Zealand cadence can lead you to believe he's an innocent awash in a world too sophisticated and treacherous to accommodate him. But under that facade lurked an artist of vivid imagination, strong business acumen, and manic drive. Obsessed with *The Lord of the*

Rings, he withstood endless rejections and challenges that continued to arise throughout filming and beyond.

"One of the great assets that Peter brought to this was sheer stamina. He worked eighteen hours a day, seven days a week for five years. He had almost blind self-confidence," observes Robert Shaye, cochairman of New Line, the small and autonomous company (owned by Time Warner) that financed the trilogy.

To say the gamble on the trilogy paid off is an understatement. Released in 2001, *The Lord of the Rings: The Fellowship of the Ring* brought in more than $871 million at the box office worldwide. *The Lord of the Rings: The Two Towers* grossed $926 million. *The Lord of the Rings: The Return of the King* racked up $1.1 billion worldwide, making it the second-highest grossing film of all time.

And that doesn't even include revenue streams for DVDs, merchandising, videogames, television, and other sources.

J. R. R. Tolkien, the man without whom this cinematic tidal wave would never have happened, was a cult author who created a vast mythological universe of elves, hobbits, wizards, and monsters, complete with a new language, Elvish. While Tolkien was an expert and vivid storyteller, before Jackson proved otherwise his tales seemed too sprawling and metaphoric to be adapted to film. His universe was simply too daunting.

His books were published starting in 1954 in England, and the following year in the United States. They didn't achieve legendary status until a revised and enhanced edition was printed in the United States in 1965.

Tolkien was haunted by his experience as a soldier in World War I. "By 1918, all but one of my close friends were dead," he wrote in a foreword to the second edition. After combat in France, he returned to England and remained a professor at Oxford for most of his life. He wrote *The Hobbit* in 1937, originally as a story for his children. He spent fourteen years writing the darker, more complex *The Lord of the Rings*, which was conceived initially as a single work.

Though set in mythical lands 7,000 years ago, the books reflected Tolkien's effort to conjure up heroes who would challenge the evils of the twentieth-century world. Hence it tells the story of the young hobbit, Frodo Baggins, who inherits a magic ring from his elderly cousin, Bilbo. Frodo soon learns that the ring's original maker, the Dark Lord Sauron, is seeking the ring, which will enable him to enslave the people of Middle Earth. The solution: Frodo, accompanied by a wizard, an elf, two humans, a dwarf, and three fellow hobbits, must travel to the Crack of Doom and throw the ring into the volcanic fires.

Tolkien insisted that all this was neither allegorical nor topical. He merely wanted to tell "a really long story that would hold the attention of readers." To Vietnam War protestors and back-to-the-earth hippies, however, it was a revelation.

The author died in 1973, having lived long enough to witness the morphing of his books into mythic status and to grasp the ramifications of becoming a cult author. Tolkien's trilogy has sold more than 50 million copies worldwide and has been translated into twenty-five languages. Tom Shippey, a Tolkien scholar, has said Tolkien was amazed by the books' popularity, but that his fans also caused him increasing problems: "They came to gawk at his house or telephone him from California at 3 AM demanding to know whether Frodo had succeeded or failed in the Quest, and whether or not Balrogs had wings."

Mindful of the groundswell, United Artists snapped up movie rights in 1965, when the second edition came to the United States, but no one could figure out how to mold the material into a film.

Enter New Zealand-born film geek, Peter Jackson, who began making films at age eight and was influenced by fantasy epics such as *King Kong* and the works of Ray Harryhausen.

In 1986, the twenty-five-year-old Jackson, wrote, directed, produced, and appeared in his first full-length effort, *Bad Taste*, a campy splatterfest that became a cult hit at the Cannes Film Festival. His breakthrough film was *Heavenly Creatures*, distributed in the United States by Miramax. The 1994 film, starring a young Kate Winslet, was based on a true story of two teenage girls accused of murdering one of their mothers. The film features several sequences in which the girls slip into their fantasy world.

Jackson and his long-time partner, Fran Walsh, won a screenplay Oscar nomination for that film, and Jackson was invited to make *The Frighteners*, for Universal in 1996.

Following *Creatures*, there were discussions with Casey Silver, then Universal's studio chief, about Jackson directing a remake of *King Kong*. Jackson was affronted when the studio did a sudden U-turn and cancelled the deal. One reason was that Silver was nervous about *Mighty Joe Young*, another simian movie that was in preparation at Disney. Another reservation related to Jackson's inexperience with big films. (Eight years later, Universal would come back to Jackson on *King Kong*, offering an exponentially more expensive deal.)

Jackson thus learned that his tastes—and appetites—went beyond what Hollywood was willing to offer. He yearned to re-create Tolkien. And he told his agent, Ken Kamins, who then worked for International Creative Management, to secure the rights for him.

The problem was that Saul Zaentz, a septuagenarian producer who had made his money in the music business, still controlled the rights and had done little with them. Zaentz was an old San Francisco hippie and not particularly accessible to Hollywood agents.

But another plot was unfolding. When Zaentz was trying to levitate *The English Patient* in 1996, a major portion of his financing suddenly dropped away. Harvey Weinstein stepped in and now Harvey, who liked both Peter Jackson and Tolkien, was willing to intervene on the hobbits' behalf. Miramax would pay Zaentz $3 million and offer him a percentage of the gross in exchange for the rights.

Given this breakthrough, Jackson proposed making *The Hobbit* as a prequel. Following that, he would make two films covering the three books that comprised *The Lord of the Rings*. After lengthy discussion, Miramax proposed dispensing with *The Hobbit* and moving ahead with the Big Show— *The Lord of the Rings*.

Elated, Jackson returned to New Zealand and started writing with Fran Walsh, who was also the mother of their two children. Soft-spoken and shy, Walsh is better-read and wittier than her life partner, and also a disciplined writer. She, in turn, brought in her friend, Philippa Boyens, a playwright who was a devotee of *Rings*, but who had never worked on a script.

But Jackson instinctively knew that pages alone would not bring his project to life. He mobilized a squadron of some fifty artisans to create a reel of special effects to prove that *Rings* was indeed a viable undertaking.

Jackson was correct in his judgment. The projected budget soon escalated to $130 million for the two films. Harvey Weinstein by now was on the hook for $10 million in script costs plus his substantial investment in Jackson's new special effects facility. "I was absolutely passionate about bringing his project to the screen," Weinstein recalls. "Unfortunately I couldn't get Michael Eisner to share my passion."

Given the cost of Jackson's dream, Eisner, CEO of Disney, Miramax's corporate parent, had to sign on to the venture, but he made it clear that he simply did not "get" the project. Tensions already were rising between Eisner and Weinstein—an abrasive relationship that ultimately would lead to a bitter corporate divorce—and these tensions doubtless contributed to the standoff.

Still determined, Weinstein tried a different tack. Piecing together Miramax's solo backing plus substantial foreign pre-sales, he approached Universal with a new scheme: *Rings* would now be wrapped in with *King Kong*, with Jackson committed to direct both projects. Casey Silver, then production chief at Universal, seemed intrigued after several meetings, but grew nervous over the magnitude of the overall commitment. This was, after all, an enormous bet on a young, still-untried filmmaker. (Universal, of course, would ultimately make a much more generous deal for *King Kong*).

With the Miramax situation falling apart, Jackson's lawyer, Peter Nelson, and Kamins, his agent, informed Weinstein they wanted to try their luck elsewhere. The disappointed Miramax chief, always a stalwart negotiator, offered tough terms. He wanted his $10 million investment to be repaid within 72 hours of the signing of a possible new deal.

Weinstein also asked for 5 percent of first-dollar gross (eventually split with Disney) and executive producer credits for himself and his brother, Bob Weinstein.

"He insisted on such a tough deal, because he really didn't want to let the project go, and he thought no one else would agree to his terms," remembers Kamins, who felt that $10 million in turnaround fees and 5 percent of first dollar gross was an unprecedented request in Hollywood. "Most studios would ask 5 percent of the net, not the gross."

Kamins proceeded to take the screenplays and scripted storyboards, along with a temporary music score, to every studio in town. Meanwhile, Jackson returned to New Zealand to start work on a thirty-five-minute presentation film, investing $50,000 in preparing the materials.

Despite the effort, the major studios all said no. They liked the presentation, but were still scared of its scale.

The entire exercise thus came down to appointments with two semi-independents: Polygram, the British studio whose Working Title label had made *Four Weddings and a Funeral*, and New Line, owned by Time Warner.

Kamins was already looking around for other directing jobs for Jackson. "I could see that the studios just didn't think he had the experience, and some didn't want to pay Harvey's terms," said Kamins. "However the Polygram people had been very aggressive about *Rings*. Stewart Till was an enormous believer in its international potential. The meeting with them went very well, but then we got a call that blew us away. Polygram wouldn't be a buyer, after all. It seemed Universal was in discussions to acquire Polygram. They were frozen."

Thus when Jackson and his group walked into New Line's offices on Robertson Boulevard in West Hollywood, they knew this was the only game in town. They were at the mercy of this unpredictable little company, and its cochairman, Bob Shaye.

They had nothing going for them except their "visual aids"—the presentation film, an array of photos, a tentative budget they knew the company would challenge—and their passion. They fully understood what was lacking: Any form of cofinancing or completion guarantee—a commitment from a financial source covering possible costs beyond the existing budget. For any major picture, these financial elements were usually vital components.

Would Bob Shaye, a famously skeptical, tough-minded executive, go along with all this? "We were numb," said Kamins.

Shaye himself was a quirky, unpredictable man. A skilled attorney and serious art collector who could schmooze both bankers and artists, Shaye also was a man given to petulant outbreaks. He could switch from friendly philanthropist to confrontational studio boss at a moment's notice, often catching colleagues and filmmakers off balance.

He had founded New Line in 1967 to distribute low-budget films like *Reefer Madness* and *Pink Flamingos* to college campuses and art houses, and he had built a reputation for cost-effective productions. But Shaye was also a maverick who went on instinct: He was impressed by Jackson's presentation reel. He also felt he could offset some of his risks by lining up advances from foreign distributors.

Most important, he was impressed by Jackson. Shaye felt that the New Zealander's background as an independent filmmaker would help him bring in the project as efficiently as possible. "I knew that the guy didn't have the experience, which he clearly didn't, but I very much liked *Heavenly Creatures*. It showed how to bring fantasy and reality together, and I believed that our people could give him the proper support to bring it off, even if he faltered," said Shaye.

New Line at this moment was urgently looking for another franchise to follow the lucrative *Nightmare on Elm Street* and *Austin Powers* films. The company had tried to develop Isaac Asimov's *Foundation* for a year and a half, but it had fallen apart. Attempts to make sequels to hits like *The Mask* and *Dumb and Dumber* also proved frustrating. But here was a filmmaker offering built-in sequels.

When Shaye summoned Jackson alone into his office for a one-on-one conversation, Kamins, left in the waiting room, wondered if he was trying to let him down gently or even proposing another project to direct. An aide of Shaye's, Mark Ordesky, who had known Jackson for ten years, warned Kamins that if the famously abrupt Shaye wasn't interested in a project, he could abruptly switch off a tape after five minutes and bring the meeting to a quick, and rude, close. In actuality, all Shaye was doing alone in the room with Jackson was assuring him that if things worked out, fine, but if not, nothing personal.

Shaye finally finished his one-on-one and called everyone in. The tape began. "We were nervously waiting for him to switch it off at any point," Kamins recalls. "Then Shaye suddenly said, 'Why are you making two movies? Aren't there three books? Why don't you make three?'" The clouds had suddenly parted.

Miramax and New Line lawyers began negotiating. A few weeks later, a deal was hammered out. On August 24, 1998, New Line issued a press release announcing the trilogy, saying the films would be released as a Christmas-summer-Christmas series during the 2000–2001 calendar year.

Most in Hollywood were astonished. *Variety* reported on August 31, 1998, that New Line had set the budget at $130 million for the three films. The article pointed out that Jackson hadn't made a film since *The Frighteners*, which grossed a disappointing $16 million.

New Line quickly reminded everyone that the trilogy would not get an official green light until its production executives flew to New Zealand and carefully reviewed what they thought the production would actually cost. Translated, this meant that the company also wanted more time to take the temperature among foreign distributors. New Line was adept at the art of preselling films to foreign markets. Rolf Mittweg, New Line's chief of marketing and distribution, a two-decade veteran of the sometimes brutal foreign sales business, guessed international subdistributors might ultimately provide about 60 percent of the production costs. Another 10 percent of the budget would come from merchandising rights. Tax incentives from New Zealand would also kick in.

Aside from tax incentives, New Zealand was the perfect setting for Tolkien's tales. The untouched virgin landscape encompassed snowcapped mountains, volcanoes, rivers, lakes, deserts, and rolling green hills. But New Zealand was thousands of miles away from New Line. The company felt it needed a strong production team to support Jackson. It selected Barrie M. Osborne, who had been production manager on *Apocalypse Now* and had worked on such ambitious films as *The Cotton Club, Dick Tracy*, and *The Matrix*. Ordesky, the executive producer, was steeped in the Tolkien books. He had also vigorously championed Jackson.

After careful study, New Line finally green-lighted the project, revising the budget up to $210 million, a figure that was to continue to escalate.

The back-to-back production schedules, while risky, nonetheless offered several advantages. The filmmakers wanted to shoot in remote regions of New Zealand and hence needed to build roads. This would require assurances to the government that they would remove all traces of their intrusion when they left—it made no sense to build and then unbuild a road three times. Then there was the question of avoiding the logistical and fiscal nightmare entailed in renegotiating actors' salaries and schedules for follow-up films. Back-to-back sequels could result in substantial economies, provided the actors and their agents went along with the scheme.

It was a production of unprecedented scope, with 274 days of principal photography. A production team of over 2,400 worked on the films for five years. The walled castle city of Minas Tirith was the largest set ever built in the Southern Hemisphere. The elephant-like mûmakil was the largest prop ever built, and had to be transported to the set in pieces in more than a dozen trucks.

A vegetable garden was planted a year before filming, to make the hobbits look at home. Meanwhile, more than 120 technicians worked on makeup and prosthetics, armor and weapons, miniatures, and model effects while 200 others created computer-generated (CGI) creatures.

New Line and Jackson quickly agreed they didn't want an all-star cast. They felt stars would distract from the story. Plus, nonstars would be more likely to sign on to several years' commitment to one project.

Still, at the eleventh hour New Line pursued one marquee name: Sean Connery was the first choice as Gandolf. He turned them down. Ian McKellen was the next choice, but he had committed to appear in *X-Men*, which was shooting at the same time. Shaye encountered him at a London restaurant and said he was sorry to hear the films' schedules conflicted. "I went back to my table, and then a few minutes later I decided to go back and ask, 'Just for the record, what the hell is the scheduling conflict?' He said, 'Well, you're starting *Lord of the Rings* three days before I finish *X-Men*.'" They didn't take long to adjust their schedule.

The only other casting snag occurred when Stuart Townsend was replaced as Aragorn just days before the start of shooting. During two months of rehearsals and physical training in New Zealand leading up to the start date, it became apparent to the studio and the filmmakers that Townsend was simply too young to credibly convey the haunted, battle-hardened Aragorn. "We had five days in which to cast the right person, make the deal and get him on a plane for New Zealand—for 15 months," said Ordesky.

Viggo Mortensen was reluctant to take the role, because he would have little preparation time and didn't want to leave his son for a long period. Ironically, it was his son, who knew the books and convinced him to accept the role.

Elijah Wood, an eighteen-year-old former child actor, was cast as Frodo, the 3-foot-six-inch hobbit who leads the Fellowship to destroy the One Ring. Sean Astin, son of actress Patty Duke, was the loyal hobbit, Sam. Other members of the cast included Cate Blanchett, Orlando Bloom, Ian Holm, Christopher Lee, and Liv Tyler.

Despite his total immersion in the production, Jackson proved adept at dealing with his benefactors and ameliorating their panic. Shaye visited the set several months into production, bringing a group of international distributors who were eager to see where their advances were going. Jackson surprised them by showing a half hour of footage with just the actors, and no effects. The gamble paid off; the distributors were persuaded that, unlike other effects-heavy films, this one would feature nuanced performances along with spectacle. Said Michael Lynne, New Line's cochairman: "There was a dynamic between the characters themselves—forget the digital effects, because they weren't there, or the scenery, because there wasn't much of it. But the pure, compelling nature of the story and its characters got to us."

Still, the scope of the movie created a relentless pressure. As cowriter Walsh said, "It was like laying tracks ahead of a moving train. Enormous decisions had to be made and made quickly and there was no margin for error." The screenwriters worked each day to polish scenes for three movies simultaneously. They had learned to be wary whenever they saw an actor carrying a copy of the book, knowing that he'd found a few lines or a scene that he wanted restored.

New Line discovered an unexpected bonus in filming in New Zealand: The entire country seemed enthused about a project for its native son. After all, thousands of extras and craftspeople were being employed for several years at a stretch. This enthusiasm translated into a more dedicated workforce. Visiting the set, Royd Tolkien, the writer's great-grandson, was impressed that everyone was working without the benefit of experience. "Their attitude was: The job's got to be done, so let's do it," said the young Tolkien.

Still, New Line was understandably nervous. Disappointments like Adam Sandler's *Little Nicky* and *Thirteen Days* with Kevin Costner, not to mention the looming disaster of *Town and Country*, starring Warren Beatty, weighed heavily on the company. Shaye's reputation as a savvy operator was coming into question. It was rumored that if *Rings* failed, New Line could be absorbed into parent company Warner Bros. and lose its long-standing autonomy. After Time Warner's merger with America Online in early 2000, every division was coming under increased scrutiny. By early 2001, New Line was required to ask permission to make any movie that cost more than $50 million. Meanwhile, New Line had laid off 20 percent of its staff and fired the president of production, Michael De Luca, who had worked with Shaye for sixteen years.

Ordesky stayed in New Zealand for most of the shoot. He and Jackson kept propping up his bosses in Los Angeles and New York via regular e-mails, but he had never supervised a movie whose budget was more than $6 million. His job was to make sure both Jackson and the studio got what they wanted.

"A big part of the job was simply conveying what was going on. Peter knew what he wanted, and I knew how to put it forward in the way that New Line would understand—and vice versa," Ordesky said. Throughout production, Ordesky made an estimated thirty flights between Los Angeles and New Zealand. He'd leave Wellington Friday afternoon, land at LAX fourteen hours later, where a car would take him directly (with no shower and no nap) to New Line's West Hollywood offices. There, he would show a videotape to Bob Shaye, take notes, and then fly to New York where cochairman Lynne was based and take notes from him. Then he would return to Wellington with the notes and the videotape, which he clutched tightly, nervous that the footage would end up on the Internet.

When Ordesky ran into friends from other studios, they would needle him about the project. Some warned he could emerge as the new Steven Bach—the executive at United Artists whose career ended when he oversaw production on *Heaven's Gate*.

Ordesky also understood the fragile state of his international distributors, some of whom could lose their business if the films didn't succeed. On May 12, 2001, New Line Cinema was ready to give these distributors and the media a first glimpse of their multimillion-dollar baby. At the Cannes Film Festival, the company scheduled two daytime screenings for hundreds of distributors, film critics, and journalists, who saw twenty-five minutes of *The Lord of the Rings*. After the screenings, the media was bussed to a chateau to join the film's stars, executives, and foreign distributors at a lavish $2.5 million party. The expansive grounds had been transformed into Tolkien-land, featuring sections of the film's set, such as a walk-through hobbit house, a swan boat floating in the misty swimming pool, performers dressed as Middle Earthlings, and an abundance of food and drink.

The party chatter confirmed the positive mood. "Media reaction ranged from upbeat to wildly enthusiastic," said a report in the Cannes edition of *Variety*. "It's hard to remember a pic with a splashier launch here."

Indeed, the foreign distributors seemed more than pleased. Ordesky wept with relief that the gamble might actually have paid off. Even those distributors who had not signed on caught *Rings* fever. Representatives from Warner Bros. snapped up rights for Germany after the screening. One exhibitor grabbed Ordesky and kissed him on the mouth.

Still, New Line, by now, was forced to raise the budget yet again to accommodate postproduction. The final total for all three movies had moved to $330 million, before marketing costs, which could total another $210 million. The extra money was needed to create visual effects of a magnitude that hadn't been seen before. Added expenditure would go into the CGI-created character of Gollum, who is barely glimpsed in the first film, but is a key player in the second and third. Wearing special gear, an actor played the role on camera, but effects mavens morphed him into "the most realistic animated creature ever on screen," according to producer Osborne.

The initial movie, *The Fellowship of the Ring*, was released on December 19, 2001, just three months after the terrorist attacks of September 11. The audience, gripped by the clash of good and evil, seemed hungry for the film. In Wellington, New Zealand, over 100,000 fans streamed into the street to watch a cast and crew parade.

But *Rings* faced stiff competition at the box office, particularly from another film based on a best-selling fantasy novel: *Harry Potter and the Sorcerer's Stone*. Both were kicking off vast film franchises and insiders questioned whether either could break out beyond their fantasy niches to wider audiences.

In the end, *Sorcerer's Stone* hit $974 million dollars worldwide, while *Fellowship* racked up $861 million. The first three *Harry Potter* films grossed $2.6 billion, compared with the *Rings* total of $2.9 billion.

The fan buzz on the Internet—a key component of the company's marketing strategy—was very strong for *Rings*, and the good reviews seemed like gravy. "Jackson keeps a firm hand on the work's central themes of good versus evil, rising to the occasion and group loyalty in the face of adversity, and always keeps things moving without getting bogged down in frills or effects for effects' sake," said *Variety*'s Todd McCarthy. The *Boston Globe*'s Jay Carr concluded, "Not since the original *Star Wars* trilogy has film dipped into myth and emerged with the kind of weight and heft seen in Peter Jackson's first installment of J.R.R. Tolkien's *Lord of the Rings* trilogy." The website RottenTomatoes.com, which tallies critical reaction, showed *Fellowship* with a nearly unprecedented 97 percent positive rating.

Even positive notices pointed to reservations, though. Roger Ebert could not ignore the film's long, episodic quality. "The film is remarkably well-made. But it does go on, and on, and on—more vistas, more forests, more sounds in the night, more fearsome creatures, more prophecies, more visions, more dire warnings, more close calls, until we realize this sort of thing can continue indefinitely."

Even before *Fellowship* premiered, New Line had to start gearing up for its Oscar campaign. Awards strategists warned that fantasy films had never done well at the Oscars. Not even *Star Wars* had won.

As it turned out, the Oscar constituency was more than receptive. *Fellowship* won thirteen nominations and ultimately won four awards: cinematography, visual effects, makeup, and original score. (*A Beautiful Mind* took best picture and Ron Howard won for best director.)

The following year *The Two Towers* opened in the United States December 5, 2002, and earned an astonishing 100 percent positive review rating from the Rotten Tomatoes web site. Total domestic box office for *The Two Towers* climbed to $342 million, second only to *Spider-Man*'s $404 million, and considerably higher than *Fellowship*. It nonetheless suffered a slight sophomore slump in Oscar attention. *Two Towers* earned six nominations and two Oscars, for sound editing and visual effects.

Expectations were high for *Return of the King*, which opened December 17, 2003. *Variety*'s McCarthy called it "decisively the best of the lot," reminding readers that the third installments of *The Godfather*, *Star Wars*, and *The Matrix* hadn't matched their predecessors.

"As a model for how to bring substance, authenticity and insight to the biggest of adventure yarns, this trilogy will not soon, if ever, find its equal," wrote Ken Turan in the *Los Angeles Times*. Even the positive reviews, however, carped about the proliferation of endings. The *Christian Science Monitor*'s David Sterritt praised "the most exciting special effects of the series. . . . But it can't sustain such power for a whopping 201 minutes, and has there ever been a movie with more endings?"

Still, the movie grossed $377 million in the United States alone, ahead of the first two films.

At the Oscars, *The Lord of the Rings: The Return of the King* was pitted against *Master and Commander*, *Lost in Translation*, *Mystic River*, and *Seabiscuit*. This time it was the clear front-runner, despite the fact that, as one voter told *Variety*, "I just can't bring myself to vote for a film about elves."

The film's Oscar sweep surprised even its filmmakers. *Return* ended up with eleven Oscars, winning every category in which it was nominated: picture, director, adapted screenplay, film editing, score, song, art direction, costume design, makeup, sound mixing, and visual effects.

Jackson became the fourth artist to win for best writer, producer, and director in one evening, following Billy Wilder, Francis Ford Coppola, and James L. Brooks. The film so dominated the evening that only two other films won more than one Oscar. It also took best film and three other prizes at the BAFTA awards (the British Oscars), the Directors Guild award for Peter Jackson, four Golden Globes, and best film from the New York Film Critics.

Jackson's behavior at the Oscars was typically idiosyncratic. After the Oscar ceremony, it's traditional for winners to go to the Governors Ball, the official party thrown by the Academy of Motion Picture Arts and Sciences. Jackson dutifully attended with his entourage, but later streamed to "The One Party," an impromptu celebration thrown by fans. It may have been the first time a film's cast and crew made a post-Oscar appearance at a fan-sponsored fete, but that seemed entirely appropriate. Few films had inspired such fervent fan bases as the *Rings* trilogy.

And that loyalty was demonstrated anew with the DVD release. New Line decided to release the DVD versions one year apart. It was an astute marketing decision, as each DVD included hours of bonus material, such as deleted scenes.

The DVD for the first film, *The Fellowship of the Ring*, added thirty minutes to the film. The two-disc set also included hours of documentary material on the making of the films and four commentary tracks. *The Two Towers* added forty-three minutes of more footage and *The Return of the King*, a full fifty minutes of extra footage, making the total running time of the trilogy in extended editions more than eleven hours. Jackson at some point promised an ultimate extended edition with even more deleted scenes and documentaries for die-hard fans. "Consumers spent more than $400 million buying and renting about 20 million DVD and videocassette copies of each of the first two releases," *Variety* reported.

Also helping keep the franchise alive were a series of videogames. Three games were based on the films, and a later role-playing game, "Lord of the Rings: The Third Age," also proved popular as well as a "Hobbit" game for younger players.

To some studio veterans, Peter Jackson's trilogy

represented yet a further validation of William Goldman's oft-quoted flip remark that "nobody knows anything." Quasi-independent companies like New Line supposedly don't take giant gambles like this and survive. Projects of this magnitude aren't entrusted to relative neophytes like Jackson. Hollywood companies don't shoot films in remote locations like New Zealand, far removed from executive scrutiny. Sequels to movies aren't given the green light before the success of the first film can be quantified. And after an array of major filmmakers like Spielberg and Kubrick pass on a project a company would be ill-advised to contradict these masters' reservations and take it on.

All the components of conventional wisdom weighed against a decision to push forward with the trilogy, and hence its extraordinary success brought great satisfaction to some, great confusion to others. For those corporate players who preached the wisdom of risk-averse strategies, *The Lord of the Rings* seemed to constitute the ultimate refutation. Surely the spreadsheet models of business school graduates all around Hollywood would have to be rewritten.

For those who, like Bob Shaye and Michael Lynne, believed that big returns emanate from big risks, *Lord of the Rings* provided a unique and generous validation.

Every giant hit leaves in its wake an array of mixed messages. There is hubris and self-congratulation; there is also anger.

Peter Jackson and his Medici, Bob Shaye, felt both. The spectacular success of the trilogy gave New Line a new future. It gave Jackson a new career. But when it came time for Jackson to cash in on his new status as a superstar filmmaker, he turned, not to Shaye, but to a major studio, Universal. Indeed, Shaye was left with a huge law suit rather than another Peter Jackson film.

By signing to remake *King Kong* yet again, Jackson secured the most lavish deal any filmmaker had ever achieved—topping even Spielberg. Universal agreed to pay him $20 million against 20 percent of gross receipts to write, produce, and direct the film, with a provision that his payday would be diminished if he exceeded the agreed-upon budget of $150 million. In November, 2005, he delivered his film to the studio at a running time of three hours. The studio offered to kick in a portion of the overage, thus relieving Jackson of part of his obligation.

In shifting his filmmaking activity to Universal, Jackson also was avoiding the book-keeping nightmare he had encountered at New Line. Universal was a full-fledged studio that distributed its own films around the world. By contrast, New Line was a semi-independent; to raise money for Jackson's trilogy, the company had to go hat-in-hand to sub-distributors in various parts of the world who put up advances for their territories. These dealings were the root of Jackson's argument with New Line; the allocation of fees and sales commissions were a gray area that had long stirred disagreements among production partners. On the surface, Peter Jackson seemed like the prototypical artist who didn't pay attention to business details, but his aggressive position with New Line was that the company owed him millions of dollars from its overseas dealings and he would be unrelenting in his pursuit of that money.

I picked up on some of these residual tensions one night at a special screening of *The Fellowship of the Ring* at the Egyptian Theatre in Hollywood. The cinema—a jewel of a theater that had been restored by the Cinematheque—was packed by avid fans. According to the program, I was to interview Bob Shaye prior to the screening—a prospect that left me uneasy because of Shaye's fabled mood swings. Would I encounter the grumpy, quarrelsome Shaye or the calmly self-satisfied one? I had always avoided doing onstage interviews such as this, but as a vice president of the Cinematheque and member of its board, I felt obligated to help the cause.

I had prepared two sets of questions, their tone dependent on Shaye's mood and willingness to talk candidly about the problems of the movie. Once the theater filled, I moved down the side aisle toward the stage, awaiting the signal to go on. I noticed Shaye standing further up the aisle, talking to a thicket of press agents. He waved; his face seemed taut, which was not a good sign.

Then I noticed a man huddled beside a column. He was dressed in a t-shirt and jeans and wore sandals and no socks. He had a scraggly black beard and looked like a homeless person. His eyes were fixed on me, however. I moved several steps toward him.

"Peter . . . ?" he called out.

"Peter . . . ?" I responded. I was dumbfounded. This was clearly Peter Jackson who, I had been told, was still in New Zealand. I had met him once before when we did an interview for my television show.

We shook hands. "Good to see you," he said in a near-whisper. He seemed oddly diffident.

"What are you doing here?" I asked.

He shrugged. "My plane got in a bit early so I thought I'd drop by and check out the audience reaction."

"Well, for Chrissake, come onstage with me," I blurted.

He stared at me and said nothing. I persisted. "Peter, I have to get onstage with Shaye and he looks like he's in one of his moods. Let's go on together and give the audience a surprise."

The filmmaker looked troubled. "He might feel we're stealing his show. I mean, he wants to take his bow."

"We'll give him his plaudits. But that won't cover half an hour of stage time."

Jackson smiled. "Come on, let's do it."

We walked to the side of the stage. Shaye followed us, looking a bit surprised. He and Jackson shook hands. I could feel a certain awkwardness, but both made every effort to seem congenial.

The interview began, the three of us seated side by side. Jackson and I each took turns praising Shaye for his fiscal courage. But the New Line founder offered little in the way of insight into the film he had just financed. If anything, he seemed relieved and a bit exhausted.

Jackson, by contrast, was a delight, spinning anecdotes about his performers and offering vivid descriptions of the pioneering CGI effects that he and his crew had achieved. The audience listened with avid interest. In his own hobbit-like way, Jackson was a brilliant teller of tales.

The evening was a big success. Primed for the film, the audience applauded

The Lord of the Rings

rapturously at its end. The last I saw of Jackson and Shaye, they were heading off in opposite directions. Jackson gave me an off-handed grin. "That was pretty good," he said.

I don't know if Shaye and Jackson subsequently spent any time together. One New Line executive confided that their relationship had become frosty as a result of the litigation.

I can understand why. Shaye had taken the big gamble; he ended up with a great picture, but not a great picture maker. New Line would have to find the next Peter Jackson. And Peter Jackson would have to find his next hit.

6 Geek Speak

The Blair Witch Project (1999)

The Blair Witch Project is one of the great anomalies of filmmaking history, remarkable both for its accomplishments as well as for its failures. It is the most profitable independent movie ever made (except for the porn pseudo-classic, *Deep Throat*), produced at a cost of $30,000 and grossing an astonishing $140 million. It brought celebrity to two filmmakers who were totally outside the Hollywood fraternity—indeed were not even at the bottom of the radar. It empowered an important new player, Artisan Entertainment, to capitalize on the revolution-ary promotional tool spearheaded by *Blair Witch*—the Internet. It blurred the traditional lines separating fiction from reality and con-tributed significantly to the burgeoning mar-ket for reality TV.

And because of all these factors, it demonstrated that the media had been truly democratized by the miracle of the Internet. Now anyone at any time could produce a movie at minimal cost and grab the attention of millions of filmgoers. The chokehold of the giant entertainment distribution companies had finally been broken. The great pipelines of our pop culture had been opened to the great unwashed.

The Blair Witch Project accomplished all of these things—or so it seemed at that magical moment, in 1999. Put into perspective, however, the single most astonishing reality about *Blair Witch* is that it changed absolutely nothing. Its legacy of disappointments was, in fact, devastating.

The Internet did not revolutionize promotion and marketing. The pipelines of distribution did not open wide to those outside the power circle. The cost of making movies has since escalated rather than diminished and the independent community has not significantly expanded.

And the careers of those involved with *Blair Witch* have been extinguished rather than enhanced. The two directors who created the film, Daniel Myrick and Eduardo Sanchez, have never made another successful film—indeed never made any film at all (both were separately trying again at the start of 2006). Artisan Entertainment has disappeared, devoured by another independent, Lions Gate. Bill Block and Amir Malin, the two men who were shrewd enough to acquire the distribution rights to *Blair Witch*, are no longer important players in the movie business.

The story of *Blair Witch* is one of failure—mythic failure, but failure nonetheless.

Moviegoers usually cite Alfred Hitchcock's *Psycho* as the film that turned them off showering. Not Eduardo Sanchez; it was all about Bigfoot, not Hitchcock.

"There was one particular Bigfoot documentary," Sanchez says. "I was terrified to take a shower because there was a little window in my shower, and I always thought that Bigfoot would walk by and look in."

The fact that Sanchez lived in rural Maryland, with a veritable forest in his backyard, didn't help. But neither did it stop him and his friend and collaborator, Daniel Myrick, from watching every film and TV show they could get their hands on about the Bigfoot legend, including *The Legend of Boggy Creek*, a sly 1972 semi-documentary thriller based on allegedly true stories of Bigfoot sightings.

The year was 1992—a full seven years before *The Blair Witch Project* would open—and yet the crux of the film's inspiration was already in place: A fascination with the horror of nature (and, for that matter, the nature of horror), and with the ability of the "semi-documentary" to blur the lines between fiction and reality.

At the time, Myrick and Sanchez were students in the inaugural film class at the University of Central Florida, and were trying to create a new style of horror film. Stirred by such seminal '70s and '80s horror films as *The Exorcist*, *The Amityville Horror*, and *The Shining*, they thought they might rescue a genre that had devolved into the likes of *Freddy's Dead: The Final Nightmare* in 1991 (which featured cameos by Roseanne and Tom Arnold).

"These movies were just jokes," Sanchez says. "Horror movies weren't what they were when we were kids, and they weren't what they are now."

This rescue mission was a formidable task for two neophytes with no resources. What Myrick and Sanchez eventually settled upon was the idea of a modest horror film set in the woods—a reality film in which they created the reality. They were especially keen on using handheld cameras, and were obsessed with one "killer POV shot," as Myrick described it, in which a person would approach a dark house in the woods, slowly open the door, and enter the darkness within—all in a single "creepy as hell" long take, with no cutting away to relieve the tension.

The movie they relentlessly discussed would be made up entirely of random material, shot by a documentary film crew that turned up somewhere in the woods. The movie would thus constitute what Myrick calls an "indirect chronicle" of what happened to the crew.

The Blair Witch herself had not yet entered their minds, and the project itself—which was referred to from that point on as "the woods movie"—would not get off the ground for another three years.

As film students, Sanchez and Myrick showed promise, but the films they envisioned at UCF—including an attempted trilogy—never got off the ground. Their graduation in 1994 was followed by nearly three years of struggle and outright failure. Myrick stayed in Orlando while Sanchez moved back to Maryland in 1994, but they continued to talk on the phone regularly, month after month, kicking ideas around, sending each other screenplay drafts, commiserating about all the potential financiers whose promises had fallen through.

It wasn't until 1995 that Sanchez, now working as a truck driver, decided that enough was enough. He was then twenty-six, and Myrick was in his early thirties. "I gotta get off my ass and do something," Sanchez recalls thinking as he drove down the Washington, D.C. beltway. "Let's fucking do this damn woods movie."

The decision made, Myrick and Sanchez began writing a treatment early in 1996, inventing the story of what would eventually become *Blair Witch*. As much as Bigfoot was an inspiration, they wanted their villain to be something even more mysterious—a strange force in the wilderness that needed uncovering, something that would draw the film crew into the woods in the first place.

The idea of witchcraft didn't appeal to them initially. In their minds, witches were just "women on broomsticks." Eventually, they thought better of it. Sanchez whimsically named the witch after Montgomery Blair High School in Silver Spring, Maryland, which his older sister had attended. The name *Blair Witch* seemed spookily suggestive, though it was never intended to be permanent.

Myrick and Sanchez decided to pitch the concept to their friend Gregg Hale, a former classmate who had made several short films but had no immediate access to production funding or distribution. Hale signed on as a producer, offering to help find some money.

The first "angel" turned out to be John Pierson, the writer and host of the IFC Bravo series *Split Screen*. The half-hour magazine-format show followed Pierson as he toured the country with directors like Spike Lee, Kevin Smith, and John Waters—all intended to showcase the erratic world of independent filmmaking.

In 1997, Pierson needed someone to shoot a *Split Screen* segment on the Florida Film Festival, and Myrick got the call. Shortly afterward, Myrick asked Pierson to take a look at his eight-minute trailer that posed the concept for *Blair Witch*—one he and Sanchez had shot specifically for investors. Pierson promised he would watch the tape after he returned to New York. Two days later, Myrick recalls, Pierson called him and asked, "Where did you get this footage?" After Myrick explained, Pierson asked if he could air the trailer on *Split Screen* in return for $10,000.

Myrick, Sanchez, and various friends and family members continued to throw money into the pot until, during the shoot, their friend Rob Cowie saved the day, raising $25,000 from private investors.

Eventually, Myrick, Sanchez, Hale and Cowie—all friends from UCF film school, and all of whom would share producing credits on *Blair*—came together to form an Orlando-based entity called Haxan Films. The name was taken from Benjamin Christensen's 1922 documentary, *Häxan*, about the history of witchcraft through the ages.

If Myrick and Sanchez were novices at financing, they were also foreign to the casting process. About five separate open casting calls were held over the course of a year with Myrick and Sanchez auditioning about 1,500 actors. The process, like the film itself, was highly improvisational. After signing in, the actors would be handed a situational prompt—for example, they were convicted murderers about to appear before a parole board—and then asked to act out the scenario in front of the cameras. The three winners were Heather Donahue, Joshua Leonard, and Michael C. Williams, all of whom would retain their first names in the actual story.

The Blair Witch Project's now legendary eight-day shoot began in October 1997. The company headed up to the woods surrounding Seneca Creek State Park and Black Hill Regional Park near Burkittsville, Maryland. The three actors were each given a color Hi-8 camera and a black-and-white 16-mm camera and since they, supposedly, were filmmakers making a documentary about the *Blair Witch* legend, they were instructed to keep the cameras rolling more or less at all times.

The actors also received an individual set of directors' notes specific to each character, to be kept confidential. The notes contained fairly simple instructions—get into the car at 9 AM, for example; once in their car seats, the actors each found additional notes. Through this step-by-step clue-hunt process, the actors eventually found themselves in the middle of town, where Myrick and Sanchez had cleverly stationed additional extras, programmed to answer questions if and when they were approached.

Donahue, Leonard, and Williams, of course, had no idea which interview subjects were real and which were fake. It was their job to act like documentary filmmakers and figure it out. Some of the most intriguing interviews were with nonactors who were completely clueless about the production. One local woman, not hired by Myrick and Sanchez, responded, "Oh yeah, I've heard about Blair Witch." Her segment (which also showed the woman's baby picking its nose) was so convincing that it made its way into the finished film. In retrospect, the incident seemed a vivid reminder of the theme of *Blair Witch*—the willingness to buy into a completely fictional construct. The barriers between reality and fiction were growing ambiguous.

Once in the woods, contact between cast and crew gradually lessened as the shoot progressed. During the film's thirty-day preproduction period, Myrick and Sanchez had thoroughly mapped out a clear trek through the woods that corresponded with the order of scenes in the script, and they also furnished the actors with a GPS compass so that they could follow the route. Otherwise, the directors remained essentially invisible, creeping up to the actors' campsite ("like elves," Myrick says) every night to pick up completed reels from the day, and to replenish food and film. While Donahue, Leonard, and Williams were free to improvise (and encouraged to do so), the script directions—right down to when and where they were supposed to act scared—were very specific.

By the end of the eight-day shoot, the three actors had amassed between forty and fifty hours of footage. The process of paring that down to a manageable length would last an additional eight months.

Three or four months after the shoot, Sanchez moved down to Florida to

work with Myrick editing videos during the day and that enabled them to edit *Blair Witch* at night.

It was around this time that *Blair Witch* unleashed its crucial marketing tool—the Web site. Haxan Films launched blairwitch.com in June 1998, before editing on the film was complete. The site was simple in design, but its masterstroke was to present the disappearance of the filmmakers as absolute fact, complete with images of the students "before their disappearance," stills from the recovered footage, and suspicious photos of the interior of Leonard's car after being "discovered by police on Black Rock Road."

An entire section was devoted to explaining the fake mythology of the Blair Witch, with a bogus timeline of events. It explained the story of an eighteenth-century woman accused of witchcraft and related the confession to the ritualistic murders of seven children. All of this was primarily the invention of Sanchez, who said he "didn't have a girlfriend at the time" and thus had time to fantasize.

The site was *Blair Witch*'s breakthrough. Web traffic increased daily, leading to an enormous groundswell of support for the film and for its eerily convincing mythology. Within months, several additional *Blair Witch* sites sprang up (as well as a *Blair Witch* Web ring), created by fans for whom the unfolding story had become an obsession. The first of these, a message board called the *Blair Witch* Forum, was created by a rabid fan named Jeff Johnson. In November 1998, Johnson drew attention to the film by appearing on the *Mark and Brian Show* on KLOS-FM in Los Angeles where he persuaded the morning talk show hosts to devote a half hour to navigating blairwitch.com. Sanchez says, "This was the first time a lot of the industry heard about the movie. . . . That's what helped generate the buzz that led us to Sundance."

The final stretch of editing was the most demanding for Myrick and Sanchez. Money was running low and credit card bills were piling up. Myrick says that by the time Sundance rolled around, his phone had been shut off because he didn't have money to pay the bill.

Before the Sundance Festival in January 1999, however, a test screening of a rough two-and-a-half hour cut was held at MGM Film Theater in Orlando. There Myrick and Sanchez met Los Angeles-based independent producer Kevin Foxe, who cornered the directors after the screening and told them, "You guys are gonna be celebrities." Foxe quickly signed on as executive producer and helped secure representation with the Endeavor Talent Agency. It was Foxe as well who raised $90,000 necessary to make a print (Sundance wouldn't accept digital projection).

"Kevin really saved our butts," Sanchez says. "It wouldn't have happened the way it happened if it wasn't for him."

Securing a spot on Sundance's midnight movie roster, *Blair Witch* played to a packed house. "There was a frightening amount of interest after the screening," Hale later recalled. "The distributors just couldn't schedule meetings fast enough." By 7:30 AM, *The Blair Witch Project* had become the fest's first pickup—from Artisan Entertainment, the small company that had acquired Darren Aronofsky's *Pi* at Sundance a year earlier. The deal was made for between $1 million and $1.5 million and also entailed a first-look agreement with Artisan as well as a *Blair* sequel.

As eager as Artisan was to get its hands on *Blair*, they quickly registered less than total confidence in the product's appeal. Artisan executives wanted to change the ending, which they felt was inconclusive. "They literally threw $30,000 at us to go shoot five new endings," recalls Myrick, who didn't have much of a choice. "We were still pretty broke."

So he, Sanchez, and the cast headed back to the house in the woods where the original cut of the film had ended with Heather discovering Mike in the basement, his back turned toward her, not turning around in response to her frantic screams. The five alternative endings were "endings by committee," Myrick says—one of them involved Heather finding Mike crucified. "Of course Artisan ended up not liking them," Myrick says. Bill Block, the Artisan copresident, phoned to say he wanted to keep the original ending, but regretted doing so. "I think it's going to cost us millions at the box office," Block told him.

Artisan slated the film for a limited July 14 release before going wide. Sanchez says that the company anticipated a healthy $10 million gross, no more and very likely less. They had no idea what was on the horizon.

It began with the reviews, which were almost uniformly excellent.

"An extraordinarily effective horror film . . . a reminder that what really scares us is the stuff we can't see," exalted Roger Ebert. Ebert wasn't the only one to call attention to the film's minimalist aesthetic. Writing in the *New York Times*, Janet Maslin called the film "a nifty example of how to make something out of nothing."

Capturing the approval of mainstream critics, *Blair Witch* also pleased the art-house reviewers, who praised the film's supposed integrity. In the *Village Voice*, J. Hoberman said *Blair* was "in every sense a psychological thriller . . . an absolutely restrained and truly frightening movie."

Myrick was absolutely stunned by the in-depth "intellectual treatises" and interpretations that followed in the film's wake. "Critics much smarter than me would be giving this analysis on what we were doing," he said. "My reaction was, 'Wow, I didn't know we were that smart.'"

Critical success doesn't necessarily trigger box-office results, but in this case it was supplemented by relentless word-of-mouth promotion and the continued success of the Web site, which Artisan had purchased and whose traffic, like that of its sister fan sites, showed no signs of abating.

Rather than follow the usual route of starting exclusively in Los Angeles and New York, *The Blair Witch Project* opened Wednesday, July 14, on twenty-seven screens in twenty-four cities. On July 19, *Variety* reported a $1.5 million gross, for a boffo per-screen average of $57,700. In less than a week, the film had recouped not only its budget several times over but also Artisan's acquisition price.

It was only the beginning. *Blair* opened wide July 30, in 1,101 playdates, and grossed a staggering $28.5 million—a $25,885 per-screen average that far outpaced the $21,822 earned by *Star Wars: Episode I—The Phantom Menace* in May. As Artisan co-president Amir Malin told *Variety*, "It's almost an out-of-body experience looking at these numbers."

The excitement surrounding the film, even after its limited release, was so formidable that both Universal and Warner Bros. adjusted their release schedules to get out of *Blair*'s way. Universal postponed *Mystery Men* one week, while Warner pushed *Deep Blue Sea* up from July 30 to July 28 to get a head start on the weekend.

It didn't hurt *Blair*—and indeed, probably helped—that it opened less than two weeks before Jan de Bont's lavish but toothless horror remake of *The Haunting*.

"What is it about *The Blair Witch Project* that taps into such primal emotions?" David Edelstein wrote in the online magazine *Slate*. "Even if the script weren't so tin-eared and the direction so clunky, *The Haunting* still wouldn't come within screaming distance of *The Blair Witch Project* . . . de Bont, who thinks that movies can do anything if you throw enough money around, wants to scare you by showing you stuff. Myrick and Sanchez want to scare you by not showing you stuff—and by reminding you how much you can't see and will never know."

At the end of its run, *The Haunting*, made by DreamWorks for an estimated $80 million, grossed about $91 million domestically. By the end of November, *The Blair Witch Project* had grossed more than $140 million and became the most profitable independent film of all time (beside the aforementioned *Deep Throat*).

"The movie was never meant to have made $140 million," reflects Sanchez. "When Dan and I had the idea, we thought, this is gonna be perfect for video. You go home and you pop it in late and you fucking go crazy watching it by yourself. The fact that it even worked for some people in the theater is amazing."

"Ed and I actively tried to maintain a sense of perspective for the audience," Myrick says. "Whenever we did an interview, we tried to remind people that this was a $35,000 film, shot on twelve Hi-8 tapes. This was not *Lord of the Rings* . . . With all the hype that's surrounding this movie, try and keep that in perspective."

But if hype takes on a life of its own, so does anti-hype. Some audiences lured to the theater by all the "scariest movie ever" buzz were left wondering what all the fuss was about. Myrick, who was prepared for the backlash, admits, "I can't blame people for being kind of underwhelmed."

"You can see it in the box office," Sanchez says. "The first two weekends were huge, and even the third one was pretty good. And then it just completely dropped off, it had no legs at all. The people who'd loved it had already seen it a couple of times."

The reactions of those who didn't love it, Sanchez says, were somewhere along the lines of "That was a piece of shit! What the fuck was that?"

Entertainment Weekly even ran a short piece on the film's motion-sickness-inducing handheld cinematography, citing an Associated Press report that theater employees from Atlanta to Boston found themselves having to clean seats and bathrooms. "Before heading out to *The Blair Witch Project* this weekend, better pop a couple of Dramamine and bring an empty popcorn bucket," Josh Wolk wrote in the magazine. "Across the country more and more viewers are vomiting after getting motion sickness from the shaky camera work and grainy footage."

While Myrick and Sanchez played on the reality-fiction ambiguity, milking it for all the paranoia it was worth, they both blanched at the idea that the *Blair Witch* legend was intended as a hoax. Instead, they hoped that even viewers who knew the truth would find the film absorbing enough for them to be able to suspend disbelief.

"We aren't trying to pull a hoax here," Myrick told *Entertainment Weekly.* "You go to our Web site or look at any of our other marketing and it looks and feels real, but in every interview we've done we've told about the process of how we made the movie."

On August 4, 1999, *Variety* quoted Jeff Berg, the top agent at ICM, as predicting that studios have been slow to use the Internet as anything more than a promotional tool, *Blair Witch*'s innovative Web campaign and superb opening could be the green light Hollywood's major studios have been waiting for to devote a larger percentage of their marketing dollars to the

Internet." (Blairwitch.com had recorded 647,997 visitors and 10.4 million page views alone for the week ending August 1, making it the forty-fifth most used site on the Internet.)

The flurry of ongoing traffic around blairwitch.com and its various bastard offspring was enough to provoke a *Salon* piece by Patrizia DiLucchio with the headline "Did Blair Witch Project Fake Its Online Fan Base?" The article stated that the film had spawned more than twenty fan sites and it also cited the film's massive exposure on "Ain't It Cool News," floating the suggestion that the twelve reviews posted on Harry Knowles' Web site in advance of the film's release—raves like "the most creepy fuckin' mockumentary made . . . ever"—had been initiated by someone from within the Myrick–Sanchez camp.

The Blair Witch Project also spawned a legion of parodies, many of them pornographic, such as *The Erotic Witch Project*. Then there was *The Bear Witch Project*, a Web site retelling the *Blair* legend using teddy bears. Two parody sites were titled *The Blair Bitch Project*—one was an extended rant at the filmmakers, the other billed itself as "Bitchology." Then there was *The Watts Bitch Project*, about three white kids looking for a legendary "crack ho."

"That's the sincerest form of flattery," says Myrick. "To this day, I knew I made it when I opened up *MAD* magazine and there was a parody of *Blair Witch* in there. I said, 'Dude, we're in. The hell with *Time* and *Newsweek*—*MAD*! We've made it!'"

Despite the many parodies, however, *Blair* is unique in that it hasn't produced any serious imitators (aside from its ill-fated sequel, *Book of Shadows: Blair Witch 2*). The low-budget 2004 thriller *Open Water*, whose filmmakers employed digital cameras and real sharks, was cited by a number of critics as "*Jaws* meets *Blair Witch*," but Myrick, an *Open Water* fan, puts them in separate categories.

"I think *Blair* was such a specific kind of conceit, it would be hard to replicate that without looking like you're directly ripping it off," he says. "*Blair Witch*, outside of the parodies, kind of stood on its own."

Myrick also resists the temptation to credit *Blair Witch* with prompting the wave of reality TV, pointing out that MTV's *The Real World* had already been on the air. He agrees, however, that the film helped legitimize digital filmmaking as a commercial force, convincing distributors that "things that are shot on video . . . can break into the mainstream."

On January 26, 2004, *Newsweek* ran a wistful where-are-they-now piece titled *Curse of the Blair Witch*, reporting that Michael C. Williams had been unable to find work as an actor and was making a living as a furniture mover, while Heather Donahue and Joshua Leonard were still "working mostly under the radar."

Myrick and Sanchez also have yet to make another film. Had *Blair* only grossed its expected $10 million, Sanchez speculates that he and Myrick, free from the pressure of high expectations, would have made two or three more films by now—perhaps even their proposed romantic comedy *Heart of Love*, which was intended to go into production in 2001, but was eventually shelved. Quips Sanchez, "At least we haven't made a horrible movie."

Myrick, Sanchez and Hale all share the distinction of marrying the women who saw them through *Blair Witch* from genesis to execution. "The thing about everybody's girlfriends is that they helped to support us while we went off into the woods and shot this goofy movie," says Myrick, who credits the women with not only chipping in to pay the bills but also weaving the stickmen figures that became representative of the *Blair Witch* legend. "They were just wonderful. And still are to this day."

While the major studios continue to pump money into promotion over the Internet, expectations from the medium have become more realistic in the years since *Blair Witch*. In launching each of their "tentpole pictures," studio Web sites are dutifully established and the studio in-house geeks flood the Internet with thinly veiled promotional material. Fan Web sites, too, are all but overwhelmed with studio-generated blurbs. Online critics and bloggers are courted and catered to, invited to studio screenings and jetted to Hollywood junkets.

But while *Blair Witch* was essentially a creation of the Web, no film since has replicated that experience. The Internet is no longer thought of as a promotional miracle; it is simply another tool in the studios' arsenal. And even hardcore geeks understand that just because a story is unfolding before them on the Internet, it isn't necessarily more credible than if it were whispered to them at school.

Blair Witch was a great story, but a bogus one.

7 Global Beach Party
Baywatch (1989)

It is impossible to travel anywhere in the world without encountering some fragment of American pop culture. It may be the torpor-inducing strains of CNN; it may be a trailer for the next Tom Cruise *Mission-Even-More-Impossible* blockbuster; but as likely as not, it will be yet another overseas rerun of the ubiquitous *Baywatch*.

Watching the endless iterations of *Baywatch* around the globe, I've occasionally asked myself, "Won't this series ever end? Won't these middle-aged lifeguards ever stop chasing beach babes and retire to their used surfboard shop?" And then, the inevitable business question: Which network financed so many segments of this brain-dead show that it can afford to run forever in syndication?

The answer to the last question is even more confounding: No United States network ever believed in *Baywatch*—not for long, anyway. CBS flirted with it, then dozed off. NBC actually put it on for one season, then ran like hell.

In point of fact, *Baywatch*, the show that won't go away, probably ranks as the most rejected show in the history of television—except, that is, in the nebulous world of international syndication. Though United States networks may think it's a snooze, programmers around the world can't get enough. It's all about the beach, the babes, sunshine, just a little bit of sex, and a very, very little amount of jeopardy. It's American, but harmlessly American. And it's a cash cow.

Not surprisingly, the man behind *Baywatch*, whose dogged persistence year after year kept the show's prospects alive, is a benign Southern Californian who's not quite a writer, not quite a producer, but whose obsession is simply hanging out at the beach. To him, life is lifeguarding. And his stubbornness has made him a multimillionaire and, as a by-product, injected his soporific sensibility onto TV schedules around the world.

The story of Greg Bonann ranks right up there in the highlight reel of show-biz get-rich legends—an improbable triumph over critics, network suits, and just about everyone else active in the television world.

Bonann's love affair with the beach began when he was a kid, suffering from severe asthma. Bonann's parents decided it would be best for him to live close to the water, so his family settled in Pacific Palisades. When an allergy ruled out playing baseball, Bonann decided to try out for the Palisades High swimming team. By his senior year he was competing against the best high school swimmers from all over Los Angeles.

In April 1970 he took the test to become a lifeguard. He made the initial cut, survived the physical exam, and wound up graduating first in his rookie lifeguard class. Bonann took on lifeguarding duties at Will Rogers State Beach, later moving to Playa del Rey. Meanwhile, he earned a journalism degree from Cal State Long Beach in 1974, and his MBA from UCLA business school in 1977.

The story of *Baywatch* begins that same year—and it starts off, naturally, with a lifeguard rescue. Bonann had performed countless rescues since becoming a Los Angeles County lifeguard in 1970. But one changed his life.

At Will Rogers State Beach in the summer of 1977, a little boy and girl, aged about six or seven, were caught in a riptide. Bonann jumped in the water and brought them in to shore. They were fine, just a little shaky. Their father came to the lifeguard headquarters to fill out the rescue card. The children were named Tommy and Jacey Erwin; their father's name was Stu. Bonann recognized the name. Stu Erwin was an actor who'd starred in films from the 1936 *Pigskin Parade* to the 1964 Disney film *Son of Flubber*. To baby boomers, he was best remembered for a 1950 sitcom *The Stu Erwin Show*, which ran in syndication for years under the title *Trouble With Father*. Bonann asked if he was the *Trouble with Father* star.

"No," Stu said, "that's my father." Stu said he worked for Grant Tinker, the head of the TV production company MTM.

Tinker began his career at NBC radio in 1949 and served as a programming executive at the network for most of the 1960s. In 1970, Tinker and then-wife Mary Tyler Moore founded MTM and the production company, known as a friendly haven for writers and producers, quickly took off. Its first hit was *The Mary Tyler Moore Show*.

Bonann thought, "Gee, this might be a great guy to know."

When Erwin told Bonann to let him know if there was anything he could ever do for him, Bonann took him up on his offer. A few months later, in November 1977, Bonann visited Erwin at MTM's offices in Studio City on the CBS Radford lot. Bonann got the grand tour—including a meet and greet with Tinker. Besides *Mary Tyler Moore*, MTM was then riding high with shows like *Rhoda*, *WKRP in Cincinnati*, *The Bob Newhart Show*, and *Lou Grant*.

Bonann finally told Erwin of an idea he had for a TV show: one based on lifeguards. Erwin told him to come back in a week and make a real TV pitch, explaining what the show is about and who the characters would be.

Bonann raced out to Larry Edmunds cinema bookshop on Hollywood Boulevard, where he bought everything he could about the business of television. One week later, he was back in Erwin's office pitching a show called *A.C.E.S.*, an acronym for "Aquatic Corps for Emergency Service." Erwin liked the idea—but worried it sounded too much like *Emergency*, which had recently left the airwaves after five years. MTM had also soured on the action-adventure genre after developing an unsuccessful show with Brian Clemens (*The Avengers*). If Clemens couldn't make it, they reasoned, a newcomer like Bonann surely couldn't pull it off.

Erwin didn't buy the pitch, which was the first of many doors to slam shut on the project. "It was far less of a pitch meeting and more of a tutor session," Bonann says now. "Stu took me under his wing, and coached me through the whole process. What network is it for? What hour of primetime is it for? Is it a star vehicle or an ensemble piece? Question by question, over the course of the next year I honed my pitch down."

Meanwhile, Bonann put the lifeguard idea on the back burner as he pursued his other obsession: The Olympics. In 1980, he put together a film about the Winter Games called *Fire and Ice*. Bonann had qualified for the 1972 Olympic trials in the pentathlon, but failed to make the team. Instead, he went to work for John Hennessy, the owner of JJH Productions, which made industrial, educational, and documentary films. Bonann and Hennessy became close colleagues, and Bonann worked for JJH for several years.

Fire and Ice won several awards and established Bonann as an Olympics filmmaker. The following year, JJH decided to branch out beyond its documentaries. Bonann decided it was time to dust off his lifeguard project, now called *Baywatch*, and the rejections began to flow yet again.

He was told that the *Baywatch* concept was dull. And he found that few

Hollywood types even made it to the beach, increasing their prejudices against the show.

Bonann also discovered that his reputation as a documentarian hurt his shot at getting *Baywatch* made. In his book *Baywatch: Rescued from Prime Time*, Bonann remembers, "In my naïveté, I didn't realize that the industry loves to 'niche' people. That is, they lock a person into a tight little pigeonhole. No one took me seriously. I would have been better off coming from nowhere, in the manner of Quentin Tarantino."

As Bonann worked for JJH shooting both the Summer and Winter Games in 1984, he continued to lifeguard on the weekends. Every time he'd hear about some lifeguard tale—a small plane crashing on the beach or some other exciting rescue—it strengthened his resolve to bring that action to TV.

Meanwhile, Erwin's old boss, Grant Tinker, had left MTM to take over as chairman of NBC in 1981, then decided to return to independent production, partnering with the media company Gannett in 1986 to form GTG Productions. Tinker bought the old Laird Studios in Culver City, renamed it the Culver Studios, and developed new programming, including a syndicated version of Gannett's *USA Today* newspaper.

Also renting space on the Culver lot was a production company, where Bonann's sister, Deborah, worked as a receptionist. Bonann would regularly stop by the lot to visit his sister and Erwin, who had reconnected with Tinker.

His sister met and married a writer named Doug Schwartz, who with his writing partner (and first cousin) Michael Berk had written several series and TV movies. Schwartz and Berk asked Bonann to introduce them to Erwin and eventually the scribes ended up developing new projects for GTG.

The stage was now set. Comments Bonann: "All the key elements were coming together. I knew Grant Tinker, who ran his own studio. I knew his trusted associate, Stu Erwin, Jr. A member of my own family and his first cousin were now working as writers at GTG."

At this point, late summer 1987, Bonann had pitched *Baywatch* to Schwartz and Berk dozens of times. Each time they had said, "What else do you have?" Bonann decided to convince Schwartz to attend the annual Lifeguard Games. Held over two nights, the event comes complete with bonfires, helicopters, rescue boats, and thousands of spectators.

Schwartz took it all in, as Bonann called it, "an unrestrained riot of action." It worked. Schwartz finally got it, and brought Berk to the beach as well. All three began interviewing lifeguards and learning the ins and outs of the profession.

Bonann by now had launched his own production company, Tower 18 (named, naturally, after his favorite lifeguard tower). He called up his

Olympics film crew to shoot that year's annual lifeguard tryouts. Pieced together with the Don Henley song "The Boys of Summer," Bonann finally had a presentation tape—something that would prove to be an invaluable selling tool.

Tinker, meanwhile, landed a ten-series commitment from CBS. Under the deal, CBS would pick up ten shows from GTG over a five-year span.

By spring 1988, CBS had several slots to fill, including Friday night at 10 PM. Erwin told Bonann, Schwartz, and Beck to start developing *Baywatch* for the network. A month later, Erwin called the trio into his office. Tinker was sitting there. He said GTG had chosen *Baywatch* as one of its CBS shows.

Bonann remembers: "Champagne. Everything was great. *Baywatch* was going to be on the air. This particular CBS version of *Baywatch* did not match my original vision, but I didn't care, not after ten years of pitching. We walked out of Stu's office hardly bothering to touch the ground. The feeling was almost as good as winning the rookie lifeguard tryouts."

When CBS agreed to the show, the network imposed a few restrictions: No CPR, no mouth-to-mouth resuscitation, no horsing around. The network wanted a serious show.

The trio developed a two-hour script, handed it to CBS, and waited. On July 1, they received the news that CBS had passed. CBS was turning its back on GTG's ten-series deal as well.

Tinker called in Bonann and said he wanted to shop *Baywatch* to Brandon Tartikoff at NBC. Bonann finished writing a presentation and, together with Schwartz and Berk, the trio shot a new presentation on 35mm film. The Coast Guard lent use of their helicopter. The shot list extended from Will Rogers State Beach to the Palisades Cliffs, from Venice to Marina del Rey.

A week later they heard the news. Tartikoff loved it, and bought a two-hour *Baywatch* pilot. NBC wanted murders and the lifeguards to wear guns like policemen. Bonann and his group fought to retain something of the lifeguard's world, which has nothing to do with murders, committed or solved.

Tartikoff, Warren Littlefield, and Perry Simon finally approved the script "Baywatch: Panic at Malibu Pier." It was *Fatal Attraction* at the beach. The script focused on a woman who is rescued by a lifeguard. She begins stalking him and eventually tries to kill him. The secondary storyline was a tale of an older lifeguard who dies while saving people on an exploding fishing boat.

Bonann had to fight even to keep the *Baywatch* name. NBC worried that viewers would be confused—is the show taking place in a bay? Bonann convinced them that the title referred to the rescue boats that patrol Santa

Monica Bay, which stretches fifty miles from Point Vicente to Point Dume. Like all good titles, *Baywatch* was easy to remember, he argued.

Now, they needed a star to play the lead role, Mitch Buchannon. Actors like Tom Wopat (*Dukes of Hazzard*), William Katt (*Greatest American Hero*), Adrian Paul (pre-*Highlander*), Lorenzo Lamas (*Falcon Crest*) and Jack Scalia (pre-*Pointman*) were considered. The producers needed an actor they not only liked, but someone who could handle the physical demands of the role.

NBC suggested former *Knight Rider* star David Hasselhoff. The *Baywatch* team liked him. Parker Stevenson also signed on, as did Erika Eleniak. Eleniak, however, had just shot a spread for *Playboy* as a July 1989 Playmate. NBC was outraged, and wanted her cut from the show, fearing the wrath of conservative affiliates. But Bonann and company prevailed, and Eleniak stayed.

With the casting out of the way, the pilot "Baywatch: Panic at Malibu Pier" was scheduled to begin shooting on January 4, 1989. But there was yet another final problem: Finding a director. The A-list directors didn't want to touch *Baywatch*. The B-list seemed busy with other projects. The producers finally agreed on Richard Compton, who had directed a few episodes of *Miami Vice*.

Now, the network suddenly had a change of heart yet again. Having pushed hard to keep costs down, the decision was now handed down to shift the shoot to Hawaii. The price tag quickly jumped to $6 million from the original budget of $2 million.

The pilot aired on Sunday, April 23, 1989. NBC promoted it vigorously and viewers tuned in. *Baywatch* became the month's top-rated movie, at a 17.1 rating and 34 share. With the upfronts (the annual gathering at which the television networks present potential new shows to media buyers) fast approaching, the big question was: Would they be getting a pickup for a series?

Word came down three weeks later. Tinker called Bonann into his office and gave the news: NBC had picked up twelve episodes of *Baywatch*.

With a staff in place, Bonann decided to take the writers on a tour of his beloved bay. They stopped at Zuma Beach, then Malibu and Santa Monica's Will Rogers beach. From there, they headed to Venice, home of the lifeguard division headquarters.

As they were leaving, a teenager frantically came up to the group, screaming for help. His brother was drowning. A fierce riptide had sucked the young boy underwater. Bonann dropped to his underwear and swam out. Visibility was near zero, but he managed to find the boy underwater, close to death.

He gave the boy mouth-to-mouth, and he eventually started to breathe. Bonann started swimming back to shore, but the force of the waves nearly knocked the boy out of Bonann's arms.

The *Los Angeles Times* wrote about the rescue the next day and Tinker personally called Bonann to congratulate him.

Things weren't going as well with the show. After clashing with the network and GTG, Berk had quit. Schwartz had expected to be named showrunner—the writer-producer who supervises the show—but that didn't happen. So now Bonann had lost his two biggest supporters. "Without a doubt, this was the most hectic, unpleasant time of my life, especially because this is what I had been working to achieve for so many years," Bonann recalls.

When NBC's *Baywatch* debuted on September 22, 1989, most critics were underwhelmed. The *Variety* review read, "Script by Michael Berk and Douglas Schwartz contains lines like 'You're more trouble than most riptides,' but the inanities are mostly uttered by attractive men and women in bathing suits, so presumably it doesn't matter." TV critic Matt Roush, writing for *USA Today* called the show a "wet blanket" and argued that "surfer dudes the world around might relate, but who else is likely to give a fin?" The *Los Angeles Times'* Howard Rosenberg was even harsher, noting that the show "Isn't even treading water. You suspect that the creators of *Baywatch* are lifeguards moonlighting as writers." Still, *Variety's* reviewer predicted that the show would do well, considering "the nice bods, the sun-and-sand setting, and the frequent musical interludes. For audiences who were geographically challenged when it comes to hitting the beach, or who were in the midst of winter freezes, it was the perfect TV fantasy."

Variety's review was correct. The show would prove to be an overwhelming success, but not on NBC.

"NBC was comfortable with cops-and-robbers shows," Bonann says. "They'd had success with them before. That's what they wanted, so that's what they made."

Still, the show was working enough in its first season that NBC opted to pick up the "back nine" order, beyond the original thirteen episodes. With a caveat: The network wanted former soap star John Allen Nelson to join the show and add a little more "hunk factor."

GTG gave in on the condition that NBC pay Allen's $17,500 per episode salary. The network agreed. But it didn't matter in the end—NBC had lost interest in the show, and decided not to renew it for a second season. Bonann got the news from Tinker on May 7, 1990: "It was over. Finished. As far as Grant Tinker, GTG, Brandon Tartikoff, and NBC were concerned, *Baywatch* was history," he remembers.

The cancellation hit Tinker hard. He had helped make Tartikoff a super-star as head of NBC, and Tartikoff hadn't even called Tinker personally to let him know *Baywatch* had been canceled.

Bonann went back to lifeguarding, but his parents kept nagging him: Talk to Grant Tinker. Ask for the show back. "I was desperate," he says. "I didn't have a job, didn't want to go back to making documentaries." Bonann called up Berk and Schwartz, who had by now set up a deal at Reeves Entertainment after leaving *Baywatch*. The scribes were inter-ested in trying to revive the show—if nothing else, to prove the network wrong.

It wouldn't be easy. Even if they got the rights back, they'd need money to produce the show and to set up distribution. Bonann again met with Tin-ker, who agreed to sell back his stake in the show—for $10. Next stop: Gan-nett. Much to Bonann's relief, the company wasn't looking for money to cover the first season's deficits, which would have equaled $8 million. The company wanted $5,000 per episode for any future shows that might be produced—and said that they wouldn't spend another dime on the show. Gannett exec-utives made it clear that they thought Bonann was wasting everyone's time by trying to refloat *Baywatch*.

Bonann now turned to the Fremantle Corp.'s Paul Talbot, a venerable ex-ecutive whose company had distributed the first season of *Baywatch* inter-nationally. Fremantle had paid GTG just $75,000 an episode then, but this time out agreed to an astonishing $400,000.

The reason: Talbot understood the international popularity of Hasselhoff, particularly in Germany. Talbot stipulated that Hasselhoff appear in at least seventeen episodes (out of twenty-two). Bonann also agreed to give Talbot a big cut of *Baywatch* merchandise in continental Europe (a savvy move that made Talbot very wealthy).

Bonann was halfway there. He had crunched the numbers and figured that the show could be produced on a weekly budget of $800,000 (compared to the first season's $1.3 million) by cutting overhead, writing staff, and salaries.

"I immediately called David Hasselhoff," Bonann says. "We needed him, badly. Without Hasselhoff, no new *Baywatch*." The solution: Hasselhoff was made a full partner, an executive producer along with Berk, Schwartz, and Bonann. Ultimately, this proved to be an exceptionally profitable move by Hasselhoff. "And by being vested in its success, Hasselhoff over the years would be an indefatigable promoter of the show," Bonann adds.

Meanwhile, the British network, ITV, was looking for a show that could play at any time of day, not just in the evening. The ITV executives told Bonann that *Baywatch* would have to meet British TV standards: No violence against women or children; no guns.

Says Bonann: "Herein lies the secret to *Baywatchs'* runaway, worldwide, ongoing success: By adhering to ITV's rules, we made a show that appealed to a broad range of viewers and it could play in any timeslot, on any day, anywhere in the world. It's not a tits-and-ass show. It's about heroes. If there was a single reason why it was so popular, it's because it was so family-friendly, you could play it in any day part."

Domestically, *Baywatch* faced a bigger challenge. ABC and CBS passed, as did the then fledgling Fox. Bonann and company also pitched the show to cable outlets like Lifetime, USA, TNT, and even the Playboy Channel, to no avail.

Enter syndication. Since the earliest days of TV, the syndication market existed to fill the various timeslots outside of network primetime with original fare (like the early *Seahunt*) or reruns of network shows.

A small distributor, LBS, run by Paul and Henry Siegel, got on board to distribute *Baywatch* for a fee and piece of the profits. LBS convinced Chris-Craft, which owned WWOR in New York and KCOP in Los Angeles, among other stations, to take a look. Chris-Craft was interested and became partners, taking a 6 percent ownership in the show. Now the domestic distribution was there, but *Baywatch* still needed funding—and the loan guarantor wasn't going to be LBS, which was near bankruptcy. The show's producers talked to several sources, including Syd Vinnedge, an executive at Scotti Brothers Records. Scotti Brothers had produced one TV show, *America's Top 10*, but was looking to increase its TV presence.

Renamed All-American Television, Scotti came on board. At that point, Berk, Schwartz, Bonann, and Hasselhoff owned 50 percent of the show, with the other half split among LBS, Chris-Craft, Fremantle, and ITV. All-American took over the *Baywatch* copyright and trademarks.

It was finally time to sell the show at the annual gathering of the National Association of TV Program Executives (NATPE), where syndication deals are made or die. "At the 1991 NATPE, *Baywatch* came in through the front door, guns blazing. The guarantor, All-American, had its point man, Syd Vinnedge, in the booth. The star, David Hasselhoff, was hovering nearby," Bonann remembers.

And it worked. *Baywatch* managed to clear 89 percent of the country in its first season in syndication. (In comparison, network series can be seen in around 98 percent of the country.)

As always, a deal still had to be finalized and All-American's lawyers kept uncovering sticking points, particularly regarding control. Finally, the lawyers hammered out a compromise: Berk, Schwartz, and Bonann would get creative control, unless they exceeded budget. Then All-American would take over.

The deal was signed on May 10, 1991. The producers set about reining in the show's expenses. Hence the crew, which had worked on the NBC *Baywatch*, was told it would need to take pay cuts, beginning with the executive producers and the actors.

Beyond Hasselhoff, returning actors were Billy Warlock, Erika Eleniak, and Richard Jaeckel, all at reduced fees. In an effort to keep the cast and crew happy, the producers pointed out the magic of residuals. Given that first-run syndicated shows are constantly repeated, sometimes twice in one week, actors stood to collect backend money. Bonann also vowed that the workday would never exceed twelve hours. No exceptions. "We were all tremendously overpaid and we knew it," says Bonann. "As long as the cuts were equitable, everyone agreed to sign on."

Meanwhile, *Baywatch* continued to save money by renting equipment at low prices, and even building a concealed set above the actual lifeguard headquarters at Will Rogers State Park.

The first episode of syndicated *Baywatch*, the two-parter "Nightmare Bay," was loosely based on the rescue Bonann had made in front of the original *Baywatch* writers two years earlier. The episode began shooting in July 1991 and aired the weekend of October 5, 1991.

Without a network, the *Baywatch* producers didn't have to worry about suggested changes from network executives (euphemistically called "notes"), which can force producers to spend money and time by reshooting or re-editing scenes.

In the middle of season one, LBS, the distributors, went bankrupt, so All-American took over distribution in addition to its duties as the show's guarantor. By the end of the year, Bonann and company went back to NATPE and convinced several network affiliates to pre-empt regular programming to give the show a shot. *Baywatch* wound up in 94 percent of the country.

Then came season two, and a key casting change. With Eleniak opting to leave the show, *Baywatch* needed a new leading lady. Enter Pamela Anderson. The four executive producers asked the Canadian-born actress, who'd made a minor splash as the "Tool-Time Girl" in the ABC sitcom *Home Improvement*, to read four lines from the script. She peeled off her sweater and slipped off her skirt, standing before them in a tight, one-piece bathing suit. That was her idea. "I guess you could say Pamela was already into the part," recalls Bonann.

Anderson got the role and promptly became a hot poster pinup, contributing greatly to the show's hype. *Baywatch* was on its way to becoming a global phenomenon. It was now on the air in 145 countries, more than any other TV show (*I Love Lucy* was next, in around one hundred markets). The series' PR company, the Lippin Group, began pitching the show as the Number One series in the world. The press ate it up. *Entertainment Weekly* featured the cover story "The Most Popular TV Series in the History of the Planet Is . . . *Baywatch?*" *TV Guide* also put it on the cover, a rarity for a syndicated series.

"The planets had aligned," Bonann concludes. "*Baywatch* was king. In one week, more people watched an episode of *Baywatch* than saw some of Hollywood's biggest blockbusters in the total life of the film."

There were occasional setbacks. Anderson departed in 1997. That same year, the spinoff, *Baywatch Nights* disappeared after two seasons.

In its tenth season, *Baywatch* needed a jolt, both creatively and financially. The producers thought a change of locale might help. They had all but settled on Australia when Hawaii kicked in incentives, ponying up roughly $7 million for free airfare, hotel rooms, production and infrastructure support. Local unionized truckers and stagehands also got into the mix, agreeing to cut their pay and benefits up to 30 percent.

Baywatch relocated to Hawaii in time for its 200th episode, complete with a new name. *Baywatch Hawaii* lasted two more seasons, but it finally ended at the end of the 2000–01 season, with the last episode airing the weekend of May 14, 2001. With 243 episodes in the can, it just didn't make financial sense to continue. The show had already produced twice as many episodes than necessary for off-network syndication.

At a Honolulu press conference soon after the cancellation, Bonann told the *Advertiser* that the show was no longer making money. "[But] it's not because the costs [locally] went up, but because the ratings went down," he told the paper. "The costs exceeded our ratings. I was really surprised when we got a second year [in Hawaii]."

The success of *Baywatch* will always be singled out by students of television for a number of reasons. First, it represented yet another reminder that the networks—all networks—can be dead wrong in predicting audience reaction to a show. *Baywatch* also signaled the fascination of viewers around the world with the effluvia of American pop culture. The tide of anti-Americanism may rise and fall, but that fixation remains a constant. Finally, the saga of Greg Bonann has inspired producers and wannabe producers to believe there is no such thing as a final pitch. It's always worth trying one more time, irrespective of the pile of rejections. The only rejection that's really damning is self-rejection.

8 Controlled Reality

Real World (1992)

From its inception, the billion-dollar boondoggle known as reality TV has been a study in marketing alchemy. Reality shows were sold as unscripted, but they were in fact carefully laid out—indeed, the writers of the "non-scripts" eventually demanded union representation. Reality entries had breathless titles like *Fear Factor* or *Survivor*, yet offered a minimum of peril or suspense as the episodes unfolded—just a great deal of random intermingling. As the genre proliferated to suffocating proportions, each scrambled for a new gimmick—*Fear Factor* went interactive, *The Amazing Race* went global—in recognition of the fact that their formulas offered meager doses of wish fulfillment.

The entire exercise owes its origins to a curious MTV show called *The Real World*, which is basically a faux exercise in video vérité filtered through the sensibility of a soap opera producer. The conceit of *Real World* is downright simplistic compared with the elaborate setups of later network reality shows: Plunk a group of unintentionally exhibitionistic kids in a confined situation and keep the cameras rolling as they make idiots of themselves.

As stripped-down and basic as this formula seemed, its success, in 1992, sent shock waves through broadcast television. How could any idea so straightforward and inexpensive not have been exploited till now?

Once the wheels started turning at the networks, the reality genre quickly morphed into a burgeoning industry led by brilliantly hyperactive shlockmeisters like Mark Burnett. Meanwhile, *The Real World* managed to build its franchise as the most-watched series on cable among the MTV target audience of twelve-to-thirty-four-year-olds, sucking new generations of viewers into its gauche love affairs and adolescent intrigues.

TV aficionados would argue that some manifestations of reality television predated *The Real World*. Unscripted shows like *America's Funniest Home Videos* and *Cops* existed before. Some might even trace the genre back to the Roller Derbies of TV's baby-step years, when oddball types skated in circles, now and then colliding like rush-hour travelers on the New York subway system.

But *The Real World* took "reality" to another level—one that would ultimately not only spawn a long-lasting series, but would become a genuine pop culture phenomenon. Indeed a casting call for *The Real World*, once a strenuous struggle, has itself become a pop event, attracting hundreds of thousands of young people hoping to live rent-free for six months while achieving a measure of post-pubic immortality.

Like every great idea, this one grew out of a combination of need and desperation.

By 1990, MTV had much to be proud of—and apprehensive about. At the age of ten, it was reaching more than 50 million subscribers, one of a small cluster of cable networks that, like ESPN, had managed to hit pay dirt. But while it could boast advertiser-friendly demographics, there was no signature series on MTV that could claim "appointment viewing." Madison Avenue wanted a show that would attract younger viewers on a more predictable basis. A steady diet of hosted video blocks could not make that pitch.

At the same time, a certain tension existed between the network and both the music and movie industries. MTV needed music videos and nurtured its close ties to the record labels. Whenever it ventured into shows like *Remote Control* or *The Ben Stiller Show*, it could all but hear the sighs of exasperation from the music mavens who were wondering, "Why not just play more videos?"

Movie companies, meanwhile, were dependent on running various forms of thinly disguised promo reels on MTV, again hoping to reach that magical young demographic. Rival companies had become suspicious that Paramount's products had easier access on the network because Paramount and MTV were both parts of giant Viacom.

Lauren Corrao, the head of development at MTV, felt she had the answer to MTV's dilemma: launch a soap opera for teens. She even came up with the producers who, in her view, were ideally equipped to develop just the right sort of show—Mary-Ellis Bunim and Jon Murray.

Bunim, daughter of a rice importer and a nurse, started her career in television in 1967 as a secretary for the CBS soap opera *Search for Tomorrow*, one of the earliest programs in the genre. Fiercely ambitious, she rose through the ranks to become one of the youngest daytime executives in television. She spent the next twenty years supervising production for *Search*, *As the World Turns*, *Loving*, and *Santa Barbara*, earning a reputation for revving up ratings.

In 1987, Bunim was introduced to Jon Murray by their agent, Mark Itkin, who thought the two might mesh. With a shared love of storytelling, they were eager to nurture a new genre of television that would combine Bunim's dramatic sensibilities with Murray's news training. Murray had started as a newsman in local TV, working his way into programming. He then became what's called a TV "rep," working with local stations in buying and scheduling syndicated programming. His first love, however, was producing occasional news specials focusing on topics of social interest—a doomed housing project, for example. Once Bunim/Murray Productions was founded, the two found they were like-minded in their TV work, even placing their desks side-by-side in their always frenzied office.

In the beginning, the pair shot several prototype pilots, but none of them took off. First there was *Crime Diaries*, which they conceived as a daily half-hour series that featured fictional detectives solving actual crimes. Another was *American Families*, a docu-soap inspired by the highly influential *An American Family*, the 1973 PBS documentary that chronicled, and some say exploited, the family of William and Pat Loud, a Santa Barbara couple who filed for divorce on the final episode of the twelve-hour series. *American Family* was the show that would grab the attention of MTV executives, which were on the hunt for a teen soap and would later take a chance on Bunim and Murray to develop the project for them.

Encouraged by her friend, MTV's Corrao, Bunim worked for a year to develop a straightforward scripted soap for MTV, mindful that it might prove to be too expensive for the cable network. The cost of hiring union writers and crew was inconceivable for the network, which at the time relied on a diet of 90 percent music videos.

The idea was abandoned and then Bunim and Murray came up with a better one—a hybrid soap-documentary series. As MTV's Corrao remembered it, Bunim and Murray had said simply, "What if we could do a soap opera with no actors or writers?" Perhaps with the right editing, music, and a quicker pace, an *American Families*-style show could play to the MTV audience.

They pitched the idea to Corrao over a breakfast and she bought it by lunch. She had seen the Fox pilot for *American Families*, and was "shocked at how natural people were in front of the camera." She, herself, had been through a *Real World*-style situation after college: "I lived in an architect's loft with six other people. Some of them I knew, but some were friends of friends. We stayed there for four months. It was amazing in terms of the parties and conflicts we all had. All these things became very clear to me in terms of possibilities for good television—how a group of people who had never met before would react when forced to live together."

In order to "sell" the rest of the MTV staff—including Judy McGrath, the MTV president, and the nonmusic programming head Doug Herzog—Corrao decided she needed to show some footage. Again, MTV had never done a narrative-driven series of any sort, scripted or otherwise, and "no one would have believed it would work if I had tried to sell it verbally," Corrao said.

So Bunim and Murray went about shooting something resembling a pilot. They rented a loft for a long Memorial Day weekend with a practice cast of seven strangers that Murray had chosen mostly himself. Casting a documentary series—essentially, one without a theme or driving narrative—was difficult. An ad in *Electronic Media* from December 1991 read: "MTV has hit the streets here [in New York] in search of three males and three females between the ages of 18 and 26 willing to take part in a 13-week video experiment. The producers of the show don't want actors. Once selected, the six people will share a 3,000-square-foot loft with room and board paid by MTV in addition to a small stipend. The six will wear wireless microphones and be filmed 30 hours a week." The ad concluded: "The only time we'll respect their privacy is when they're in the bathroom or on their way to second base with someone they're very interested in."

The ad was not successful, so Murray took to the streets to find his cast.

Murray recalls, "It was hard walking down Broadway and asking people to participate. A lot of them thought we were making porn. We put up signs with the tear-off phone numbers in laundry rooms. We went on radio shows and MTV put ads on the air. We also went through modeling and acting agents."

New York was chosen as the location because it's a place where "young people go to find themselves and pursue their dreams," Murray says. It wasn't by chance that the initial cast members were all aspiring artists. "MTV wanted a bit of a wish-fulfillment angle. So we tried to play to the fantasy of the viewers. That's what a good soap does. The idea of someone wanting to become a rock musician that plays to the fantasy of a lot of fifteen-year-old kids out there.

"We didn't start with the idea of having all young 'artists,'" he continues. "We interviewed a broad spectrum, but the people who were attracted to this project were generally these more open-minded, artistic people. The stock broker, the telephone operator—they didn't pound down our doors. And those who did, frankly, weren't that interesting."

But that didn't mean that Bunim and Murray weren't tempted to do some prompting in the beginning, as they acknowledged to authors Hillary Johnson and Nancy Rommelmann, in *MTV's The Real Reel World*. Says Bunim, "The original concept of the show was that if not enough happened, we would encourage the drama by 'tossing pebbles into the pond,' so to speak. MTV wanted that guarantee. So our first 'toss' was to ask Peter, a cast member from the original pilot, to invite Becky on a date. Becky found out and was very uncomfortable with being set up like that. The same thing happened with Eric, who'd appeared in Bruce Weber's *Bear Pond* book without clothes. We planted the book in the loft, and Heather, another cast member, teased Eric, and this added to his paranoia. We realized we couldn't manipulate what we were going to get, so we stopped 'tossing pebbles' and promised not to use the footage. Besides, the unprompted drama was much better than anything we could set up."

She adds: "Cast members had to agree that every part of their lives was open to viewers. We really fully expected someone to break under this scrutiny—that was OK, as long as they made the decision in front of the camera. Fortunately, that didn't happen, but we were prepared for it."

As producer–director George Verschoor observes: "It takes an incredible amount of character to accept the truth. When you're twenty-two years old, you live by what's going to get you through the day. *The Real World* is a difficult mirror to look into. And here I am asking them, 'Please tell me everything about your life, the good, the bad, the ugly; whatever you can tell me . . . If you turn your back to me, you're going to see your butt.'"

Inevitably, the biggest obstacle was getting the cast comfortable enough with the situation that they ignored the ubiquitous cameras. "When we first got there, we knew they were there," a season one cast member admits. "But after awhile it was like they were a piece of furniture."

Sasha Alpert, who has been casting *The Real World* since its early years, says her challenge in casting the show was sheer volume. "We'd have these huge open calls. We'd get 2,000 per call sometimes, especially in college cities like Boston. In the beginning, we'd meet applicants in groups of ten. We'd look for people who weren't self-conscious on camera."

Alpert, whose background was in feature documentaries, acknowledges casting is a particularly subjective art. "I'd choose people that I was interested in talking to. The people that worked were the ones who held my attention interview after interview. Also, if they're struggling with an issue it helps. Twenty-four is the cutoff age, so a lot of these kids are asking themselves, 'Who am I? What is my place in the world?' People who struggle with that more actively are more likely to get cast. In other words, anyone who is at a turning point in their lives."

Building chemistry was also important. "It's always challenging to figure out what chemistry will work best. We wanted to make sure everybody felt connected. If you have seven people who can't find common ground, then it's not a good show. That's why it's important to get rid of people who you think are doing this for publicity," she observes.

Sometimes that's a losing battle. Says Murray, "In the second season, set in L.A., Beth S. hid the fact that she was an aspiring actress. She was constantly trying to create a character, posing in each shot. The cast picked up on it and started calling her 'Drama Queen.'"

Still, Murray acknowledges, "Some of the cast thought doing the show would lead to other opportunities in the entertainment business, but other than Eric, it really hasn't. We tell everyone who applies to this show not to do it for the fame or exposure. Do it because it's an incredibly cool experience."

At the outset, Bunim and Murray shot two test episodes over four days for Corrao to take back to her bosses at MTV. Herzog was a quick ally, won over by the "plain good, compelling television" he saw on the tapes. But still it was a first-of-its-kind effort—one that would cost more than the network was budgeting on any other programming. Approval ratings were strong on two initial pilots, but the network still took all of its nine-month option time before ordering thirteen episodes, which would be shot in SoHo, New York.

Having decided not to interfere by "tossing any more pebbles" into the show, Bunim said no activities were planned or suggested, other than planting certain props to stimulate conversation, including a Ouija board and a *Love & Sex* book of party questions.

The first season's cast included Norman Korpi, twenty-four, a partner in a struggling design firm; Rebecca (Becky) Blasband, twenty-four, a waitress/aspiring singer; Julie Oliver, nineteen, a dance student; Kevin Powell, twenty-five, a freelance writer and poet; Eric Nies, twenty, a model and aspiring actor; Andre Comeau, twenty-one, the lead singer of a band; and Heather B, twenty-one, a rap singer.

The cost of the show during the first season was about $110,000 per episode. "That was unheard of for us," Corrao said. "We had spent about $15,000 to 20,000 for *Remote Control*, and $110,000 for basic cable at the time was a very large sum. To get that much money took a lot of support internally." Each cast member received a small stipend (around $250 per week), plus their house expenses paid (not including food). Anything else they wanted they'd have to pay for.

Mindful of MTV's relationship to the music industry, producers also spent a lot of time choosing the right music to lay over scenes. "We wanted to make our viewers feel comfy with this show and make it feel like our air—not PBS," Corrao says. "So from frame one to the end, montage scenes were all driven by music."

By using songs from music videos that MTV already had clearances to play, the network also avoided expensive music rights for the contemporary pop songs that underscore the adventures of the cast members.

Their ratings were unprecedented for a series and were all the more impressive because MTV hadn't spent any money to market the show off-air.

"The kids who were watching the show saw themselves on TV without stilted dialogue. It was really and truly of its time. And that's why the show continues to rate well till this day. It's always timely. It's always a reflection of what's going on in the culture," Corrao says.

Variety's original review of the series when it premiered in May 1992 seemed to agree: "MTV, the arbiter of style and music for today's younger generation, has come up with another winning idea in this half-hour reality drama tracking the lives of seven people living together. MTV went out and found seven attractive, hip, twenty-something people and thrust them together in a happening Manhattan apartment so the network could film their every move. Result is a compelling, immensely interesting and thoroughly addicting thirty minutes of television. Done in the "traditional" MTV style of music-laden quick cuts with head-on interviews, the program is mesmerizing. It's *Cops* without the police and violence."

Jon Murray says the show stays relevant because it is "always reflecting the currency of the times. Critics say real people don't live in lofts and aren't this attractive. I say to them that TV is an escapist medium, so you need to have a nice loft. But it doesn't take away from Pedro's story, or the racial discussions. It didn't take away from Tami [from the second season] dealing with an unplanned pregnancy."

Verschoor also defends the series as less *90210* than most people would believe: "We've captured issues ranging from leaving home, to family illness, romance, racism, roommate relations, living with AIDS, looking for work, abortion, or simple practical jokes, slacking, and sticking your finger in the peanut butter jar."

In the eyes of MTV, the series needs no defense. *The Real World* elevated the network to a whole new level of success. Besides expanding the MTV empire around the world, the company has continued to build the scope of its operations and by 2005 was pushing aggressively into motion-picture production. Meanwhile, in 2005, its founder, Tom Freston, became CEO of half of the newly-divided Viacom empire, presiding over Paramount Pictures as well as MTV and Nickelodeon.

Keeping pace with the ever-evolving reality genre they helped launch, Bunim and Murray went on to produce *Road Rules* in 1994, a road-trip spin-off involving sports contests, which pioneered the new subgenre of competitive reality series. Their credits also include *Making the Band*, in which teenage boys vied for the chance to be the next 'NSync and *The Rebel Billionaire*, a show in which Richard Branson sought to take on the robust aura of Donald Trump.

Mary-Ellis Bunim died of breast cancer in 2004 at the age of fifty-seven. At the time of her death, Brian Graden, her boss at MTV, praised her "great insight" as revealed in the casting of *The Real World*. "She and Jon were absolutely pioneers in showing how people learn by interacting with one another and being with people who are different than themselves," he says.

Tom Freston, president of the Paramount arm of Viacom, later observed that *The Real World* became a classic example of how poverty could nurture creativity—in short, MTV's lack of resources to do a scripted show forced its staff to come up with something vastly more interesting and innovative. "It's a reminder that throwing money at a project is not always the answer," he says. "Throwing fresh ideas at it can often be more productive."

In any event, the unique "world" that MTV, through Bunim and Murray, created is now being shared with millions of viewers around the globe. It is an edgy world, an immensely profitable world, but by no means is it a "real world."

9 Feel-Good Felines

Cats (1981)

It was not until the dawning of the '80s that I finally succumbed to the Message of the Moment. Mind you, it had been right there, staring at me for some time. Indeed, I had been living through it but had still been fighting it off, as though it were some alien concept. And in a way it was. The Message of the Moment was as unsettling as it was obvious, because it would change the way we would all think about popular entertainment—even, change the way pop culture and its practitioners would think about themselves. Movies and plays and TV and pop music were no longer about that simple process that we had all come to understand: Artists writing and composing and directing; producers and random hustlers flailing about, exploiting the clumsy apparatus of distribution and promotion; companies battling for market share; all of them hoping for the hit, fearing the flop, praying for the payoff, dodging the debacle.

That was yesterday. Now it was something very different. At some invisible moment pop culture had been transmogrified into a multinational, multicultural, all-engulfing monster mega-industry. It had all become grist for giant corporate conglomerates for which entertainment was just one additional product, which they chose to label "content." The focus of their attention was not on the artists but the delivery systems—the pipelines and who would control them.

The world had changed, and I felt I was the last to take notice; yet, just about everyone I knew shared that glimmer of self-doubt, as though we all were standing on the *Titanic* and were loathe to talk about that sinking feeling.

It was, oddly enough, a cat that triggered my awakening—not a real cat, but rather a grotesquely costumed and bewhiskered dancer playing a cat who materialized suddenly and startlingly before me. For reasons that escape me, I had decided to be part of the opening night audience at an Andrew Lloyd Webber musical. I was expecting very little and in fact feared the worst. The advance buzz on *Cats* had not been good. There had been rumors that a terrified Webber had tried to call the whole thing off. There had been cast changes and even reports (incorrect) that T. S. Eliot's widow wanted to withdraw her authorization to adapt the poems into an expensive musical.

And now this hideous, writhing cat had appeared before me and I could sense that what was unfolding was not an ordinary experience. This was in-your-face show business. This was loud and even belligerent. This was not so much the opening of a musical as it was the launch of an industry.

That would figure, considering the events of the moment. Michael Jackson's *Thriller* was then more a phenomenon than a conventional CD (forget the term "album"). Some 45 million copies had been swept off the counters and seven of its nine songs appeared in the Top Ten. And then there was Spielberg's *E.T.*, which wasn't behaving like a normal hit but more like a pop culture phenomenon. Hollywood had had its big hits before this—films like *Jaws* and *Star Wars* most recently—and *Variety* had even coined a word for them: blockbusters. But they were thought to have been aberrations from the norm, phenomena that likely would never happen again. Yet suddenly here was *E.T.* and *Raiders of the Lost Ark* and *Thriller* and even *Cats* exploding all over the landscape. And the studio "suits" were telling themselves, "This is good, it's the new world order and who says we cannot sustain it?"

Newsweek observed in 1982 that *Cats* was "the theatrical parallel to Steven Spielberg's film, *E.T.*, a sharply intelligent popular entertainment that resonates at many levels all the way down to the heart." A couple of critics even took note of the vaguely similar imagery in the Webber and

Spielberg pieces—*E.T.*'s kids riding their bicycles toward the moon even as that tired old puss, Grizabella, rose toward heaven in a tire at the end of *Cats*.

Some highbrow pundits were predictably put off by these theatrics. Writing in the *New Republic*, Robert Brustein wondered whether all this "could have been manufactured by Disneyworld." One character in John Guare's 1990 play, *Six Degrees of Separation*, gripes, "Aeschylus did not invent theater to have it end up with a bunch of chorus kids wondering which of them will go to Kitty Cat Heaven."

On April 17, 1981, four days before the first

public performance of *Cats*, in London, composer Andrew Lloyd Webber and producer Cameron Mackintosh agreed they had to pull the plug on the show.

It was during the first technical run-through on Good Friday at the New London Theatre: "I went to Cameron," says Lloyd Webber. "He said, 'I know what you're going to say. We've got to close this now. It's going to be an ignominious shame.' So we took [the director] Trevor Nunn out to Joe Allen's, which was the only restaurant in those days open on a bank holiday, and we said, 'We're closing this.' I said, 'I'm sorry, Trevor. I have money in this show, but I can't go through with it. The reputation—it's going to be too awful.'"

"Trevor said, 'OK, you close it, but I'm going on with it.' Trevor took us through that weekend. I tell you, Cameron and I were shaking like leaves with worry."

It's ironic that the show was saved by director Nunn, since his two collaborators had had a difficult time convincing him to take it on to begin with. "I confess I was fairly doubtful about whether it could be the basis of a large-scale musical and I was also fairly doubtful that I was anything like the right director to be involved with it," Nunn recalls.

In early 1980, Nunn and Lloyd Webber went to lunch to discuss the project. Nunn was the artistic director of the Royal Shakespeare Company, one of the most important subsidized theaters in the world. He and John Caird had just finished the famed eight-hour adaptation of Charles Dickens' *Nicholas Nickleby* for the RSC. He was a serious, classical director.

As it turns out, Nunn had studied T. S. Eliot at Cambridge under F. R. Leavis, a renowned Eliot scholar. This made him an ideal choice for director—and as it turns out, his Eliot knowledge would become crucial at many points during the creation of *Cats*.

While Nunn was intrigued, he felt nervous about venturing into commercial waters with such a risky project. Plus, the show had no shape. Was it a book musical? A song cycle? A dance show? As Mackintosh recalls, "Trevor did tell me it was very nice to meet [with] Andrew, but what a shame it was that it was a bad idea." He later reconsidered, albeit reluctantly.

Their fears were warranted. Here was a show based on poetry by T. S. Eliot, not exactly a hot commercial prospect, to be directed by a Shakespearean director who'd never done a musical. It was being staged at the New London Theatre, a venue that seemed cursed as a legit house and that was used mostly as a business and conference center. And, perhaps most crucially, all the actors were dancing around dressed as cats.

The show's creators were getting little encouragement from newspapers and those in the theater world. "It was considered to be—and all the theater queens knew it would be—the biggest disaster that had ever been presented in the history of time. We opened with half its investment missing and I had a second mortgage on my house to guarantee the deal," says Lloyd Webber.

Reminiscing at the Beverly Hills Hotel twenty-four years later, Lloyd Webber is smiling at the memory. At this point, he can afford to smile. The show has become one of the biggest theatrical smashes of all time.

The final statistics transcend reality for its backers: a total of 8,950 performances in London's West End, some 7,485 on Broadway, additional companies in thirty countries seen by 30 million theatergoers, resulting in an ultimate total gross in the range of $3 billion. These numbers defied the dimension of success and gave new heft to the term blockbuster.

Born in 1948, Lloyd Webber grew up with T. S.

Eliot's, *Old Possum's Book of Practical Cats.* "They were read to me by my mother. I'm also a cat man" Lloyd Webber says and grins. "It's something you remember from childhood. And [later] I would read them and laugh at the sheer wit of them. I always thought they were very fun. Even back in the *Jesus Christ Superstar* days, I thought that would be fun to set those poems to music. But I never thought it would be a stage show. I thought it would be a record album or a concert piece, a bit like *Peter and the Wolf.*"

He can't remember the first song he wrote. "But the interesting thing for me was that I was setting poetry, or existing 'lyrics,' if you like, to music. And I use that term advisedly, because Eliot was American and if you ever have to set anything to music, I think you can tell an American because he used irregular meters, and played around with scansion.

"I started doing it out of intrigue, to see if I could do it the other way around," because with Tim Rice and his other lyricists, the music came first.

Lloyd Webber might never have shown the songs to Mackintosh if they hadn't gone drinking together. When *Evita* won the prize as best musical at the 1978 Society of West End Theatre Awards (renamed the Oliviers in 1984), Lloyd Webber had mocked the evening's entertainment, describing it as "abysmal cabaret." "I said it'd be great if Hal Prince [one of the original producers of *West Side Story* and director of the original productions of *Cabaret*] could come in and stage these awards in the future." The remarks offended Mackintosh, who had produced the show. The two exchanged six months' worth of "very rude letters" and then Lloyd Webber invited the producer to lunch at London's venerable Saville Club. "I had no idea who Cameron Mackintosh was. I assumed I was going to meet this ancient, wizened Scotsman." In fact, Mackintosh was thirty-one years old. He'd begun producing in 1967, with his shows including the London revue *Side by Side by Sondheim*, a touring production of *Godspell*, and London revivals of *Oklahoma!* and *My Fair Lady*.

According to Lloyd Webber, "It was the funniest lunch of all time. It started at quarter to one in a rather prickly way and ended at seven with me saying, 'Cameron, let's go have another drink, this was the most enjoyable meeting. I've got this ridiculous idea about a musical about cats.' Then I went home and played him the bare bones of the score. God knows what state I was in."

Mackintosh recalls that Lloyd Webber had been pitching the idea for three years, and "everybody thought he was out of his mind." But Mackintosh saw something in it.

According to Lloyd Webber, "All this material came together rather quickly; Cameron and I thought about it a lot. 'Who is the one person who understands the most about popular-theater staging?'"

Nunn had directed the Kaufman–Hart comedy *Once in a Lifetime*, and a version of *The Comedy of Errors* that included quite a bit of music and song. The composer and producer decided he would offer commercial savvy while protecting the integrity of the Eliot poetry. Nunn recalled that he, at first, wanted the musical to be "a small piece with something like eight performers and two pianos and [Lloyd Webber] said, 'No no no, I'm thinking of something much more spectacular than that.'"

Some of the songs were tried out at Lloyd Webber's annual arts festival at Sydmonton, his country home, where he's tested new material for thirty years. "There was probably about an hour of material," Webber says. "But we didn't have Grizabella and we didn't have the Jellicle Ball."

He had secured rights to the book of poems, but "there was a wooing process with Valerie Eliot [the poet's widow] to convince her to take it from a concert piece to a theater piece," and to convince her that her husband's work would not be violated.

In fact, when she heard the songs, she told Lloyd Webber, "You ought to look at this other material." There were other works, about dogs and cats, and something mysterious Eliot called the "Heaviside Layer." "Suddenly, there was the germ of something bigger. Also, there was the story of Grizabella the Glamour Cat, which was not in the original book at all, and a whole load of other unpublished poetry about animals that she gave me. One was the ballad of Billy McCaw, the parrot."

Lloyd Webber envisioned a big dance piece, though conventional wisdom said that the London stage was not known for its dances. And suddenly he felt he had the seed of "an emotional story, because of Grizabella."

Eliot had written a poem called "Pollicle Dogs and Jellicle Cats." Lloyd Webber asked Valerie Eliot, "Why were they called that?"

"It's because the upper class in England talk about 'poor little dogs, jolly little cats,'" replied the widow.

Thomas Stearns Eliot seemed an unlikely source for a commercial blockbuster. A native of St. Louis, Missouri, he was educated at Harvard, the Sorbonne, and Oxford, then settled in London in 1914, working as a clerk at Lloyds Bank while writing poetry. His seminal works included "The Love Song of J. Alfred Prufrock" (1915), about a painfully self-conscious man ("Do I dare to eat a peach?"), and "The Waste Land" (1922). It's hard to imagine a poem causing a sensation even in 1922 but his mixture of slang and scholarly phrasing caught the postwar mood. His "The Hollow Men" (1925) contains the now famous lines "This is the way the world ends / Not with a bang but a whimper."

Not exactly the kind of stuff you want to sing along with. But the man who wrote the 1948 *Notes Towards the Definition of Culture* was the same man who loved whoopee cushions and exploding cigars. And he exhibited that earthy, whimsical side in his 1939 *Old Possum's Book of Practical Cats*, evocative poetry about the secret lives of felines.

Lloyd Webber and Mackintosh now were convinced that dance would play a large part in their show and even offered it to a few dance companies, all of which promptly rejected it. Early on they selected Gillian Lynne as choreographer and associate director. She had worked with Mackintosh on *The Card* and *My Fair Lady* and had collaborated with Nunn on *The Comedy of Errors*. Mackintosh admired Lynne and thought her participation would help sustain Nunn's enthusiasm.

"Trevor took a while to get to the altar," admits Lloyd Webber. "Gillian Lynne was very pro it from the beginning. I think Trevor knew it was a huge step for him, to be the director of one of the most important subsidized theaters in the country at the time and having been incredibly successful."

Now contemplating a larger-scale work, Nunn concluded that "we would have to find a way of extracting a narrative from those poems suggesting some central characters and an environment."

Lloyd Webber proposed a return to Eliot's idea about dogs versus cats. "He never got around to writing all the dog stuff, thank goodness, but he did write about the battle of the pekes and the pollicles. That's the only poem that survives, apart from this bit that was never published. Trevor said we can't possibly do that. It's not going to be about dogs. So we used all the Eliot ideas in 'Jellicle Songs for Jellicle Cats.'" As the musical became a show about a tribe of cats. A character in another poem, Macavity, emerged as the tribe's enemy.

Though "Jellicle Songs for Jellicle Cats" became the opening number, the song needed about twelve crucial lines to help set up the narrative for the rest of the show. So Nunn and lyricist Richard Stilgoe appropriated lines from Eliot's "The Man in the White Spats," adding some of their aim.

The creators worried that Valerie Eliot would not approve of using any lines that weren't written by her husband. So they set up an "absolutely crucial" meeting, Nunn recalled, in a restaurant on the piazza at Covent Garden. Nunn decided to pull out all his Eliot know-how.

"I was able to talk with some relative ease about T. S. Eliot's more ob-scure work," Nunn recalls. "I think she was able to trust that we were reliable people and that we weren't going to injure his tone or voice."

Lloyd Webber also told Valerie Eliot, "We do intend to use very sexy young people in the dance numbers. It's going to be quite raunchy in vari-ous places. The ball itself is not going to be about anything other than what cats get up to. I thought that I was going to be shown the door at that point. And she said, 'Oh, Tom would have liked that.'" The composer was startled. "You know, Tom turned down the biggest offer of his career from Disney. They wanted to animate *Old Possum's Book of Practical Cats*. It was to be the follow-up to *Fantasia*. And I said, 'Why did he not want to do that?' and she said 'Tom thought *Fantasia* was . . .'" Lloyd Webber pauses and discreetly explains, "a four-letter-word."

He laughs, "Blimey, I'm listening to the sixty- or seventy-year-old widow of T. S. Eliot! She said, 'He just didn't like it.' She then said, 'Tom would not have wanted his cats turned into pussycats. They were always about the street.'"

Cats

"And that's when she said, 'You can have Grizabella.'" Eliot had mandated that the poem was "not to be included in the volume *Practical Cats* because it is too sad for children."

Reading Grizabella's poem was a "eureka moment" for Nunn. "It was a little poem about mortality, it was about old age, and how beauty doesn't last, and how we're all heading for the grave," Nunn says. "I remember phoning Andrew and saying, 'This changes everything.'"

The major emotional arc of the show could be the story of this aging, Norma Desmond-like cat that mourns her faded beauty but then ascends into heaven and is reborn. Realizing this, Nunn assured Mackintosh he was in for the long haul.

The unpublished Grizabella poem solved many problems with the show, but a few questions remained. Nunn recalls, "We needed for that cat to appear and to have a statement of her own. I remember writing a note to Andrew, 'If ever one of your great Puccini-like tunes was necessary, it is here. You need to give a really emotional ballad to this cat."

Later, Nunn says, "We were at some ballet center in South London, and we'd had quite a successful audition session . . . At the end of this session, Andrew said, 'Look, I've been thinking about what you said, I've got this tune, just tell me what you think.' And he sat down at the piano and we all heard the tune that we now associate with 'Memory' for the first time, and I remember saying to everybody, 'Check the date, check the time, and remember it, because that's going to be for your memoirs. That's going to be the first time you heard a tune that would become famous, that swept the world.'"

The lyrics were another story. Initially no one could get them right. Nunn says they first approached Lloyd Webber's former writing partner Tim Rice, who turned them down. They asked poet Roger McGough, who wrote what was "a good poem but was completely unsingable," Nunn says. "We reminded ourselves of the difference between a lyricist and a poet." Eliot's poems adapted remarkably to music, with their "brilliantly clever rhymes, sometimes on-purpose bad rhymes that lyricists can do," according to Nunn. They tried several other famous lyricists, all of whom failed to come up with anything that could match the quality of Eliot's poetry.

Finally, a frustrated Nunn found himself at home alone one Saturday afternoon. The onetime Eliot student decided to read the entire works of T. S. Eliot from beginning to end, from 2 PM to 11 PM. "There was this poem called 'Rhapsody on a Windy Night' and during the course of it, Eliot apostrophizes the word 'memory' and I thought 'I wonder if that's a basis.' And I started to play around with the lyric, and got very sleepy and went to bed. I woke up at 6 AM and said 'I have to go on with this . . .'

"I showed it to Andrew first thing on Monday morning, we were doing a talk-through of the second act, and Andrew's reaction was extraordinary. He said, 'Well you've got it, it's exactly what we want.' I said, 'Is it the right idea?' He said 'No, I don't want to change it at all.' I was very confused and slightly flattered."

With the show taking shape, the search for an appropriate venue took on urgency. The producers, Mackintosh and Lloyd Webber's Really Useful Group Ltd., considered many traditional theaters. Lloyd Webber liked the New London, where he had taped an episode of *This Is Your Life*. He recalls, "They had it as a business and conference center, having been a disaster as a theater, we really thought it was the theater for us. Finally that old impresario, Bernie Delfont, brokered a deal providing that the longer we ran, the more we'd have to pay to close. Old Bernie knew I was guaranteeing the money."

The rehearsal period was extremely difficult. Though the actors were all trained dancers, the feline movements required contortions that weren't used in most dance and ballet pieces.

Meanwhile, press reports started appearing that denigrated the show and excoriated Nunn for joining a childish endeavor. "It struck many people as odd, indeed," Nunn says. "They couldn't keep themselves from laughing in my face. It was a prediction of disaster everywhere. 'You mean human beings are going to play cats,' they would snicker."

Not surprisingly, Mackintosh was having trouble finding the £400,000 needed to fund the show. He didn't raise the final £10,000 until the night of the first preview.

Then came the Good Friday technical rehearsal, which entailed a run-through of all the sound cues, lighting, and set changes. It's a start-and-stop process in which there is no flow to the work. And the process is particularly grueling when the tech demands are heavy. Mackintosh calls the *Cats* session, "the longest, most manic tech in history." Mackintosh and Lloyd Webber promptly panicked and tried to convince Nunn to pull the plug. As Nunn recalls, "I said, 'You've got to trust theater practitioners to bring things together.'"

Lloyd Webber now says, "If you are the author of a musical, go away during the technicals."

At the first preview, Tuesday, April 21, Lloyd Webber and Mackintosh were too nervous to watch, fearing the audience's reaction even as the actors emerged in their cat costumes. Lloyd Webber recalls, "We stood, Cameron and I, at the back of the theater and there were all these kids, young people, dressed as cats! Cameron said to me, 'We're either going to witness the worst moment of bathos in the history of theater or something will happen.' We heard them go onstage, we didn't watch it—and there was no laughter.

"And suddenly we got to the end of 'Jellicle Songs for Jellicle Cats.' There was supposed to be no applause at this point; we didn't want any because it goes right into 'The Naming of Cats.' And the whole audience went into an uproar of applause. The first act went wonderfully and the second act went appallingly. And the next night, the second act went very well but the first act went badly. And the third night, it coalesced completely and we knew then."

The problems weren't over, though. Playing Grizabella was Judi Dench, a veteran of musicals. She played Sally Bowles in London's first production of *Cabaret* (1968) and had appeared in the Andre Previn–Johnny Mercer production *The Good Companions* in the West End. During previews, however, Dench snapped her Achilles tendon. The two weeks of previews were extended to four weeks, to allow for her recovery. The producers released photos of Dench in a cast to show that her injury wasn't a ploy to gain time.

Dench returned, but during a rehearsal at Her Majesty's Theater, she took a stumble and realized she wasn't up to the role. The producers scrambled to hire Elaine Paige, the original Eva Peron in *Evita*, as Dench's replacement. That's when Tim Rice, who was close with Paige, decided to try writing a lyric to substitute for "Memory."

"It was a lyric of high quality," Nunn recalls. "The problem was that it really didn't fit with the show." Paige sang Rice's lyrics for seven previews. Nunn said, "The moment didn't pay off, it didn't happen, it seemed to be disconnected." Mackintosh agreed with Nunn, and Nunn's lyrics were restored.

The song "Memory," as it turned out, melted audiences, and it was followed by the show's spacey climax. Inspiration for the ending stemmed from a letter Eliot had written to his publishers, Faber & Faber, speculating "maybe I should bring all the cats together at the end and they all should get into the basket of a huge balloon and should go 'up up up past the Russell Hotel—up up up to the Heaviside Layer.' "

"Heaviside Layer," is the scientific term for the layer of the space just beyond the stratosphere. In Eliot's mind, the cats would award a new life to Grizabella. John Napier, who designed the sets and costumes, came up with the idea of carrying Grizabella to heaven in a tire, and designed a hydraulic lift to levitate the tire with her in it.

"When we first did it, we had smoke pouring down, and you absolutely couldn't see any support for it, everybody just absolutely gasped," says Nunn. "It seemed like pure magic."

Napier also designed a stylized trash heap, which Nunn says was inspired by "The Waste Land." The set was placed in the middle of the audience and rotated; so did the first several rows of the audience.

That movement became a big selling point for the show. "If you have an advertisement for the show that says 'Latecomers will not be admitted while the auditorium is in motion,' you've got to go just to find out what it means," Nunn says.

The show debuted on May 11, 1981. "Frankly, it would've been better for us if we'd opened on the date that we'd originally scheduled," Lloyd Webber reflects, "because the show had settled by then. It was right. By the time it got to the new date, everyone was even more jittery."

The response from critics was mixed. In the *Guardian*, Michael Billington praised the songs and the "dazzling staging" adding, "it never simply becomes a series of isolated feline spectaculars." Michael Coveney in the *Financial Times* called it "triumphant," and John Barber in the *Daily Telegraph* called it a "sparkling concatenation of multi-media theatrical talent."

Critics such as Milton Shulman in the *Evening Standard*, and Benedict Nightingale in the *New Statesman* were less exuberant. Wrote Nightingale, "Wasn't it all, well, rather a lot of fuss to make about the minor doodles of even a major poet?"

Lloyd Webber says, "We didn't open to great reviews, but it took off so completely with the public. Then we had 'Memory,' which was out as a single—and that got up the noses of a lot of critics." The song hit number six on the British charts and was ultimately recorded by the likes of Barbra Streisand, Judy Collins, Barry Manilow, and Johnny Mathis, and immortalized in department store elevators everywhere.

"While Brit audiences were enthusiastic," says Lloyd Webber, "on the second night, some famous Americans walked out at half time saying, 'This is the most appalling thing!' I'm not going to mention their names, because I worked with one of them subsequently. Some people didn't get it. But the Brits did."

That incident planted the seed of doubt that Americans would not "get" the show. That attitude was reinforced by Harold Prince. When Prince first heard Lloyd Webber's songs for *Cats*, he says, "I listened to it all, and I said, 'Andrew, is this something I don't get? Is this about Queen Victoria, she's the main cat, and Disraeli and Gladstone are other cats, and then there are poor cats, and am I missing this?'" Lloyd Webber took a terrible, painful, long pause and said, "Hal, it's about *cats*." They never discussed it again.

New York remained the great unknown to Lloyd Webber and Mackintosh. Though the composer had seen three of his works play Broadway— *Jesus Christ, Superstar* (1971), *Evita* (1979), and *Joseph and the Amazing*

Technicolor Dreamcoat (1982)—other producers, notably Robert Stigwood, had done the work.

Despite dire expectations, the New York opening was finally scheduled. *Cats* was to be Mackintosh's initial production on Broadway. He and Lloyd Webber's Really Useful Group joined with the Shubert Organization and with David Geffen, who had previously produced *Master Harold . . . and the Boys* on Broadway and whose record company would produce the *Cats* album. Geffen's million dollar investment would ultimately yield him a $30 million return.

David Merrick, the legendary producer, had been so desperate to get involved that he offered to trade Mackintosh his smash hit *42nd Street* in return for the opportunity to produce the New York production of *Cats*. Mackintosh turned him down.

As it turned out, however, Mackintosh and his team had determined that *42nd Street*'s then home, the Winter Garden, would be the best fit for *Cats*. The Shuberts owned the theater and persuaded Merrick—"or, I would think, crossed David Merrick's palm with a great deal of gold," Mackintosh says—to move *42nd Street* to the Majestic.

The producers waltzed into the Winter Garden with a $5.5 million initial capitalization. "We were cutting into the ceiling and the roof, slapping black paint everywhere," Mackintosh recalls, "but the Shuberts didn't bat an eye." Positive word of mouth from London had propelled the Broadway production to a $6.2 million advance, the largest in history at the time.

The show premiered October 7, 1982, at the 1,482-seat theater, with a top ticket of forty dollars. Reviews again were mixed. Frank Rich in the *New York Times* declared, "Whatever the other failings and excesses, even banalities, of *Cats*, it believes in purely theatrical magic, and on that faith it unquestionably delivers."

Richard Hummler in *Variety* similarly said that the show "takes Broadway legit to a new plateau of technologically enhanced spectacle," and that it "makes up in sensual impact what it doesn't have in emotional involvement."

But Walter Kerr in the *Times'* Sunday edition panned the show, writing that he didn't believe the poems justified "so much bigness, so much busyness, such a massive sweeping of sounds and bodies."

Kerr ultimately was outvoted. The show won seven Tony Awards: for best musical, score (Lloyd Webber and Eliot), book (Eliot again!), director (Nunn), featured actress (Betty Buckley), costumes (John Napier), and lighting (David Hersey). It went on to gross over $400 million and be seen by 10 million people on Broadway alone.

Productions of the show around the world stayed remarkably faithful to the original staging, replicating the original set, direction, and choreography. By mid-1985, the show was running in New York, London, Los Angeles, Toronto, Sydney, and Vienna and in repertoire in Budapest, with other productions touring the United States and Japan.

Inevitably, *Cats* set off a major invasion of Brit tuners, and a few met with success: *Les Miserables*, *Miss Saigon*, and Lloyd Webber's *The Phantom of the Opera*, which ended up breaking the *Cats* longevity record on Broadway. All featured faux Puccini scores, throbbing arias, and complex sets. The tyranny of British musicals was born.

Lloyd Webber proudly points out, "*Cats* was responsible for bringing forth a new generation of performers, one of whom was the ex-Mrs. Lloyd Webber, Sarah Brightman. The show also advanced the career of Elaine Paige and gave boosts to actors such as Paul Nicholas, Wayne Sleep, and Finola Hughes from the original London cast, and Betty Buckley and Harry Groener from the Broadway litter."

So, was there something in the air during those years that inspired Nunn to create Grizabella's rise to heaven in a tire and prompted Spielberg to have *E.T.* lift the bicycle into the air and fly past the moon? "It's a lovely thought," Nunn muses. "I really do believe that inspirations are in the ether."

Paradoxically, some fifty years after Disney first wooed T. S. Eliot, *Cats* would inspire Disney to start its own theater pieces. The Disney 1991 cartoon feature *Beauty and the Beast* and the 1995 *The Lion King* were turned into extraordinarily successful stage tuners that emulated the spectacle, feel-good fun, and lucrative merchandising of its 1981 forebearer.

The "Disneyfication" of Times Square finally helped fuel a *Cats* backlash. Theater pundits singled out the show as the beginning of the blockbuster musical, when extravaganza began to overshadow story and character. In a 2000 piece when *Cats* closed, Bruce Weber wrote in the *New York Times*: "Its monumental success is so remarkable as to be laughable, an enduring (now and forever) joke on the theme of nine lives. How many Leno and Letterman monologues has it salted? How many New Yorkers, even those who have seen it (and perhaps claimed not to), have disavowed its allure as tourist fodder?"

Critiques such as this don't faze Lloyd Webber. "They really don't matter. There was something so extraordinary going on with the alchemy. It's that thing you can't quite put your finger on when everything comes together in one moment and I don't believe any of the people involved in that moment necessarily know that they're doing it, except they have a complete belief that they *should* be doing it."

10 Queen of Daytime
Oprah (1986)

In January 2006, storm clouds gathered around Planet Oprah. Within a few days she had endorsed, then re-endorsed, then renounced a best seller by James Frey called *A Million Little Pieces*. Her lightning shifts had made page one news in major newspapers. One editorial denounced her as "a sanctimonious bully" while Maureen Dowd chided her in the *New York Times* for trying to be "The Empress of Empathy."

For months Oprah Winfrey had been caught up in a rising crescendo of publicity. There was her feud (and reconciliation) with David Letterman, her strident campaign against child molesters, her bizarre interview with Tom Cruise, who bounced on her couch proclaiming his love for his fiancée. And then came her ringing recommendation of the James Frey memoir (or faux memoir, as it turned out to be).

The Frey endorsement quickly became an embarrassment when it was revealed that the author had, in fact invented key episodes about his inspirational recovery from addiction. Thanks to Oprah, the book already had become a major best seller, so when Frey went on Larry King's CNN show to acknowledge his imaginings, Oprah impulsively called in to defend him. "The underlying tone of redemption" in Frey's book was so persuasive, she argued, that readers could well afford to overlook his flights into fiction.

The phone call produced a firestorm, and Oprah promptly reconsidered. The call to King had been a dreadful mistake, she admitted—a rare admission of fallibility from the titan of talk. Her comments had falsely created the impression that "truth doesn't matter," she said, and this was terribly wrong. "I felt duped," she said, charging that Frey had "betrayed millions of readers."

Oprah's vulnerability came as a shock to viewers and media critics alike. Robert Thompson, an historian of pop culture, pointed out that during her sudden emergence as a sort of "punitive national matriarch" understandably shook up her followers. This was the Oprah who had prompted viewers to pick up *Anna Karenina*; now suddenly she was revealing her own inner conflicts before an audience.

Would Planet Oprah ever recover?

Throughout the history of television, each decade has offered up its succession of talkers, charmers, hucksters, pitchmen, and random sociopaths to preside over their own "gabfests," as *Variety* chooses to call them. Among the more memorable talk show hosts have been loveable neurotics like Jack Paar, spiteful ideologues like Joe Pyne, neighborly goofballs like Arthur Godfrey, or silver-tongued celebrities like Dinah Shore.

But there's never been anyone like Oprah. More life-force than TV personality, Oprah Winfrey re-invented the talk show format into a new genre that can only be called the Oprah format.

A billionaire, her show has been in the number one spot in the United States for some seventeen years and is broadcast in 121 countries overseas. She owns her own show and, when she wants to, makes her own movies. Bored with her studio facility, she spent $10 million to build a new one, then another $10 million to enhance it and add a restaurant. When it comes to TV "gets," she essentially can access anyone she wants, though guests can be wary of the fact that Oprah's presence is so imposing there is hardly room for anyone else.

She was actually born Orpah, not Oprah, named after a woman in the Bible, but the name was incorrectly spelled on the 1954 birth certificate. It was but the first of many mistakes in her young life.

She was raised primarily by her grandmother in Mississippi. Her mother, Vernita, left to find work in Wisconsin when Oprah was just four years old. Encouraged by her grandmother, Oprah began memorizing passages from the Bible and other religious texts. Her memory skills were so impressive that her grandmother would make her recite passages in the local church in Kosciusko.

Oprah was an avid reader. "Getting my library card was like citizenship . . . it was American citizenship," Oprah says. She continued to speak at churches all over Nashville, where she moved a few years later to live with her father and stepmother. She became known there as "The Speaker," before she was nine years old. "From the time I was eight years old, I was a champion speaker. I spoke for every woman's group, banquet, church function—I did the circuit," Oprah says. She moved back and forth between parents several times before enrolling in college.

Oprah's childhood was tainted with sexual abuse. When she was nine years old, her nineteen-year-old cousin raped her. A couple of years later, she was molested by a family friend, and then by an uncle. She escaped through books—an early favorite was Betty Smith's *A Tree Grows in Brooklyn*, the story of Francie Nolan, a lonely but hopeful girl growing up in Brooklyn in the early 1900s. Oprah also became hooked to TV shows including *Leave It to Beaver* and *I Love Lucy*. Oprah partially credits Lucille Ball with her early desire to become an actress.

By the time she started high school, the abuse had taken its toll on Oprah, and she began skipping school and stealing money from her mother. She ran away from home on several occasions. On one of her escapes, she ran into Aretha Franklin's limo; she conned the singer with a wild story that her parents had kicked her out of the house and she needed to buy a bus ticket to stay with relatives in Ohio. Duped, Franklin gave her $100, which Oprah used to stay in a hotel room, ordering room service and watching TV.

Still, Oprah's passion for public speaking put her on the path that would eventually lead to her career as a talk-show host. At seventeen, she was offered a part-time job as a news reader for radio station WVOL in Nashville. The station had sponsored Oprah at the teen beauty pageant called Miss Fire Prevention—where she was the first black winner. The station had also "auditioned" her after she'd attended the White House Conference on Youth, where she represented the state of Tennessee.

She enrolled in Tennessee State University, an all-black school in Nashville, majoring in speech and drama and continuing to work at WVOL. It was 1971, the middle of the Vietnam War. College students were staging protests against United States involvement; at Oprah's college students were also rallying for "Black Power."

"It was a weird time," Oprah reflected to Katherine Krohn, who wrote, *Oprah Winfrey* in 2002. "This whole 'black power' movement was going on, but I just never had any of those angry black feelings. Truth is, I've never felt prevented from doing anything because I was either black or a woman." Her attitude earned her the nickname "Oreo"—an expression for a black person who is considered "black on the outside and white on the inside."

Oprah

In 1973, the station manager of WTVF-TV, the CBS affiliate in Nashville, offered her an audition to be a reporter for the evening news. She was nineteen years old, and because she was afraid she wouldn't be able to balance both college and a full-time job she declined the offer. The station manager persisted. He sensed Oprah was still dreaming of becoming an actress, not a newscaster. Her speech professor scolded her: "Don't you know that's *why* people go to college? So that CBS can call them?"

During her audition, she tried to do her version of Barbara Walters. "I would sit like Barbara, or how I imagined Barbara to sit, and I'd look down at the script and up to the camera because I thought that's what you do, how you act. You try to have as much eye contact as you can—at least it seemed that way from what I had seen Barbara do."

It worked for her. She took the job at $15,000 a year. Since it required her to work evenings only, she was even able to stay in school. Some viewers accused the station of hiring Oprah as a "designated black person," but it didn't bother her. Oprah became the first black female—and youngest— newscaster in Nashville history.

The warmly casual style she exudes on *The Oprah Winfrey Show* today was forged on that job. She worked on her news delivery by studying videotapes of herself, working on her timing, rhythm, and ease in front of the camera. Soon she had weaned herself away from Barbara Walters. She began mailing out her tapes to bigger stations, including market leaders New York and Los Angeles.

In 1976, just three years after she began at WTVF, she received an offer from an ABC affiliate in Baltimore, WJZ-TV, to be a news reporter and anchor. Taking the job meant leaving her father and stepmother (she'd been living rent-free while attending college) as well as dropping out of college months before she would graduate. Still, determined to advance her career, she moved to Baltimore. She was met by billboards around the city that read "What's an Oprah?"

Presiding over the six o'clock news brought problems. Oprah would get emotionally involved in her stories. She'd sometimes change words from the teleprompter, making the reports sound more personal. She would even cry on the air. "My openness is the reason I did not do so well as a news reporter," she explained. "I'd say to people at fires who had lost children, 'That's okay. You don't have to talk to me,'" according to Krohn.

The news director soon yanked her from the evening news and relegated her to a five-minute segment at five thirty in the morning. "I was devastated because until that point, I had sort of cruised. I really hadn't thought a lot about my life or the direction it was taking. I just happened into television, happened into radio . . . I was twenty-two and embarrassed by the whole thing because I had never failed before."

Her bosses also decided she needed a makeover and voice lessons, which depressed her further and got her thinking more about returning to her first love, acting. Still, she continued on at WJZ, determined to see it through.

When a new station manager, Bill Carter, was hired at WJZ in 1978, he decided Oprah's easygoing nature made her perfect to co-host a morning talk show called *People Are Talking*. She would interview Baltimore personalities and do features both lighthearted and serious and personal.

Oprah found her niche. On *People Are Talking*, she could be herself and talk to guests about their feelings. Her reaction: "The day I did that talk show, I felt like I'd come home. My very first interview was the Carvel Ice Cream Man, and Benny from *All My Children*—I'll never forget it. I came on the air thinking, 'This is what I should have been doing.' Because it was . . . like breathing to me. Like breathing."

People Are Talking debuted in 1978. And although it was up against *The Phil Donahue Show*, a popular nationally syndicated show, Oprah's ratings surpassed Donahue's in the Baltimore market.

Donahue had established the format many, including Oprah, would emulate with varying levels of success. The host went into the audience and invites people to make comments or ask questions. His style was straightforward and somewhat impersonal, much like that of a news reporter. But Oprah's style was to get more personal, sharing her own feelings and insecurities. On a show about weight loss, she would reveal her struggle with food addiction. She'd hug or hold hands with a guest who'd gotten upset.

"The most personal thing that Phil Donahue ever talked about was the fact that he was a wayward Catholic. Other than that, talk show hosts didn't talk about themselves. Oprah opened up a lot of new windows because [viewers] could empathize with her," observes Maury Povich.

Female viewers constituted *People Are Talking*'s biggest following. Oprah hosted the show for six years until she was thirty years old.

Then came another career opportunity. In 1983, Debra DiMaio, one of the producers for *People Are Talking*, sent a tape of the show to WLS-TV in Chicago and she was hired to produce the station's morning show, *AM Chicago*. The show happened to be looking for a new host. DiMaio encouraged the station manager, Dennis Swanson, to give Oprah a shot.

Oprah flew in to Chicago on Labor Day and recorded an hour-long audition tape as reported in *TV Week Magazine*. Swanson later recalled the session and his reaction: "The problem for WLS-TV and *AM Chicago* was that we were head-to-head with the highly successful *Phil Donahue Show* being produced live across town at WBBM-TV. At that time they were the highest-rated CBS-owned station in the country. I thought one of our problems was that we were trying to out-Donahue Donahue, rather than provide an alternative. I urged the staff to look for someone totally different so we might give the viewing audience a distinct choice."

He continued: "As I sat in my office and watched a mock version of the *AM* show hosted by Oprah, I realized she was the best I had ever seen. Oprah came down to visit afterward. She wanted to do this show and do it solo. She seemed to me to be almost desperate for the chance."

Oprah was hired in 1984, and her salary skyrocketed to $200,000 a year, *Variety* reported. The addition of Oprah sent ratings through the roof. Within weeks, *AM Chicago* regularly beat Donahue in the ratings race. "[Swanson] opened this door wide enough for me to come through, in terms of broadcasters understanding women. . . . Had a male not made the decision, I don't know whether I would have been able to come from nowhere," Oprah would later say.

The Oprah Winfrey Show—the title it took even before it moved into national syndication in September 1986—had an impact on WLS, way out of proportion to that of normal morning programs. TV stations are "like battleships, taking years to change course," said Tim Bennett, promotion manager at WLS when Winfrey started. (He is now president of Harpo Productions, which Oprah owns.) "She turned this thing around in eighteen months. It was Oprah who was the greatest catalyst."

Typically in television, a popular morning show can pull viewers to other shows in the morning, but Winfrey created a "halo effect" that spread over the entire station. WLS rebroadcast her show in late night, where the 11 PM repeat more than held its own against the network comedy programs.

Oprah also enhanced her guest list to include celebrities like Stevie Wonder, Shirley MacLaine, Tom Selleck, Christie Brinkley, and Candice Bergen. She tackled tougher, more controversial issues, including incest, child abuse, and eating disorders.

That year she also met with Quincy Jones, who helped land her a role in *The Color Purple*, a feature based on the book beloved by Oprah. That role would earn her an Oscar nomination.

Her daytime show, meanwhile, continued its ratings winning streak and in spring 1985, she signed with the TV syndication company, King World, becoming the first black host of a national TV talk show.

Oprah was by now a national celebrity, but in the hardscrabble world of syndicated television, her career still needed some King World-style hard sell.

When "selling" Oprah, King and his brother Michael, did not leave the decision to put a then-plump black woman on the air to the station managers, most of whom were white males over the age of fifty. When the Kings screened their tape of *The Oprah Winfrey Show*, they insisted that secretaries and other women at the station be invited into the room.

Oprah once spoke about a general manager in Iowa who phoned King to warn him that Oprah might play in Chicago but she would never play in the heartland. "He'd get a better rating by sitting a potato in the chair than a black woman," the misguided man said. King World decided to launch *Oprah* in the 1986–87 season, when she drew national attention as a costar of *The Color Purple*. The show went on the air on 130 stations (she is now on more than 200), representing a near 100 percent market penetration.

"Oprah worked her butt off to get that show going," King said. "She would do the show in Chicago, then fly to Cleveland to do promos. The next day she would do the show, then fly to Detroit to do promos. No sacrifice was too great for her." Revenues from the show totaled $125 million in its first season.

Life with Oprah wasn't always peaceful. Periodically, she let it be known that she wanted to leave the show, that she was disgusted with all of the Oprah clones vying for airtime, such as Star Jones, Bertice Berry, and Rolanda Watts.

Talks to renew *Oprah* through 1997 stalled as Oprah wanted the "no-compete" clause dropped from her contract. This would allow her to distribute the show herself or go to another syndicator after 1997. King World, at the time, was contracted to syndicate the show—now grossing $175 million annually—through 1995. Oprah and King World finally reached a five-year deal, resulting in Oprah's receipt of 500,000 additional shares of King World stock added to the one million she already owned.

Her earnings, by then $60 million per year, were said to increase over the life of the contract, and she was given the option of picking up yet another 250,000 King World stock options every year she re-upped. Additional stock options would make Oprah one of the largest, if not the largest, shareholder in King World. The company also reduced its percentage of syndication fees below the 40 percent level.

Starting with the May 1994 sweeps, Oprah began to face competition tabloid competitors like *Ricki*, *Jenny Jones*, and *The Montel Williams Show* that populated the airwaves. Oprah had switched to softer topics and her rivals were biting at her heels.

After a ratings slippage, Oprah hired a new president for her Harpo Productions. Later in 1994, Oprah was sued by former publicist Colleen

Raleigh, who quit after eight years of service. Longtime executive producer Debra DiMaio and personal assistant Beverly Coleman had also exited. Raleigh claimed she could no longer foster an image of the show that was "harmonious and humane." The battle was met with a flurry of attention from the press, but Oprah continued, without comment, business as usual.

Nothing, it seemed, could slow Oprah. A year later, in October 1995, she signed a four-year deal with ABC to produce made-for-TV movies, TV series, and theatrical films as well as videos, books, and ABC Radio Networks programs. "The breadth of our deal with Oprah is unprecedented in our business," said Bob Iger, then president of ABC.

From that point on, Oprah each year said she would consider stopping production on her talk show. In 1995, she even asked for her September 15 deadline to be extended for a few weeks so she could further weigh her decision. "I wavered from week to week, day to day," she told the *Chicago Sun-Times*. A personal visit from Iger proved "a major, pivotal deciding factor for me." She ultimately decided to keep going and signed on for another two years. And by March 1996, her show was grossing $200 million for King World—a third of the company's total revenue. An average of 10 to 15 million people were watching her show every day.

When *Rosie O'Donnell* debuted in 1996, O'Donnell became the number two talk-show queen, but overthrew Oprah just once during her six-year run.

When Oprah's twelfth season began in fall of 1997, TV insiders again looked to see if she would extend her contract with King World. Warner Bros., the producer of *Rosie*, quietly began securing deals to move *Rosie* into Oprah's lucrative timeslots, should Oprah announce retirement; but Oprah, once again, re-upped for another two years, through the 1999–2000 season. This time, she announced her decision theatrically, during a live show.

Oprah's Harpo Entertainment Group, formed in 1988, was meanwhile buying up rights to some of her favorite books including Toni Morrison's *Beloved* (which she would later turn into a movie starring herself), Zora Neale Hurston's *Their Eyes Were Watching God*, starring Halle Berry, and Dorothy West's *The Wedding*.

Along the way, Harpo also bought the rights to *The Oprah Winfrey Show*, giving Oprah the power to produce her series the way she wanted. She opted to change the live format to a pretaped one, making her schedule more flexible.

And Oprah, of course, also had been busily creating Oprah's Book Club, assigning books for viewers to read and later discuss with the authors. Book publishers were not prepared for the extraordinary demand generated by this innovation. Philip Pfeffer, former CEO of Borders, termed the

"Oprah phenomenon" the biggest change to hit the publishing industry in fifteen years. "The thing that's amazing to me is that *Oprah Winfrey* airs at 4 PM so the show is not watched by what we consider our core customer base. But Oprah's viewers still go out and buy the books featured on the show," says Pfeffer.

Sometimes the "Oprah phenomenon" worked against her. On the April 16, 1996, show, she commented that mad cow disease "stopped me cold from eating another burger." A vegetarian activist also spoke about the dangers and effects of the disease. A group of Texas cattlemen sued Oprah, claiming that she had "wrongfully defamed" American beef and thus cost the industry $11 million dollars. She spent six weeks on trial in Texas, where she taped her show during the process, and emerged the victor.

Given Oprah's extraordinary resiliency, it's hard to imagine a scenario in which she truly loses interest in her show, or her audience loses interest in her. At the same time, her annual ritual of self-scrutiny and renegotiation is clearly significant to her. Despite her vast wealth and celebrity, she still feels a need to hear her value reaffirmed, or so it would seem, and to reap the reward of that re-affirmation. Perhaps her self-doubts are real; her whims and neuroses are impossible to analyze because there has never been another Oprah to study. That is the source of her astonishing strength, and also of her inscrutability.

11 Revenge of the King Nerd

American Graffiti (1973)

It is one of history's anomalies that artists seem to appear in clusters. At a given moment, in a given space, an extended family of poets or painters, song writers or filmmakers, will suddenly emerge from the cultural underbrush. It is not as though smoke signals are emitted to encourage the ingathering; indeed, the community at large may not even be aware of, or come to terms with, the new subculture until the artists have been devoured by their own mythology.

Such was the case in Hollywood in the late '60s when a feisty, freewheeling, iconoclastic aggregation of filmmakers suddenly surfaced, beating at the doors of the Hollywood studios. They were children of the sixties with all that that entailed—Vietnam, political assassinations, rock 'n' roll, the sexual revolution. They were enamored of film as the new language of storytelling. And they were keenly aware that the existing lexicon of filmmakers had lost its impact.

The old-line studios had run out of both money and ideas. Movie attendance had tumbled from 78.2 million people a week in 1946 to 15.8 million in 1971. Managements were being overthrown. Sliding uneasily into the seats of power were tough-minded young pragmatists who were keenly aware of the fact that television had stolen the studios' "habit" audiences, that resources were scarce, and that there was no time to summon up marketing gurus or commission management studies to analyze the problem.

The filmmakers who had arrived hopefully to create a brave new world in Hollywood were a disparate lot. Francis Ford Coppola was nerdy but brilliantly persuasive. He could not only summon up bold ideas to startle veteran producers, but could almost instantly bring forth script pages to bolster his arguments. Peter Bogdanovich was erudite and well-mannered, having written thoughtful profiles for *Esquire* and other publications about the leading stars and filmmakers of an earlier generation. Steven Spielberg was gawky and unsocialized, but he presented his ideas with messianic zeal and exuded a boyish confidence that he could deliver, if given the opportunity.

George Lucas did not share these traits. He was as nonverbal as his friend Coppola was loquacious. He was as shy as Spielberg was audacious. He had none of Bogdanovich's polish. He presented like an engineer, not a poet. It was difficult to imagine him commanding a crew or coaxing a performance from a recalcitrant actor.

And Lucas's early work seemed to reinforce these impressions. A short made at USC's film school, *THX 1138: 4EB* was as uninviting as its title— a bleak glimpse of the future heavily influenced by *1984* and *Brave New World*. It played like a techie kid's fever dream, but it reflected a budding mastery of the filmmaking process and attracted the attention of his peers. Coppola connected with Lucas's youthful pipe dreams and resolved that they would ultimately create something together.

Coppola already had learned the craft of "pitching" the studios. Some of the newly installed studio executives had liked Coppola's first feature, *You're a Big Boy Now*, a quirky pre-*Graduate* effort that reflected the sensibility of a young man who knew more about the camera than he did about women. Though *Big Boy* was, at best, a marginal success, the young turks who had recently taken over Warner Bros. decided to anoint Coppola with a deal to adapt the musical, *Finian's Rainbow*. The decision itself reflected the awkwardness of the transition taking place in Hollywood—marrying a hot twenty-seven-year-old filmmaker to a thoroughly conventional Broadway property.

Coppola was destined to fail in bringing *Finian's Rainbow* alive, but, in return for his efforts, he succeeded in hitting on the studio for $300,000 to develop material that would better reflect his taste. One of these pieces became *The Conversation*, which Coppola ultimtely directed at Paramount. Another was *THX 1138*, for his friend Lucas to direct. In fact, Warner Bros. finally wrote a check for $300,000 to help back the Lucas movie, but when studio executives saw Lucas's first cut, they took the film away from the young director and demanded that the money be paid back.

Lucas was devastated by this rejection and by the fact that virtually no one outside the film community would get to see his film. Determined to prove the validity of his vision, he talked about prepping yet another dark sci-fi mini-epic, but Coppola, learning from his own disappointments, urged him to try something more commercial. The debates between the two were less than classic—the exuberantly Italian Coppola serving up pasta and rich conversation and Lucas, dead-on serious, reserved in both word and emotion, listening, sparring, and ultimately yielding. As Lucas recalls it, the issue came down to a wager: Coppola bet his friend he couldn't "do a silly, warm, funny comedy," and Lucas both offended and stimulated by the challenge took him on. Offended because it seemed like an affront to his techie nature, but stimulated because there was a side to Lucas, a repressed side, that was still the small-town kid who loved cars and remembered cruising as a teen. He'd even made a little film about car racing at USC film school.

And thus was born one of moviedom's most enigmatic sleeper hits, a movie that celebrated life in the '50s even though it was set in the '60s and filmed in the '70s; a teen comedy shot like a documentary, with lighting so gritty the characters were occasionally barely visible, their dialogue competing (sometimes unsuccessfully) with background soundtrack. It was a movie that embraced the talents of obscure young actors who would go on to distinguish themselves in varying careers—Ron Howard, Harrison Ford, Suzanne Somers, Richard Dreyfuss—and would launch Lucas himself into superstar status, but not before running yet other gauntlets of rejection that would make *THX* seem like the proverbial walk in the park.

American Graffiti was thus the ultimate coming-of-age experience, both in terms of its story and its impact on its filmmaker, as well as the Hollywood establishment. Ned Tanen, then the young head of Universal, and John Calley, who ultimately became his coequal at Warner Bros., were both essentially square business types who were nonetheless alert enough to understand the void in pop culture of the era, and the opportunity it offered. They were cognizant of the emerging generation of filmmakers and rock stars, but they couldn't quite figure out how to fit the talent into the opportunity. Thus they found themselves courting the bright, young artists, flattering them, and smoking dope with them, yet, finally rejecting their work. They were akin to dysfunctional fathers, encouraging their kids, then swatting them down.

Tanen, a tough-minded, thoroughly neurotic young Universal careerist, was prone to temper tantrums and was frustrated by the narrow vision of his boss, the fabled Lew Wasserman, a genius as a business manipulator but a man with rigidly prosaic taste in film and TV. Calley was the bearded young bon vivant, a glib and witty one-time advertising executive who interacted smoothly with his corporate bosses, yet also knew how to massage the talent. It was Calley who cultivated Kubrick and Nichols and "hung" with the Coppola–Lucas gang, but who also was often exasperated by their output. As such, Calley, like Tanen, was a transition figure who thrived in transitional times. (While Tanen ultimately all but disappeared from the Hollywood landscape, Calley, after a decade-long period of unemployment, resurfaced in the late '90s as a production chief at MGM and then Sony.)

The fact that *Graffiti* got made at all was an extraordinary accident of history. It was not the product of corporate meetings; studio advertising and distribution specialists did not study its potential in overseas markets or ponder its worth in video. (No one even thought about video then.) *Graffiti* essentially slipped between the cracks. It got made because no one at Universal was paying attention and because some of the younger executives thought it would be cool to gamble on a couple of the "kids" who'd been hovering around the studio gates and even infiltrating the editing rooms. *Graffiti* wasn't so much a decision as it was an accommodation—the same phenomenon was taking place at other studios as well; witness *Harold and Maude* at Paramount.

The screenwriting process reflected this sort of guerilla filmmaking approach. Lucas had written a twenty-page treatment that was rough and ill-formed. He asked his friend, a film-school classmate, Willard Huyck, if he and his new wife, Gloria Katz, would help him refine it. A longer treatment was prepared, which was shown to a few associates and low-level studio personnel, but no one was particularly excited by it. Yet another Lucas friend, Richard Walters, then prepared a full screenplay, but Lucas felt it had a teens-on-a-rampage tone that didn't mesh with his vision for the picture. He imagined a car culture film packed with '60s songs—a movie about small town kids who were about to emerge into the real world and were trying to mask their nervousness about it.

And so the filmmaker went back to his friends, Huyck and Katz, who churned out a 180-page screenplay. Lucas liked it. His friend, Coppola also liked it and, more important, thought he could get it financed. Lucas knew he needed Coppola's backing, but he was still nervous about the length of the script. "Do I have to shoot all of it?" he asked Willard Huyck.

"Don't worry, we'll type it small," Huyck assured him.

Given his extraordinary success with *The Godfather*, Coppola, a born optimist, persuaded himself that he would have no trouble getting Warner

Bros. to finance *American Graffiti*. The studio promptly turned him down. So did United Artists, whose savvy young chief of production, David Picker, liked the material but not enough to make a deal. Besides, Picker seemed distracted by the success of his bigger, glossier films, like the *James Bond* sequels, which were now taking off.

Coppola's final stop was Universal, where there was an appetite to back a Coppola film. None of Ned Tanen's executives were especially interested in Lucas, to be sure. To them, this was a very small bet for a studio that was desperate to seem hip. The most attractive part of the project was the music. (Lucas had already secured rights to several big rock 'n' roll hits for a modest sum of money.)

The studio felt that the frivolous nature of the project, set in 1962, would also seem a welcome distraction in 1973 from the tensions of the day. 1962 was the year of the Cuban Missile Crisis, when global war seemed an imminent possibility. Rival studios were putting out a steady agenda of dark films, such as *The Manchurian Candidate, Whatever Happened to Baby Jane,* and *Birdman of Alcatraz*. The list of Oscar-nominated screenplays would include films like *David and Lisa, The Miracle Worker,* and *Last Year at Marienbad*.

When Lucas finally got the green light to make *Graffiti*, he seemed more stunned than pleased. As he set about to cope with his lengthy screenplay and scrawny budget, he recognized that the omens were both good and bad. On the plus side, it was clear that studio executives would not meddle with the production. This was a shoot that was well under the radar. They looked to Coppola to deliver a film of professional quality. On the negative side, no one involved in the production—not even the cast or crew—really seemed to believe in the movie, save Lucas and Coppola. "The atmosphere was like that of a USC student film," recalls Huyck.

Reflecting these mixed messages, the original budget for the film was set at $600,000, including music rights, cast salaries, and $50,000 for Lucas to direct. Lucas's agent at the time, Jeff Berg, persuaded Tanen to push the budget to a more realistic $750,000. The studio agreed, provided it could option Lucas's next project, whatever the hell it was (Universal didn't really care; the studio's business affairs executives just wanted to say they had snared an option).

The casting process was similarly off-putting. Lucas decided to work with Fred Roos, a taciturn but knowledgeable casting agent who had the blessing of Coppola. Roos tried to elicit from Lucas some insights as to what sorts of actors he would like to work with, and what character "types" he favored. Lucas either could not articulate his preferences or was still struggling to form an image of his characters in his own mind.

Roos started to bring in young actors for various parts, realizing all the while this would be a torturous casting process. For one thing, Lucas had difficulty interviewing actors. They would come into the room, ready to do their shtick, and Lucas would peer at them, assessing them warily, but not conversing with them. Roos had been accustomed to Coppola's chatty style—Francis would tell them stories of his childhood and even cook meals for them, as though intent on creating one big Italian family. Lucas, however, did not possess Coppola's conviviality. Further, when an actor finally left the room Lucas would not tell Roos whether he liked or disliked him. He would simply ask, "Who's next?"

In the end, the cast was an idiosyncratic assemblage of actors who would go on to their own exotic destinies. Harrison Ford, who Roos all but forced on Lucas, would become a major star. Richard Dreyfuss would appear in some of his generation's most important films, such as *Jaws* and *Close Encounters*. Ron Howard would become a major filmmaker in his own right, winning the Oscar for *A Beautiful Mind*. At the time, however, they were all kids—anonymous kids, with the exception of Howard—who had been assembled to do a curious film in a curious location for a curious director.

American Graffiti was set during one evening in Modesto, California, in 1962—precisely ten years before it started shooting—and focused on high school grads who were about to leave small-town life forever. To a degree, the narrative drew upon Lucas's own boyhood, years when he himself was obsessed with cars. The year 1962 had personal meaning for Lucas: He graduated from high school in Modesto in 1962. The year also saw one of the key turning points in his life.

On June 12, 1962, just before graduation from Thomas Downey High School in Modesto, Lucas was returning home from the library in his Fiat Bianchina and, as he made a left turn into his driveway, was hit broadside by seventeen-year-old Frank Ferreira. As the Fiat flipped over several times, Lucas's racing belt snapped at its base and he was thrown out of the car through the open roof. The car flipped again then crashed into a walnut tree: If Lucas had remained in the car, he almost certainly would have died.

After two weeks in the hospital, he returned to his parent's home to recuperate for the rest of the summer. Instead of pursuing his dream of being a race-car driver, Lucas decided to enroll in Modesto Junior College and from there went on to USC's film school.

In the book *Skywalking: The Life and Films of George Lucas*, the filmmaker tells biographer Dale Pollock, "You can't have that kind of experience and not feel that there must be a reason why you're here. I realized I should be spending my time trying to figure out what that reason is and trying to fulfill it. . . . The accident made me more aware of myself and my feelings. I began to trust my instincts. I had the feeling that I should go to college, and I did. I had the same feeling later that I should go to film school, even though everybody thought I was nuts. I had the same feeling when I decided to make *Star Wars*, when even my friends told me I was crazy. These are just things that have to be done, and I feel as if I have to do them."

American Graffiti follows four parallel stories. Ron Howard and Cindy Williams are high-school sweethearts who must deal with the understanding that, once he goes away to college, they will inevitably start seeing other people. Their pal, Richard Dreyfuss, will be leaving Modesto the following morning for college in the East and has cold feet about this transition. Charles Martin Smith, a geek, is puffed up with pride at being given custody of Howard's cool car and is coming on to bubble-gum blonde, Candy Clark. Hot-rodder Paul Le Mat rides around in his bright yellow deuce coup, accompanied by a pesky, eager-for-fun pre-teen (Mackenzie Phillips) as he searches for the hot-shot driver, played by Harrison Ford, who wants to challenge him to a drag race.

Lucas wanted an unglossy look for his film and, with a tight schedule of twenty-eight shooting days, couldn't afford "slick" anyway. Instead of a "name" cinematographer, he hired Ron Eveslage and Jan D'Alquen to operate two cameras simultaneously. (The two are credited as directors of photography.)

Much of the action took place in cars, as teenagers cruised the streets of Modesto. The primary location, in fact, turned out to be the town of Petaluma. (San Rafael, Lucas's first choice, revoked its agreement to let him shoot there after only one chaotic night. The teenagers taunt, woo, bully, and moon each other while their cars slowly traverse the streets. Lucas wanted a camera on the side of each car so both sides of the conversations could be shot simultaneously.

The filmmakers quickly realized that shooting low light at night created depth problems—the characters were blurry when they moved—so Haskell Wexler was hired as visual consultant. Wexler, then forty-six, was a successful, if trigger-tempered, maverick in Hollywood, a former apprentice of James Wong Howe (*The Thin Man, Sweet Smell of Success, Hud*). Wexler had built up an impressive body of work, having shot such films as *Who's Afraid of Virginia Woolf?, In the Heat of the Night*, and *The Thomas Crown Affair*. He also directed *Medium Cool*, a 1969 film that assimilated events at the Democratic National Convention in Chicago into a fictional narrative. Though he was shooting commercials, Wexler flew up to Petaluma for five weeks to nurture the neophyte director and his neophyte cameramen.

Since the entire film took place between sunset and dawn, the all-night shooting was wearisome. There were no trailers for the actors, not even a folding chair to sit on. The one trailer housed makeup and costumes. Howard and Williams were given a mere five minutes' notice to prepare for their climactic reconciliation scene, which had to be shot in one take because the sun was about to rise.

Arguably, the sheer down-and-dirty nature of the shoot worked in its favor. When a young filmmaker is faced with no time to shift locations or even camera angles, he must rely on his gut.

"When you're faced with a tight schedule and budget pressures, you fall back on your instincts," observes Mike Nichols, whose second film, *The Graduate* (1967), was shot under similarly difficult conditions. "On one level, it becomes your subconscious communicating through the medium of film with the audience's subconscious. And either it all works or there's a terrible disconnect."

In the case of *Graffiti*, there seemed at the time no way to tell whether it was working or not. Lucas was focusing on the camera, rather than on his young actors. The filmmaker and his primary advisers saw their dailies on the fly when they were bleary from the night shooting. Verna Fields, their experienced and very talented editor, who had edited other guerrilla films such as *Medium Cool*, was encouraging but somewhat inscrutable. Getting it done was the key objective; getting it right seemed a distant task. Assisting her was a friendly, warm spirited, and thoroughly inexperienced young woman named Marcia, who was Lucas's wife.

Marcia and Verna Fields did their first cut on *Graffiti*, working in the garage of a house Coppola had rented in Mill Valley to keep the studio at bay. When Tanen and the other members of Universal's cadre finally saw a cut, they made no effort to mask their disdain. They hated the film, its performances, its sensibility, even its score. The initial meeting played out like a sour '60s generation-gap melodrama. Coppola and Lucas hadn't just betrayed their backers; they had betrayed their craft. While the Universal executives presented their list of mandated cuts and edits, they did not disguise their opinion that the film was, in their mind, unreleasable, even as a possible movie for television.

A hastily organized test screening in San Francisco in January 1973 did not change their minds. The audience's reaction was very positive. Kids started whooping it up from the moment they heard the initial strains of "Rock Around the Clock." Tanen had flown up for the screening, but even before it began he told associates that he felt the test was rigged, that Coppola had filled the audience with friends and allies. He exchanged some tense words with Coppola, then hurried for his plane back to Los Angeles.

Hollywood is a tight-knit community and news that *Graffiti* was a problem child traveled quickly to other top players in town. Some of the more senior studio executives seemed almost pleased by Lucas's dilemma. Their apprehensions about this latest wave of rebellious newcomers were validated; "kids" like Lucas and Coppola were confident that they had all the answers, but they were wrong. *Graffiti* had been billed as a hot new movie, but it was a cold dud.

Universal was guarded about letting other studios see the film. Paramount told Coppola it would offer to buy the negative from Universal if he could arrange a screening for the studio, even a surreptitious one. The studio promised to guarantee a million-dollar check to serve as a down payment. Nervous about these inquiries from rival studios, Tanen persuaded Wasserman that *Graffiti* should be tested one more time before an audience—one that included teenage filmgoers—to determine whether the film had some mysterious appeal that had eluded the executives.

Coppola and Lucas had mixed feelings about this idea. Tests of this sort were commonly conducted at conventional movie theaters before paying audiences who would not have a preconceived bias. Tanen, however, had scheduled his test screening at the Writers Guild Theater on Melrose (since torn down), which normally served elite, older audiences of industry members.

But Coppola and Lucas had run out of leverage. Indeed, Coppola resolved that at the end of the screening, which he expected to be disastrous, he would offer his check and hope Universal would acquiesce. That was his only hope.

But the screening did not go as anticipated. Universal had in fact invited a substantial number of teenagers, and their enthusiasm for the movie was unabashed and contagious. They got the jokes, they loved the tunes, and their applause at the end left the studio executives in a state of astonishment. And this time they couldn't charge that the audience had been rigged. Here was a film that truly connected with its prime demographic. Suddenly the project from hell became a hot property. The most staid, conservative studio in town had become edgy and forward-looking.

Coppola was ebullient. Lucas was relieved, but wounded. Response from the critics was supportive. On June 20, 1973, Murf., the normally caustic critic of *Daily Variety*, gushed, "Of all the youth-themed nostalgia films in the past couple of years, George Lucas's *American Graffiti* is among the very best to date . . . an exceptionally talented cast of relatively new players." He added, "There is brilliant interplaying and underplaying of script, performers and direction which will raise howls of laughter from audiences, yet never descends on the screen to overdone mugging, pratfall, and other heavy-handed devices normally employed."

The reviewer correctly predicted, "Without exception, all players fit perfectly into the concept and execution, and all the young principals and featured players have a bright and lengthy future. And so does Lucas. *American Graffiti* is one of those rare films which can be advanced in any discussion of the superiority of films over live performances; the latter can vary from show to show, but if you can get it right on film, you've got it forever."

In the August 31 issue of the *Wall Street Journal*, Joy Gould Boyum praised the film's "special quality" and added that "the film goes far beyond the mere re-creation of time and place and atmosphere." Referring to Dreyfuss's character, Boyum said, "Through Curt, the film does touch on the universal theme of painfully putting away childish things, a theme which lifts it out of its specific locale and helps to make it meaningful to us all."

In August, Stephen Farber wrote in the *New York Times*, "The nostalgia boom has finally produced a lasting work of art. . . . Lucas's technical flair was already visible in his first movie, *THX-1138*, but his work with the actors in *American Graffiti* is a revelation. His gifts are prodigious; at 28 he is already one of the world's master directors. . . . That sense of impermanence gives the comedy its undercurrent of pathos. Everything seems precious because we know it can't last."

A few weeks later, Vincent Canby in the *Times* described *Graffiti* as a movie about "young lives going nowhere in particular but with a debonair manner, a good deal of humor and a lot of decent feelings."

Despite this response, the experience filled Lucas with an anger that was to alter the future course of his career. No longer would he look to Hollywood for support or succor. In the future he would not even trust its agents or lawyers. Henceforth, Lucas would go it alone. And the *Star Wars* franchise represents that legacy.

George Lucas's turbulent career arc from techie to titan stands as a metaphor for the cinematic advances of his time, but he was fortunate to survive until his moment finally arrived. His survival strategy stemmed from his unique stubbornness and his commitment to his vision. It stemmed as well from the curious Puritan attitude that drove him: He was not the high-living sybarite, like his friend, Coppola. He did not feel the need, as a young man, to try and establish a new studio, as Coppola did. He ultimately built his empire when the opportunity and the resources presented themselves. While Coppola remained the poet and the promoter, Lucas sustained

x

himself as the stalwart technophile, a quiet propagator of digital dogma. He seemed to sense instinctively when the time had come to make his big moves, first in the rolling hills of Marin County, north of San Francisco, then at the immense Presidio in San Francisco. Even the address of his first venture carried some irony: The 4,700 acre facility was nestled along Lucas Valley Road, but contrary to myth, this was not a road named for Lucas; it was Lucas who chose to build there. Perhaps with Coppola it would have been the other way around.

The miracle of George Lucas is that his willpower and dedication brought him monumental success despite his acknowledged limitations. To filmmakers like Nichols and Coppola, the key skills of the filmmaker are, first, the ability to work with actors and, second, the talent to tell a story. Lucas was not especially gifted in either area—a fact that many critics harp on. But Lucas understood that technology was the greater tool, and that great storytellers throughout history have always wielded this skill, even if they were merely carving on stone. Lucas believed he, too, had a Great Story to tell, one that would change his own fortunes and would become a central experience to two generations of filmgoers. And he also believed he would find the means of telling it.

12 Archie's Last Laugh
All in the Family (1971)

By the late 1960s, it was becoming increasingly difficult to relate what you saw on the street to what you saw on the tube. The country was gripped by racial tensions and angst about Vietnam. Frank Zappa was singing, "There's no way to delay, that trouble coming every day." Filmgoers were crowding into *Easy Rider*, a movie that would not have even found a distributor five years earlier.

But in the face of all this, television was still a playpen. The top-rated sit-coms of the 1969–70 season were *Mayberry R.F.D.*, about a rustic who dispenses down-home wisdom, and *A Family Affair*, about a softhearted bachelor who becomes a surrogate dad to three cute-as-a-button kiddies.

To network executives at the time, the gap between the real world and the world of TV translated into good ratings. To a growing number in the creative community, however, the discrepancy was numbing. "Looking at shows like *Father Knows Best* or *Leave it to Beaver* or *Green Acres . . .* you would think that America had no blacks, no racial tensions, that there was no Vietnam," reflects Norman Lear. An especially curmudgeonly writer–producer, Lear's career in film had picked up some heat thanks to such relevant comedies as *Divorce American Style* and *Start the Revolution without Me*. He was even offered a three-picture deal at United Artists.

On the other hand, he was tempted by what he saw as a void in TV. Lear had read in *Variety* about a comedy series broadcast by the BBC called *Till Death Us Do Part*. It focused on a bigoted Cockney dad, a well-meaning mom, and a liberal son and his wife, sharing a house in the East End of London. Developed by a writer named Johnny Speight, it depicted fiery arguments about social problems of the day, with the father offending everyone within earshot. This was material that could translate to the United States.

Lear had a difficult decision to make—the movie deal or the tough TV project. "There wasn't anyone in my life who didn't beg me to take the three-picture deal," he says. "But there was so much of my own dad in this series. I was emotional about it. I had to do it."

As Lear was wrestling with his decision, a new CBS president named Robert D. Wood was doing some serious housecleaning. Gone were the long-running variety shows of Ed Sullivan, Jackie Gleason, and Red Skelton; also out were *The Beverly Hillbillies*, *Green Acres*, and *Petticoat Junction*. Advertisers wanted younger viewers, so Wood had a mandate to reduce the average age of the CBS audience and to bring more contemporary shows into the mix.

Thus he was inclined to take a shot at a show that ABC had toyed with and abandoned. It was touchy, it was worrisome—but it was undeniably funny.

The new show was the creation of Lear, who took inspiration from his own childhood. Lear's father referred to him as "dead from the neck up," an invective that was used in the pilot episode when Archie hollers at Mike and gives him his nickname: "You're a Meathead. Dead from the neck up."

"He would call me the laziest white person he ever met, putting down a whole race of people just to get at his son. Then he'd call me the dumbest white person he ever met," Lear says. "One hundred pages of notes spilled out of me in a few days."

After ABC rejected a pilot for Lear's show, he and partner Bud Yorkin took it to CBS. The programming chief at CBS at the time was Fred Silverman, a mercurial executive renowned as "the man with the golden gut" because of his reputation for anticipating audience response. Mindful of his network's mandate, Silverman was an early supporter of Lear's idea. He also knew that ABC allegedly had passed because the network brass disliked the cast of the pilot, which originally boasted the clunky title *Those Were the Days*. Carroll O'Connor, then an experienced Broadway actor, was the lead opposite another theater veteran, Jean Stapleton. The younger roles were played by Kelly Jean Peters and Tim McIntire.

Lear was skeptical of the official ABC explanation. "They were roaring with laughter at the pilot," he recalls. "But they were simply afraid of it."

In casting the new show for CBS, Lear still wanted to go with O'Connor and Stapleton, but he agreed to consider other actors. Mickey Rooney was a leading candidate to play Archie—the network thought he would attract viewers—but the aging actor was skeptical that the show would ever succeed. "They're going to kill you in the street," he warned Lear. A young actor named Harrison Ford was approached to assume the role of Mike, whose ethnicity had by now been changed from Irish to Polish. Ford made it clear he also wasn't interested, possibly because he found the Archie character too repulsive to play against.

All this gave a clear field to Lear's choices: Rob Reiner, and Sally Struthers, who, by coincidence, had been dating Reiner. Struthers's main competitor for the role was Penny Marshall, who later was to marry Reiner. Reiner, meanwhile, was fretting that he'd seem too young for the role, despite his already receding hairline. He grew a mustache so he could look twenty-four, his actual age.

O'Connor was by now everyone's choice to hold down the role of Archie, but he was a difficult man, even in his Broadway days. O'Connor was living in Rome and he insisted that he and his family be provided roundtrip tickets to Los Angeles. He was certain the show would never be picked up and this was his insurance.

Stapleton, too, still worried about her role. "Why would someone like Edith put up with Archie's bombast for so many years?" she wondered. "Norman reminded me that Edith had learned to turn him off. She shut out Archie's abuse. This was the clue I needed to play the role."

Once the cast had been set, other issues soon arose. Lear wanted the show to be shot in black and white; CBS argued for color. Lear responded by making the set full of drab, muted colors: beige, brown, dusty pink. The set decoration included a TV with furniture arranged around it, the first time that the glowing box was the center of a typical family's living room. Archie's treasured recliner was bought at a Goodwill store in Los Angeles (it now sits in the Smithsonian). While Archie's upstairs toilet was never shown, it does go down in history as the first toilet flush to be heard on TV.

Not surprisingly, the show had its share of corporate doubters, among them CBS chairman William Paley. Paley knew a fine line existed between controversial and vulgar, and he was concerned not only about Archie's blathering, but about other elements of the show. Surely certain sectors of the country would object to a white family inviting a black family to visit their home as friends, for instance.

Years later, in his autobiography, Paley acknowledged his concerns but said he was pleased in retrospect that he had let the show go forward. "We felt the time had come to catch up with some of the developments that had been taking place in this country," he wrote. As an example, "Interracial friendships might have been rare at the time, but it was important to show them on national television."

According to Donna McCrohan's book on the show, CBS audience researchers lobbied for Archie to be more likeable and supportive instead of combative when he dealt with his family. CBS standards and practices, not surprisingly, also had a laundry list of things they wanted to change in the show. William Tankersley, the vice president in charge of the Department of Program Practices, felt that "explicit sex" was implied in the first episode and he wanted the second episode of the show to be shown first. Lear refused. It wasn't until twenty-four hours before the first show was ready to air that CBS capitulated. The *TV Guide* blurb about the show's premiere reflected the battle: "True to the series' controversial nature, the subject matter for tonight's episode was undecided at press time—CBS executives might even change the program's title."

"I had written the first script to show 360 degrees of Archie Bunker. All of the vituperativeness, all of the fear of the future, all of the fear of anything he didn't understand and all of the love of family," Lear says.

Although Lear says no cuts were made to the show, *Variety* at the time reported otherwise: In the original version of the pilot, Mike and Gloria are interrupted during foreplay by Archie and Edith when they return home from church. A shot of Mike zipping up his pants was deemed offensive and was excised. The version that aired showed Mike and Gloria on the way to bed, but decidedly not in the middle of any action.

When the network showed the first two episodes to reviewers, some were stunned and offended. While *Weekly Variety*'s critic called it "the best TV comedy since the original *Honeymooners*," *Daily Variety* declared, "Nothing less than an insult to any unbigoted televiewer . . . something for every prejudice." (The two papers had separate critics until the mid-'90s.)

The *New York Times'* reviewer Fred Ferretti said he preferred the British version; the *Washington Post's* William C. Woods said it was "all shock and no story . . . every racial epithet and prejudiced social stance available in the long catalogue of ways we find to be cruel to each other."

All in the Family was given a slot at 9:30 PM on Tuesday nights, after *Hee-Haw* and before CBS news. It premiered January 12, 1971, without much promotion. CBS executives admitted they were baffled on how to market the show. CBS set aside extra operators, anticipating a deluge of irate phone calls.

A voiceover opened the premiere: "The program you are about to see is

All in the Family. It seeks to throw a humorous spotlight on our frailties, prejudices, and concerns. By making them a source of laughter, we hope to show—in a mature fashion—just how absurd they are."

When the show was over, CBS tallied 1,000 calls. More than 60 percent were favorable. Lear recalls: "I got some letters from people I quite respect and were very unhappy. They thought I was wrongheaded about this, because they knew I didn't want to make bigotry a living art. They thought it just didn't make sense to do what I was doing."

For its premiere, *Family* received a 15 percent audience share, putting it third in its timeslot against the telefilm *Assault on the Wayne*, starring Joseph Cotten and Leonard Nimoy (38 percent share) and the theatrical film *Secret Ceremony* with Elizabeth Taylor and Mia Farrow (30 percent share).

"I've often blessed the fact that they put us on in January," says Lear. "It was a midseason show and in those years, when they contracted for thirteen, they aired thirteen. People who had been watching whatever their favorites were on other networks turned to us. The ratings started to pick up. Bob Finkel was producing the Emmy show that year and told me that he'd like to start the Emmy show with a cold opening on the four principals of *All in the Family*, sitting at the television set before the Emmy broadcast starts, do four minutes of that and then into the show . . . that was enormous exposure."

In the early days of the show, Lear would literally pull his hair out while writing episodes. His wife finally bought him a hat to prevent the early onset of complete baldness. Yet he had assembled a team of writers that held impressive credits, and all had the ability of writing under the quick turnaround deadlines of TV. Milt Josefsberg had written for *The Jack Benny Show*. Mort Lachman worked on two decades' worth of Christmas specials. Hal Kanter was the writer, director, and producer of *The George Gobel Show*. Bob Schiller and Bob Weiskopf wrote for Danny Thomas, Lucille Ball, Red Skelton, and Flip Wilson. Michael Ross was the program editor for the Sid Caesar vehicle, *Caesar's Hour*, where he worked with head writer Mel Tolkin, who also joined the *Family* scribe tribe.

All were Emmy winners. Yet, as with most sitcoms, rewrites were relentless. When asked, "What is the best outcome you can conceive of a script coming in from an outside writer?" Lear replied, "One where I would say, 'This will really rewrite well.'" Ad-libbing among the cast was also encouraged, with O'Connor devising one particular Archie bon mot on the spot, calling his neighbor "the queen of the women's lubrication movement."

Lear made it a policy that whoever wrote the first draft of the episode got the on-screen credit, even if barely a word of the original script made it to air, but story meetings produced a stressful environment. Lear even gave two writers $25 toward the cost of therapy sessions. He figured what they talked about with their shrink could come to light in a really good script down the road. The use of topical humor, incorporating headlines from Vietnam and Watergate, required last-minute rewrites of scenes before they were taped. A copy of the *New York Times* was given to each writer every day.

Lear says, "I still don't know when I stopped being afraid that every script might not work. It took a long time."

As was the common sitcom practice of the day, each episode was taped twice; the version that finally made it to air generally was a combination of the two. The first taping, before a live studio audience at CBS Television City in Los Angeles's Fairfax district, would begin at 5:30 PM, with rehearsals concluding at 5:15. Lear superstitiously introduced the actors to the crowd before the new taping.

The show was taped straight through, like a play, with no stops for flubs or errors. The second taping began at 8 PM. Afterward, Lear would question the audience about what made them laugh and what didn't, and asked their opinion on tweaks they made in the few hours between the first and second tapings. Then they did retakes for flubs. The show didn't use a laugh track. The laughs that were heard came from the studio audience.

Although ratings remained low for the first few weeks, CBS ran reruns of the show throughout the summer, and the audience steadily grew. That fall, Jean Stapleton won an Emmy as best comedy actress. By September 1971, *All in the Family* was number one in the Nielsen ratings, with 50 million people watching the show every week, a record for a regularly scheduled series. In some urban areas, like New York, it hit a 70 percent share.

Besides the ongoing subtext of racism, *Family* dealt with rape, euthanasia, murder, breast cancer, infidelity, and homosexuality. While the black family next door, the Jeffersons, are referred to from the first episode, only son Lionel was awarded a regular, recurring role from the outset. Isabel Sanford's Louise became Edith's best friend, but Sherman Hemsley's George didn't appear on the show until two years into its run.

As the show gained more viewers, audience response wasn't always as Lear expected. One letter from a women's rights group asked, "What does Gloria do? What's her job, her education? Is she just around all the time?"

Lear and director John Rich agreed that the character had been underwritten. The result was one of the early controversial episodes, "The Battle of the Month," centering on an argument between Gloria and her mother. Gloria was moody because she had her menstrual period. According to writer Michael Ross, "We needed Gloria irritated to the point where she would blow up at Edith. In fact, we got the idea from Sally herself. When she has her period, forget it . . ."

Edith continued to take a number of knocks for being the happy housewife in an era when the Equal Rights Amendment was a topic of furious debate, according to Donna McCrohan. The writers and Stapleton felt that it would be out of character for Edith, who scurries to the kitchen to get her man a beer, to become a bra burner, but her attitudes changed slowly over the course of the show.

"I think that by showing Edith as she really is, we are doing more good than an instant out-of-character liberationist would accomplish," Stapleton said in 1974. "There's a slow development going on with Edith and that's the way it's really going to happen in the country."

The show used Stapleton's character—"Edith the Good," as Archie snarkily refers to her—as the all-encompassing innocent to deal with these issues. In "Edith's Christmas Story," she suffers a breast cancer scare, but receives comfort from a neighbor who has had a mastectomy. The result of Edith's tests were given only after the character had gone through the gamut of possible reactions: fear, denial, hope, anger. The audience responded in kind—if it can happen to loyal Edith, the perpetual optimist, it can happen to anybody. After the episode with Edith's breast cancer scare, doctors saw a substantial increase in the number of women who made appointments for mammograms.

While the show tackled serious subjects, it always did so with humor. When Archie is being driven crazy by Edith's menopause symptoms, he explodes: "If you're gonna have the change of life, you gotta do it right now. I'm gonna give you just thirty seconds. Now c'mon and change!"

Edith: "Can I finish my soup first?"

Her menopause attracted one of Lear's favorite anecdotes, which he often used to warm the crowd up for live tapings. A viewer sent in a postcard complaining about the episode. In a different handwriting underneath the rant was written, "Please don't pay any attention to this person. This person does not know where it's at. Signed, the Postman."

It was the rape episode in 1977, however, that became national news. Run as a one-hour special, "Edith's 50th Birthday" has Edith attacked by a man posing as a police officer who claims he is questioning folks in the neighborhood about a rape. He tries to force himself on her, and Edith begs him to leave his clothes on to make the attack as impersonal as possible. Edith manages to escape when a cake she is baking starts to burn in the oven and she throws it in the assailant's face. Archie tries to dissuade her from reporting the crime to the police, arguing that "nothing happened." Gloria insists that she report the assault; Edith complies in the hope that her information will prevent others from being attacked.

Lear took over a year pondering the episode. Originally it was tossed around as a plot development for Bonnie Franklin's character, Ann Romano, on another Lear production, *One Day at a Time*. He instead decided that the topic would have more impact if it happened to Edith. He interviewed the director of a rape treatment center in Santa Barbara and screened the tape for police and social workers around the country.

Despite his research, it took a great deal to sell the script to the actors. In the first read-through several felt some of the jokes were tasteless, including a secondary plot that had a party going on next door at Mike and Gloria's house. The actors came together a day later and agreed they wouldn't do the show unless some of the dialogue was changed. Lear brought in a social worker from a rape crisis center, but to no avail—it wasn't the topic they were upset about, it was the way it was handled on the show. Lear then agreed to add a half hour to the episode, making it a one-hour special that could set a slower pace and allow for a less jokey, more dramatic tone.

David Dukes, the actor hired to portray the rapist, and Stapleton practiced their choreography so that the show could be taped straight through without mishap. Paul Bogart, the director, opted for five cameras and three boom microphones to make sure nothing was missed. The reaction from the audience when Edith escapes her attacker was so loud at the 5:30 taping that the crew had to pause before the next scene or else Edith's next lines, where she tells her family what happened, would be drowned out.

Upon airing, many critics were outraged. Harriet Van Horne of the *New York Post* wrote, "This historic episode demonstrates anew what a fine actress Jean Stapleton is, and how far down Norman Lear and CBS will reach to push up the Sunday ratings a point or two." Val Adams of the *New York Daily News* offered a similar viewpoint: "There are some who think that Lear . . . is a genius. A more moderate view is that he's a good showman." But Cecil Smith, TV critic of the *Los Angeles Times*, wrote, "The attack was not treated lightly; the humor was hysterical and in keeping with the Edith character. A number of letters I have received [against the show] seem to be from people who did not see the program."

Over time, Norman Lear's relations with his cast became ever more turbulent. In the summer of 1973, O'Connor threatened to leave the show, citing several instances where his idea of the Archie character differed with the plan that Lear had in mind. Lear explains: "I was dealing with an actor who just was going to be unhappy. It was just in his nature, and then we would fight about a script for a couple, three days. When Carroll O'Connor realized he had to embrace the script, without the wholesale changes he would insist upon, that's when he finally accepted it and slipped into character. Now he was in serious rehearsal. None of us could write Archie Bunker the way it flew out of him, in his understanding of the character and the idiom, the language, the malaprops. He was gifted as an actor and writer of that character. It was worth all of the aggravation to get to that moment. Carroll was utterly devoted to the character and the mission."

Meanwhile, O'Connor himself still felt he had much to attain. He wrote a note to Jackie Gleason praising the energy he brought to his portrayal of Ralph Kramden on *The Honeymooners*. "I know I'm doing some of the things you did." Gleason wrote back, "I wish I had done some of the things you're doing."

Still, with each new season O'Connor's critiques increasingly made news. O'Connor refused to perform a scene that Lear deemed critical: Louise Jefferson, the black next-door neighbor played by Isabel Sanford, was standing under mistletoe, and her son Lionel suggests that Archie kiss her. O'Connor thought the entire scene was inappropriate, but when he raised the issue, Lear turned a deaf ear. O'Connor was galled by the lack of heft his opinions were given, and said in an interview, "When Norman picked me up from what was supposed to be 'Nowhere Land,' I was further along in my profession than he was in his. It was really a question of who did what for whom." Eventually the scene was whacked.

And O'Connor was placated with a new, richer contract.

However, in July 1974, O'Connor walked off the show. He sued Lear and Yorkin's production company, Tandem, for $65,000 in back salary and, reputedly, to get his name above the title of the show. Lear, in response, won an injunction that prevented O'Connor from working in TV or any other medium until the dispute was resolved.

The first two episodes of the 1974–75 season were shot without O'Connor. Archie supposedly had traveled to Buffalo on business and had disappeared. The character would have been killed off in the third episode if the lawsuit wasn't resolved. When the dispute was settled, O'Connor's and Stapleton's names were now emblazoned before the title and O'Connor was back on set.

But only for two months. The next incident of "Archie interruptus" occurred in September when the International Brotherhood of Electrical Workers went on strike at CBS. O'Connor refused to cross the picket line; Lear disapproved and O'Connor went public with his unhappiness, declaring, "I've been a trade union man all my life. I cannot work with strikebreakers . . . Norman's tack, and you may quote me, seems always to be to question my sincerity and my goodwill and to imply that my actions are against the best interests of the case and company of *All in the Family.*" The strike was settled, O'Connor again went back to work in the first of a four-part story in which Archie went on strike.

The next season, Struthers tried to get out of her contract to concentrate more on film work. The case went to arbitration, and Struthers was ordered not to seek outside work in TV, radio, or film until her deal ran out in two years.

Next it was Lear's turn to balk.

In 1975, CBS asked for *Family* to start airing reruns in daytime. While the FCC had dictated that primetime shows could air a maximum of three minutes of ads for each half hour, daytime shows had six minutes per half hour. Lear balked at making the cuts, noting, "It is enormously destructive to the intent of the original show, and I think it is a terrible crime against all the people who worked so hard to make the original show."

He offered to pay CBS whatever money the network could lose from the three less minutes of ad time. CBS wouldn't buy it and Lear relented.

Despite Lear's occasional protestations, *All in the Family* inevitably became big business. According to Spence Marsh's book *Edith the Good*, Gloria's pregnancy gave *Family* another ratings boost and when son Joey was born on December 22, 1975, a new age of promotional marketing dawned. A baby Joey doll ("physically correct" according to advertisements) hit store shelves. The doll caused less controversy than the actual birth of the child and its presence in the show's storyline. The notion of the baby's naughty bits being flashed during diaper changes sent the CBS censors into a frenzy, and they requested that the gender of Mike and Gloria's baby be changed to a girl. The request was shot down: Joey remained a boy, and civilization did not end.

The birth of Joey also led to a spin-off from the series. As early as the first season, Lear created a character that inspired the first of the series' seven spin-offs. Maude originally served as a foil for Archie. "It was time after eight or ten shows, to have somebody on the show that would kill Archie verbally," Lear says. "Mike fought with him all the time, but Mike was as poor a liberal as Archie was a conservative. So I thought, given my family life, it had to be somebody out of his past that could hammer him over a twenty-year period. I've always loved my friend Beatrice Arthur, so we wrote in the character of Maude, a cousin of Archie's, who never wanted him to get married, who knew him that long. We brought her on and we were three days into rehearsals when I knew that I would hear from Silverman and others to do a show with this woman."

So the era of Lear spin-offs had begun. *Maude* ran from 1972 to 1978; *The Jeffersons* from 1975 to 1985. These two spin-offs created their own spin-offs: *Good Times* (1974–79) featured Maude's maid Florida Evans (Esther Rolle), while *Checking In* (1981) starred the Jeffersons' maid, Florence (Marla Gibbs).

More than 120 million Americans watched at least one of these shows—more than half the country's population at that point.

"I don't know how it was with other companies, but we were in profit on every single show," Lear says. "We didn't have a syndication department at Tandem, so we relinquished the syndication rights to CBS. We had to wait a long time to regain those. CBS sold them to Viacom. We felt we were just adrift, whichever way the wind blew, we couldn't control them."

In 1979, when the other three actors left the show, O'Connor starred in *Archie Bunker's Place*. For the 1982–83 season, Struthers returned to the character, Gloria, with her son Joey. In the 1994 *704 Hauser*, a black family now lived in the old Bunker residence.

In the 1970s and '80's, Lear and Tandem became a sitcom factory cranking out other hits including NBC's *Sanford and Son* (1972–77) and *One Day at a Time* (1975–84). In 1975, Lear had seven network shows on the air as well as *Mary Hartman, Mary Hartman* in syndication. (That record was matched by Aaron Spelling for two seasons in the mid-1980s and was broken by Jerry Bruckheimer with nine series in the 2005–06 season).

With the development of new hits on other networks, *All in the Family* ultimately saw its ratings reign come to an end. The show became *Archie Bunker's Place* in 1979 and started to focus more on Archie's antics and friends at the bar.

Says Lear: "I never heard from Bill Paley until I wanted to retire the characters, tie a ribbon around them, and put them on a shelf. That's when he chose to deal with me, when he wanted Archie Bunker back. I thought we had done it. I thought we had said it. We've had it and I wanted to hang it up . . . no show should be on for over five years. It makes no room for fresh talent."

In 1978, the final episode of the season was a classic tearjerker. Struthers said at the time, "I felt the way you do after you'd been to a friend's funeral. The weeping has stopped, but you're not adjusted to the loss." Reiner supposedly starting crying on the freeway while he was driving home and Lear watched the final taping in sunglasses to hide his tears.

Stapleton reduced her presence to a recurring role on *Archie Bunker's Place*, but in 1980, she said she wanted out of the show altogether. Lear announced that Edith would be killed off. There was an immediate outcry—

a "Save Edith Bunker Committee" was founded and Stapleton was forced to issue a statement: "It's like talking about something that really doesn't die. Edith still exists in the imagination . . . We must encourage people to realize that Edith doesn't die because she never really lived. You can't kill something that's an idea, can you?"

The public was not placated. Newspapers published eulogies. Lear's Tandem Productions eventually created an "Edith Bunker Memorial Fund" and donated $500,000 dollars to supporters of the ERA. The show had Edith die of a stroke in her sleep.

By 1983, *Archie Bunker's Place* was twenty-sixth in the Nielsen ratings and CBS decided to cancel the show. The first offer O'Connor got after the wrap was to play Khrushchev in a miniseries.

Clearly, *All in the Family* and its characters had long since become something greater than simply a TV show. In its own quirky, often irritating way, the show had insinuated itself into the national experience. The Bunkers had become part of our lives.

As Norman Lear reflects, "I learned my biggest lesson about the country when the network used to say 'This won't fly in Des Moines,' or 'There'll be a knee-jerk reaction in the middle of the country.' I thought, 'Don't hand me that.' I feel like I'm from Des Moines. The American establishment always underestimates the American people. I think they're dead wrong. We are not as well educated as we might be, but we're a people wise of heart."

13 Kaleidoscope of the Sixties
Easy Rider/Hair (1969)

Great shows are supposed to reflect (and reinforce) the mood of their times. What happens,
therefore, if the times are utterly schizoid?

The '60s were a time of anger and ecstasy, an uneasy co-existence between
the hubris of sex, drugs and rock 'n' roll on the one hand and the despair of
Vietnam, political assassinations, and violent demands for black power on the
other. Pop culture amplified the noise level of these contradictions. On television, the nightly news, full of stories of turmoil and unrest, collided with
Gomer Pyle USMC and *Bonanza*. Filmmakers brought forth *Bonnie and
Clyde* and *Midnight Cowboy*, but the biggest grosses came from *The Love
Bug*, a Disney comedy about a Volkswagen with a mind of its own. Audiences
were moved by the aggression of Mrs. Robinson in *The Graduate*, but they
also responded to a sheepish Rex Harrison as *Dr. Dolittle*, singing a tender
love song to a seal that's dressed as a woman.

The conflicts and contradictions of the '60s reached their fullest expression, I believe, in the film *Easy Rider* and the play *Hair*. Both reflected the
anger and optimism of the times. And both served as a wake-up call for their
target audiences.

Hair was the brainchild of James Rado and Gerome Ragni, two unem-
ployed actors who met while job hunting. They wanted to create a show
that reflected life as they observed it in the East Village. The musical might
have been a footnote to the history of musical theater were it not for
Michael Butler, the young heir to Butler Aviation, who bought a ticket to
the show, mistakenly thinking it was about Native Americans.

With no credentials as a producer, Butler decided to reinvent *Hair*,
or at least trigger a chaotic process through which it was redesigned,

re-costumed, relighted, re-orchestrated, and mostly recast. He also hired a new director.

America's first "tribal love-rock musical" opened at the Biltmore Theater on Broadway on April 29, 1968, six months after its debut at New York's Off-Broadway's Public Theater. *Hair* ended up playing 1,742 performances on Broadway, closing on July 1, 1972. It had the fourth-longest run for a Broadway musical of the 1960s (after *Fiddler on the Roof, Hello, Dolly!*, and *Man of La Mancha*).

Easy Rider was conceived in a marijuana haze. Though countless young people in the '60s came up with, like, wow, really "heavy" ideas while stoned, Peter Fonda actually followed through on his inspiration. On a budget of only $360,000, *Easy Rider* began filming with 16mm cameras, no final cast, no final script, and a crew that had been assembled in five weeks. Dennis Hopper was a first-time director, who, as Fonda wrote in his 1998 book, *Don't Tell Dad*, began the first day of shooting with a two-hour rant to the crew that began, "This is *my* fucking movie and *nobody* is going to take it away from me!"

The cinema graveyard is littered with incoherent movies from stoned filmmakers, but *Easy Rider* was to have its own special destiny. Viewed from today's perspective, it seems at once disoriented and disorganized, an example of mood over matter. Yet in its time, *Easy Rider* was revered by its audience, not so much as film, but as instant folklore. Grossing an astonishing $60 million worldwide, it fired a warning shot at the already hobbled Hollywood studios. A new lexicon of filmmaking had arrived to serve the mythos of the times—if only someone could figure out what that embodied.

Rado and Ragni wanted to create something new and different for the theater. As Rado says, "The times were experimental and so we decided to experiment." The two pitched the idea to theater maestro Joseph Papp, who was interested, provided they come up with a good score. Nat Shapiro, the agent and music publisher who represented the duo, introduced them to another client, Galt MacDermot.

MacDermot was relatively new to the New York scene and seemed utterly incompatible with crazed characters like Rado and Ragni. He was born in Canada, received his musical education in South Africa, and wrote a modern-jazz work, "African Waltz," which won two Grammys. Before meeting Rado and Ragni, he didn't even know what a hippie was and admitted as much. Still, the three had a kind of chemistry and managed to compose a few songs they could present to Papp.

The producer liked what he heard. The show, under the direction of Gerald Freedman, launched Papp's partly subsidized New York Shakespeare Festival Public Theater. The first of its fifteen previews began on October 17, 1967, and it opened October 29 for fifty performances, at a top ticket price of $2.50 (the cost of a Ziegfeld Follies ticket in 1907). But even at these prices, the show didn't seem to work. It also seemed out of synch with a Shakespeare Festival.

The discordant scenes started to come together when the show found a new (and more appropriate) home at a disco called the Cheetah. To Rado and Ragni, their show had now reached the point where they were ready to take it to Broadway. No one else thought so, however.

Enter Michael Butler. A handsome Brahmin from Chicago, Butler, who owned a few discos of his own, saw an ad for *Hair* featuring actors wearing beads and feathered headbands. Since he was interested in Native Americans, he decided to take in the show. What he saw both excited and baffled him.

Butler had been raised in Oak Brook, Illinois, a private preserve that encompassed stables for 400 horses, a golf course, and several compounds. The Butler family, having been driven out of Ireland by Cromwell in 1654, founded Butler Paper in the 1840s and built it into one of the nation's biggest privately owned companies. The family later expanded into ranching, banking electronics, and finally aviation, establishing Butler Aviation, which serviced the airline industry.

Butler himself was a restless young man who traveled on his own through Mexico and Africa and mingled with other wealthy and restless young men. One of his friends was John F. Kennedy, the two spending time on the Kennedy compounds, hooking up with girls and occasionally seeing to it that the elder Kennedy, Joe, also found female companionship.

In his early thirties, Butler was at a turning point in his life. "I was a member in good standing of the military-industrial complex," he deadpans. In short, he was a polo-playing, fox-hunting jet-setter.

Butler found himself working in the family business and, at the same time, handling special missions for a family friend, Illinois governor Otto Kerner. He even ran for state senator in DuPage County on a Democratic ticket and lost.

It was Robert Kennedy who encouraged him to run for the United States Senate. In the spring of 1967, Butler was preparing for a Senate campaign when he became intensely involved in the politics of the Vietnam draft. The antiwar movement, he realized, had become the overriding issue of his time.

When he happened upon the first preview of *Hair*, therefore, Butler's response was one of shock. "This curious show was the strongest antiwar statement I'd ever seen," he says. "I wanted to take the show to Illinois and force people to see it. *Hair* was more powerful than any political speech I could make."

Butler talked to Joe Papp, who had gone on to other shows and was uninterested in extending its run. The enthusiasm of Butler and others changed his mind. Indeed, Butler confided to him that he was now going to end his flirtation with politics and try his hand at producing. Most important: he was willing to finance *Hair*'s Broadway run.

Butler had previously been an investor in *West Side Story*, but otherwise had no background in the theater. Still, he thought of himself as a showman. And now he was determined to shape up *Hair*.

Butler revamped the production. The cast was largely overhauled, with Rado and Melba Moore among those added. In a key move, Butler hired director Tom O'Horgan to reinvent several scenes. Butler felt Freedman was a good director who understood beatniks, but not hippies. "I don't think he'd ever smoked grass," Butler says. O'Horgan had been working in avant-garde theater, helming such plays as *Futz*, about a loveless farmer who "marries" his pig, Amanda. But in a way he felt that he was preaching to the choir by working in plays with limited audience appeal, and he welcomed the chance to shake up the Broadway scene.

The input of O'Horgan energized the production, but *Hair* played oddly flat even during a final rehearsal, with the audience applauding politely but indifferently. "Opening night on Broadway," Butler recalls, "was akin to witnessing the birth of an entirely new show. From the opening number the audience seemed enthralled. By the end, the applause was tumultuous. *Hair* had become an instant hit."

As audiences entered, they saw no curtain on the stage, a rarity at that point on Broadway. There was open scaffolding, with several levels of playing area; otherwise, the stage area featured graffiti and not much else. As the lights dimmed, actors emerged from various areas of the theater—the lobby, the balconies, and various exit doors. When music started, they moved toward the stage in slow motion.

Then came a series of striking moments: Claude enters on a motorcycle, wearing a gorilla costume; three black women enact the Supremes, in apparently identical costumes, and then separate to reveal that they're all stuck in one gigantic dress. A black woman dressed as Abraham Lincoln recites a mock Gettysburg address. As she's shot, she walks away saying, "Shit, I ain't dyin' for no white man!"

At the end of the first act, several members of the tribe burn draft cards at a "be-in." The cast then disappears under a tarp that covers the stage. As Claude sings "Where Do I Go," the tarp is dropped and several of the cast members are exposed, literally, standing onstage naked. After the song, there is an immediate blackout, the sound of sirens, and two men in police uniforms walk to the front of the stage to announce that everyone in the theater is under arrest—the cue for intermission.

The nudity in *Hair*, of course, proved to be a big selling point. A positive review from Clive Barnes in the *New York Times* didn't hurt.

Not everyone was swept away. In a May 1, 1968, review, *Variety's* Hobe frowned on the show's "jeers at patriotism, religion, morality, and the traditional idea of respectability, such as the belief that the people should be clothed in public." He seemed amazed that "few opening performances have ever been received with such noisy encouragement. Every number, indeed almost every line, was greeted with loud cheers or laughter, or both."

Word of mouth, needless to say, was exuberant. Butler and the show's other backers were thrilled, but still weren't sure if they could get away with it. Their attorney regularly came to the theater with $10,000 in his pocket, in case the cast and creators were hauled off to jail.

But there were no arrests. Indeed, the show not only attracted typical theatergoers, who were enthralled by its boldness, but also brought in new and younger audiences.

The *Hair* spirit spread. Before long, there were twelve productions of *Hair* in the United States alone, including seven simultaneous touring companies. Soon after, it opened in other countries, too, where it was a phenomenal success. Productions were shut down in Japan and Acapulco, but never in the United States.

Meanwhile, *Hair* was creating gyrations in the music business. When the show debuted at the Public Theater in 1967, RCA recorded an original cast album, but when the musical moved to Broadway the following year with a mostly new cast, RCA released another album that was considerably more commercial. It became the number one album in the United States for twenty weeks and ended up in the bestseller charts for 151 weeks. Within a year, disc sales of all the *Hair* recordings had grossed $20 million with an astonishing sixteen songs released as singles. The Fifth Dimension's medley "Aquarius/Let the Sunshine In" remained number one for six weeks, with two million records sold. Selling a million each were "Good Morning Starshine," by Oliver, and "Hair," by the Cowsills. *Hair* would turn out to be the last Broadway show to land multiple singles on the hit parade, though

Broadway albums continued to sell well after that (as with *A Chorus Line*, *Cats*, and *The Phantom of the Opera*).

In his 1998 autobiography *Don't Tell Dad*, Peter Fonda says the idea for *Easy Rider* came to him when sitting in a Toronto hotel in September 1967, smoking a joint and drinking a Heineken. He looked at a photo of himself and Bruce Dern from the recently completed *The Wild Angels*. They were both on a motorcycle, and, writes Fonda, "I understood immediately just what kind of motorcycle, sex, and drug movie I should make next."

Fonda had starred in several biker films for American International Pictures, which achieved box office success by following rigorous genre requirements. They had titles like *Glory Stompers*, *Hell's Angels on Wheels*, *Angels from Hell*, and *Cycle Savages*. Though Fonda had signed a deal for further genre pictures, he had something else entirely in mind. He wanted to do an update of the John Ford movie *The Searchers*, in which John Wayne and Jeffrey Hunter go hunting for young Natalie Wood, who's been abducted by Indians. "America would be our Natalie Wood," Fonda decided.

Instead of two cowpokes heading west, these two would head east. In a perverse American dream, they would make a huge amount of money with one mega-drug deal, then retire to Florida. The two would be named Billy and Wyatt, after Western icons Billy the Kid and Wyatt Earp. And the film's tagline would be: "A man went looking for America, but couldn't find it anywhere."

The first thing that crystallized for Fonda was the ending: "We would be blasted to bits by the narrow-minded, redneck poachers at dawn, just outside of Heaven, Florida." It would be a vision of, in his words, "America the Ugliful," and he soon sketched in a beginning and a middle.

When he told his wife, Susan, the outline, she responded, "That's the corniest story I've ever heard." Fonda didn't see it her way. He called his old friend Dennis Hopper and asked him to direct. Hopper had done some second-unit directing for *The Trip*, and his acting career seemed at a dead end.

Fonda next traveled to Roscoff, France, a fishing village where he and sister Jane were starring in a segment for the anthology film *Spirits of the Dead*, directed by her then husband, Roger Vadim. He spent four hours a day staring at the sea and working on the story.

When novelist and screenwriter Terry Southern arrived for a meeting with Jane and Vadim, Fonda told him the idea, saying he and Hopper were looking for a writer for the material. Southern was enthused: "It's the most commercial story I have ever heard. I'm your man." Fonda was stunned. He didn't see it as that commercial. But Southern, in his mid-forties, was a very successful writer, thanks to his novels (*The Magic Christian*) and screenplays (*Dr. Strangelove*). Southern's fee at that point was $100,000 per script, but he agreed to work for scale (about $350 a week) knowing his name would lend credibility to the project.

In New York, Hopper, Southern, and Fonda spent five days talking through the story. Before committing anything to paper, Southern suggested recording the story verbally. Fonda taped a forty-minute pitch, which Southern's secretary transcribed and edited to twenty-one pages.

After Christmas 1967, Fonda and Hopper paid a visit to Sam Arkoff and Jim Nicholson, the heads of American International Pictures. They assumed the two partners would be receptive, because they relished genre pictures. When *Beach Party* was a success, it led to *Beach Blanket Bingo* and other surfing films, but AIP also was smart enough to hire genuinely talented people, including Jack Nicholson, Francis Ford Coppola, Martin Scorsese, and Vincent Price.

Even renegade AIP was wary of this project, however. Hopper's directing talents were unknown. What's more, the idea that the "heroes" were selling cocaine was troubling. AIP suggested that the characters should not be smuggling hard narcotics, but that marijuana might be acceptable. They also warned that if Hopper fell three days behind, AIP could take away the movie.

Fonda and Hopper were offended. First, the protagonists were smuggling the drugs in the gas tank of a motorcycle so it would take a truckload of marijuana to give them enough money to justify their retirement. They had toyed with their heroes selling heroin, but came up with cocaine as a compromise. And they felt, probably correctly, that the general public didn't know enough about cocaine to be offended by the notion. (Years later, Hopper claimed to Peter Biskind, author of *Easy Riders, Raging Bulls*, "The cocaine problem in the United States is really because of me. There was no cocaine on the street before *Easy Rider*. After *Easy Rider*, it was everywhere.")

Even more upsetting to the would-be filmmakers, however, was the notion that AIP would keep such a tight rein on Hopper. Neither side would budge.

Jack Nicholson, who had written the script of *The Trip*, suggested that Schneider and Hopper take their project to Raybert, a production company run by Bob Rafelson and Bert Schneider. From the first meeting, it seemed like a perfect match. All four occupied some niche in the Hollywood mainstream, but still saw themselves as rebels. And *Easy Rider* embodied their maverick fantasy lives.

Bert Schneider was born in 1933 and raised in New York, the son of Abe Schneider, a tough, frozen-faced accountant who eventually became head of Columbia Pictures. He was dubbed "Mount Rushmore" by subordinates.

Bert grew up in New Rochelle, a New York suburb. Tall (six-foot-four), with striking good looks and a cool charisma, he'd started work at Screen Gems, the TV division of his father's company. He and his wife, Judy, seemed the personification of a '50s success story, attractive and bland. Below the surface, though, Schneider was restless. Rafelson, a recent transplant to Los Angeles who had been Schneider's friend from their New York days, encouraged him to move west and find a new job. Schneider, his wife, and two children moved to Southern California and within a short time, he was smoking dope and embracing radical politics.

He and Rafelson started Raybert ostensibly to encourage maverick filmmakers. Rafelson, supposedly the creative partner, grew up on Manhattan's Riverside Drive, near Eighty-first Street and was expected to inherit his father's haberdashery business. But at Dartmouth, he got hooked on Sartre and Kerouac and became something of a hipster. Through a friend at his parents' country club, he landed a job writing for TV and in June 1962, he and his wife moved to Los Angeles, where he worked for Revue Productions, the TV arm of Universal. When Universal's überboss Lew Wasserman, reprimanded him for injecting "degenerate" subplots into scripts, Rafelson knocked everything off of Wasserman's desk. He was escorted off the lot.

As independents now, Schneider and Rafelson went on to invent *The Monkees*, a 1965–67 TV series. The show and its best-selling records made Schneider and Rafelson very wealthy. "Monkee money made *Easy Rider*," Fonda later said.

Hipsters sneered at the series, because the half-hour comedy about a wacky, lovable singing quartet so blatantly imitated *Hard Day's Night*. Even worse, it was revealed that the actors didn't always play their own instruments. *Easy Rider* thus represented a big leap for Schneider and Rafelson. Though Schneider obviously had contacts at Columbia, there was no guarantee that the company would release the film. Columbia's fare at that point was decidedly mainstream—*Guess Who's Coming to Dinner*, *Funny Girl*, and *To Sir With Love*, for example, placed their hopes on the talent of Fonda and Hopper.

Hopper was born in Dodge City, Kansas, but began acting in San Diego, where his family had moved when he was a kid. At age eighteen, he was put under contract to Columbia, but rebelled against their strict control. Moving to Warner Bros., he costarred in *Rebel Without a Cause* and *Giant* and grew to idolize James Dean and his rebellious aura. When Hopper hassled Hollywood veteran director Henry Hathaway while shooting the 1958 film *From Hell to Texas* and challenged his decisions, the director saw to it that his "bad boy" reputation was known all around town.

Hopper fell back on underground projects and activism, even marching in Montgomery, Alabama, with Martin Luther King Jr. Both *Vogue* and *Harper's Bazaar* ran his photographs of musicians and artists. He hung out with poet Allen Ginsberg and began an art collection.

Hopper and Fonda found they had much in common. Fonda was expelled from private school and raised by an aunt and uncle in Omaha. He studied acting, appeared onstage in New York in *Blood, Sweat and Stanley Poole*, and made his film debut in *Tammy and the Doctor* (1963). He found a few more roles, but was keenly aware that he hadn't lived up to the legacy of his famously cold father, Henry, who'd starred in such groundbreaking films as *The Ox-Bow Incident* and *The Grapes of Wrath*. Peter hadn't even achieved the success of his sister Jane, who was an established name via *Barefoot in the Park* and *Barbarella*.

When Fonda and Hopper gave their outline to Schneider and Rafelson, their proviso was that the filmmakers would get one-third of the picture, $40,000 to get started, and an ultimate budget of $360,000.

With the Mardi Gras "season" underway, Fonda and Hopper now pulled together a crew in five weeks. On February 22, they flew to New Orleans to begin six days of filming. They had an outline of scenes but no final cast and no script.

According to Fonda's book, *Don't Tell Dad*, the first day ended when Hopper broke Karen Black's guitar over the head of cinematographer Barry Feinstein. "I got Hopper back to our room, made him smoke a doob—he'd been doing whites and wine all day—and I told him he needed to calm down," Fonda says. He also gave Hopper 1,000 mg of Placidyl, which he described then as "a heavy central nervous system drug."

The second day, Hopper began to rant anew, and Fonda labeled him "a little fascist freak." After the disastrous New Orleans shoot, the company returned to Los Angeles, regrouped, and restaffed. Paul Lewis became production manager and assistant director. William Hayward was hired as associate producer. They hired a new cinematographer, Laszlo Kovacs, and started filming with 35mm cameras (as opposed to the 16mm they'd used in New Orleans). The crew was composed of artisans who normally worked in television. All of the actors agreed to work for scale, meaning their salaries would be well below-market.

Crucially, Fonda kept his producer title, but Schneider became executive producer. Fonda rationalized that Hopper felt insecure, because the film was Fonda's idea and Fonda had hired Hopper, and was on the set, watchful, each day as producer.

Several events caused further tension between the friends, however. In a New Orleans cemetery, Hopper insisted that Fonda improvise a speech talking to his dead mother. Fonda was horrified at giving voice to personal matters he'd carefully kept secret in his life. (His mother, Frances Seymour Brokaw, had committed suicide. Henry Fonda typically had tried to ignore the entire incident.) Fonda eventually improvised a monologue, and the footage was kept in the film, but it would be some time before he could forgive Hopper for the embarrassing intrusion.

When he returned to L.A., he played tapes of Hopper's rants to Schneider, insisting that Hopper be replaced. Schneider refused, although he clumsily warned Hopper of Fonda's indignation.

The rift widened further over financial negotiations. Under the original deal, Fonda and Hopper were both to get eleven percent of the profits and Southern would get ten, with Schneider receiving the rest. When Southern quit the picture, his points were up for grabs: Fonda gave half to Bill Hayward, who was Hopper's brother-in-law and associate producer on the film, and the other half to Pando, which was Fonda's production company. Hopper was livid. Later, he filed a suit alleging Fonda owed him money.

A later dispute erupted over writing credits and casting. Southern says he wrote the part of lawyer George Hanson specifically with Rip Torn in mind, and the actor had committed to play it. There are varying versions of why this failed to happen. One is that Torn had pulled a knife on Hopper; or Hopper, according to different accounts, pulled one on Torn. Fonda says that, when they had been in New York working on the script, they all went out to dinner. Hopper and Torn got into an argument and soon "gripped each other's shirts and brandished butter knives."

Years later, the *New York Times Magazine* ran a story stating that Torn had walked off the set. He demanded and got a retraction, stating that he'd read the script, but never committed to the movie. Therefore, he couldn't have walked off the set because he was never on it in the first place.

Against Hopper's instincts, Schneider cast Nicholson as the lawyer. However, casting Nicholson restored a needed degree of professionalism to the production. He was a member of the AIP fraternity and had earned his share of acting credits in schlocky biker and horror pictures. He'd even tried his hand at writing and directing a few low-budget films and, since his acting career hadn't taken off, had contemplated a behind-the-camera life.

On the other hand, *Easy Rider* represented an easy payday. He knew Dennis Hopper was talented, but also hot-wired—a volatile and hyper individual whose behavior was erratic even without the benefit of drugs. He had an actor's instinct and an artist's eye, but could he actually run a film company and prepare his shots?

There was an immediate clash about drugs. Though Nicholson and Hopper had dropped acid together in New Mexico when visiting the grave of D. H. Lawrence—a macho hippie ritual of the '60s—Nicholson resisted smoking dope during his acting scenes. During one lengthy monologue, Hopper apparently kept passing him joints, but Fonda nonetheless rated his performance "letter perfect and very stoned."

In Flagstaff, Arizona, on the start of filming, a morale party was held in Fonda's motel room. "Many of the crew had never smoked pot, but that night was all about getting high," Fonda recalls.

When the filmmakers entered a Morganza, Louisiana, diner to prepare a scene, a group of locals (read: rednecks) began muttering about the actors' long hair. Hopper insisted that they be hired to repeat their insults on film. The "lynch mob," as Hopper called them, was delighted to be on film, and they hung around during the entire shoot.

Through principal photography, Hopper's appetite as an artist clearly exceeded his mastery of the camera. In his mind, he was creating what he later described as "the first American art film." He said he'd modeled his technique after that of Satyajit Ray (*The World of Apu*) and Luis Bunuel. He favored jump cuts and zooms. Key scenes, he felt, would be stronger if they were improvised rather than scripted. It didn't matter to him if lighting didn't match from scene to scene. He was more concerned with specific images—pop art inserts of the American flag, motorcycles, buckskin, and football helmets. These, in his mind, were "symbols of a time and of pop culture." The movie, he insisted, was "a fable about this moment of time."

After what seemed an eternity to cast and crew, the movie finally wrapped. Back in Los Angeles, however, Hopper and Fonda realized they'd forgotten to include a crucial campfire scene in their shooting schedule. The scene was subsequently scheduled. In the scene, Fonda's character says what ultimately became the most famous line of the film: "We blew it, man."

For twenty-two weeks, Hopper edited his film to a four-hour cut, then slashed it to two hours and forty-five minutes. Finally, Schneider sent a reluctant Hopper away and a team including editor Donn Cambern, Schneider, Rafelson, Nicholson, and Fonda spent six weeks getting the cut down to ninety-six minutes. By all accounts, the shorter version was more commercial, but when Hopper returned from Taos, he cried, "You've ruined my movie!" In his version, for example, the five-minute scene in the diner ran for twenty-five.

Henry Fonda was invited to a screening of the shorter version of his son's film. He fretted that no one would ever come see it. He was wrong, but his hesitance was a clue that the Hollywood establishment couldn't connect to the piece. In spring 1969, the filmmakers took a print to New York and screened it for the Columbia executive staff. Predictably, they didn't understand the film at all. After its success, Abe Schneider intoned that if *Easy Rider* was the way the industry was going, he "didn't want to be part of it."

Also at the screening, however, was a programmer from the Cannes Film Festival, who saw to it that the picture became an official entry in the May 1969 event. The invitation of a biker movie seemed odd, except that *The Wild Angels* had premiered at the 1966 Venice Film Festival to a good reception. *Easy Rider* was, on the surface, a road movie. But it was also a political statement, and the Cannes screening lent it gravitas. Though the Palme d'Or went to Lindsay Anderson's *If*—a British film about a private school that also embodied a spirit of revolution—*Easy Rider* was given a special prize, as best film by a new director.

Two months later, the film debuted in the United States. Opening at the Beekman Theater in Manhattan on July 14, 1969, it played to sold-out houses and quickly became a rallying cry for protest.

Columbia was dazed at the film's success. It offered a multi-picture deal to the newly formed BBS (the new Schneider–Rafelson company), stipulating that none of the films could be budgeted at more than $1 million. BBS's output turned out to be remarkable, but short-lived: *Five Easy Pieces* (1970, directed by Rafelson); *The Last Picture Show* (1971, Peter Bogdanovich); *Drive, He Said* (1970, Nicholson); *A Safe Place* (1970, Henry Jaglom); and *The King of Marvin Gardens* (1972, Rafelson).

After that, David Begelman replaced Abe Schneider at Columbia, and BBS did a quiet fade-out. Bert Schneider produced a few more films, including Terrence Malick's *Days of Heaven* in 1978, but generally stepped away from Hollywood. He joined anti-Vietnam war efforts, supported George McGovern's presidential campaign, and used his money to back the Black Panthers. Tom Wolfe ultimately coined the phrase "radical chic" to describe wealthy, white Americans who made it fashionable to be seen in the company of political radicals.

Schneider finally seized center stage during the 1974 Oscar ceremonies. In accepting the documentary-feature Oscar for *Hearts and Minds*, a searing look at the Vietnam War directed by Peter Davis, Schneider read a message of "greetings of friendship to all American people" from Ambassador Dinh ba Thi, chief of the Provisional Revolutionary Government delegation to the peace talks. The Academy audience was stunned by this bold infusion of politics into the customarily benign proceedings.

After *Easy Rider*, Hopper's directing career ground to a halt. Universal financed *The Last Movie*, a tale of filmmakers in Peru. The script by Stewart Stern worked well, the studio felt, but Hopper preferred improvisation. The film became renowned as one of Hollywood's legendary fiascos. It received only a symbolic release.

Hopper appeared occasionally in films, but didn't make a significant comeback until the '80s with *Blue Velvet* and *Hoosiers*.

In 1982, Fonda raised money for a sequel to *Easy Rider* called *Biker Heaven*, in which Wyatt and Billy descend from heaven to a post-apocalyptic Earth. It was never made, but as recently as 2004 there was further talk of *Easy Rider* remakes.

The long-term winner from the film, to be sure, was Nicholson, who carved out a long career as a superstar, winning three Oscars and creating numerous indelible characters. While succeeding generations still "get" Jack Nicholson, the same cannot be said for the film that brought him to the public's attention. Viewed today, *Easy Rider* seems more about caricature than character. Its attitude is vastly more interesting than its woolly-headed dialogue. Though Dennis Hopper wanted to create a protest movie, instead he conjured up a druggy road movie, which is hard to take any more seriously than the Bob Hope–Bing Crosby road movies of a generation earlier. As such, *Easy Rider* remains the ultimate example of zeitgeist cinema: it not only reflected the moment, but galvanized it. But its moment was fleeting.

In the same vein, *Hair* is the classic embodiment of zeitgeist theater; yet its themes, like its melodies, continue to resonate. There is an antique charm in its determination to shock, like a small child demanding attention. And as the experience of Iraq blends into our memory of Vietnam, the emotional zeal of its antiwar message may likely find a new audience.

One inadvertent impact of shows like *Hair* and *Easy Rider* was to glamorize drug use. Grass and coke seemed an intrinsic element of the good life, '60s-style, for this cast of characters. Dope made you more creative; at least, it made you feel better about yourself and your work, no matter how illusory that judgment.

As the principals of these two shows grew older, to be sure, many of them cleaned up their acts. Dennis Hopper, who was both a drunk and an addict, became a health fanatic and a conservative Republican, and still works in film and TV well into his seventies. Michael Butler, too, became fanatical about his health and remained trimly handsome. However, drugs played a poignant role in foiling Butler's ambition to create a motion picture based on *Hair*.

Butler decided the ideal director for his project would be Hal Ashby, who was himself a '60s hippie. Ashby's films like *Harold and Maude* and *Coming Home* appealed to Butler's sensibility. I knew both Ashby and Butler very well, and encouraged them to spend time together. A bond soon developed; both agreed that Colin Higgins, the young writer who was responsible for *Harold and Maude*, would be ideal to adapt the play to film.

The project was about to go into preproduction when I got a call from Ashby. Much as he wanted to do the *Hair* film, he said, it had become imperative for him to withdraw. The reason was simple: Ashby felt his own cocaine dependency had reached the point where he did not trust his ability to command a cast and crew and deliver a film on schedule. "I've lost it," he said. "I need time away." Butler was living in Santa Barbara during this period, and when he got the same phone call, he and his then girlfriend started driving to Los Angeles to commiserate with Ashby. Half an hour into their trip, a state trooper, driving behind Butler, saw smoke drifting through the sun roof of his Mercedes. The trooper pulled him over, and found marijuana in the girlfriend's purse. He promptly arrested them both.

Control of *Hair* ultimately drifted to another producer, who put the film together under the direction of Milos Forman. It didn't work. Ashby, meanwhile, took some time off and when he returned, continued to do excellent work, though drugs still impinged periodically upon his career. Butler went to work on other plays, but he remained convinced that his film version of *Hair*, with Ashby directing, would have been a great success, if only drugs had not intruded upon his plans.

14 Alpine Sing-Along
The Sound of Music (1965)

If a how-to book were written about the art of creating a blockbuster, surely *The Sound of Music* would make a tempting case study. Its "rules," however, might seem keenly perplexing:

- Find a property that succeeded financially both as a book, a foreign-language film, and a Broadway musical, but is critically panned each step of the way.
- Place it at a studio in a state of collapse, whose management has just been fired.
- Hire a director who is superbly talented but harbors a profound disdain for the basic property and considers it saccharine and inane.
- Produce a movie that not only alienates key critics but causes the respected Pauline Kael to threaten retirement. ("It's all hopeless," she said in her review, "I give up.")

These "rules" might seem aberrant, but they resulted in one of the most beloved and abhorred movies of all time—a movie that grossed a then aston-ishing $163 million, won five Oscars, and is still shown at "sing-along" events, which have a way of raising audiences to rapturous heights.

The legacy of *The Sound of Music* is sufficiently perverse that, while it saved Twentieth Century Fox in the short-term, it also planted the seeds of its later implosion. That's because the studio's management actually tried to apply the supposed lessons of the mega-hit in devising subsequent musicals. The results were catastrophic for all involved.

The story of *The Sound of Music*, a movie that warmed the hearts of millions of filmgoers, was created in a cauldron of angst and pain. The project that was given no chance to succeed, in fact, succeeded beyond the wildest of expectations and achieved its own unique immortality. And it came to symbolize Hollywood's anachronistic approach to filmmaking—an approach that would undergo a revolutionary change in the turbulent '60s and '70s.

In the early '60s, Twentieth Century Fox was in desperate trouble. Though some members of the board of directors had been grateful when the dynamic but egomaniacal Darryl F. Zanuck departed as studio chief in 1956 to start his own independent company, he left in his wake a tradition of profligacy and a series of box office flops. Television was picking up more and more viewers and Spyros Skouras, the chairman of the company, was considering the possibility of selling his back lot and renting space to MGM.

The movie that finally broke the camel's back was the big-budget behemoth *Cleopatra*, which started principal photography in 1960. Originally intended as a modest production, the film ultimately took nearly two years to finish (not counting additional battle scenes shot in 1963) and was beset by every disaster possible. Elizabeth Taylor contracted pneumonia, shutting down production for six months. Directors quit, the producer was sacked, and the production itself went monstrously over budget (the final tally approached $44 million). Amid the chaos, Skouras was ousted, clearing the way for Zanuck—who still had a major stake in the company—to make his grandly theatrical return to power.

The aging titan promptly delegated his twenty-seven-year-old son, Richard, as his chief of production and laid off some 1,000 employees. In the words of writer Ernest Lehman, "Fox became a haunted studio." Yet Zanuck father and son still had every intention of keeping the place alive. There were several promising projects in preparation: the Shirley MacLaine vehicle *What a Way to Go!*, a Doris Day–James Garner picture, *Move Over, Darling*, and *The Sand Pebbles*, directed by Robert Wise. All the studio needed was one big, colossal hit to put it back on its feet.

Ernest Lehman first saw *The Sound of Music* on Broadway in November 1959, then starring Mary Martin. Despite the critical drubbing it had received, he was enthused about its movie potential and pitched it to David Brown, Fox's story czar and Zanuck's confidante. In June 1960, three months before *Cleopatra* got under way, Fox bought the rights to the musical for $1.25 million plus a participation in the film's gross—the largest sum a studio had ever paid for a literary property. The contract had been orchestrated by Irving "Swifty" Lazar, the agent who represented Richard Rodgers and Oscar Hammerstein along with Howard Lindsay and Russel Crouse, who wrote the book.

The studio also secured a six-year option on *Die Trapp Familie* and its United States-set sequel, *Die Trapp Familie in Amerika*, two German films that had been adapted from the Trapp saga in 1956 and 1958, respectively. Directed by Wolfgang Liebeneiner, they'd been the most successful films produced in Germany since World War II. Fox combined the two films into one, dubbed it in English, and retitled it *The Trapp Family* for a March 1961 release. The resulting film was roundly panned by critics. *Daily Variety* said its "uncompromisingly sentimental nature has a tendency to slop over into naiveté."

Since the contract for the musical stipulated that the film based on *The Sound of Music* could not "be released in the United States or Canada until all first-class stage presentations have closed, or until December 31, 1964, whichever is earlier," the studio was forced to put its most expensive acquisition on hold while its own financial straits grew increasingly dire.

By 1963 Richard Zanuck saw *The Sound of Music* as a major opportunity, since the musical was still a hit on Broadway, and the film itself would have huge family appeal upon its release. Zanuck hired Lehman to write the script and he seemed a natural for the project: Lehman had just been nominated for an Oscar for his screenplay for *West Side Story*, and in 1955 he had written the film version of *The King and I* for Darryl F. Zanuck. He'd also written *North by Northwest* (1959) and the caustic *Sweet Smell of Success* (1957). Some of Lehman's friends felt he was now jeopardizing his reputation on an altar of schmaltz. Burt Lancaster, upon finding out that Lehman had taken on *Music*, blurted out, "Jesus, you must need the money!" The director Billy Wilder went so far as to tell Lehman, "No musical with swastikas in it will ever be a success!"—a remark that stung Lehman into writing the scene in which Captain von Trapp tears down the Nazi flag.

Stubborn, but shrewd, Lehman was hardly blind to the softness of the material: Indeed both he and Richard Zanuck favored Robert Wise to direct the project, hopeful that his naturalistic style could offset the film's sentimental whimsy. Lehman and Wise had collaborated before on *Executive Suite* and *Somebody up There Likes Me* as well as *West Side Story*, for which Wise had won directing and picture Oscars.

Wise, however, had his hands full at the time with *The Sand Pebbles* for Fox and wasn't interested in *Music*. Nor was Stanley Donen, despite having been an investor in the Broadway show. Next Lehman approached Gene Kelly, not only a singer and dancer but an accomplished filmmaker in his own right. A gracious, good-spirited man, Kelly told Lehman, "Ernie, go find somebody else to direct this kind of shit!"

Lehman and Zanuck next set their sights on William Wyler. Lehman personally took Wyler to New York to see the musical, which Wyler hated. They nonetheless talked for hours afterward, walking the streets until 2 AM. Zanuck told Lehman to continue pressing Wyler, and for the next two weeks the writer was in the director's office and home, reiterating how successful the musical could be and how Wyler could give the material the substance it needed.

One of the elements that appealed to Wyler, an Austrian Jew, was the possibility of making an anti-Nazi statement. He even considered staging a full-blown Austrian invasion, tanks and all. Lehman noticed a stack of books in Wyler's office about the Anschluss, which further heightened his concern that Wyler was bent on making a war movie, not a musical.

"Willy, I know you hated the show," Lehman said at one point, "but just tell me one thing. What did you feel at that moment when Captain von Trapp started singing 'The Sound of Music' with his children?"

Said Wyler: "Funny you should bring up that moment. I almost cried."

Lehman: "Willy, that's it! That's what it's all about!"

Finally, Wyler agreed to direct and produce, though he still innately distrusted the project. Location scouting in Austria began, even as Lehman suspected that Wyler was going through the motions. As further evidence, Wyler seemed lukewarm to Lehman's suggestion that Julie Andrews play Maria and instead tried to interest her in another project, *The Americanization of Emily.*

In the meantime, Lehman was occupied with the script. His most exhaustive overhauls concerned the placement of the songs. He moved the title number up to the beginning, before the title credits (the opening shot of the Alps was Lehman's inspiration). Maria and the children would now sing "My Favorite Things," instead of Maria and Mother Abbess. "The Lonely Goatherd" would come later in the movie, and peripheral characters like the Baroness and Max would lose their numbers. Finally, the "Do-Re-Mi" sequence would be shot on several locations so as to open it up cinematically.

According to *The Sound of Music: The Making of America's Favorite Movie* by Julia Antopol Hirsch, it was Lehman's intent to showcase Rodgers and Hammerstein's score to the fullest. "This picture is not to be approached as a 'play with music,'" he wrote to Wyler. "It is not to be a picture in which we feel slightly apologetic every time someone sings. On the contrary, our aim is to be slightly apologetic every time someone talks."

Another of Lehman's inclinations, in contrast to Wyler's, was to remove

THE LORD OF THE RINGS (2001)

The idea of three films simultaneously
was one of the biggest gambles in film
history, all in the hands of a director
who had never had a commercial hit

CSI (2000)
The "procedural drama" was too dark and
technical for most networks, but it
proved an immediate hit and spawned
a slew of spinoffs and imitators.

MAMMA MIA! (1999)
Love 'em or hate 'em, Abba songs are the
motor that has driven the phenomenon to a
worldwide gross of more that $1 billion,
making it the world's number one musical.

BLAIR WITCH PROJECT (1999)
Although it was one of the most
profitable films of all time, its creators,
briefly lauded, took ten years to get
another picture off the ground.

REAL WORLD (1992)

The conceit of *Real World* is downright simplistic: Plunk a group of unintentionally exhibitionistic kids in a confined situation and keep the cameras rolling as they make idiots of themselves.

BATMAN (1989)

Somewhere in the studio's collective subconscious there was an instinctual recognition that *Batman* was not so much an inspiraction as an inevitability.

Cats (1981)
In-your-face show business, loud and even belligerent, *Cats* was not so much the opening of a musical as it was the launch of an industry.

THE GODFATHER (1972)

Mario Puzo once said, "I wanted this book to have sex and murders and all the stuff readers wanted to wallow in. I wanted to make some money. I never thought it would lead to all the craziness . . ."

Essentially slipping through the cracks,
American Graffitti got made because no one
at Universal was paying attention and
because some of the younger executives
thought it would be cool.

EASY RIDER (1969)

Disorganized and feuding incessantly, Dennis
Hopper and his partner, Peter Fonda, seemed
unlikely candidates to foster a mega-hit, but
the zeitgeist ruled in their favor.

Facing Page
ALL IN THE FAMILY (1971)

When the network showed the first two
episodes to reviewers, some were stunned
and offended, but *Weekly Variety*'s
critic called it "the best TV comedy
since the original *Honeymooners*."

HAIR (1969)
Reflecting both the anger and optimism of the times, *Hair* served as a wake-up call for its target audience.

THE SOUND OF MUSIC (1965)

The legacy of *The Sound of Music* is perverse; while it saved Twentieth Century Fox in the short-term, it also planted the seeds of its later implosion.

BEN-HUR (1959)

In the end, *Ben-Hur* did not save
the Hollywood studio system, nor did it
save MGM. Sword-and-sandal epics
vanished from production schedules,
only to reappear generations later
in films like *Gladiator* and *Troy*

GUNSMOKE (1955)
For over 640 episodes,
stoic Marshal Matt Dillon survived a
seemingly endless succession of
rustlers, ambushers, bushwackers,
and random lawbreakers.

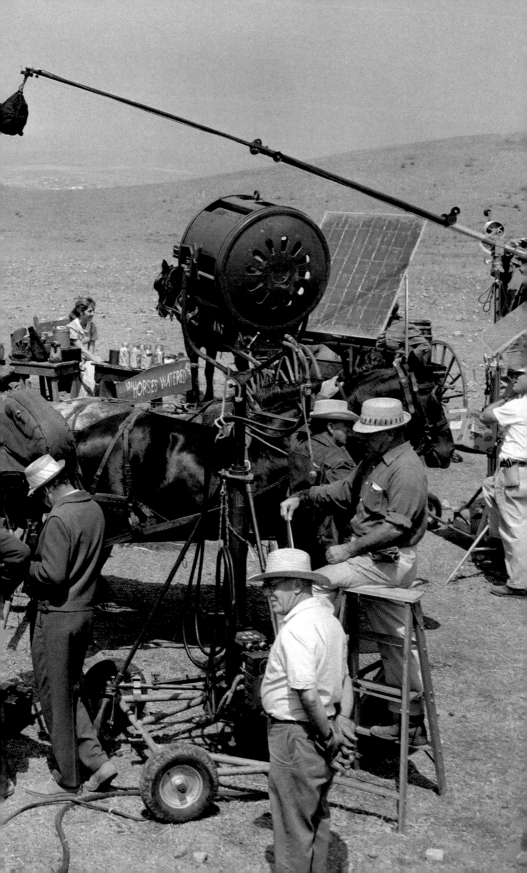

Psycho (1960)
Alfred Hitchcock wouldn't let studio executives even read a script, and the secrecy was carried over into the film's marketing.

I LOVE LUCY(1951)

Nobody set out to make a series that would endure for more than 50 years. *I Love Lucy* was designed simply to save a marriage

THE BEST YEARS OF OUR LIVES (1946)
Nearly unthinkable: Only a year after the
war ended, a drama about returning vets.
But audiences found it cathartic.

Facing Page
CASABLANCA (1942)
The stars didn't get along,
nobody liked the director,

LIFE WITH FATHER (1939)

Even the creators were surprised by
the record-breaking success of *Life with
Father*. But during World War II,
it presented family life in a way
that was both memory and fantasy.

SNOW WHITE AND THE SEVEN DWARFS (1937)

Snow White and the Seven Dwarfs was
the wrong project at the wrong time,
and everyone around Walt essentially
told him so with relentless persistence.

MODERN TIMES (1936)
The era of silent pictures was over, yet Chaplin's *Little Tramp* was a creature of the silent era who had delighted his audience in *The Gold Rush*, *The Circus*, and *The Kid*.

Director King Vidor wanted to make a film that would last more than one week at the theaters. It ended up running 96 weeks.

THE BIRTH OF A NATION (1915)
Best remembered as a racist tract,
this was a turning point, making the
moviegoing experience something
respectable for the first time.

<small>KING KONG (1933)</small>

Would the public accept a scary love story
involving a five-foot blonde and
an eighteen-foot gorilla?

some of the play's political elements. One scene, in which the Captain is aroused by Maria's patriotism, was cut, and the roles of the Baroness and Max were depoliticized. Lehman also introduced some elements not in the play—the children's early hostility toward their new governess and the scene in which the children attempt to visit Maria at the abbey. He also added more comedy to the barbed courtship between the Captain and Maria.

Lehman completed his outline in May 1963, but between the outline and the finished script, the film's ending changed considerably. Lehman had originally written a car chase in which the Nazis pursue the von Trapps on their way to the music festival for Rolf, Liesl's young-love-turned-Nazi, to help the family escape. In the final script, the car chase was removed, and Rolf ends up informing on the von Trapps, albeit too late to stop their happy ending.

In writing the stage musical, Lindsay and Crouse had already restructured the narrative, condensing the time frame and removing a subplot in which the von Trapps convert a farmhouse in the Green Mountains of Stowe, Vermont, into a ski resort called the Trapp Family Lodge. They also had changed Maria's maiden name from Kutschera to the more digestible Rainier and renamed all of the children. They'd also conceived the romance between Liesl (in real life, the eldest von Trapp child was a boy named Rupert) and Rolf. Father Wasner, the von Trapps' friend and musical mentor, was reborn as the worldly and sophisticated Max. Not surprisingly, the Nazi conflict was not much of an issue in the German films, whereas it figured more importantly in the Rodgers and Hammerstein musical.

Lehman finished his first draft on September 10, 1963, and sent it to Wyler, who replied that it was "a perfect first draft" and he couldn't think "of a single thing to improve." Lehman knew that Wyler was toughest on writers when he was most invested in a project so this instant affirmation was a bad sign. Later, during a party at Wyler's house in Malibu, the writer noticed several copies of a script for another project, *The Collector*, then in preproduction at Columbia.

Lehman warned Zanuck that Wyler was going to defect. Together they decided to rush a copy of the *Music* script to Robert Wise's agent, Phil Gersh.

As expected, Wyler requested that Zanuck delay *Music* until after he finished another project. According to Hirsch, Zanuck refused. "I think he got scared," Zanuck said of Wyler. "Maybe he thought the movie was too 'saccharine.' Maybe that's why he needed to insert this whole military aspect into it that I thought was unnecessary. So, when we finally had to let Willy go, I didn't think that it was that great a loss. Oh, we ranted and raved about how awful it was, but deep down inside I was a bit relieved."

Fortunately for Zanuck, Wise had run into production delays on *The Sand*

Pebbles, which had to be postponed for a year, freeing him to take on *The Sound of Music*. Wise read Lehman's script, liked it, listened to the music, liked that, and finally signed on, bringing with him Saul Chaplin, a veteran of musicals who had been associate producer on *West Side Story*. Wise and Chaplin weighed in with their own thoughts and rewrites for the project. Wise in particular was skittish about the opening aerial shot, fearing that it would smack too much of *West Side Story*, though it ultimately stayed. He also overruled Lehman, cutting the song "An Ordinary Couple," sung by Maria and the Captain after they confess their love. Richard Rodgers had the contractual right to approve any alterations to the score and also the option of composing new songs himself (Hammerstein had died by this time). Wise and Lehman were aware that they had to present their suggestions carefully. Fortunately, Rodgers agreed; "Couple" was scrapped, and in its place Rodgers wrote "Something Good," which was happily accepted.

Rodgers was also asked to write a song with the working title "Walking Soliloquy," to capture Maria's initial anxiety and growing confidence on her way to the von Trapps estate for the first time. The song, which eventually became "I Have Confidence," went through several rewrites and was ultimately written partially by Chaplin himself, a fact that Chaplin concealed from Julie Andrews, fearing she wouldn't agree to sing a song that hadn't been entirely written by Rodgers. Andrews didn't find out the truth until after filming was completed, and by that point she didn't care.

The second draft was completed December 20, 1963, but more changes were to come, several from the real Maria von Trapp. Maria sat down with Lehman and told him about her life in the abbey; several details made it into the beginning of the film. She also protested that the Captain's character had been portrayed in the play as too dull and strict and suggested that her husband become an adviser on the film. Wise put a stop to that idea.

If Maria proved to be brittle and tough-minded, so did Julie Andrews. Ironically, Andrews had played Maria before, in a TV special in which she costarred with Carol Burnett at Carnegie Hall. One skit was called "The Prutt Family of Switzerland," and Andrews had performed the satiric piece with relish. She had finished her role in Disney's *Mary Poppins*, but the film hadn't been released yet. Wise, Chaplin, and Lehman had seen some footage and they were enthusiastic about her performance, though some at Fox were concerned whether her screen presence was frosty and mechanical; in meetings, she came across as rather steely and distanced—not the warm-hearted nanny type so evident in *Mary Poppins*. In point of fact, this flintiness in her performances hurt her later films, such as *Darling Lili*, an expensive musical that subsequently flopped at Paramount.

Though Wise was convinced she would be empathetic in *The Sound of Music*, Andrews's concern was that her character seemed "saccharine." At one point she said, "What can you do with nuns, seven children, and Austria?" She demanded of Wise, "How are you going to get all the sugar out of this picture?" Wise must have satisfied her with his response, but, in fact, her reservations were valid.

Regardless of all this, no one else had been considered for the part. Mary Martin, at fifty, was clearly too old, though she'd lent her character great verve on stage. Names like Leslie Caron, Grace Kelly, Anne Bancroft, Angie Dickinson, and Shirley Jones had been bandied about the studio, but no one had made any firm offers. During his stint on the film, Wyler had suggested Audrey Hepburn, who, of course, had bumped Andrews from *My Fair Lady*, but as far as Wise was concerned, Julie Andrews was the first and only choice.

In fact, Fox initially wanted to sign her to a four-picture commitment, but her agent balked; they ended up agreeing to two films, and received a flat fee of $225,000, with no share of the profits.

Christopher Plummer was also a first seed from the beginning. A successful stage actor at the time with modest Hollywood credentials, Plummer was more interested in theater, and disliked the way the role of the Captain was written—a dull, stiff man whose sole purpose, it seemed, was to come onstage periodically and yell at the children. "I knew Maria von Trapp, and she couldn't have married a dull man. . . . She had too much humor and too much naughtiness and spark to her," Plummer observes.

When he turned down the role, Wise considered others—Sean Connery, Stephen Boyd, Richard Burton, David Niven, Peter Finch, Walter Matthau, and Patrick O'Neal—but none seemed a good fit. Yul Brynner lobbied hard for the role, but Wise felt he'd be too reminiscent of *The King and I* and, besides, he had the wrong accent. So Wise revisited Plummer and gave him a hard sell, explaining his ideas for the film and promising to work with Lehman to improve the character. While still not enthused, Plummer eventually was signed to the role in January 1964.

Plummer would turn out to be one of the more contentious forces on the set, at one point nearly stopping the production before it started. He was determined to do his own singing in the film, even taking daily voice lessons, and threatened to walk off the set when told he would be dubbed. Lehman was brought back in to talk to Plummer, but the conflict went all the way to Zanuck, who told the actor he could do the prerecordings and, if his voice was good enough by the end of the shoot, he could be rerecorded.

The rest of the cast quickly fell into place, with Richard Haydn and

Eleanor Parker tapped to play Max and the Baroness, and veteran Peggy Wood signed for the role of Mother Abbess.

A few of the children who auditioned for roles would later become famous in their own right—the Osmond brothers and, in the role of Liesl: Mia Farrow ("lack of energy," as Wise assessed her at the time), Lesley Ann Warren, Teri Garr, and Sharon Tate. The part ended up ultimately going to a girl with no singing or acting experience named Charmian Farnon, who at twenty-one (a secret she kept until after she'd been signed to a seven-year contract with the studio under the name of Charmian Carr), was a bit old for the part of a sixteen-year-old.

Production began March 26, 1964, on Stage 15 of the Fox lot. The first scenes to be shot were the thunderstorm/bedroom sequence and the "My Favorite Things" number; for the chemistry of the characters to feel natural, Andrews and the child actors had to "bond" and feel at ease with one another. Next came scenes at the abbey, including the Maria number, and the graveyard escape.

Then cast and crew packed off to Salzburg, Austria, for a carefully planned six-week shoot that, due to continual lousy weather, ballooned to eleven weeks.

It was here that Plummer's obstreperousness once more emerged, as related by Julia Hirsch. The intense actor started calling the film *The Sound of Mucus*—a title he insists everyone else used as well—and remained at a chilly remove from the children. Said Chaplin, "He behaved as though he was a distinguished legendary actor who had condescendingly agreed to grace this small, amateurish company with his presence." Kym Karath, the actress who played the youngest child, Gretl, says, "I remember absolutely nothing about Christopher Plummer. He stayed so far away from us."

For the film's final shot, where the Captain is carrying Gretl on his back, Plummer protested that Karath was too heavy and requested a double. According to one newspaper article at the time, Plummer's exact words were "I'm not carrying that bloody fat kid."

Plummer and Andrews maintained a civil working relationship, however. Andrews was in more scenes than anyone else, and the presence of her nineteen-month-old daughter, Emma, provided an excuse not to socialize with the rest of the cast and crew.

Meanwhile, Zanuck began pressuring Wise to get everyone back to Hollywood; the film was twenty-five days behind schedule and $740,000 over its $7,995,000 budget. The location shoot was simply getting too expensive. When cast and crew finally returned home July 3, 1964, almost all of the exterior shots had been finished in Salzburg, although the "I Am Sixteen" and "Something Good" numbers had to be shot on the Fox lot, necessitating a gazebo to be built on a soundstage.

The shoot wrapped officially on September 1. At the start of post production, the issue of Plummer's singing voice quickly re-emerged. As he'd been promised, Plummer was allowed to rerecord his tracks, with the hope that they'd work for the film. After listening to the tracks, Wise told the actor, "I don't think it's good enough for our picture . . . it will bring down the level of the marvelous performance you gave as the Captain." Having lost his leverage, Plummer agreed, especially since his imperfections really stood out against Andrews's silky delivery. A singer, Bill Lee, was hired October 1 to dub his voice.

When *The Sound of Music* was previewed on February 1, 1965, at the Mann Theater in Minneapolis, Zanuck recalls there was a standing ovation at the intermission. The critique cards all read "excellent," with the exception of three that said "good." "Suddenly we were all focusing in on those three 'good' cards, trying to figure out what we did wrong," Zanuck said.

Zanuck sent an exultant telegram to his father, Darryl, closing with: "There is no question in my mind but that we have a great commercial hit." Still, Wise returned to the editing room, trimming shots and tinkering with the audio dubbing. Despite the rapturous reception, he was still far from certain of his film's success.

The Sound of Music premiered March 2, 1965, at the Rivoli Theater in New York. During the screening, Wise and Fox publicity chief Jonas Rosenfeld retreated to the theater lobby to read an advance copy of the next day's *New York Times*. Critic Bosley Crowther's review read, "The fact that *The Sound of Music* ran for three and a half years on Broadway, despite the perceptible weakness of its quaintly old-fashioned book, was plainly sufficient assurance for the producer–director Robert Wise to assume that what made it popular in the theater would make it equally popular on the screen." He praised Julie Andrews, speculating that the actress seemed to realize that "the whole thing was being staged by Mr. Wise in a cozy-cum-corny fashion that even theater people know is old hat." Crowther had little good to say about Plummer, however, claiming he looked "as handsome and phony as a store-window Alpine guide" and that the singing of "Edelweiss" was "painfully mawkish." Crowther's final barb: "Mr. Wise seems to run out of songs toward the end of the picture and repeats two or three of the more familiar ones . . . Business-wise, Mr. Wise is no fool."

Judith Crist's review in the *New York Herald Tribune*, and on the *Today* show, was even more withering. "Icky sticky" was her verdict; she added,

"The movie is for the five-to-seven set and their mommies who think their kids aren't up to the stinging sophistication and biting wit of *Mary Poppins*."

Young Zanuck was so incensed by Crist's review that he wrote Seymour Poe, Fox's chief of distribution, that the critic "has built her reputation with a knife and the evil skill of an abortionist." Poe replied that "an industry effort should be made to dislodge Crist from her spot on the *Today* show," to which Zanuck replied, "I would thoroughly enjoy the pleasure of inserting the toe of my ski boot in Miss Crist's derriere."

Pauline Kael's blasts were still to come. Writing in *McCall's* magazine, she termed the movie "the big lie, the sugar-coated lie that people seem to want to eat." She demanded: "Wasn't there perhaps one little 'von Trapp' child who didn't want to sing his head off, or who screamed that he wouldn't act out little glockenspiel routines for Papa's party guests, or who got nervous and threw up if he had to get on a stage?"

Readers were so incensed by Kael's review that *McCall's* fired the critic, who promptly went on to more hospitable pastures at the *New Yorker*.

Yet the film also attracted its share of supporters. In the *Los Angeles Times*, Philip K. Scheuer wrote, "They have taken this sweet, sometimes saccharine and structurally slight story of the von Trapp Family Singers and transformed it into close to three hours of visual and vocal brilliance, all in the universal terms of cinema."

And *Daily Variety* hailed the film as "one of the top musicals to reach the screen . . . a warmly-pulsating, captivating drama set to the most imaginative use of the most lilting R-H tunes, magnificently mounted and with a brilliant cast." The paper concluded, prophetically, that the film "bears the mark of assured lengthy runs and should be one of the season's most successful entries."

The Sound of Music opened in 131 American theaters as a road show—a 70mm movie with six-track stereophonic sound, released in a limited number of theaters. The idea was to sell the film more in the manner of a Broadway musical than a general release, with reserved seats, two showings a day, and an intermission.

The movie quickly proved to be critic-proof. In four weeks, after playing only twenty-five theaters with ten performances per week, *Music* became the number one movie at the box-office. By December 1965, nine months after its opening, it had been number one for thirty out of forty-three weeks and grossed $50 million in worldwide receipts. The movie's run as both a road show and a general release would last a remarkable four and a half years in the United States. The key was strong word of mouth and repeat business.

The Sound of Music opened in 261 theaters overseas a few months after its United States run began, but there were two countries where it was decidedly not a hit: Germany and Austria. Shortly after the film opened in Germany, a newspaper ran a story with "Will Hollywood's Hate of Germany Never End?" as its banner headline. Wolfgang Wolf, the Munich branch manager of Twentieth Century Fox, cut the film's last third entirely, ending it after the wedding scene. Wise and the studio were horrified that a United States company was bowing to perceived pressures. Wise told *Variety*, "I abhor any kind of cut made in my film by an exhibitor since he is, in fact, setting himself up as a judge of my work." Wolf, who said he was only "testing" to see if the new version would draw more audiences, was immediately fired. The cut material was restored, but the film still bombed.

In Salzburg, the film ran for three days before theater owners yanked it; it has never been reissued since. (This despite the fact that most of the film was shot there, pumping a total of $900,000 into the Austrian economy.)

According to Pia Arnold, the film's German production manager, the biggest reason *The Sound of Music* sank in Austria and Germany was that *Die Trapp Familie* and *Die Trapp Familie in Amerika* had been so popular (and continue to be). They couldn't handle a Hollywoodized remake.

The Sound of Music went on to win a total of five Oscars, for best picture, director, film editing, sound, and music adaptation. It was nominated for five others: best actress (Andrews), supporting actress (Wood), art direction, cinematography, and costume design.

The film also won Golden Globes for best motion picture-musical/comedy and actress (Andrews).

Other prizes included the DGA (for Wise), the WGA for best-written American musical (for Lehman), and the ACE Award for cinematography (for William Reynolds).

Needless to say, it won no critics' awards.

In reflecting on his reign at Fox years later, Richard Zanuck still reveled in the excitement that followed the release of *The Sound of Music*, but harbored deep regrets about the events it spawned. The success of the film gave the studio a jolt of energy. Briefly, it seemed as though young Zanuck and his savvy story guru, David Brown, would be able to usher in a new era at the studio. But this was not to be.

Zanuck and Brown were brilliant, young executives, but the times were against them. While they remained committed to mainstream movies, the filmgoers who paid to see traditional studio films were migrating to television. Expensive musicals like *Dr. Dolittle*, starring Rex Harrison and *Hello, Dolly!*, starring Barbra Streisand, appeared to follow the business models of *The Sound of Music*—or so the financial types thought—but they failed at the box-office. The sorts of films that were destined to turn around Hollywood's fortunes, such as *Midnight Cowboy, Bonnie and Clyde, The Godfather,* or *Rosemary's Baby*, were not being developed at Fox.

Zanuck's father, the feisty Darryl F. Zanuck, was abruptly put out to pasture by the corporate powers at Fox and Richard always regretted the manner in which this was done and the fact that, given the tensions of the moment, he did not display the appropriate empathy toward this difficult, but brilliant man. Richard himself was to lose his job at Fox in 1970, but he, like David Brown, went on to create an extraordinary body of work—movies like *Driving Miss Daisy, The Sting,* and *Jaws*. Brown was still producing a formidable slate of plays and films well into his eighties.

The Sound of Music represented a big, if evanescent, boost to other careers. Robert Wise continued to turn out films, but none approached the magnitude of this success. Julie Andrews became an instant superstar as a result of *The Sound of Music* and *Mary Poppins*, but her subsequent career in movies proved erratic. The era of the big musical was over, and she never established her credibility in romantic roles.

The success of *The Sound of Music* did not mark a trend, but rather an aberration. The elements contributing to its amazing success have never been replicated. There has been no genre of sugary musicals. Achieving bad reviews does not automatically stamp future films as potential blockbusters. Studio chiefs do not go out of their way to sign actors who hate their roles going in.

In becoming a mega-hit, *The Sound of Music* did not establish a new set of rules. It loudly proclaimed: Rules are there to be broken.

15 Sword-and-Sandal Swan Song

Ben-Hur (1959)

From today's perspective, the exercise of making *Ben-Hur* in the late '50s seems intrinsically preposterous. The Hollywood studio system was already in clear decline, with audiences gravitating to that sinister little box that was starting to pop up in everyone's living room. The genre of Biblical, sword-and-sandal epics, most of them made in Spain or Italy, was already becoming creaky. (After completing *The Silver Chalice,* Paul Newman swore that he'd "never again wear a cocktail dress in a movie.") *The Robe* and *The Ten Commandments* had run their course in the early '50s.

Ben-Hur itself was a curious antique—it was a novel written in 1880 by a Civil War general, and had already served as the basis for two plays and two movies. The story was a lame twist on *The Count of Monte Cristo* by Alexandre Dumas, involving a highborn hero thrown into prison by an evil villain and ultimately gaining his gory revenge.

Lew Wallace's novel had a sort of pseudo gravitas because of its religious overtones. Actually, the full title was *Ben-Hur: A Tale of the Christ,* though Jesus made but a few cameo appearances and Wallace himself would not have passed muster with Mel Gibson: He'd always professed that he never went to church and lacked religious conviction. Nonetheless, during Wallace's lifetime his book outsold every other except for the Bible.

Indeed, the decision to remake *Ben-Hur* itself seemed like a religious statement: Old Hollywood's final death-defying act. Corporate control of the venerable MGM already was shifting from one power block to another (Kirk Kerkorian was to seize the remains a few years later).

Louis B. Mayer, MGM's czar, had been fired in 1951 and Dore Schary, the succeeding studio chief, had lasted until 1956, when the company ran an operating deficit of $3 million (paltry by contemporary standards). The corporate boss, Nick Schenck, was himself canned a year later. There was a brief movement to restore Mayer to his throne, but he died in 1957 while these intrigues were still aboil.

Ben-Hur kept rolling along, as though the studio had gone on autopilot. Within only a few years, another MGM regime headed by former CBS chief Jim Aubrey would systematically extinguish some fifteen projects including every big-budget spectacle still in the pipeline—movies like *Taipan* to be produced by the fabled Carlo Ponti, and *Man's Fate*, to be directed by Fred Zinnemann, both based on famous novels. But *Ben-Hur* managed to beat the deadline, albeit at a formidable cost. By the time the $15 million epic had wound down, its producer had suffered a fatal heart attack, its production manager had been forced to resign due to heart problems, and the already wounded studio hierarchy had gone through yet other rounds of turmoil.

And with little wonder. Despite MGM's fragile finances, *Ben-Hur* managed to scrounge up a cast of 8,000 with 365 speaking parts. It occupied the biggest set ever built, a five-story Roman coliseum which required the services of 1,000 workers.

In the end, it turned out to be a bonanza, breaking box office records with a world gross of $73 million, the equivalent of a Spielberg–Lucas-type $600 million-plus blockbuster by today's standards. Besides big numbers, it also left in its wake some delicious spats, including the famous Charlton Heston versus Gore Vidal exchange about the film's supposed homoerotic subtext.

Though *Ben-Hur* became one of the most honored films of all time, with eleven Oscars, much of it today seems stagy, if not downright clunky. Nine of its 212 expansive minutes achieved a special immortality: the chariot race. And, oddly, that sequence wasn't even shot by the film's esteemed director.

Wallace, a Civil War general in the Union Army, spent five years researching and writing *Ben-Hur*, most of it underneath a beech tree near his residence in Crawfordsville, Indiana. The novel was published by Harper on November 12, 1880.

In *How I Came to Write Ben-Hur*, Wallace writes that he wanted the novel to show the religious and political condition of the world at the time of the Crucifixion. Wallace was never a formal member of any church and, when he began the work. "I had no convictions about God or Christ. I neither believed nor disbelieved in them," he admits.

Wallace created Messala, the centurion, to represent Roman politics and Ben-Hur and his family to represent Jewish culture and faith in a messiah. He decreed that Ben-Hur's mother and sister should be lepers to demonstrate the "awful power underlying a miracle."

Defining himself as a novelist rather than a theologian, Wallace was determined to avoid sermonizing. To give the book dramatic tension, he withheld the appearance of the Christ until the end. Yet, his book's impact was formidable. There was, for a time, a national fraternal organization known as the Supreme Tribe of Ben-Hur, which was later formed into Ben-Hur Life Insurance. American towns were even named after Ben-Hur.

At first, Wallace was doubtful *Ben-Hur* would translate into a successful stage play. How could the chariot race be accomplished in a theater? Without a chariot race, it would hardly be *Ben-Hur*.

Producers Marc Klaw and Abraham Erlanger managed to convince Wallace otherwise. Jesus Christ would only be depicted as a beam of white light. They utilized eight trained horses, pulling two chariots, which ran on treadmills in the floor of the stage. The background scenery was installed on a cyclorama and moved behind the racing chariots to complete the illusion.

Ben-Hur opened at the Broadway Theatre in New York City on November 29, 1899, adapted by William Young and directed by Joseph Brooks. The stars were Edward Morgan as Ben-Hur (though William Farnum soon replaced him) and William S. Hart as Messala. (Hart went on to great success as a silent-screen cowpoke, as did Farnum's brother, Dustin.)

The play ran for 194 performances on Broadway before it took to the road. At a time when touring companies often played one or two nights in each city, *Ben-Hur* sometimes held for two weeks. The show ran for twenty-one years in the United States, with an estimated 6,000 performances seen by 20 million people. The final performance was in April 1921, but later companies played Europe and Australia.

In 1907, the Kalem Company, a silent-film company based in New Jersey, produced a twenty-minute version by using some shots of a mock chariot race that the Brooklyn Fire Department staged at a fireworks show at Sheepshead Bay, Brooklyn. They then added some interior shots.

There was one minor oversight: Kalem failed to acquire the motion picture rights; indeed the precept of motion picture rights was unknown. One day a process server appeared at the Kalem office with legal papers, notifying the producers that the estate of Gen. Lew Wallace was suing. A precedent-making action, the suit was to establish the legal protection of a motion picture as a medium of dramatic and literary expression.

Fighting their battle through to the Supreme Court, Kalem's attorneys made an effort to show that the screen production was "merely a series of photographs," which served as a good advertisement for the book. "Nonsense" ruled the court. A final decision handed down in 1911 ordered Kalem to pay $25,000. The ruling meant that, forever after, authors would have to be paid for film adaptations of their works.

In 1912, a year after the Kalem case was decided, Wallace's son, Henry, received offers to sell the film rights to his father's literary works. He responded, "I will oppose in every way possible all attempts to produce any of General Wallace's work in moving pictures. The reason is because the average moving picture shows are wretched exhibitions, utterly unworthy of dignified consideration."

However, in 1915, Henry Wallace happened to watch D. W. Griffith's *Birth of a Nation*. Perhaps the memorable "Ride of the Klan" scene convinced him that *Ben-Hur*'s chariot race could be filmed. He affixed a price tag of $1 million for movie rights. In 1921, Wallace closed a deal for $600,000 with a group headed by Abraham Erlanger, who had also been responsible for bringing *Ben-Hur* to the stage. The rights were eventually passed to Metro-Goldwyn-Mayer.

Kevin Brownlow, in his book on the silent era, *The Parade's Gone By*, described the 1925 silent version of *Ben-Hur* as "the Dunkirk of the cinema, a humiliating defeat transformed, after heavy losses, into a brilliant victory."

The production had several false starts. It began shooting in Italy with director Rex Ingram and star George Walsh. Production delays convinced Irving Thalberg to return the production to California. Fred Niblo took over as director; (William Wyler, who would remake the story in 1959, was an assistant director). Ben-Hur was a breakout role for the twenty-five-year-old Ramon Novarro, only three years after his first starring role. Francis X. Bushman played Messala.

The production was so impressive that some top actors visited the set to gape; a few served as extras during the chariot race, including Douglas Fairbanks, Mary Pickford, Harold Lloyd, Myrna Loy, Lillian Gish, Colleen Moore, Marion Davies, and John Gilbert.

The arena for the chariot race was built on what is now the corner of Venice and La Cienega Boulevards. An astonishing forty-two cameras captured the action as twelve four-horse chariots took part in the race. A cash prize for the winner ensured some hectic driving and spectacular accidents. The final film captured a genuine pileup that injured horses and actors. Legends were passed along the years about the deaths of more than 100 horses and the death of a stuntman, but there's no hard evidence of these casualties.

The silent *Ben-Hur*, well-paced and handsomely mounted, ended up costing MGM approximately $4 million, one of the most expensive films of the silent era. It opened on December 30, 1925, at the George M. Cohan Theater in New York City and received rave reviews. Under the headline: "Ben-Hur—Greatest Picture" the January 6, 1926, *Variety* gushed, "The word 'epic' has been applied to pictures time and time again, but at the time there was no 'Ben-Hur,' therefore, you can scrap all the 'epics' that have been shown prior to 'Ben-Hur' and start a new book. . . . 'Ben-Hur' will go down the ages of the picture industry to mark an epoch in its progress."

Studio ads proclaimed: "The Picture Every Christian Ought to See!" The film grossed an impressive $9 million, not as much as *The Big Parade*, which cost only a fraction of *Ben-Hur*'s budget. Yet both films helped solidify MGM's reputation as a major studio. For another quarter century, the MGM brand was to signify movie quality, at any expense.

The film also reminded Hollywood about the expense of location work: For the next quarter of a century, the studios preferred to build everything from the Vatican to the Alamo on their own back lots.

But now it was time to start over. And once again, foreign locations beckoned. More precisely, Italy. Sets could be constructed in Rome that would be prohibitively expensive at the studio. Legions of extras could be recruited. Besides, those studio executives who had managed to survive the power shifts in Culver City could look forward to some enjoyable European vacations. While visiting the set, of course.

The first order of business was to find someone qualified to oversee the production. The choice would have to be politically sensitive. He would have to be someone who was trusted by all the various factions—Nick Schenck and his bankers in New York, Louis B. Mayer's allies in Hollywood, and also those of Dore Schary.

Early on, the project was assigned to producer Sam Zimbalist, a veteran studio hand in his mid-fifties who had started as a second assistant director at the old Metro Studios. Zimbalist remained at Metro when it merged with the Goldwyn Company in 1924 and morphed into MGM. He worked on the editing of the 1929 *Broadway Melody*, which went on to be the first talkie to win an Oscar. That same year, he was promoted to assistant producer under Hunt Stromberg. Working with Stromberg, one of the top producers on the lot, he became a full producer in 1936, starting out with modestly budgeted programmers like *Navy Blue and Gold* and *Tarzan Finds a Son!* Over the years, he chalked up twenty-four features, but it was his work on such big-scale films as *King Solomon's Mines* (1950) and *Quo Vadis* (1951) that convinced MGM he was the man for the job.

The first task related to the script. Zimbalist and his colleagues had to preserve the sweep of the epic genre and at the same time find a contemporary context for their project. The stilted dialogue of the silent *Ben-Hur* would have to be reworked, the conflicts strengthened. A further problem: The film censors were becoming ever more tyrannical, reacting to the uptight attitudes of '50s society. As screenplay drafts emerged from the studio, the admonitions became ever more ominous. In October 1954, the code warned: "The portrayal of the Christ presents a very serious problem from a public relations standpoint. . . . It would be unacceptable to quote Christ in any way other than directly from the Bible . . ." This decree was solved by never showing the face of Christ or hearing him speak directly. Shots were always from behind, and showed the look of joy or beatitude on people's faces.

A month later, the censors warned Dore Schary, the studio chief, "It will be necessary to indicate affirmatively that the character of Iras is not nude in his bathing sequence . . ." Another "advisory" went, "We assume there will be nothing unduly gruesome about the people of the leper colony. . . ."

As the script was going through several revisions, Zimbalist approached King Vidor, who passed, and then William Wyler to direct the massive film. The Wyler choice turned out to be an inspired one.

In the Wyler biography *A Talent for Trouble*, Jan Herman suggests that Wyler wanted to "out-De Mille De Mille." Wyler also enjoyed living in Rome and was eager to return. Moreover, MGM had guaranteed him 8 percent of the gross with an upfront payment of $350,000.

The son of a prosperous Swiss dry goods merchant, Wyler had been studying the violin in Paris in 1922 when he met Universal Pictures executive Carl Laemmle, a distant cousin of his mother, and decided to try his luck in Hollywood. He worked his way up to assistant director at Universal, finally graduating to director for the two-reel Western *Crook Buster* (1925). Over the years he earned a reputation as one of the most meticulous directors in the business, shooting extensive retakes on even the simplest scenes. His painstaking methods and autocratic on-set behavior exasperated many, but he built up an imposing list of credits including *Wuthering Heights* (1939), *The Little Foxes* (1941), *The Heiress* (1949), *Roman Holiday* (1953), and *Friendly Persuasion* (1956).

Despite Wyler's reputation as an actor's director, one star after another turned down the *Ben-Hur* remake, including Paul Newman, Burt Lancaster,

Kirk Douglas, and Rock Hudson. Sword-and-sandal epics, it seemed, had become an anathema to the big stars.

Common sense would suggest that the studio take notice and possibly scrap the project, or at least delay it until more auspicious circumstances surrounded it. But MGM, in its then chaotic state, decided to push ahead anyway. A green light had been flashed and some sort of a cast would be assembled, even if it did not consist of the hottest stars of the moment.

Throughout 1957 and 1958, Rosalind Russell was considered for the part of Ben-Hur's mother. Charlton Heston tested for the role of Messala, as did Stewart Granger and Victor Mature. Anna Maria Alberghetti and Carroll Baker tested for Esther. The gossip columns said Princess Grace was almost lured out of royal retirement to play the Virgin Mary. Finally Charlton Heston agreed to play Ben-Hur and Stephen Boyd was cast as Messala.

British actors were eventually cast as Romans and, for the most part, American actors were cast as Jews. This reflected Wyler's theory that the Romans were like the British in their ruthless colonization, and the Jews were like Americans in their combative attitudes.

Even as the first day of filming approached, the script still hadn't come together. Respected playwrights like Maxwell Anderson, S. N. Behrman, and Christopher Fry had all given it a shot. In desperation, the studio now brought in Gore Vidal to help with some pivotal scenes between Messala and Ben-Hur.

Wyler was alarmed that there was insufficient motivation for all the fury the characters felt toward one another. A mere argument over politics may have played in a simpler time, but audiences now needed more. Vidal's idea: Add some homoerotic intrigue. The two men had been lovers as youths, and now it was Messala's unrequited love for Ben-Hur that fuels his rage.

In his autobiography, *Palimpsest*, Vidal said that when he told Zimbalist and Wyler his idea, "Sam was behind his desk; eyes narrowing and enlarging as he puffed on a large cigar, his normally ruddy face was now an olive color; his heart was preparing to shut off."

"How do we show this . . . uh, love affair?" asked Zimbalist.

"By never mentioning it," replied Vidal. "There won't be a line of dialogue anyone can question. It will all be in their reactions."

According to Vidal, "We'd inherited a javelin-throwing contest between Ben-Hur and Messala. This was supposed to symbolize the contest between Zionists and Roman overlords. It could also, as easily, represent male sexuality either in contest or collusion. I learned from my days in heavily censored television how to write dialogue that sounded like one thing, to mean quite another."

They agreed to give it a try. "Anything is better than what we got," said Wyler. "Just tone down the off-stage directions. I'll talk to Chuck. You talk to Boyd. But don't you say a word to Chuck, or he'll fall apart."

According to Vidal, he and the director were depressed after watching the two actors play the scene. "Chuck hasn't got much charm, has he," Vidal said.

"No," said Wyler. "And you can direct your ass off and he still never will."

In the early '90s, when both published their autobiographies, Heston and Vidal had a war of words in the press regarding this story.

Heston wrote in *Time* magazine on May 13, 1996:

What are we to make of Gore Vidal? He has earned a respectable reputation as an essayist and novelist, but now he's irrationally determined to pass himself off as a screenwriter for *Ben-Hur*. This past year his obsession has grown like crabgrass. Your story on homosexuals in film and the documentary "The Celluloid Closet" said that in *Ben-Hur* "writer Vidal got actor Stephen Boyd to suggest, 'sub rosa,' a homoerotic tryst with Heston." That demands a response for the record. Vidal was, in fact, imported for a trial run on a script that needed work. Over three days, as recorded in my work journal, Vidal produced a three-page scene that William Wyler rejected after Steve Boyd and I read through for him. Vidal left the next day. His ludicrous claim that he somehow slipped in a scene implying a homosexual relationship between the two characters insults Willy Wyler and, I have to say, irritates the hell out of me.

A month later, Gore Vidal responded in the *Advocate*:

In numerous accounts of a marvelously dull life, Chuck has told us of his triumph as Ben-Hur. With each version he adds, alas, new lies. The facts: *Ben-Hur* was the third picture that I, as a contract writer at MGM, wrote for producer Sam Zimbalist. I arrived with Zimbalist and Wyler in Rome not for a "trial run" but as The Writer. Since I could stay only a couple of months, Christopher Fry was on hand to replace me. Zimbalist died in the middle of the picture, and credits were totally confused.

Now my eight weeks in Rome become three days, according to Chuck. This is very bold. But then, recently, in *Palimpsest*, I did describe how no one at MGM wanted him for the film. Only after Paul Newman and Rock Hudson were unavailable did Zimbalist, glumly, accept Heston.

Despite Chuck's denial of the famous "love scene," the reviewers who watched *The Celluloid Closet* saw very clearly what I had done and said so.

Incidentally, one *Celluloid Closet* producer got a message from homophobe Heston, assuring him that a character he had also "acted" on the screen, Michelangelo, was in no way homosexual. But what is one to do with the spokesperson of the National Rifle Association, who, when he "acts" now, wears two toupees, one on top of the other, in the interest of verisimilitude?

Heston decided not to pursue the issue further.

During the filming of *Ben-Hur*, the tales of its size and scope turned Rome's Cinecitta Studios into a tourist attraction. Over 25,000 visitors came to watch the making of this epic, with tour busses arriving every hour.

The design of the Circus Maximus stadium had been a major bone of contention. MGM asked an archaeologist what the stadium in Jerusalem had looked like. "Roman," came the reply. A second archaeologist volunteered, "It was in a Phoenician style." Since Hollywood is essentially self-referential, MGM eventually based its designs on the 1928 silent version's stadium.

When Wyler began principal photography on May 20, 1958, no footage had been shot of the chariot race, even though there had been a year of preparation and weeks of rehearsals. The chariot race, budgeted at $1 million, was created by second-unit directors Andrew Marton, Yakima Canutt, and Mario Soldati. The nine-minute sequence took five full weeks to shoot, spread out over a period of three months.

One of the most spectacular stunts in the sequence was the result of an accident. Ben-Hur is seen being tossed from his chariot onto the horses in front of him. That's because Joe Canutt, the stunt supervisor's son, was accidentally bounced in the air and managed to grab the crossbar that held the horses together. The accident looked so great on film that Marton wanted to include it, covering with a shot of Heston climbing back into the chariot.

Wyler did not see dailies of the chariot race until they were trimmed to a rough cut with temporary sound effects. Marton and his colleagues were nervous, because Wyler was known as a perfectionist. On the first day of filming *Jezebel*, Bette Davis had a scene in which she was required to dismount from her horse and rush into the house. For this "simple" scene, Wyler forced her to do forty-eight takes. Davis was livid, but learned to appreciate his direction. They feared that the director would demand a reshoot.

But when Wyler and Marton screened it together, Wyler sat quietly for a moment, then simply patted Marton on the shoulder and said, "Good job." This was good enough for Marton. Wyler was renowned for stinginess in his praise; assistant directors and actors alike had long since learned not to seek words of encouragement.

Toward the end of the shoot on *Ben-Hur*, Wyler and Heston were leaving at the same time when Wyler said, "Good night, Chuck. You were good today." The actor was dumbstruck: "It was the only time in *Ben-Hur* that he ever said that."

On November 4, 1958, nearly six months after filming began, Zimbalist suffered a heart attack and died. Wyler was devastated. "It was as though the roof had fallen in on me. I felt alone. I'd never felt alone with Sam around," Wyler recalled.

According to the November 12, 1958, obituary in *Variety*, "Zimbalist had been prepping for his assignment on 'Ben-Hur' off-and-on for five years and intensively for the past two. J. J. Cohn, Metro VP now in Rome, will now take over production helming in association with director William Wyler, who expects to wind film late next month."

Still, two months of additional shooting would be required to finish the film. The *Ben-Hur* budget for the eight-month shoot ran twice its initial $7 million estimate. And six months of postproduction remained on the schedule.

A fight over writing credits further complicated things. On screen, the script was attributed to Karl Tunberg, but the director and producer wanted to credit Christopher Fry. As Vidal writes in *Palimpsest*, "The [Writers] Guild, with its secret arbiters, has always been famous for denying credit to those who actually write the scripts, preferring to assign credit to one of its own. In our case, this proved to be a former president of the Guild, who claimed that he had been mailing [the now-deceased] Sam [Zimbalist] pages from Hollywood."

Wyler lobbied to get Fry back on the credits. He appealed to the Guild, claiming there was additional material that had not been submitted that would prove Fry was the primary writer. After a lengthy arbitration, the motion was denied.

At last, the movie was ready for its unveiling. Though residents of Crawfordsville, Indiana (where Wallace wrote the book), were eager to host the film's premiere, the movie opened instead on November 19, 1959, at the Loew's State Theater in New York City. The stars of the silent version were trotted down the red carpet with the cast of the new movie.

In Los Angeles, the red carpet at the premiere featured a parade of stars including Edgar Bergen, Gary Cooper, Irene Dunne, Jimmy Durante, Clark Gable, Cary Grant, Audrey Hepburn, George Montgomery, Dinah Shore, Edmond O'Brien, Tony Perkins, Tony Randall, Ronald Reagan, Debbie Reynolds, and scores of others.

While Bosley Crowther in the *New York Times* raved, "There has seldom been anything in movies to compare with this picture's chariot race," some critics nonetheless carped about its unprecedented length (four hours including intermission), the wooden acting, and clunky dialogue. The problems so apparent in the silent version had not been overcome.

The December 5 *New Yorker* groaned, "Charlton Heston is remarkably sinewy, but speaks English like he learned it from records." According to the November 30 *Newsweek*, "*Ben-Hur* is grindingly slow and the dialogue is no more than utilitarian; in moments of crisis, it is almost abandoned altogether for some rudimentary music. Finally, so much time is spent watching people survive ordeals (battles, whippings, leprosy) that the audience is apt to have a hard time remembering what many of the ordeals were."

Standup comic Mort Sahl had a brief, sardonic review: "Loved him, hated *Hur*."

The movie was released amid a blizzard of publicity, and merchandising. There was a *Ben-Hur* push mobile scooter-type chariot, plastic toy breastplate, and shield, Ben-his and Ben-hers towel sets, children's chariot whips, sword and buckler, cut-out toys, chariot hobby kits, toy dagger and sheath, chariot race board games, children's bow and arrow set, assembled plastic chariots, adult paint-by-number sets, biscuit and cookie arrangements, and jigsaw puzzles, record albums, umbrellas, scarves, sun suits, sweatshirts, jewelry, and candy bars.

In the end, *Ben-Hur* was a huge hit, for which pundits offered a number of explanations. Amid the Cold War, Biblical epics seemed a bulwark against communism, some suggested. They were patriotic and pro-American. And with the advent of television, epics seemed to provide the only reasons to go back to the movie theater. Finally, in the morally conservative climate of the '50s, sword-and-sandal epics were about as erotic and full of sexual tension as you were going to get. As Dwight MacDonald said in his review in *Esquire* magazine, "The only real reason you went to these movies was the possibility of a Roman orgy scene."

In the end, *Ben-Hur* did not save the Hollywood studio system, as it was then constituted, nor did it save MGM. Sword-and-sandal epics for a long time vanished from production schedules, only to reappear generations later in films like *Gladiator* and *Troy*. Indeed, the genre was ultimately to prove a feast for the special effects gurus who were to play such an important role in post-2000 Hollywood.

Will there be yet another *Ben-Hur*? Given Hollywood's dependence on remakes, a project of this sort seems inevitable. But irrespective of the technological wizardry, the chariot race will never be more riveting or the homoerotic subtext more complex.

16 Caught in the Shower

Psycho (1960)

When Alfred Hitchcock walked onto a set, the cast and crew took notice. His was an imperious presence, a portly, pink-faced man habitually clad in a dark gray business suit, his movements studied and deliberate. When he chose to speak, his cadence was Churchillian and he coveted the aphorism. His gaze, however, seemed at once strict and impish, as though hinting at his willingness to defy convention. For Hitchcock was at once the stern Jesuit, yet also a wit and occasional voyeur. He was a fiercely disciplined filmmaker, yet also a rebel—a man determined not so much to break the rules, but, rather, to set his own.

In a sense, therefore, *Psycho* is a splendid metaphor for Hitchcockian behavior. The project was based on a book of no special importance—a pulp fiction novel by Robert Bloch that had a modest first printing of 10,000. When the novel was first submitted to studios, the door slammed quickly. "Impossible for film," said the Paramount reader, whose name was William Pinckard. "Too repulsive and shocking even to a hardcore reader."

However, Hitchcock had bought a copy at an airport on the way to

London and, by the time the plane had landed, had decided it would be his next film. Years later, he observed that "the suddenness of the murder in the shower, coming out of the blue" had sparked his imagination. But the subplot of voyeurism also grabbed him. Having pushed the censorship boundaries with nudity, transvestism, and other non-'50s indiscretions, the filmmaker was eager to venture into new forbidden territory.

But he wanted to do it on his own terms. Purchasing film rights to *Psycho* with $9,000 of his own money, Hitchcock sent forth his troops to buy every copy in the bookstores to protect the secrecy of the plot. Indeed, the deal had been done anonymously. Hitchcock didn't want to show his hand even to the studio. He well understood that the studios, circa 1959, had ceded their audience to television and were desperate to shock their remaining filmgoers with UFO's, giant tarantulas, and teenage werewolves. What could be scarier than monster movies? The blandly smiling neighbor next door, thought Hitchcock.

Hitchcock's contract at Paramount was winding down. His deal allowed for control of screenwriter, story, cast, editing, and publicity for any project costing $3 million or less.

It was a dream deal for any director, but he had earned it. Hitchcock was on a roll in the '50s, creating some of his greatest films. Most of them centered on ordinary people thrust into extraordinary circumstances. Farley Granger says hello to someone in the 1951 *Strangers on a Train* and finds himself framed for murder. Doris Day and James Stewart are friendly to a stranger and are thrust into a political assassination attempt. Madison Avenue drone Cary Grant is enmeshed in a world of international spies and microfilm. The underlying moral: Be careful who you're friendly to.

It was Hitchcock's plan to spend time and money on preproduction, then shoot the film quickly and inexpensively, almost like an expanded episode of his TV series *Alfred Hitchcock Presents*. The series, which Hitchcock hosted, ran from 1955–62, first in half-hour versions on CBS and later in an hour format on NBC. It featured stories of suspense, adapted from short stories by top-tier writers including Eric Ambler, Ray Bradbury, and Roald Dahl (Dahl's story led to one of the series' most famous episodes, in which a housewife bludgeons her husband to death with a frozen leg of lamb, then roasts it and feeds it to the investigating officers), Robert C. Dennis, Ira Levin (who later wrote *Rosemary's Baby*), Richard Levinson, and William Link (who later created such shows as *Columbo* and *Murder She Wrote*). Directors included Robert Altman, Paul Henreid, Ida Lupino, Norman Lloyd (an actor Hitchcock venerated), and Hitchcock himself.

By 1955 Hitchcock had become a brand, and he knew it, lending his name to a regular anthology of short stories, *Alfred Hitchcock Mystery Magazine*. And though he only directed seventeen episodes of the TV series, his profile and his personality became well known to TV viewers via his mannered, black-humor vignettes that introduced each episode.

Despite Hitchcock's remarkable track record and a deal guaranteeing him a high degree of autonomy, Paramount executives declined to green-light *Psycho* unless Hitchcock elaborated on his story line. These were stressful times in Hollywood, and secret plots simply didn't do.

Stubbornly implacable, Hitchcock refused to disclose the plot, but agreed to cut his budget. He even offered to deploy the crew on his TV show to shoot the film on a quick schedule. Paramount didn't budge. Hitchcock next offered to waive his normal director's fee of $250,000 provided that Paramount grant him 60 percent of the profits. No movement. He offered to shoot on the Universal lot, where his TV show was produced, permitting the budget to be reduced to a mere $800,000. Now the studio was agreeable, but nervous. Earlier Hitchcock films had been shot in high style, in bright Technicolor with glamorous Edith Head wardrobes and flashy sets. *Psycho* was going to be down and dirty. Paramount was still uncertain, but top executives did not want the embarrassment of passing on a Hitchcock movie. *Psycho* was to go forward, despite the fact the studio still didn't even know its real title.

Hitchcock surreptitiously hired one of his TV writers, James Cavanaugh, to adapt the novel, but felt Cavanaugh's first draft petered out in the final act and lacked black humor. Agent Ned Brown suggested a veteran TV writer named Joseph Stefano. Hitchcock was skeptical. He'd seen a few things Stefano had written and wasn't impressed; moreover, he wasn't excited at working with new writers, but agreed to meet him. The meeting was a success.

A central question was how to show Mrs. Bates without really showing her. The book begins with an apparent conversation between Mrs. Bates and her son Norman. It's easy to cheat in a book and later explain that Mrs. Bates is long dead, that both voices come from the psychotic Norman and that he is the murderer. It's harder to do that in a movie.

Stefano came up with a magician's trick: Distract the audience by making them concentrate on something else. In the book, the first victim (called Mary Crane) arrives at the motel in chapter two and is killed in chapter three. Stefano suggested starting not with the Bates household but with the victim. The audience would think this was a movie about her.

The victim's name was changed in the movie from Mary to Marion Crane. The film begins with her and her lover Sam, whom she wants to marry. Sam cannot fully commit to her because of his large alimony debt to his ex-wife. The audience is thus hooked on Marion's story—a good girl gone bad! Will she get caught stealing $40,000? Will she return the money? Then she's suddenly murdered, forty-five minutes into the film.

Hearing the pitch, Hitchcock said, "We could get a star to play that part." Stefano said, "I knew then I had the job."

The first scene of Marion and Sam was crucial. Hitchcock took the script home and the next day reported to the writer, "Alma loved it." That was the official seal of approval. Alma Reville had been Hitchcock's wife since 1926; she was a film editor who became his closest collaborator, consulting on script, storyboards, casting, and every other element of his films. If she didn't like it, it wouldn't get done.

Though Stefano had passed the crucial test, Hitchcock played it safe and hired the writer on a week-to-week basis.

In the book, Norman is a fortyish, pudgy, mother-dominated alcoholic whose flights of madness are fired up by liquor and pornography, plus the music of Saint Saëns and Beethoven.

Stefano wanted to make the killer more interesting. He suggested that Norman be lonely, young, and sympathetic. "Imagine Anthony Perkins," he suggested.

Perkins was only twenty-seven at the time, but a hot commodity. The son of Osgood Perkins, a stage actor who appeared in the 1932 *Scarface*, Anthony Perkins had made a big impact in Broadway's *Look Homeward, Angel* and received an Oscar nomination for his second film, the 1956 *Friendly Persuasion*.

Bloch's 1959 novel had been, as they say, ripped from the headlines—except the headlines were too demure to give details. Bloch's Norman was based on Ed Gein (1906–1984), aka the "Butcher of Plainfield," who also inspired the Leatherface family in the 1974 *Texas Chainsaw Massacre* and the character of Buffalo Bill in Thomas Harris's novel *The Silence of the Lambs*. Brothers Ed and Henry Gein were raised on a farm outside Plainsfield, Wisconsin, by an alcoholic father and an overbearing, fiercely religious mother who tried to keep her sons away from women, warning that they were temptresses who would lead to damnation. Gein's father died in 1940, his brother in 1944, and his invalid mother in 1945 after two strokes. Living alone, he became obsessed with books about the female anatomy and medical experiments at Nazi camps. He began digging up graves, retrieving various female body parts for "research," including the body of his mother.

When the police searched his house in 1957—using flashlights and oil lamps, since the house had no electricity—they found the body of a fifty-eight-year-old hardware store owner hanging from rafters. They also found various other body parts from an estimated fifteen women along with a bowl made from a human skull, four chairs covered in human skin, and a refrigerator full of human organs. But his pièce de résistance was his female body suit. Using women's body parts, Gein had created a face-and-scalp mask, a vest made of female breasts, and "pants" including female genitalia. Gein was only charged with two murders: The 1954 killing of fifty-one-year-old tavern owner Mary Hogan and the 1957 murder of Bernice Worden. Both were said to resemble his mother.

For the role of the first victim, Marion, Hitchcock cast Janet Leigh, easily the biggest star of the film. She'd started as a contract player at MGM, with her fame rising in her teaming with then-husband Tony Curtis: *Houdini*, *The Black Shield of Falworth*, *The Vikings*, *The Perfect Furlough*, and *Who Was That Lady?* Hitchcock hired her for three weeks; one of them was devoted to the forty-five-second shower sequence. The fact that she filmed forty-five minutes' worth of other scenes in less than two weeks is a testament to Hitchcock's promised fast shooting schedule, which encompassed fourteen to eighteen setups a day.

The crew was drawn mainly from his TV show (black-and-white series move with far greater alacrity than Technicolor features). The director of photography on *Psycho* was John L. Russell, who'd been cinematographer on the 1953 *The Beast from 20,000 Fathoms*. The art directors were Robert Clatworthy and Joseph Hurley. Together they created a house that reflected Gothic menace with San Francisco's Victorian gingerbread look; it's never specified where the fictional Fairfield is, but assistant director Hilton A. Green in the DVD documentary says they figured the film takes place near the town of Tulare in central California.

Hitchcock bypassed many of his usual feature crew, such as Edith Head, who helped contribute to the glamorous look of films like *To Catch a Thief* and *Vertigo*. But he retained two key big screen collaborators: editor George Tomasini and composer Bernard Herrmann.

For the role of Marion's sister, he cast Vera Miles, who'd starred in *The Wrong Man* for the director and was under personal contract to Hitchcock.

Meanwhile, Hitchcock and Stefano continued to polish the script, fretting over the smallest details, trekking through a used-car dealership in Santa Monica, looking at real estate offices, probing into taxidermy. His theory, according to Stefano was, "Think what the audience is going to ask and answer it as fast as possible."

Stefano was in Freudian analysis at the time and Hitchcock was a strict,

Jesuit-educated Catholic. The combination was irresistibly cheeky, as they attempted to break taboos and debunk myths. The movie's very first shot peeks through a hotel window at a shirtless John Gavin in bed with Leigh, wearing only a white brassiere. Though audiences had seen Elizabeth Taylor in a slip in the 1958 *Cat on a Hot Tin Roof*, a mere bra and half-slip was groundbreaking. And while earlier films had depicted bathrooms, they only showed someone in the tub or shaving. No major film had ever depicted a toilet; Stefano thought the mere sight of one would be unsettling to the audience. Hitchcock showed Leigh flushing it.

But the most daring taboo may have been their depiction of the mother. The theme of the saintly, self-sacrificing mother was a favorite in the film world, including the 1931 *The Sin of Madelon Claudet* (in which Helen Hayes won an Oscar for playing a woman who becomes a prostitute to put her son through medical school). In *Stella Dallas* Barbara Stanwyck plays the lower-class mom who doesn't want to embarrass her daughter at her high-society wedding, so she stands smiling in the rain outside a window watching her daughter's ceremony.

But by the late '50s, moms were coming under attack. Perhaps we can assign it to the growing popularity of Freudian analysis, but in any case they were no longer immune to monsterous motives or insensitivity. Lana Turner in the 1959 *Imitation of Life* was oblivious to her daughter's needs; that same year, on the Broadway stage, Ethel Merman exploded as Mama Rose in *Gypsy*.

And then there was Mrs. Bates, the real villain of the piece, the little mother that Norman carries inside of him, tormenting him. In Stefano's script, the house becomes Norman's mind and buried deep within it, behind a secret door, in the root cellar is the root of his problems: Mother. Marion and her coworker, Caroline (played by Patricia Hitchcock, the director's daughter) also make passing references to nagging mothers.

The tyrannical mom motif must have appealed to Hitchcock, who had used it in some of his early films. Jessie Royce Landis in *To Catch a Thief*, Marion Lorne in *Strangers on a Train*, and Leopoldine Konstantin in *Notorious* were not the friendliest of mothers, although they were sometimes played for laughs, but Mrs. Bates brought America's mother fixation to center stage.

Even after production on *Psycho* began on November 30, 1959, Hitchcock continued to keep a lid on details. It was referred to simply as "Production 9401" at the studio, or sometimes as "Wimpy," after the second-unit cameraman Rex Wimpy, whose name appeared on clapboards. Hitchcock even refused to allow the chief of the studio's still photography department, William "Bud" Fraker, to shoot anything that might allude to the subject matter or plotline of the film. To quell questions, he even spread the word that he was having casting calls for the central role of the mother.

However, Hitchcock carefully allowed smidgeons of advance publicity. In a *Variety* article on December 27, 1959, Hitchcock said the picture would "open with the longest dolly shot ever attempted by helicopter." He wanted a "four-mile scene" that would even top the bravura dolly with which Orson Welles opened *Touch of Evil*. He wanted the audience to be as voyeuristic as Norman Bates: The film would open with a pan across Phoenix, zooming in to a hotel and peering through a window.

But the shot was abandoned due to budget limitations, so clever cutting blended a pan of the city, a zoom into a hotel, a shot of a window, and then Leigh and Gavin in bed—all so seamless that it seemed like one shot.

Variety reported on the intricate and detailed planning. "Mr. Hitchcock will rehearse with film, staging the scene and photographing it simultaneously from several angles with hand-held IMO's (old-style newsreel cameras). The results obtained will be assembled, edited, and then used as the basis for Mr. Hitchcock's sketches from which he will later photograph the grisly scene with a regular camera."

When the reporter asked the director whether he feared that the sensational aspects of the scene might bring forth the censors, Hitchcock replied, "Men *do* kill nude women, you know."

Graphic artist, Saul Bass—who designed the striking credits on the film—was also called on to storyboard the entire shower sequence. Costumer Rita Riggs came up with the idea that Leigh could wear moleskin over her breasts and "over the vital part—and that's it."

Hitchcock later told François Truffaut that there were seventy camera setups for the forty-five-second sequence. "I used a naked model that stood in for Janet Leigh. We only showed Miss Leigh's hands, shoulder, and head. All the rest was the stand-in. Naturally, the knife never touched the body; it was all done in the montage. I shot some of it in slow motion so as to cover the breasts. The slow shots were not accelerated later on because they were inserted in the montage so as to give an impression of normal speed."

Hitchcock said he decided on a model because he thought she would be more comfortable standing around naked during the camera set-ups and shots than an actress or stand-in would.

The blood that ran down the tub's drain consisted of chocolate syrup in a plastic squeeze bottle. Costume supervisor Helen Colvig recalls, "Even the unit manager (Lew Leary) said, 'He'll never get away with this scene.' Frankly, we all thought he'd cut it to just show Mother coming into the bathroom, the knife raising, the blood, the girl falling, and that's it. We thought the bits-and-pieces montage approach lent itself to any censorship or editorial changes he had in mind. It was *so* outrageous for its time."

The last shot of the shower sequence starts on Leigh's open, dead eye and pulls back, angles, and pans out of the bathroom and to the nightstand to show the $40,000 untouched—pointing out that this was not a murder of greed. There were more than twenty takes of that shot.

One rumor at the time suggested that Bass directed the shower sequence, a rumor that he fostered. In 1981, Bass told *Variety*, "I showed it [the test footage shot with the IMO newsreel camera] to Hitch and he very graciously said, 'You do it.' He was on the set. It was really a very generous gesture. It was a thrill for me." However, assistant director Hilton Green and Janet Leigh both say that Hitchcock directed every shot and would never let anyone else direct such a key moment in a film of his. Chimes in Stefano: "I *know* he shot it. Because one of my favorite memories of the whole experience was of Alfred Hitchcock standing there talking seriously about camera angles with a naked model." (Other witnesses insist the model wore a body stocking.)

When it came time to edit his film, Hitchcock marked the shower scene for immediate attention. Because he normally shot so little extra footage, his films tended not to take more than a few weeks in postproduction.

In the meantime, he had to decide who would be the voice of Mother. According to Perkins, "While Hitch was very eager to play fair; he also didn't want the audience to see through the whole thing." Perkins wanted to record the lines himself in a faux female's voice, but the director wouldn't budge. So Perkins recommended friend Paul Jasmin, a twenty-three-year-old budding actor who had created a female alter ego, "Eunice Ayers," that he would use to call friends on telephone practical jokes. Hitchcock hired Jasmin as well as actresses Jeanette Nolan and Virginia Gregg. All recorded Mother's lines but there was some dispute as to whose voice was ultimately used.

Said Jasmin, "Hitchcock had the whole town talking about this strange, disturbing movie he was making. Everybody wanted to know what he was up to, but he asked all of us not to talk about it."

One critical reason for *Psycho*'s enduring success is its music. Hitchcock had worked with composer Bernard Herrmann on his five previous films. The filmmaker originally intended to have as little music as possible, relying heavily on the natural sounds of the streets and the environment.

Recalling a rough cut screening of *Psycho*, Herrmann told director Brian De Palma, "Hitch was nervously pacing back and forth, saying it was awful and that he was going to cut it down for his television show. He was crazy. He didn't know what he had. 'Wait a minute,' I said, 'I have some ideas. How about a score completely for strings? I used to be a violin player, you know . . .'"

The director was so pleased with the score that he doubled the composer's salary to nearly $35,000. Herrmann considered it a "black and white" score, since it was very understated.

Stefano says, "When I saw the rough cut, I thought it was a truly terrible movie." But after the film was tightened in editing, and Herrmann's music was added: "I nearly fell out of my seat."

After the censors screened *Psycho* for the first time, they reacted the same way Hitchcock anticipated. They were shocked at the shower scene and demanded to examine it closer, sure that they had seen a naked breast. Hitchcock was smart enough to know his limits. He had wanted Leigh to be topless in the opening hotel-room scene, but knew he couldn't get away with it. Ever the strategist, he added a few moments of material that he guessed would never pass muster to use as bargaining chips. He then sent a supposed "re-cut" of the shower scene that was, in fact, identical to the first. He further proposed that the censors leave the shower scene as is and he would reshoot the opening scene where Leigh appears in bra and slip, under the condition that they be on-set that day to approve.

They agreed, but when the day arrived, none of the censors showed up. Hitchcock had won the protracted battle with the motion picture code and he hadn't changed a single shot in the film.

Maintaining the secrecy that had been part of the filming became a key marketing tool. For one thing, the film was not prescreened for the press or the industry, ignoring a time-honored tradition. As a result, critics had to review the film the day it opened, which resulted in some grumpy reviews. More important, no patron could be admitted after the start of the film. Hitchcock worried that filmgoers would arrive halfway through *Psycho* and wonder "Where's Janet Leigh?" His practical concerns were transformed into a gimmick.

In the '50s, movies were often on double features and audience members had no qualms about entering in the middle of a movie. They'd walk in, sit through the end of the movie, and then stay until the moment in the film when they arrived. With *Psycho*, however, magazine and newspaper ads stressed that "No one . . . BUT NO ONE . . . will be admitted into the theater after the start of each performance of *Psycho*." Hitchcock insisted that the theater owners enforce this rule in a contractual prerequisite for booking the film. He wrote, "I believe this is a vital step in creating the aura of mysterious importance this unusual motion picture so richly deserves."

Theater owners, especially of major chains, feared that customers would rebel at having to show up at an assigned time. Hitchcock sent a manual titled "The Care and Handling of *Psycho*" to the theaters. In it, he writes, "As you read the copy . . . please note that my own firm but non-belligerent stand on the top-secrecy policy was recognized in the editorial cooperation of the mighty [New York] *Times* itself. I might add that this same pictorialized pastiche must certainly have piqued the curiosity of millions coast-to-coast."

Also included in this package were tips on hiring Pinkerton guards to enforce the admission policies, order forms for large lobby clocks to remind the audience of start time, and five-foot cardboard standees of Hitchcock. The standee held a note: "We won't allow you to cheat yourself!" The note explained that no one would be allowed in after the start of the film. "We say no one—and we mean no one—not even the manager's brother, the President of the United States or the Queen of England (God bless her!)"

In addition, theater owners were advised to mount outdoor speakers to broadcast recorded messages from Hitchcock. In one of them, the director says: "I must apologize for inconveniencing you this way. However, this queuing up and standing about is good for you. It will make you appreciate the seats inside. It will also make you appreciate *Psycho*. You see, *Psycho* is most enjoyable when viewed at the beginning and proceeding to the end. I realize this is a revolutionary concept, but we have discovered that *Psycho* is unlike most motion pictures, and does not improve when run backwards."

He also said, "The manager of this theater has been instructed, at the risk of his life, not to admit to the theater any persons after the picture starts. Any spurious attempts to enter by side doors, fire escapes, or ventilating shafts will be met by force. I have been told this is the first time such remarkable measures have been necessary . . . but then this is the first time they've ever seen a picture like *Psycho*." Posters, some using the work of graphic artist Tony Palladino, who'd designed art for the book jacket, proclaimed "Please don't tell your friends its shocking secrets."

The audience ate it up; Hitchcock had created an event in movie going. Of course, he wasn't the first to come up with such gimmicks. The acknowledged master of this was William Castle (1914–1977), whose marketing artistry surpassed the artistry in his direction. For *Macabre* (1958), each audience member was insured with Lloyd's of London in case of "death by fright." In 1961, Castle's *Psycho* knockoff, *Homicidal*, had a "fright break" in the middle of the film so anyone with a weak heart could leave, or at least go to the nurse in attendance and have her monitor his or her blood pressure.

Psycho opened June 16, 1960, in New York, then had a prerelease engagement in Philadelphia, Boston, and Chicago. The reviews weren't uniformly enthusiastic. The *New York Times*' Bosley Crowther said, "It does seem slowly paced for Mr. Hitchcock and given over to a lot of small detail." Without ever mentioning the screenplay, Crowther raised the question "whether Mr. Hitchcock's points of psychology, the sort of highly favored by Krafft-Ebing, are as reliable as his melodramatic stunts." He added that the director's "denouement falls quite flat for us. But the acting is fair." Still, Crowther included the film in his year-end Top Ten list, saying "it represented expert and sophisticated command of emotional development with cinematic techniques. Aptly performed by Anthony Perkins, Vera Miles, and Janet Leigh."

Audiences couldn't care less what the critics thought. Theaters saw long lines of people waiting to see the film. Stories surfaced about people passing out in their seats because of the fright, and ticket holders threatening to tear down the Woods Theater in Chicago if the manager didn't let them in to get out of the intense summer heat. When Hitchcock learned of this, he was quoted as saying, "Buy them umbrellas." The theater manager did so, and the quote gave Hitchcock even more free press.

Also helping the film was its "B" rating from the Catholic Church's Legion of Decency, which meant that the movie was objectionable for people of any age. Audiences couldn't wait to see what was so naughty.

Fueling interest further were the three trailers that Hitchcock made, costing him nearly $10,000. The first two were essentially brief teasers that reinforced the rules of getting there on time, and not divulging the ending, because, as Hitchcock says, "It's the only one we have."

The third was far more innovative. In the six-minute trailer (available for viewing on the DVD), Hitchcock gives a tour of the Bates mansion and motel, with no footage ever shown of the film. The script concludes with Hitchcock pulling back the shower curtain. With the sound of Bernard Herrmann's screeching violins, it reveals Vera Miles in a blonde wig. The voiceover cuts in and says, "The picture you must see from the beginning—or not at all!"

Fawcett World Library reprinted *Psycho* in paperback, with a new cover design that tied in with the movie. Pictures of Janet Leigh were included, as were cast credits. Hitchcock did many interviews to promote the film, including one for *Life* magazine.

The movie broke box office records, to the amazement of Paramount executives. The New Brunswick Drive-In in New Jersey reported a waiting line of cars three miles long. The film was held over second and third weeks, with only 5 percent drop-off. It eventually played 3,750 United States dates.

As art director Robert Clatworthy said, "What surprised me was it probably looked a little better than we thought it would. It was a helluva picture and turned out to be the only picture I've ever been on that I heard people talking about in supermarkets, banks, everywhere."

The movie grossed $9.5 million from its first theatrical engagements, and another $6 million internationally. That year, only *Ben-Hur* made more money in America, but of course cost vastly more to make—sixteen times, to be exact. By the end of its first year, *Psycho* had tallied $15 million domestically—in an era when the average movie ticket cost seventy cents.

The timing of the film was perfect. With the population booming and postwar housing thriving, people flocked to new suburbs where they often didn't know their new neighbors. As *Psycho* showed, one of our greatest fears is that a nameless, faceless person in the crowd turns crazy—and lethal.

Horror films had originated in Europe, with *The Cabinet of Dr. Caligari*, *Nosferatu*, and *The Golem*. When Universal produced the lavish Lon Chaney version of *The Phantom of the Opera* in 1925, it was unsure how to sell it: There was no horror genre and they weren't sure audiences would enjoy being scared.

Chaney made other macabre films for the studio, but horror didn't really click with audiences until Universal's Tod Browning-directed *Dracula* in 1931, starring Hungarian actor Bela Lugosi repeating his stage success. The studio followed that with the 1931 *Frankenstein* and a slew of other classics: *The Mummy*, *The Invisible Man*, *The Bride of Frankenstein*, and then a series of *Wolf Man* movies in the 1940s and *The Creature from the Black Lagoon* in the 1950s.

The horror genre changed shape over the decades, always reflecting the subliminal fears of the generation: Giant insects in the wake of nuclear bombs, hideous creatures invading the body (a fear of pollution or cancer?) such as *Alien* and *Rabid* in the 1970s, and teenage slasher films in the 1980s.

That subgenre was partly inspired by Ed Gein, whose story had triggered the novel *Psycho*. Tobe Hooper's 1974 *Texas Chainsaw Massacre* popularized the genre of teenagers being tortured by nearly inhuman humans, a theme that was picked up four years later by John Carpenter with the huge hit *Halloween* (starring Leigh's daughter, Jamie Lee Curtis). And the 1991 *Silence of the Lambs*, directed by Jonathan Demme and written by Ted Tally, became the first "horror" film to win the best picture Oscar.

Hitchcock never felt he fit into this category. He made a clear distinction: He didn't direct mysteries or horror movies—he directed suspense films. In the 1958 *Vertigo*, Kim Novak apparently dies, then James Stewart sees a woman who looks identical to her. Many filmmakers would hold back the truth until the twist ending: Novak hadn't died, but had just changed her identity. But Hitchcock immediately reveals the truth. The audience is not asking "What's going on?" The suspense comes from their question, "What is James Stewart going to do when he finds out?"

After *Psycho*, Hitchcock directed six more films, including the 1963 hit *The Birds* (which also set off a chain of films featuring eco-imbalanced animals attacking humans) and the 1972 *Frenzy*, in which he returned to London lensing after thirty years for a tale about a rapist–strangler.

Universal revived the *Psycho* franchise in the 1980s with three sequels, all of them starring Perkins, who also helmed *Psycho III*. The first two, in 1983 and 1986, were theatrical releases. *Psycho IV: The Beginning* was a 1990 TV-movie starring Henry Thomas (*E.T. the Extra-Terrestrial*) as young Norman, with Olivia Hussey (*Romeo and Juliet*) as his slutty mom. While they're no worse than many slasher movies, they certainly never became more than footnotes to the *Psycho* legacy.

In 1997, Gus Van Sant did a remake of the classic film, retaining Stefano's script with only a few words altered. Critics were outraged at Van Sant's audacity, but it was an interesting exercise to see how different actors interpret the same material. The film is, unsurprisingly, inferior to Hitchcock, but there are little touches that are interesting: Sam, as played by Viggo Mortensen, actually seems more like someone who runs a hardware store than did John Gavin. And the film shows, in fact, that Stefano's script has held up to the test of time surprisingly well.

But overall the exercise proves a vivid reminder that there can be no Hitchcock after Hitchcock. The small, hobbit-like Brit was a complete original. His wonderfully perverse view of the world was so idiosyncratic as to defy imitators. Many films would be described as "Hitchcock-like," but they wouldn't be Hitchcock.

It was indeed a curious irony that the old master, upon reading the novel *Psycho* bought and hoarded all the published copies to keep everyone away from the story. Surely his singular approach, combining style and suspense, was something no one else could mimic. Or, for that matter, even want to.

17 Return of the "Oater"
Gunsmoke (1955)

Long before *Deadwood*, there existed on television a somewhat more orderly, cosmetically appealing version of the Old West in which even the bad guys avoided profanity and, at the point of death, no one ever uttered the "F" word. That version of the West was epitomized by *Gunsmoke*, which began on radio in 1952 and made its TV premier three years later, where it resided for a record-breaking twenty years—the longest for a primetime series. For over 640 episodes, stoic Marshal Matt Dillon survived a seemingly endless succession of rustlers, ambushers, bushwhackers, and random lawbreakers only to be finally done in by something he never saw coming: It was old man Nielsen who finally dispatched him to Boot Hill.

It was a surprising end for the *Gunsmoke* legend, which had been universally respected as a network staple. By its fourth season, it was the top-rated show, a title it held for four consecutive years. Even in its final year, the Nielsen ratings showed it was still attracting abundant viewers, but CBS felt they were the wrong viewers. In fact it was a sort of hellhole of viewership: Farmers and blue-collar workers with household incomes of under $5,000, many in the fifty-and-older age group. It was a rustic show, appealing only to rustics, and advertisers were fleeing in droves.

When *Gunsmoke* died, it took down with it one of Hollywood's most beloved genres. On radio and TV, the Western had nurtured a generation of cowboy heroes going back to *The Lone Ranger*. In movies, John Wayne's 1969 fade-out in *True Grit* signaled the end of the superstar Western, which traced its origins back to Gene Autry and before.

Gunsmoke's demise was more than the end of a show; it was a sort of rude awakening, a cultural cold shower reminding us all of the generational changes that we'd chosen to ignore. What had started as a serious, adult glimpse of the Western now seemed musty and irrelevant. And many asked: Did all this reflect a loss of innocence or simply an absence of civility?

The radio *Gunsmoke* began April 26, 1952, and ran through June 18, 1961—a late addition to the genre of radio dramas.

The show fell under the supervision of producer–director Norman MacDonnell, who, at thirty-one, had worked on *Escape* for CBS, the suspense show that adapted famous tales from Joseph Conrad, Edgar Allan Poe, and Daphne du Maurier for radio.

MacDonnell had become fixated on nurturing an "adult Western" on TV. Radio Westerns at that point were uncomplicated, cowpokey shows like *The Lone Ranger*. MacDonnell wanted something that wouldn't have a neat and clean ending each week. He brought in writer John Meston, also an *Escape* veteran, to flesh out ideas.

Unbeknownst to them, Bill Paley, the founder and chairman of the board at CBS, was looking for the same kind of TV project. He told the top CBS programmer, Hubbell Robinson, to look for a "Philip Marlowe of the early West," a reference to the then popular radio show based upon Raymond Chandler's detective anti-hero of 1930s Los Angeles.

Given the green light, MacDonnell and Meston brought in other writers who had worked with them on *Escape*, including Les Crutchfield, Kathleen Hite, Anthony Ellis, and Sam Peckinpah (this was before he found his calling as the director of blood-splattered Western feature films).

The opening narration in *Gunsmoke* was to be read by the sonorous-voiced William Conrad, who had been radio's Matt Dillon. The series was to be set in real-life Dodge City, Kansas, with the action unfolding after the Santa Fe Railroad came to town in 1872.

CBS felt that, with a dedicated following on the radio, *Gunsmoke* could transition quickly to TV and be popular. Executives were nonetheless leery of MacDonnell and Meston, who'd had no experience on filmed projects. So the network brought in Charles Marquis Warren as supervising producer—Warren had written the screenplays for *Streets of Laredo*, *Springfield Rifle*, and Paramount's *Pony Express* and had directed *Arrowhead* with Charlton Heston and Jack Palance.

Though CBS thought the new hire would have the fresh vision to make the transition from radio to TV, Warren himself had trepidations about the new medium of TV. In fact, he didn't even own a TV set. Warren liked to describe how he and neighbor John Wayne sat around reviling television. "Tiny little motion pictures. What is that," Warren asked. "The budgets were ridiculous." Still, CBS made him the proverbial offer he couldn't refuse. Of the $25,000 per episode budget, Warren was paid $7,000.

According to *Gunsmoke: A Complete History*, by Suzanne and Gabor Barabas, tensions inevitably started to mount between Warren and MacDonnell, who was associate producer of the TV show at the same time he produced the radio program. Warren decided not to allow MacDonnell on the set because he found him distracting and "felt his resentment."

Between 1955 and 1961, the two formats overlapped and much of the action in the TV episodes was lifted from the radio scripts. The radio staff grumbled, but no formal complaints were lodged to CBS. The TV writers were told to go to Room C at CBS Television City and pick from a shelf full of radio scripts. If they adapted one from radio, they would receive $450. If they wrote a script from scratch, their pay would be $550.

According to network folklore, the role of Matt Dillon was first offered to John Wayne. Though Wayne was never a serious candidate (the network could never afford him), he made a pivotal casting contribution: He suggested that James Arness be tried for the lead role. Wayne also narrated the introduction to the first show: "Good evening. My name's Wayne. Some of you may have seen me before. I hope so—I've been kickin' around Hollywood a long time. I've made a lot of pictures out here, all kinds. Some of 'em have been Westerns, and that's what I'm here to tell you about tonight—a Western. A new television show called *Gunsmoke*. When I first heard about the show *Gunsmoke*, I knew there was only one man to play in it—James Arness. He's a young fella and may be new to some of you, but I've worked with him, and I predict he'll be a big star. And now I'm proud to present *Gunsmoke*."

Despite Wayne's advocacy, Arness wasn't the only one considered to play the marshal. Raymond Burr was a candidate, but, as Warren colorfully put it, "I couldn't use him because when he got out of the chair, the chair came with him." Among the others considered were Richard Boone, John Pickard, and Denver Pyle.

Arness was wary of his new role. The actor, thirty-one, was even reluctant to audition, wanting to concentrate on a film career. He'd appeared in twenty-six mostly low-budget films by the time *Gunsmoke* debuted and his biggest role had been in the 1951 *The Thing From Outer Space*. Arness was unrecognizable under the monster makeup he wore as a murderous vegetable from outer space (who is eventually fried by the protagonists).

Though he clearly had the gravitas and the craggy looks for Matt Dillon, Arness stood six-foot-six and CBS feared he was too tall. Wayne eventually persuaded Arness to accept the role of the marshal, telling him it "may be the best shot you'll ever have in this town."

Arness finally read for the part two weeks before the pilot was to start. William Dozier, a producer, recalled that he still had to call Arness hours before filming to "pump some sunshine up his ass," according to *Gunsmoke: A Complete History.*

Years later, Burt Reynolds (who joined *Gunsmoke* in 1962) confirmed Wayne's role in getting Arness into the show. "John Wayne was the one who talked him into doing it, got him drunk, actually . . . got him smashed and made him sign the contract. And when I came on the show, Jim had made more money in that amount of time than Wayne had made in his entire motion picture career."

Amanda Blake won the role of Kitty by sitting outside Warren's office until she got an audition. "I had wanted other actresses, but I should have known that they were a little too refined, a little too beautiful," Warren said. "But Amanda looked just cheap enough and tough enough to play the part. Her hair was a bit too red. She was just right. I got the message to CBS, 'We found Kitty, let's make a deal.'"

In the transition from radio to TV, Kitty's occupation was sanitized from hooker to saloon owner. Still, it was logical to ask exactly what went on upstairs from Kitty's saloon. That logic got Blake in trouble. In an early interview she was asked what Kitty's job was and she replied, "Why, she's a tramp." CBS brass threatened to fire her, and the writers started turning out scripts that downplayed her scandalous past.

Milburn Stone was cast as Doc Adams and Dennis Weaver as Chester Goode. Warren had Weaver in mind to play the deputy, having worked with him on *Seven Angry Men*. On his first audition, Weaver didn't speak in what became famous as the "Chester drawl." Warren said he wished he would play the part with a little more humor. "When he said that, I remember that at the University of Oklahoma, I used to have a lot of fun at parties doing this dialect," Weaver recalls. "So I said, 'Well, let me go out in the hallway, and I'll take another approach to it. Just let me read it once more.' And he said,

'Fine.' Then I came back in and I gave it the 'Chester' thang and he jest fell right thar on the floor." He became the first principal actor to sign for the show. Weaver stood at six-foot-four and thus seemed a good match to Arness.

The question of the limp came up when Warren was seeking an explanation as to why Chester was just hanging around Arness instead of getting a job. After Warren approached Weaver about adding a limp, they repaired to the Fairfax Bar across the street from CBS Television City, where Weaver practiced the limp until the bar owner kicked them out.

Stone had clashed with Warren from the time the two met on the set of *Arrowhead*. After Stone read for *Gunsmoke*, Warren said: "I hated him, but damn, he was good . . . he was the best. So I sat him down and said, 'I know you don't like me and you know I don't like you. But you can do it. I want you to do it.'" He agreed. For his role, Stone received honorary membership in the Kansas Medical Society, one of the few non-doctors to do so. "Of all the principals, he was the most protective of his character," Warren said. "He had no reluctance to suggest changes in dialogue and could be difficult with an unheeding director. He once refused to appear in a scene that he felt was out of character and told the producer "I'm too old to scare and too rich to care."

In late summer 1955, CBS announced that *Gunsmoke* would air on TV at 10 PM. It would remain in that Saturday-night berth for twelve years. That same season, one other adult Western made its debut: *The Life and Legend of Wyatt Earp*, starring Hugh O'Brian. That show lasted six years.

The sponsors of *Gunsmoke*, Chesterfields and L&M Tobacco, were happy with the implications of the show's title and with the voiceover narration that introduced it: "Around Dodge City and the territory out west there's just one way to handle all the killers and the spoilers, and that's with a U.S. marshal and the power of . . . *Gunsmoke*."

Two pilots were filmed, one darker than the other, and, in a reminder of the link that has always existed between Hollywood and commercial sponsors, the two cigarette companies were given the choice as to which pilot would air. Surprisingly, they went with the darker episode, "Matt Gets It," in which Dillon loses a gunfight and almost dies. The notion that the lead character was fallible was totally new to the genre. According to MacDonnell, this became a recurring theme. "Sometimes we sit down and say to ourselves, 'You know, this fellow Dillon is just getting too noble. Let's fix him.' So we do. John [Meston] writes a script where poor old Matt gets outdrawn and outgunned and pulls every dumb trick in the book. It makes him, and us, human."

The level of violence on the radio show was systematically dialed down for television. In the radio episode "The Guitar," a mule has its ear cut off.

For TV, the mule has white stripes painted on it. In "The Queue," the radio version has a Chinese immigrant strangled with his own pigtail. On TV, the immigrant is beaten, but survives.

It took nine months for the TV *Gunsmoke* to crack the Nielsen Top Ten, which it finally did in July 1956. One year later it pushed *I Love Lucy* out of first place.

The show also drew overseas audiences, developing a large fan base for dubbed versions in Germany and Japan. The inevitable result was a rush of Western-themed programming, including *Maverick; Wagon Train; Tales of Wells Fargo; Cheyenne; Broken Arrow; Jim Bowie; Sugarcoat; Bronco; Have Gun, Will Travel; Restless Gun; Colt .45; and Tombstone Territory.*

By 1957, there were more than twenty-five Westerns on TV, with advertisers spending $60 million annually on those shows alone. Viewers could watch sixty-four hours of Western content each week on the three networks. By January 1958, seven of the top ten programs were Westerns, but *Gunsmoke* remained the leader.

And Jim Arness was emerging as a TV superstar. After the first three years of the series, Arness complained about his share of the profits. An agreement was reached whereby the Arness Company took over as the production entity of the show—which set him up to be the star of the series as long as he wanted to be. He also mandated that Stone, Blake, and Weaver stay in their roles as long as they wanted. Weaver left the show several times, but always returned. Arness and Stone stayed for the whole run, with Amanda Blake on the show for nineteen years and Dennis Weaver for nine.

In 1962, however, MacDonnell decided he needed a younger cast to attract a better demographic. Burt Reynolds was hired to play Quint Asper, a half-Indian blacksmith. Reynolds's actual grandmother was a full-blooded Cherokee, and he was comfortable in his debut. He received 4,000 letters of fan mail in his first week.

Reynolds remained on the show for three years before leaving to pursue a career in film. As Reynolds puts it, "You can't be a leading man when you're standing next to a guy six-foot-eight and his name is Matt Dillon. I mean, I was the blacksmith and people used to call me a dirty half-breed and spit on me for fifty-eight minutes and then Arness would come back from Hawaii and beat 'em up. So it wasn't a terrific role in terms of really shining."

As the years wore on, the network inevitably began to worry about *Gunsmoke*'s ratings dip. New executives were brought in. In 1964, the network hired British-born Philip Leacock as producer and John Mantley as story editor.

The two inaugurated a series of changes, introducing new writers and new characters. Ken Curtis joined as Festus Haggen in 1964, and lasted through-out the rest of the show's run. Roger Ewing played Clayton Thaddeus Green-wod from 1965–67. In 1967, the last regular joined the show, Buck Taylor, who played Newly O'Brien from 1967 to 1975.

As Leacock and Mantley rose in seniority, CBS booted Norman MacDon-nell from his position as top producer. MacDonnell's dismissal came suddenly, at the hands of James "The Smiling Cobra" Aubrey, who had become head of CBS Television. A member of Aubrey's team told MacDonnell that Jack Palance would be cast as a foil to Arness, because Palance had a strong fan base. MacDonnell balked at the idea and was very vocal about it.

As John Mantley explained it, "*Gunsmoke* in the early days was almost a no-drama show. There was a shorthand: 'I'm going to kill you, because you killed my brother' and there was a necessary shoot out at the end of each show. Toward the end of MacDonnell's reign, he became so frustrated with this sort of format that he began experimenting with somewhat unusual forms of shows. The audience didn't want that. They wanted the traditional no-drama. I suspect that's why the ratings were slipping."

At the end of the 1967 season, *Gunsmoke* was canceled. The reason, as Michael Dann, vice president in charge of programming at CBS put it, was "program fatigue." It had slipped in the ratings between 1963 and 1967, and eventually fell to thirty-fourth place. Demographics also were a concern. Axing *Gunsmoke* would make room for younger-skewing shows.

Dann made the announcement of the cancellation while Bill Paley was on vacation in the Bahamas. This was effectively an end-run around Paley, who still considered *Gunsmoke* one of his favorite shows.

Mantley received a call from the network saying, "*Gunsmoke* has been can-celed. Go down and tell your people." It wasn't a total surprise to Mantley—he had been warned two days earlier by a reporter at *Variety*. There was an immediate outcry; one senator denounced CBS on the Senate floor for remov-ing a classic. Several midwestern stations threatened that they would not carry any CBS programs if *Gunsmoke* was canceled.

When Paley was informed that the show was canceled, he called Tom Daw-son, president of CBS Television Network, and ordered him to put the show back on the air. Dawson said the Saturday time slot that *Gunsmoke* occupied had already been filled, so Paley canceled *Gilligan's Island* and a new com-edy, *Doc*, to make room for the return of *Gunsmoke* on Monday nights. The network issued a crow-eating press release saying it had "re-evaluated the situation." A spokesman said, "Our affiliate stations had an affectionate feel-ing for the program. . . . There's life in the old boy yet."

The publicity over the near-cancellation, in tandem with new night, served

Gunsmoke well. It returned to the top of the ratings and, incredibly, stayed there for five more years.

The individual most distressed by the show's death sentence and reprise had been Amanda Blake. Hearing of the cancellation, she'd arranged to have the set of the Long Branch Saloon shipped to her home in Arizona. She was so devoted to the actors, the crew, even the characters, that she wanted to hang out on the set even though the show would no longer be filming. "I went totally to pieces," she explained. "They did it in the typical way that all the networks do. Nobody tells you. You just pick up the paper one morning and see '*Gunsmoke* canceled.' No warning, no anything. Demographics . . . what the hell are demographics? Some dumb machine was telling us that they don't like us out there . . . that they're not watching us . . . that we're not reaching the proper age bracket . . . like the thirty-five-to-fifty year olds don't buy anything."

When *Gunsmoke* began in the Monday time slot, Marshal Dillon found himself fighting more than demographics and CBS executives. There were problems with rising costs, and rising concern about TV violence. When Mantley took over as producer in 1966, an episode cost $178,000 to produce. By 1971, in part because of the expense of the show's many guest stars, he was receiving $250,000. There was also more travel to locations in South Dakota, New Mexico, Utah, and Oregon.

Further, the assassinations of Robert Kennedy and Martin Luther King Jr. triggered an outcry against violence on television. *Gunsmoke* toned down the violence in its new shows, and cut out anything that might be deemed objectionable from old shows now being aired as reruns.

In 1969, after John Pastore's Senate subcommittee on communications started hearings on violence and sex on television, the surgeon general also threatened to get involved. The networks insisted they'd be more serious about restricting content. A point system known as the "violence quotient" was adopted by the network in 1971. Mantley said: "There were so many points for clean killings, so many for killings with blood, so many for slaps, and so many for kicks and punches. If the total was too high, the script was rejected."

The network had been intimidated, and Mantley knew it. They would have to rethink *Gunsmoke* with fewer guns and less smoke. So Mantley brought in guest actors and introduced subtler, more personal stories. Guests who found themselves in the *Gunsmoke* corral included Charles Bronson, Robert Redford, Bette Davis, Harrison Ford, Betty Hutton, Richard Dreyfuss, Jon Voight, Ellen Burstyn, Loretta Swit, and Buddy Ebsen. Whenever Ebsen appeared on the show, the ratings went up by two points.

Though the program was commended for its kinder and gentler motif, with awards coming from the President's Council on Mental Retardation and another from the National Conference of Christians and Jews, ratings were still falling. Moreover, Arness was getting less screen time. "He is a marshal with a gun on his hip, and I cannot just have him snoozing in the sun or tipping his hat to the ladies . . ." Mantley explained, but Arness was amenable to the change because it meant he could spend more time with his family.

In May 1975, CBS announced its official, final cancellation of *Gunsmoke*. It was still number twenty-five on the Nielsens when it was replaced by *Rhoda* and *Phyllis*.

Could there be another *Gunsmoke* today? According to John Mantley, "We know more about the reality of the West today and so the myth is a lot harder to sell. We know about Wounded Knee, and about Chief Joseph's magnificent march, so we can't have the Indians circling the wagons anymore and we can't keep portraying bloodthirsty savages who scalped everybody. Nor can we portray the Indians as the glorious, brilliant savage, for that has been done, too. A portion of our society now knows the truth about the West and, therefore, is not prepared to accept any part of the myth. I did the myth and I guess it worked for a while."

A long while.

18 Saving the Marriage
I Love Lucy (1951)

I remember attending a dinner party years ago at which Lucille Ball and her husband, Desi Arnaz, were present. My impressions were as follows: They were funny. They were abrasive. They were loud. They loved spinning stories of incidents in which they intimidated network executives or random agents. They were acutely conscious of who they were. As dinner guests, they were there to perform and I was there to admire their performance.

Such is the protocol with stars. And stars they were.

On one level, Lucy and Desi eventually came to represent the classic Hollywood success story. She was the wannabe actress who came to Hollywood, struggled to get noticed, started getting promising roles, and met a naughty Cuban party boy who was a nightclub performer six years her junior. They quarreled and struggled some more, then fell into an amazing television deal that they did everything they could to mess up. And out of the mess came showbiz immortality.

I Love Lucy was not just another successful TV show. It was a milestone. It changed the medium in fundamental ways. Its following was vast and astonishingly loyal.

And it was all accomplished for basically the wrong reasons. Lucille Ball agreed to do the show because she thought it would save her marriage. She knew that when Desi toured with his band, their union became a sham. And even though the network brass and agency suits didn't want to deal with a brash Cuban who claimed to know more about comedy than they, Lucy made it clear there would be no show without Desi.

A ferocious infighter, Lucy got her way. What followed was a classic tale of clashing egos, grudge fights, and battles over money. And what emerged was a multicamera sitcom filmed before a live audience in Hollywood, not New York, (where the network had wanted to make it) that became an instant money machine, still churning out millions some fifty years later.

In 1951, however, when television was still suffering through the pangs of adolescence and just starting to win eyeballs from the movie screen, *I Love Lucy* was a wake-up call. The TV set, it seemed, could become not just a distraction, but a habit. It couldn't sell tickets but it could move products. Madison Avenue, which scorned *I Love Lucy* at first, quickly came to embrace it, realizing that amid all the screaming and yelling, Lucy and Desi were absolute masters of their craft. All the more reason why the suits resented them, and why audiences craved their presence.

To millions of TV watchers around the world, Desi Arnaz was the guy in the ruffled shirt singing "Babalu" and popping his eyes at his zany redhead wife. Although every episode centered on the clowning of Lucille Ball, it was Arnaz and Jess Oppenheimer, the producers, who masterminded the TV show into a groundbreaking mega-hit.

Oppenheimer knew his mandate: Develop a TV show that wouldn't require Lucy to move to New York from her Chatsworth, California, home. Lucy wanted a show, wanted to be flatteringly photographed, and most important, wanted to save her marriage. Arnaz brought a fiery ego and shrewd business instincts to the planning; Oppenheimer brought common sense and organizational skills.

Lucy and Arnaz met in 1940 when both were starring in an RKO movie titled, ironically, *Too Many Girls*, a film adaptation of the Rodgers and Hart stage musical in which Arnaz had delivered a showstopping conga number.

Lucy used to joke that it wasn't love at first sight: It took her a good five minutes to fall in love with him. They married that same year, but the marriage wasn't an easy one. He lived the life of a bandleader on the road. Back at home, Lucy had several miscarriages, putting even more strain on their marriage.

In the early '50s, the networks started to succeed in translating radio shows to TV, such as the *George Burns and Gracie Allen Show*. Lucy was at that time starring in a radio comedy with Richard Denning, called *My Favorite Husband*, and the plan was to reteam the two in a TV version. But then Lucy came forth with her dictum: She would only do the show if Desi were the costar. She wanted to know where he was and what he was doing. It was all about Desi.

Desiderio Alberto Arnaz y de Acha III was born on March 2, 1917, in Santiago, Cuba, where his father was mayor. Desi's grandfather was one of the original partners in the Bacardi Rum Company. By the age of sixteen, he had his own car, boat, and stable of horses. The family had wealth and power, but lost everything in 1933 during the Batista revolution. His father was imprisoned, and Desi and his mother fled to Miami. (They were eventually successful in getting the senior Arnaz released from prison.)

Desi showed a talent for musical showmanship early on, and he was hired by Xavier Cugat, a Cuban who was known as "the king of Latin music." He soon left Cugat to form his own Latin band. He earned a living primarily as a nightclub performer, continuing to tour the country even after his marriage to Ball.

Lucille Désirée Ball was born August 6, 1911, in Jamestown, New York; her father died when she was four and her mother worked several jobs; Lucille and her younger brother ended up being raised by their grandparents.

At age fifteen, she dropped out of high school and traveled to New York City, where she studied drama at the Anderson–Milton Dramatics School. Intimidated by her classmates (one was Bette Davis), Ball was sent home after six weeks for being too shy. Sensing she didn't have the talent, she decided to capitalize on her looks.

She found modeling work at Hattie Carnegie's, and in 1933 was chosen to be a Goldwyn Girl and appear in the film *Roman Scandals*. Later, she was put under contract to RKO and soon landed solid supporting roles. She played a wisecracking blonde in the Fred Astaire–Ginger Rogers *Follow the Fleet*, not much of a stretch it would seem, and costarred with Katharine Hepburn in *Stage Door*. She was now a working actress, if not a star.

Her marriage, in November 1940, would not have pleased the matchmakers. Aside from their culture clash, there was their six-year age difference: to fix it, they both lied on their marriage license, she subtracting three years from her real age, and he adding three, so that they were both born in 1914.

Arnaz was a handsome party boy with a fiery temper and a roving eye, but was nonetheless very direct in his business dealings. Contemporaries described the business side of Lucy in much the same manner: Extremely blunt, often abrasive, capable of incredible loyalty or, conversely, dismissing someone instantaneously if she felt betrayed or disobeyed. While her career kept growing, his did not.

Lucy was good enough in RKO's 1942 *The Big Street* that MGM wooed her, casting her in *Du Barry Was a Lady* (1943), then *Best Foot Forward* (1943), and the Katharine Hepburn–Spencer Tracy movie, *Without Love.*

The quarrels between Lucy and Desi became so intense, however, that in 1944 she filed for divorce. In a bizarre twist, the divorce petition was voided, since California law stipulated that if a couple had spent the night together, the divorce could not be granted. She had been with him the night before.

In July 1948, her career took a sharp turn. Harry Ackerman, vice president and director of TV and radio for CBS, read a novel by Isabel Scott Rorick called *Mr. and Mrs. Cugat*, about a married couple trying to survive a culture clash. He thought it would be a good vehicle for Lucy and asked Frank Fox and Bill Davenport, who'd written for *Ozzie and Harriet*, to create it. The show was called *My Favorite Husband.*

Lee Bowman played a bank vice president, while Lucy starred as his madcap socialite wife (Bowman soon dropped out and was replaced by Richard Denning.) Serving as supporting foils were Gale Gordon and Bea Benaderet as an older, richer couple. The network billed it as sophisticated humor; the show was sustaining—meaning it didn't have a sponsor—and it wasn't likely to get one, given the low ratings.

When Fox and Davenport returned to *Ozzie and Harriet*, Ackerman called Jess Oppenheimer and asked if he wanted to submit a script for *Favorite Husband*. The timing was perfect: Oppenheimer was a talented radio writer whose six-year stint on the *Baby Snooks* radio show had just ended, and who needed a job.

As a struggling young writer, Oppenheimer had signed with an agent named Ray Stark, who arranged for him to write for *Baby Snooks*, the show that starred Stark's mother-in-law Fanny Brice. The former Ziegfeld star played a mischievous and precocious little girl who drove her daddy crazy because she was always getting into scrapes. By 1948, the show had run into trouble: The budgets of most radio shows were being cut back since production and advertising money were increasingly being funneled into TV. Brice was earning $5,000 each week. When the network asked her to go down to $4,000, she refused. The show went off the air, so Oppenheimer, who had just bought a new house and had a baby on the way, jumped at the chance to write for Lucy's new radio show.

His son, Gregg Oppenheimer recalls, "He essentially turned Lucy into *Baby Snooks*—a little girl in a grown woman's body. Her relationship with her husband became more like her relationship with her daddy. Basically, Lucy Ricardo was born."

The audience loved it, and soon *My Favorite Husband* was a success.

CBS hired Jess Oppenheimer as head writer, and later gave him the job of producing and directing the show.

Oppenheimer's friends warned him not to commit to it, given Lucy's difficult reputation. The previous director had been fired after a series of fights. But Fanny Brice hadn't been a picnic, either. Oppenheimer took the job and within a few weeks the show had a sponsor, Jell-O Foods.

When Lucy started the radio show her performance was very stiff, so one day at a rehearsal, Oppenheimer gave Lucy tickets to see *The Jack Benny Show*. Benny was a master at playing the audience, even on radio. When Lucy returned from the theater she told Oppenheimer she hadn't appreciated the value of the Jack Benny technique. From then on, he said, they sometimes needed a butterfly net to get her back to the microphone.

Inevitably, CBS decided to move the radio show to TV. Lucy agreed with the aforementioned proviso: She'd do the show with Desi, or she wouldn't do it at all.

"CBS wasn't interested," Gregg Oppenheimer says. "They didn't think people would be able to understand Desi, let alone accept him as her husband. And her famous response was, 'What do you mean? He *is* my husband!'"

To prove audience acceptance, Lucy and Desi embarked on an extraordinary vaudeville tour across the country, performing a series of sketches in which Desi sang and she clowned. There was even a skit in which she imitated a seal. The tour was a success. *Variety* called the opening night in Chicago "one of the best bills in recent months . . . If the redheaded gal wants to slide on her tummy for five or six shows a day, General Artists Corp. should have no trouble lining up dates."

The executives at CBS were impressed by Lucy's determination, but still skeptical about Desi. Madison Avenue allies of the couple suggested they finance their own pilot, thus ending their dependence on CBS.

At this point, however, Lucy and Desi received a stroke of luck. NBC made it known they were interested in hiring both Lucy and Desi, a fact that brought CBS quickly back to the table.

Again, Lucy came forth with her demands. The show had to be shot biweekly in Los Angeles. Jess Oppenheimer would run it. Lucy and Desi's company, Desilu, would have a 50 percent stake in it. And, of course, she wanted Desi.

CBS now succumbed to her demands. They had a deal, but still didn't have a show. Jess Oppenheimer had an epiphany about how to depict Desi: He would be a bandleader, but when he gets home at night, wants nothing to do with showbiz. The rub is that his wife thinks showbiz is the most glamorous thing in the world and wants nothing *but* it. "So there's this tension

I Love Lucy

between them, he's trying to stay out of it and she's trying to get into it," Gregg Oppenheimer points out. CBS liked the conflict, so they prepared to shoot a pilot, though Desi was still negotiating even as they were ready to shoot.

Finally, the network gave Arnaz an ultimatum: Sign the contract as is or the pilot will be shut down. Desi called CBS's bluff. When told that the pilot would cost $19,000, Desi replied, "Fine, then Lucy and I will pay for it ourselves and we'll own it." CBS executives again backed down.

On March 2, 1951, Lucy and Desi performed the still untitled pilot. In the show, orchestra leader Ricky Lopez (Desi) has a TV audition for his band. Knowing his wife will want to worm into the act, he devises a ruse to get her out of the way, whereby she will have to deliver their wills to a lawyer's office. Lucy defies this plan, however. Discovering that a clown named Pepito has fallen ill, Lucy goes to the audition and performs Pepito's routine. That routine featured some of the physical gags and dialogue from the Desi-and-Lucy vaudeville act. Needless to say, she did fine.

Lucy's agent, Don Sharpe, went to New York with a kinescope of the pilot, visited all of the major ad agencies, and they weren't interested. Sharpe finally took it to the Biow Agency. Its client, Philip Morris, liked the idea, but wanted a weekly series, not biweekly. Also, the characters' original last name, Lopez, had to be changed to Ricardo to avoid confusion with Vincent Lopez, a contemporary bandleader. Milton Biow even screened it for his friends, Richard Rodgers and Oscar Hammerstein II. Rodgers knew Desi, who had appeared in *Too Many Girls* on Broadway, but after watching the pilot, Hammerstein gave this one-line assessment: "Keep the redhead, ditch the Cuban."

Biow told Hammerstein it wasn't possible: Lucy and Desi came as a package deal. Hammerstein replied, "For God's sake, then don't let him sing. No one will understand him."

In the pilot, of course, Arnaz sings—a lot. Biow then amended his contract to stipulate that Arnaz was not allowed to sing unless it was integral to the story. As a result, the producers were very careful in the first season to make sure that Desi's numbers fit into the plot.

With plans for the first season shaping up, the three writers began writing scripts for the series, even though the series itself still needed a name. The ideas were prosaic: *The Lucy and Desi Show* and *The Lucille Ball and Desi Arnaz Show*.

Jess Oppenheimer said of Arnaz, "He just couldn't understand why we had Lucy's name ahead of his. Why couldn't he be first? After about a week of going back and forth with him on this, I finally managed to convince him that it was the 'gallant' thing to do—to let the lady go first. But even then he came back to me one more time, saying, 'I tell you what, Jess, why don't we compromise and make it alphabetical?'"

It finally was time to choose. Said Oppenheimer: "As I sat at my desk, I kept coming back to the same title: 'I Love Lucy.' That's the one, I decided. It would convey the essential nature of the show—an examination of marriage between two people who truly love each other. As I thought more about my choice, I realized that I had just solved another problem as well. The 'I' in 'I Love Lucy' was Desi. I had given him first-place billing after all."

When Biow returned from a European vacation, he phoned Oppenheimer to ask, "When are you and the Arnazes moving to New York?" Oppenheimer said there was never a plan to do the show in New York: It would be done in Los Angeles with kinescopes, just like *The Alan Young Show*.

Biow wasn't pleased. Kinescopes were not an ideal way to watch TV: They were essentially videotaped off a TV monitor, a copy of a copy. But it was necessary when shooting in the West: A coaxial cable wasn't yet in place to connect the West Coast to the East Coast. Viewers on the East Coast—who vastly outnumbered all other time zones—would have to make due with a version of the show filmed right off the TV screen. "Jess, I'm not going to sponsor a show in which 15 percent of the country sees it clearly and the other 85 percent of the country sees it through cheesecloth," Biow told him.

Once again, it looked like the whole thing was going to fall apart. Oppenheimer frantically called CBS. He knew that the TV pilot for the radio program *Amos 'n Andy* had been shot at Hal Roach Studios like a movie: filmed out of sequence and then edited together. The *Amos 'n Andy* producers had left space in the film to add audience laughter (there was no such thing as a laugh track back then).

Oppenheimer showed the *Amos 'n Andy* pilot to Biow, who agreed that *Lucy* could film in Hollywood, as long as the picture quality was as good as *Amos 'n Andy*. But if the film wasn't up to snuff, Biow would make everybody move to New York.

The decision to film the show created several new problems. First, it was more expensive; the added $5,000 per week hadn't been factored into the budget. Don Sharpe, Lucy and Desi's agent, proposed a solution. His clients' total combined pay would be $4,000 weekly and 50 percent of the profits. Desi, as usual, had a better idea. He'd take the pay cut on the first thirty-nine shows, provided CBS agree that Desilu will then own the shows in future years. Desi argued that Lucy was giving up her movie career, and he was sacrificing his lucrative career as a bandleader. "If we cut our salary," he stressed, "we have to own the negatives." He figured he could then sell the show in Canada or overseas.

Incredibly, CBS agreed. It was a decision that ultimately cost the network untold millions. At that point, of course, there was no such thing as a rerun. TV was essentially a live medium and nobody considered that someone might want to watch the same episodes at a later time.

The notion of shooting on film had also raised another issue besides finances: Where to put the audience. "You didn't want to take the audience away from Lucy, because all the energy would come out of it," Gregg Oppenheimer says. The network didn't want to emulate the *Amos 'n Andy* method of shooting in silence. (Some *Lucy* experts say they can always spot which scenes were filmed in pickups after the audience had left, since her energy is lower when she says a line.)

"The legend is that Desi had the idea to film in front of a live audience, but it really just sort of evolved," Gregg Oppenheimer says.

Some proposed a technique similar to filming early talkies when scenes would be filmed with multiple cameras. Ralph Edwards' *Truth or Consequences*, sponsored by Philip Morris, was filmed in front of an audience with three cameras. To facilitate this for *I Love Lucy*, Karl Freund, who normally only worked in feature films, devised a system of lighting that would keep the illumination evenly balanced over the entire set. Lights were suspended from a maze of catwalks which kept the power cables off the floor, allowing the three cameras freedom of movement without a break in action.

Because the producers decided to keep all three cameras rolling—creating acres of film—a special multiheaded Moviola was built with three picture heads and one sound head. After the film had been processed, the producers would sit in a closet with the machine and watch the material of all three cameras simultaneously. Without this they would never have had the time to edit the show in a week.

After the first pilot, the writers realized that the Ricardos needed some foils—namely Fred and Ethel Mertz, the Ricardos' landlords. Lucy's first choices were Gale Gordon and Bea Benaderet, who'd played the roles of the older couple on the radio show, but both were unavailable. William Frawley pursued the role of Fred, but CBS executives were wary because he had a reputation for loving his booze. Desi warned Frawley that if he ever showed up late, he was out, and Frawley was punctual throughout the run of the show.

Desi hired Vivian Vance after seeing her in a play in La Jolla, California. At the time, however, she was recovering from a nervous breakdown. When she showed up at the first reading, Lucy complained the actress didn't look like her image of Ethel Mertz. She was right. Ethel was supposed to be Lucy's older friend, yet Vance was a year younger. Though ultimately Vance won everyone over, her contract stipulated that the actress had to remain twenty pounds overweight, to make sure Ethel was frumpier than Lucy. Vance was smart enough to give in to the whims of the star. Vance said, "If this show were a hit, it would be the biggest thing that ever happened in my career, so I made up my mind: I was going to learn to love the bitch." This wasn't the case with Frawley, her on-camera husband, though. He and Ball loathed each other.

There was one final crisis before the show began: CBS had forgotten to tell Arnaz that the network had given away a piece of the show to Oppenheimer. As they get ready for the start of shooting, Oppenheimer was nervous; he hadn't seen a contract. He mentioned to Desi the fact that he'd been promised 20 percent. Arnaz became enraged with the network and threatened to cancel the whole thing.

Jess Oppenheimer remembered: "When I told Lucy that the network had simply forgotten to inform her about my deal, she started to sob. 'Jess,' she said, 'If we don't go through this show, everyone will say we failed. My entire career is at stake!'" After heated negotiation, Desi finally agreed to let Oppenheimer have the 20 percent interest.

There were still minor glitches at the filming. Fearing that an audience wouldn't sit still if there were delays in the filming, Desi insisted that the show be shot with four cameras. One camera would be covering while the other was reloading, so the shooting would be continuous. This meant the actors didn't have time for any costume changes, so they would wear all their wardrobe at once, shedding clothing between scenes. Oppenheimer realized it wouldn't work. After the first show, he told the band to entertain the audience during breaks.

I Love Lucy premiered on October 15, 1951, and earned a 38.7 rating and a stunning 56 share of the total TV audience. The critical praise was unanimous. A month later, it hit the Top Ten. *Variety* reported that an average of 29 million viewers watched every week, more than double the number of people who see the average Hollywood film during its total domestic first run.

"Some of the material they did was not totally original," acknowledges Gregg Oppenheimer. "My dad stole from himself; he took stuff from *Baby Snooks*. There was a famous routine where Lucy hires an English tutor, which was first done on *Baby Snooks*."

One explanation for the lack of original material could be that there were only three writers hired for the show, one of them doing-double duty as producer. In the first year they turned out forty shows in forty weeks. (On a contemporary TV series twenty-four shows a year may be handled by a staff of twelve to fifteen writers.) "They never would have been able to do that, except that they had a nice backlog of story ideas from the radio show," Gregg Oppenheimer says.

Audiences loved the show. So did the industry. Dozens of production companies in Hollywood studied the technical innovations, as well as the creative decisions.

During the 1952–53 season, some fourteen series tried to emulate *Lucy*, including *Leave It to Lester* and *Doc Corkle*. One direct imitation was *I Married Joan*, starring comedienne Joan Davis as the wacky blonde wife of a straight-laced judge.

Meanwhile, Desilu was becoming a training ground for writers as well as a production force to be reckoned with. When *Our Miss Brooks* was in the planning stages, Arnaz struck an agreement with CBS to take over production of the show. Other shows would soon follow.

Season two brought a new hitch: Lucy was pregnant. CBS and the Biow Agency were against the idea of showcasing the pregnancy. They offered a compromise: One or two episodes could deal with it, but that's it. Arnaz fired off a letter to chairman Alfred E. Lyons of Philip Morris, warning, "We will cease to be responsible to you for the show being the No. 1 show on television and you will have to look to your people."

Lyons then issued this confidential memo to the ad agency: "Don't fuck around with the Cuban!"

CBS still was insistent. "The network had issued a firm edict that we could not use the word 'pregnant' on the show," said Jess Oppenheimer. "We could say she was 'expecting.' She could be 'with child,' but never 'pregnant.' They were still deathly afraid that some segment of the public would find something offensive." CBS finally agreed that a priest, a minister, and a rabbi must approve each of the "baby show" scripts.

Desilu was producing thirty-six to thirty-nine shows a year, but there was no way Lucy could keep up that pace. Oppenheimer thus went to CBS and suggested rerunning some of the first-season episodes in primetime. Executives dismissed the notion, saying no one wanted to watch a rerun of *I Love Lucy*. Oppenheimer countered that they would film a new opening scene and make it into a flashback show. The characters would open the show, and reminisce, "Remember the time . . ." and then the show would fade out into a repeat.

CBS agreed, and they aired ten reruns of *Lucy* in the show's second year. They also filmed several all-new episodes that began with flashbacks. Flashback episodes have since become a staple in sitcoms.

Part of the impetus for the flashbacks was that episodes would be filmed before Lucy gave birth, but wouldn't appear until after Lucy had the baby on the show. Additional episodes were shot in August before she was showing too much and the producers pretended like it was a year earlier.

The first rerun of *I Love Lucy* came in May 1952, when a few CBS affiliates wanted to rebroadcast an episode to fill in their schedule. Lucy and Desi signed an agreement with CBS waiving all rights to payment—the last time they were to cut their fees. But with the pregnancy, reruns became more frequent, and CBS was stunned to realize that viewers liked them. The floodgates had suddenly opened.

Lucy gave birth to Desi Arnaz Jr. on January 19, 1953—the same night that "Little Ricky" was born to the Ricardos on TV. When "Lucy Goes to the Hospital" aired, a record 44 million people tuned in to witness the birth of Little Ricky, garnering a record 71.7 percent of the viewing audience. That topped even the 67.7 percent rating for Dwight Eisenhower's inauguration coverage the following morning.

As the show matured, Lucy and Desi had fewer fights with the network sponsors and even their writers. On June 10, 1954, *I Love Lucy* filmed the 100th episode and Lucy was quick to credit the writers. "I appreciate them daily, I praise them hourly, and I thank God for them every night," she said at the party. Earlier, accepting an L.A. Press Club award, she said, "Without my writers I'm dead" and she inscribed photos to Oppenheimer with "To the Boss man." That wasn't idle praise.

Jess Oppenheimer had been in charge of production and postproduction as well as overseeing casting and costumes and writing scripts in the long range.

In April 1955, the show began airing twice a week, in its usual primetime slot and on Sunday afternoons. The reruns of *I Love Lucy* even started topping first-run programming, including *The Honeymooners*, in the ratings. First-run *I Love Lucy* was still number one, while the reruns were tied for tenth.

Meanwhile, Desilu had become a major company in TV. By 1955, it was employing 3,300 people. Finally, in need of cash to fund their growing company, Lucy and Desi sold their interest in the show to CBS for $4.5 million in 1956.

They used the money wisely. General Tire and Rubber Company had bought RKO studios in 1955 from Howard Hughes for $25 million. By 1957, General Tire was ready to sell, and Desilu bought the studio for $6.15 million. Hence, years after they worked for RKO, Lucy and Desi owned their old alma mater. With the purchase, Desilu gained fifteen stages and fourteen acres. Added to their Motion Picture Center, Desilu now controlled thirty-three soundstages—four more than MGM and eleven more than Fox.

And it needed the space. In its heyday, Desilu created over fifty primetime series, including *The Untouchables*, *Our Miss Brooks*, and another series that became a phenomenon—*Star Trek*.

At the end of the 1956–57 season, Lucy and Desi decided they no longer wanted the grind of a weekly show. As their marriage began to crumble, the two opted to do once-a-month, one-hour specials, under the banner of the *Lucille Ball–Desi Arnaz Show*.

Sponsor General Foods dropped out, saying the $350,000 per hour price tag was too high. Network affiliates were also dismayed, but the shows, featuring guest stars such as Ernie Kovacs, Danny Thomas, Tallulah Bankhead, and Ann Southern, fared well.

On May 6, 1957, the final half-hour episode of *I Love Lucy* aired. In all, there had been 179 half-hour and thirteen hour-long shows. The Desilu empire officially ended in 1967 when it was sold to the Gulf + Western conglomerate.

Lucy continued to star in sitcoms, including *Here's Lucy* and *The Lucy Show*, costarring with Vance again as well as her two children, Lucie Arnaz and Desi Arnaz Jr. She again filed for divorce in 1960. This time it wasn't voided.

Desi Arnaz later wrote a candid autobiography titled *A Book*, detailing his alcoholism and infidelities. He had planned to write a sequel called *Another Book*, but he died in 1986.

Virtually every sitcom on the air has borrowed something from *I Love Lucy* but now the pace of TV production moves much slower. It wasn't uncommon for an audience to sit for five hours during the shoot of *Friends* in the mid '90s, watching the actors go through several run-throughs and pick-ups. On *I Love Lucy* the audience filed in and less than an hour later the actors said, "Thank you ladies and gentlemen, good night."

"I wish they still shot things the way they shot it back then," Gregg Oppenheimer bemoans. "Everything now is shot three times, like they haven't decided which version of a joke is better so they try it two or three ways. Back then, they thought of it as a play, an evening in the theater every time you heard the audience laugh, they're hearing jokes for first time. That's the reason it seemed that much fresher."

The producers were proud that they never "sweetened" the show—i.e., fiddled with the sound to make the laughs seem bigger. There were only two occasions when *Lucy*'s laughs were altered. The first occurred in 1953, right after TV's favorite redhead was accused of being a "pinko." Lucy had registered as a communist once, she later explained, only to please her grandfather when she was young. On the evening of filming, after the allegations were revealed, Arnaz came out and gave an emotional speech. The audience gave him and then Lucy an ovation. In fact, the audience was so supportive, that even the simplest set-up line earned a big laugh from the audience. The producers deliberately toned down the laughs and applause.

The second time was in a March 1957 episode titled "Lucy Does the Tango." Lucy raises chickens in the story, but Ricky gets irate when they won't lay eggs. Her brilliant solution is to smuggle in five dozen store-bought eggs under her clothes and pass them off as the result of her chickens' labor. On her way to unload the eggs, she encounters Ricky who says that they must practice their tango routine immediately. As he pulls her body into his, the sixty eggs break, and the audience emits a record sixty-five-second laugh. The producers cut the laughs, feeling it all had gone on too long.

The *Lucy* producers ended up with a substantial laugh library, which seemed at the time to be a bizarre resource. But when the era of the laugh track machine was born, the creators relied on the *Lucy* library of laughs.

Jess Oppenheimer finally left the show in 1956, one year before it stopped being a weekly half-hour. He went on to many further TV credits, most notably as a producer of the spy spoof *Get Smart*. But he never sold his stake in *Lucy*, as had Lucy and Desi.

"I've got memos that say 'This is probably going to run for three, four, five years at most; by that time it'll be old," Gregg Oppenheimer says. "Nobody imagined such longevity at the time they were doing the show. They were just trying to do their job each week. They knew it was a hit and they were enjoying that a great deal, but they had no clue. They never would have sold out if they sensed it would last more than fifty years. I think it's going to last forever."

19 Painful Homecoming
The Best Years of Our Lives (1946)

As with most great films, the key players involved in *The Best Years of Our Lives* initially felt it was a dubious idea. And their reasons seemed sound.

This was to be a great movie about war—indeed perhaps the definitive Hollywood film about soldiers and the price they paid. But was it destined to be the right movie at the wrong time—that was the question that haunted all the principals involved.

Three years earlier, in 1943, Samuel Goldwyn had produced another movie about World War II, *The North Star*, directed by Lewis Milestone, and it had been a failure. Goldwyn didn't like failure, and not only was *Best Years* about war, but its story was intrinsically downbeat.

MacKinlay Kantor, the author of the basic story, had just returned from flying combat missions as a war correspondent and was weary of war and war stories. Besides, Kantor, a tall, handsome man of great bravado, was anxious to shed his growing image as a wannabe Hemingway.

William Wyler, the director of the film, had himself just returned from combat only to endure an awkward and difficult reunion with his wife and family after his prolonged absence. The episode seemed disturbingly close to the plot of *Best Years*; besides, Wyler was not sure he wanted to return to Hollywood after his searing experience.

And finally, Robert E. Sherwood, the distinguished author of many plays (*Waterloo Bridge* among them), whom Goldwyn would ultimately approach to write the movie, had abandoned screenwriting after *Rebecca* in 1940. He'd been serving as head of the Office of War Information and was weighing a possible career in politics. Besides, he felt the story of *Best Years*—the agonizing adjustment of wounded veterans returning to their families before war's end—might seem badly dated by the time the movie was released.

Thus, there were abundant reasons out there not to tackle *Best Years*. Even if it turned out superbly, it would still be a movie dealing with a subject most Americans would just as soon put behind them. The war was drawing to an end. The world would soon get back to normal. Americans would want to move on.

But despite all this, *Best Years*, like most potentially great ideas, had developed a certain momentum. Though one obstacle after another kept presenting itself, other forces kept pushing it forward. And the most important force was the unique personality of Samuel Goldwyn himself.

Sam Goldwyn was a revered, if distinctly idiosyncratic, member of Hollywood's producing fraternity. Having arrived in town as Samuel Goldfish (originally Gelbfisz), a rather angular, odd-looking man, he quickly set about the task of reinventing himself as a suave connoisseur of the pop arts. As an entrepreneur, he brought it off, boldly establishing a production entity which became the "G" in MGM, then propelling himself forward as perhaps the boldest of the independents. But while respected (and feared) on a business level, Goldwyn never quite meshed on a personal one, and, indeed, used his somewhat gauche persona to his advantage.

Hollywood had long since steeled itself to the incursion of rough-around-the-edges immigrants from Eastern Europe. But Goldwyn, born in Poland, was a special case. For one thing, he never managed to shed his accent or to avoid his systematic mangling of the English language. Mindful that the community liked to cite "Goldwynisms," he made them work to his advantage.

As a young reporter, I had many lunches with him, listening to him hold forth on the ups and downs of his colorful career. He was very candid about his financial debacles, and also ecstatically boastful of his successes. At the end of one of our sessions, he asked as I was leaving, "You didn't hear any 'Goldwynisms,' did you?" I looked at him in surprise. It was unusual for a Hollywood mogul to reveal such self-awareness. "I know you reporters like to collect these things. I'm used to it."

In fact some Goldwynisms had become legendary, such as: "A verbal agreement isn't worth the paper it's written on" and "I can answer you in two words—im possible." So now, Goldwyn was going to grant me access to a newly minted Goldwynism and I felt duly privileged. "This morning my lawyer reminded me that this particular agent I'm dealing with screwed me on our last deal a few years ago." Goldwyn continued, "So I told him, 'Forget it, I've passed a lot of water since then.'" I looked at him, smiled, and quickly realized he wanted me to smile. He agreed that this was funny. His verbal faux pas were characteristic of the Goldwyn Brand. He was taking his own shortcomings and capitalizing on them.

That trait was a key part of Goldwyn's success. He read but was hardly well-read. He tried to school himself in our pop culture, but still remained an outsider. He had some great inspirations for films, but also could come up with numbing mistakes. He was awkward socially, but married an attractive and socially astute former model, Frances, who skillfully rehabilitated his social life and helped him create an ongoing "salon" of socialites, stars, and deep thinkers.

In short, Samuel Goldwyn had formed a steely resolve to become a great man in Hollywood, even if he had to advertise his faults and frailties in achieving that aim. Indeed, the entire experience of *The Best Years of Our Lives* provides a vivid demonstration of vintage Goldwyn.

For one thing, Goldwyn had never read the original material, and, when told about it, showed little interest. His wife, Frances, was leafing through the August 7, 1944, issue of *Time* magazine when she came upon a photograph of a ragtag band of soldiers hanging on to an old train clattering down the tracks in a Midwest town. The photo was titled "Home Again." The article that accompanied it described the experiences of several of the 370 members of the First Marine Division who had been sent home on a thirty-day furlough after more than two years in combat. The war was still raging and, while the soldiers were delighted about a respite, they also were filled with apprehension about the prospect of confronting their wives, girlfriends, and families after their long and traumatic absence. In their interviews, many of the men acknowledged that they could barely remember their loved ones and also were vaguely suspicious about new relationships that they might have formed—new lovers and possibly even new children. "You should make a movie about all this," Frances advised Sam. "It's a devastating story."

Samuel Goldwyn seemed more irritated than appreciative. After the failure of *The North Star*, and with World War II now drawing to a close, would the audience welcome yet another film in this genre? Goldwyn felt Americans wanted to be entertained. They wanted Danny Kaye and his double-speak, not reminders of combat.

But Frances persisted and Goldwyn noticed what was registering on the box office and best-seller charts. Rival producers had competed for the rights to John Hersey's impressive war novel, *A Bell for Adano*. David Selznick's film, *Since You Went Away*, was doing very well, and it dealt with the struggles of a wife and children when the husband goes off to war.

It was fortuitous that Goldwyn decided to meet with Kantor, a gifted novelist (his Civil War novel, *Long Remember*, had been a best seller). Having served a long tour of duty as a war correspondent, Kantor was open to taking on a Hollywood assignment and Goldwyn, despite himself, was suddenly talking about a possible film involving returning soldiers. As he talked, the story began to take on new colors. What would it be like to return from the war having never seen your baby? How would you deal with a wife who had become involved with a new lover?

Kantor was skeptical. He'd had enough of the war. He also understood that he looked like a central casting war correspondent. Kantor regarded himself as a serious writer; he wanted to find new images and a new voice.

When Goldwyn offered to write a check for $12,500 to Kantor, however, giving him carte blanche to devise a story, Kantor was seduced. But when they signed the contract, on September 8, 1944, Goldwyn was already distracted by other potential films—a life story of Dwight Eisenhower and a new vehicle for Danny Kaye. What he'd never asked Kantor, and what Kantor never volunteered, was that the novel Kantor had in mind, titled *Glory for Me*, would be written in blank verse.

Five months later, Kantor delivered his novel, which followed three servicemen, all discharged for medical causes, returning to the same hometown of Boone City (modeled after Cincinnati). The men were strangers before the war, but meet on an Army plane taking them home. Al Stephenson, (to be played by Frederic March) is an infantry sergeant returning to his wife, two children, and his banking job. Homer Parrish (Harold Russell) is a young sailor who's lost both his hands. Fred Derry (Dana Andrews) is a bombardier on his way back to his war bride, whom he barely knew before departing for service.

Goldwyn was not pleased with the manuscript, or the fact that it was in blank verse. He promptly shelved the project.

I remember Kantor railing over Goldwyn's decision one evening at his Fifth Avenue apartment in Manhattan. Kantor's son, Tim, was a school friend of mine; it was clear that Tim, too, regarded his dad as somewhat larger than life.

Like many successful novelists, Kantor was contemptuous of Hollywood. Employing blank verse to tell his tale clearly represented his defiance of the system; he wasn't going to write another "Hollywood novel."

Kantor's attitude epitomized the spirit of the time. With the war over, everyone was basically trying to start life anew and to reconsider their basic aims and values. The studios had been accustomed to issuing orders, but no one seemed in an order-taking mood any longer.

Had it not been for William Wyler, Kantor's book probably would have stayed on the stack of projects in "turnaround."

Wyler, the Oscar-winning director of *Mrs. Miniver* (1942), was discharged from the army in the summer of 1945, a changed man. "The war had been an escape into reality," he told a biographer, Jan Herman. "In the war, it didn't matter how much money you earned. The only thing that mattered was human relationships—not money, not position, not even family." Wyler felt he could no longer take anything for granted, especially in Hollywood. He had plans for a different future, but he still owed Goldwyn a picture under his old contract, a contract that had earned him $150,000 a year in 1939.

When Wyler visited Goldwyn's offices to discuss a possible final project, Goldwyn showed him *Glory for Me* only as an afterthought. In fact, when Wyler told him a week later he liked it, Goldwyn tried to talk him out of it. "He thought it was nothing—$10,000 wasted," Wyler recalled. Instead, Goldwyn was hoping that Wyler would shoot the Eisenhower project—a potential epic with superstars that would have a worldwide audience. But Wyler was adamant; Kantor's novel, he said, whatever its failings, depicted the ordinary GI—not a general. "I've come home twice from the war and I know just how these fellows feel," he said. "No man can walk right into that house after two or three years and pick up his life as before."

In fact, when Wyler returned home from battle, his wife, Talli, was waiting for him in New York. Talli, recalling their reunion, at the Hampshire House on New York's Central Park South said, "You're strangers but you're not supposed to be—yet you are for a moment. You've been very intimate, you've been away from each other for so long, and suddenly you're intimate again. It's lovely but it's awkward." Wyler would use their meeting as a model for the famous reunion scene in *Best Years*, when homecoming Al (March) surprises his wife Milly (Myrna Loy). These men must now court their wives again, yet don't have the energy to do so. They prefer to drink and hang out with buddies, though the liquor cabinets are empty and there is only enough food for mother and child. In the movie, Peggy (Teresa Wright) tells Milly that they don't have enough bacon for breakfast. Peggy, meanwhile, reveals that the maid took a night off three years ago and never came back. Earlier, Fred (Dana Andrews) asks Al, "Do you remember what it was like when we went overseas?" to which Al replies, "As well as I remember my own name." And Fred says, "I feel the same way, only more so . . . nervous out of the service."

Once Wyler got Goldwyn back on the *Glory for Me* track, they found themselves in agreement on the one person that could do this screenplay justice: three-time Pulitzer Prize winner Robert Sherwood. But, Sherwood was no longer writing screenplays. He had taken on important duties in Washington.

Goldwyn arranged a meeting in Hollywood between Sherwood and William Wyler. It seemed to go well, but soon afterward Sherwood returned to New York and sent a memo to Goldwyn passing on the project. Sherwood's concern was that the story would seem dated. It concerned men who were released, for medical reasons, before the war had ended. Their problems, however, would seem marginalized when every American city had tens of thousands of soldiers and sailors who had returned to civilian life, having already passed through the stages of readjustment before the picture could be released. Sherwood feared that the picture would arouse "considerable resentment" in suggesting that the neuroses of this minority of vets reflected, those of all returning servicemen.

Several conversations did not ease Sherwood's concerns, but a telegram from Goldwyn on September 4, 1944 did. "Dear Bob," Goldwyn wired:

> I want to restate my feelings about the story. I have more faith in it now than I did six months ago because I feel the subject matter will be even more timely a year from now than it is today. As you said, there will be several million men coming home next year, and more of them the year after and to release a picture at that time presenting their problems seems to me to be hitting it right on the nose. You had the right approach to the civilian point of view and this, coupled with your desire to inject some good American humor throughout, should make it one of your outstanding writing jobs.

By December 1945, Sherwood had delivered more than 100 pages. According to Scott Berg's superb biography of Goldwyn, Sherwood, along with his wife, was staying with the Goldwyns in Beverly Hills. Most days they did not discuss the project; Sherwood would keep the writing to himself. One day, however, Sherwood confessed to Goldwyn that one element of the plot was disturbing him. In Kantor's novel, Derry finds his wife making love to another man on his first night home. In Sherwood's screenplay, however, Derry can't find her on his first night home and does not discover her infidelity. Indeed in the script a love story develops between Derry and Al Stephenson's grown daughter, Peggy. This change allowed Derry to come home to his wife, try to pick up where his marriage had left off, and then discover that neither of them loved the other. Not until the end of the film, however, would he decide to leave her. At the same time, Sherwood enlarged on the character of Peggy.

Sherwood made sure that all of the stories served the central love story.

For example, all pivotal scenes for Derry and Peggy would happen at Butch's place, the town's main watering hole (Butch was Parrish's uncle). Another tweak of Sherwood's script involved Parrish, who was spastic in the novel but not in the movie. "I realized," Wyler said, "that no actor, no matter how great, could play a spastic with conviction."

In April 1946, Sherwood finished the screenplay—which, at 220 pages, ran twice the length of a normal script—but Wyler suddenly developed a case of nerves. The script was not ready, he insisted. Goldwyn explained that the cast had been put on salary and would be on set every day until the director showed up. Goldwyn also warned that Wyler would be expected to pay the expenses accrued by delaying production. Wyler was on set the very next day.

In casting the film, Goldwyn saw opportunities for all of his young contract players. Unlike today's independent producers, Goldwyn had his own stable, befitting his self-image that he was tantamount to a studio. As such, he was anxious to use *Best Years* to help amortize these commitments.

Dana Andrews would play Derry, and novice Virginia Mayo had, in Goldwyn's mind, taken enough acting lessons to play his bimbo of a wife. Meanwhile, Goldwyn's latest discovery, Cathy O'Donnell, could play Wilma, Farley Granger could play Parrish, and Teresa Wright would be a perfect Peggy. Goldwyn had hoped that Fred MacMurray and Olivia de Havilland would sign on for Al and Milly Stephenson. De Havilland, who was in fact not Wyler's prime choice, turned down the role. Wyler had his eyes on Myrna Loy, who was revered as the archetypal super-wife after her portrayal of Nora Charles in *The Thin Man* film series. Since the role of Milly was not large, Goldwyn had to offer Loy top billing. Meanwhile, MacMurray disdained the offer, which he had referred to as a "third banana" gig. March, whose days as a leading man were over—he had just lost out to William Powell for the lead in *Life with Father*—was cast as Al Stephenson.

Goldwyn's worst idea, of course, was Farley Granger. Both Wyler and Sherwood had expressed concerns about casting the Parrish character. Wyler soon found a solution at a war bond rally for disabled vets. A documentary, *Diary of a Sergeant*, recounted the story of Harold Russell, a former meat cutter who had lost both of his hands in a training accident. Wyler admired Russell's positive attitude.

Russell's accident happened at Camp Mackall, North Carolina, in 1944, the same day as D-Day in Normandy. He was a sergeant in a demolition squad, holding a half-pound block of TNT when it exploded. The documentary revealed the remarkable morale of the Washington, D.C., hospital where he was undergoing rehabilitation with other amputees. There was an absence of self-pity. Men with no legs were dubbed "shorty," one-legged men were "limpy," and men with one arm were "paper hangers." Within three weeks, Russell had mastered his hooks.

Prior to his discharge, he appeared in *Diary of a Sergeant*, and when a Goldwyn executive subsequently phoned him to come to Hollywood for an interview, Russell thought it was a prank. He couldn't have been a less likely candidate for pictures. He was prepared to take a job at a local YMCA. "I flew out to Hollywood on an old DC-3 and met with Wyler," Russell recalled. "He took me to lunch at the Brown Derby. When we left the restaurant, Wyler stopped to pay the bill. Somebody who knew him came up and said, 'Gee, that guy does a pretty good job with the hooks.' And Wyler said, 'Yeah, he does a fantastic job. He did the shrimp cocktails. He ate the salad. He cut the steak. But the one thing he can't do is pick up the check."

In prepping his film, Wyler's main objective was that the film seem real—even hyper-real. He told his long-term cameraman, Gregg Toland, that every scene needed to be shot with equal clarity. The scenes would run longer and there would be fewer cuts and shifts of focus. Makeup would be minimized and the cast would wear ordinary clothes from department stores, not an Edith Head-type glamour wardrobe. On the set of the Stephenson family home, Wyler insisted that the cast spend a full day in the mock apartment so that they felt at home with the furnishings. Cast members had to wear their clothes several times so that they looked lived-in. To Wyler's thinking, this was not going to be a "Hollywood movie" in the classic sense, but rather a venture into a new sort of realism.

Wyler was also adamant that March slim down for his role. Wyler wrote a memo to March saying: "You should make every effort to be as trim and wiry as possible. I know it's not easy for fellows our age. I've gained twenty pounds since coming back. But the entire approach to this picture will be along re-alistic lines. I would hate to have something like the proverbial little 'pouch' spoil the illusion."

Wyler also admonished Goldwyn when he learned that the producer had ordered Russell to take acting lessons. "I didn't hire an actor," Wyler yelled. "I hired a guy to play a role." To Wyler, there was a major difference.

Whenever Goldwyn came around to offer Wyler "advice," Wyler's re-sponse was to go into stall mode. The camera crew would assume glacial movements. Goldwyn quickly got the message that nothing was going to be shot until he left.

Russell recalled a time when Wyler arrived late one morning. "Apparently he had just had a meeting with Goldwyn and he was steamed," Russell said. "'This goddamned picture,' Wyler screamed. 'Goldwyn wants it produced by

Sam Goldwyn, directed by Sam Goldwyn, acted by Sam Goldwyn, written by Sam Goldwyn.' The fact is, it was Wyler's picture, no question about it," observed Russell. "It was Wyler's heart and soul. It was Wyler's wisdom that went into everything."

When it came time to select the model for fictional Boone City, presumably the archetypical Midwestern town, Goldwyn's production team toured the United States in a converted Army bomber, filming hundreds of feet of aerial backgrounds for process shots, and screen-testing dozens of towns. Cincinnati was ultimately chosen as the locale. Great care was also taken to keep the set true to life. The drugstore set was so completely stocked that it could have opened for business at a moment's notice and dispensed everything from *Sal Hepatica* to sundaes.

Wyler's realistic approach to his subject matter proved worrisome to the Motion Picture Code. The censors cautioned that scenes depicting drinking should be curtailed or eliminated and that when couples kissed, these kisses should not be "prolonged or lustful." The censors were also worried about the break-up of Fred and Marie: Marital breakups were not the stuff of wholesome movies.

Production wrapped on *Best Years* in August 1946, with nearly 400,000 feet of film ready for editing. The final cut was twice the length of an average film. Goldwyn was well aware that releasing a film that clocked in at two hours and forty minutes was a dicey exercise. But a sneak preview of the film in Long Beach, California, elicited a positive response and the film received applause that lasted several minutes. Thus, after very few cuts were made, Goldwyn decided to release his $2 million gamble.

An official premiere was set for November to ensure Oscar consideration, but the movie would not be released across the country until after the 19th Academy Awards—another gamble.

The gamble paid off. *The Best Years of Our Lives* won seven Oscars, sweeping best picture, actor (March), supporting actor (Russell), screenplay (Sherwood), direction (Wyler), music score (Hugo Friedhofer), and film editing (Daniel Mandell). *Best Years* beat out *It's a Wonderful Life, Henry V, The Yearling,* and *The Razor's Edge.* Russell was the only actor ever to win two Oscars for the same role, supporting actor and a special nod for "bringing hope and courage to his fellow veterans." Goldwyn tearfully accepted the first and only Oscar for best picture that he would ever receive. Billy Wilder handed Wyler his statuette, declaring *Best Years* "the best directed film I've ever seen in my life."

The film went on to gross nearly $11 million by the end of 1947, putting it ahead of *Mrs. Miniver* as the highest grossing film since *Gone with the Wind.*

The critical critic accolades were bountiful. "No synopsis of *Best Years* could begin to do justice to the good showmanship and even better taste with which the authors and producers have solved the post-war problem," said *Newsweek*. "The most admirable film I have sat in on in the year 1946 and I cannot easily see how a better one is going to come along. It has distinction without sacrificing, in the least, the mystic virtues that are supposed to make for popular appeal," wrote the *New York Journal-American*.

For Samuel Goldwyn, *Best Years* was surely his finest hour. The movie underscored his desire not just to be a purveyor of mass entertainment, but also to be a force in pop culture. Others were making escapist fare like *I Married an Angel* or *The Horn Blows at Midnight*, but Goldwyn was bringing his adopted country to its senses with a serious, well crafted cinematic statement.

To be sure, Goldwyn had backed into the project. Without the nagging of his wife, he surely never would have pursued the film. Without the surprise endorsement and passion of Wyler, *Best Years* would have remained an unread novel in blank verse. But somehow the movie had come alive, thanks to a fortunate confluence of inadvertencies. And it was Samuel Goldwyn, most of all, who stood proud.

20 As Time Goes By

Casablanca (1942)

From the first moment I met Hal Wallis, I sensed he was not someone I would get to know, or want to know. A churlish bear of a man with hooded eyes and an abrupt manner, Wallis had opted to spend the final years of his producing life at Paramount Pictures, after a long run at Warner Bros. He was clearly not happy about this decision, but was locked in now, under contract. His life had been focused on making "studio pictures" for "studio executives," and now he found himself working under a new regime at Paramount and having to confront Robert Evans, an actor who'd made his money in the clothing business, and me, an ex-reporter from the *New York Times*. Adding to his discomfort was the fact that this was 1969, an off-putting time for an old Hollywood warhorse like Wallis, a time when tastes were changing and the movie-going audience was shrinking. A deeply conservative man, Wallis did not "get" what was happening to his audience or, for that matter, to the country. Originally from Chicago, he had started as a press agent and had made many millions from his long producing career—in fact, he was known to be one of the wealthiest producers in Hollywood, thanks to good investments and prudent living.

Tough-minded and intuitive, Wallis had decided to concentrate on "play it safe" pictures at Paramount. He didn't want to venture forth into the new "youth culture," which he didn't pretend to understand. There were not many established stars left in the Hollywood firmament, and he wanted to stick to the few with whom he still connected. The safest bet in his estimation was Elvis Presley, and Wallis had turned out a series of Presley pictures, such as *Fun in Acapulco*.

Now I was coming to him with another presumed "safe bet"—a project for John Wayne. I had read the galleys of a new novel called *True Grit* by a young author named Charles Portis, and the image of Wayne playing the grizzled old cowboy tickled my imagination. Most of my attention had been devoted to the supposedly "hot" young filmmakers of the moment—Coppola, Ashby, Bogdanovich—and I was pleased by the notion of fostering a totally retro project. This would demonstrate that even a *Times* reporter understood how to put together a "traditional" studio picture.

I knew Wayne a little bit; he occasionally sat at an adjoining table in the studio commissary and he seemed both affable and larger-than-life. Like all great stars, there was a certain reserve in his demeanor. He would chat with me briefly, but there was a tacit distance between the two of us, as though to emphasize the reality that he was a mythic figure and I was a mere mortal. I considered the possibility of interrupting him amid his customary steak lunch and telling him about *True Grit*, even leaving a copy of the slender volume for him. After all, I was "the studio" in that I could authorize the purchase of rights to the book and assign the project to him if he liked it. But then I thought: I have a small window of opportunity to make this happen. Another studio may buy the book out from under me, and I was reluctant to take it off the market without the interest of the "Duke," as he was called.

And then there was Wallis. As forbidding as he was, Paramount was paying his overhead along with a guaranteed salary, clearly the studio would do well to elicit something for its money besides another Elvis Presley movie. I know that Wallis had a long-standing relationship with Wayne; they were of the same generation and mind-set. Both had made it clear to me that they hated the movies of the moment and disdained the sort of material that I had been working on—films like *Harold and Maude, Rosemary's Baby, The President's Analyst*, et al. So there it was: I would give *True Grit* to Hal Wallis with the suggestion that he read it quickly and pass it on to Wayne.

My meeting with Wallis started as I'd expected. He barely acknowledged my presence. His leonine head hardly moved as I spoke. His office was huge and filled with mementoes of the past—photos of Wallis with various stars, interspersed with all manner of awards and statuettes. He remained frozen at his vast desk. Silver-haired and stooped with age, he looked more like an inanimate symbol of a past era than a living producer. I delivered my message and placed the book on his desk. Wallis said he would assign his aide, Paul Nathan, to the task of "covering it"—no Hollywood veteran would use the expression "read." I emphasized the time constraints, turned, and left.

Returning to my office, I had no sense whether Hal Wallis really had heard me, whether he had paid attention to my message, or indeed whether he even knew who I was. Maybe he thought I was there to write a story for the *Times*. I castigated myself for not going straight to the Duke.

Two days later, Paul Nathan, Wallis's aide, was on the line. He had read it, told his boss about it and Wallis had already described the story to John Wayne, who had committed to star in the role. "Please buy us the book," said Nathan. I promptly did so.

I never again spoke to Wallis about the project, which moved into production within just a few months. Wallis never acknowledged that I'd brought this material to him, even though it turned out to be the Duke's last memorable picture. Nor did I expect that sort of acknowledgement. I knew who I was dealing with. This was the fabled Hal Wallis who knew, better than anyone, how to move things along on the Hollywood assembly line. He had battled the best—especially Jack Warner, who could be as goofy as he was dictorial—and he had won.

He was, after all, the man who made *Casablanca*.

Arguably, only Hal Wallis could have gotten that great film made. It was, in every manifestation, the movie from hell. Jack Warner, just prior to its opening, had told everyone who would listen to him that the film would be a disaster. Humphrey Bogart, Ingrid Bergman, and Paul Henreid, its stars, found the production process so excruciating that they would not talk about it even with friends. As if to confirm their suspicion, studio executives decided to rush the film into release when the Allies invaded North Africa in November 1942, because the city of Casablanca was suddenly in the news: They deemed it the film's only hope of catching the attention of the public. Only the sheer obstinacy and incessant bullying of Wallis, who had been Warner's production chief before becoming a producer at the studio, got the film into the theaters.

In the end, the project had only one thing going for it besides Wallis's willpower; it represented an absolutely ideal confluence of fortunate accidents: Perfect story, perfect cast, perfect moment.

Under the studio system, executives juggled writers, directors, stars, and even producers as if they were puzzle parts. *Casablanca* could have turned out quite differently. Imagine the film starring George Raft, Hedy Lamarr, and Philip Dorn, with Lena Horne playing the piano (but not "As Time Goes By"). At the end, Allied Forces arrive just in time to drive the Nazis out of Casablanca. If the filmmakers had made that version, it might have worked but, more likely, it would have been a snooze, one of those movies that occasionally pops up on late night TV.

Indeed, that was the fate that most of the participants felt was inevitable. Julius J. Epstein, one of the principal writers on the film, told the *Los Angeles Herald Examiner* in 1988, "To us, it was just another assignment. We worked on three scripts a year. It was just another programmer. They used to make a picture a week.... I'm prouder of my previous film, *Reuben, Reuben*, than *Casablanca*. The dialogue is better. And you can quote me on that."

Wallis had received a copy of the failed play *Everybody Comes to Rick's* in December 1941, just after the Japanese bombed Pearl Harbor. The studio paid $20,000 for the play by Murray Burnett and Joan Alison. Sam Marx, the story editor at MGM, had wanted to buy the film rights for $5,000, but his studio didn't think it worth the money.

Had the play reached Wallis's desk in August 1941 and not December, there's a good chance it wouldn't have been bought, as Aljean Harmetz pointed out in her excellent book, *Round Up The Usual Suspects*. The sparring between Rick and the Nazi representatives wouldn't have resonated. And if the play had arrived in 1939, its anti-Nazi script would have been viewed as propaganda. But now, suddenly, American movies had to change to fit America's new image of the war.

Notably, for most of the film, Rick is proud to be neutral about politics and world events, bragging, "I stick my neck out for nobody." Of course, he eventually gets involved. Rick, like America, decides to commit.

By November 1942, the month of the film's premiere in New York, Americans were cautiously optimistic about their new involvement. United States and British troops had invaded North Africa, while the United States Navy sank twenty-three Japanese ships in the Solomon Islands. *Casablanca* would help reassure people that the right decisions had been made.

The film's lucky timing continued with its national release on January 23, 1943. Just as the film opened, newspapers carried the story that Roosevelt and Churchill had held a secret strategy session—in Casablanca.

Long before the French came up with the theory

of director as "auteur," the Hollywood studio system was centered around the producer. In those days, he—and it was always "he"; there were no women producers then—would pick the director, script writer, key actors, cinematographer, even the assistant director.

Wallis had been with Warner's since its early days and for eight years was Jack Warner's number two man. He seemed to thrive under the eighteen-hour days, serving as executive on more than 200 films over two decades, and earning producer credit on projects like *Little Caesar* (1931), *The Adventures of Robin Hood* (1938), and *Sargeant York* (1941).

At age forty-three, Wallis decided he wanted more autonomy and formed his own production company, Hal Wallis Productions, which would make four pictures each year for Warner's. He was allowed to take some favorite projects with him. Among those he took was *Casablanca*.

His first choice for director was William Wyler, who had worked with the likes of Bette Davis on *Jezebel* at Warner Bros. But Wyler had just applied for a commission in the Signal Corps, so Wallis went to Michael Curtiz, who had earned Oscar nominations for *Angels with Dirty Faces*, and *Yankee Doodle Dandy*, and who happily accepted the job.

Curtiz, born Mikhaly Kertesz on December 24, 1886, in Hungary, was a respected filmmaker, but not esteemed for any trademark style. He'd directed sixty films in Europe before his 1926 arrival in America, where he did one hundred more. His record for coming in on budget had endeared him to Warner, but he wasn't liked by cast or crew because he was considered a grouch on the set. Indeed his crews often made fun of his malapropisms. On *Casablanca*, he kept demanding a poodle for the market scene; no one could understand why, until they realized he wanted a "poodle of water." Another line that was often repeated: "Next time I send some dumb son-of-a-bitch for a Coca-Cola, I go myself."

To adapt the play, Wallis hired Julius J. and Philip Epstein, twins who were known for their crisp dialogue. They'd worked with Curtiz on *Four Daughters* and also had turned out scripts for *The Strawberry Blonde*, and

The Man Who Came to Dinner over the past two years. The busy Epsteins only managed to complete the first third of the *Casablanca* script before being summoned to write patriotic training documentaries for Frank Capra. Frustrated, Wallis next hired Howard Koch, a junior writer at Warner's, who'd gained favor by working on Orson Welles's radio plays, including *War of the Worlds*.

According to Julius Epstein, there were no professional intrigues among the three: All accepted their role as hired hands. Koch was credited with sharpening the film's political point of view. He created Rick's background of fighting for the Loyalists in Spain and running guns to Ethiopia. Wallis later brought in still other body-and-fender specialists, including Wally Kline, Jerry Wald, and Casey Robinson.

No one, however, could come up with an acceptable final scene. Decades later, Julius Epstein would joke that Warner's had seventy-five writers under contract, and all of them had tried to come up with an ending for *Casablanca*.

Wallis, meanwhile, was focused on casting. For the female lead, Wallis zeroed in on Ann Sheridan, a studio contract player, then changed the character from an American to a European. Inspired by the 1938 film *Algiers*, Wallis had by this point also changed the film's title to *Casablanca*, and sought out the star of *Algiers*, Hedy Lamarr. She was under contract to MGM, however, and they wouldn't release her.

Michèle Morgan lobbied for the role, with her agent demanding $55,000. Wallis wrote to Curtiz: "There is no reason in the world for demanding this kind of money for anyone as little known as Michèle Morgan."

Wallis next thought of Ingrid Bergman, who'd made enough of an impression in *Intermezzo* in 1936 for David O. Selznick to bring her to the United States. Selznick had loaned her out for a few American movies, such as MGM's *Dr. Jekyll and Mr. Hyde* with Spencer Tracy, but was keenly aware she hadn't yet achieved star status.

It was Wallis's idea to dispatch the Epsteins to convince Selznick to loan her out to Warner's. Julius later recalled: "Wallis said to us, 'Go to Selznick and tell him the story.' So my brother and I went to Selznick. He was having lunch at his desk and he was slurping his soup. He never looked up. I said, 'There are refugees and transit visas and intrigue in our movie. It's going to be a lot of shit like *Algiers*. And Selznick looked up and nodded to me that we had Bergman." Wallis paid Selznick $25,000 for the privilege.

As it turned out, the chief reason the Swedish actress accepted the role was because she'd lost out on the part she really wanted: Maria in Paramount's *For Whom the Bell Tolls*. Though she'd met Ernest Hemingway, who'd put in a plug for her, the part went to ballerina Vera Zorina. (Ultimately, Paramount changed its mind, deciding Zorina was not robust enough, and gave the part back to Bergman, who got an Oscar nomination for that film.)

Even as all this was taking place, ego clashes between Wallis and his überboss, Jack Warner, became increasingly strident. The studio issued a press release saying that Ronald Reagan and Ann Sheridan would star in *Casablanca*. At that time, studios would send out weekly press releases touting their contract players, even when the executives had no intention of using them in the announced film. Meanwhile, Warner made no effort to conceal the fact that he favored George Raft. Wallis adamantly preferred Bogart, another contract player who, like Raft, specialized in playing villains. Warner couldn't see him as a romantic lead. "Who the hell would ever want to kiss Bogart?" Warner shouted, as though Raft were another Clark Gable.

Though Wallis won the day, a week before shooting actress Geraldine Fitzgerald had lunch with Bergman and Bogart, according to Harmetz. She recalled: "The whole subject at lunch was how they could get out of the movie. They thought the dialogue was ridiculous and the situations were unbelievable. And Ingrid was terribly upset because she said she had to portray the most beautiful woman in Europe, and no one would ever believe that. 'I look like a milkmaid,' she said."

Bogart had originally signed a seven-year contract with Warner's in 1936, at the instigation of actor Leslie Howard, who'd wanted Bogart to repeat his impressive Broadway performance in *The Petrified Forest*. Though *Casablanca* was an opportunity to change his bad boy image, Bogart thought Rick was self-pitying. He also admitted to being uncomfortable playing love scenes. On the set, he told one journalist that he was used to getting out of on-camera acting problems by using a gun. "Well, this leaves me a little baffled. . . . I'm not up on this love stuff and don't know just what to do," he said.

During principal photography, Bogart spent most of his time alone in his dressing room playing solo chess. His then wife, Mayo Methot, would often fly into rages and accuse him of having an affair with Bergman. Denying these accusations, Bergman, to the contrary, found Bogart remote: "I kissed him, but I never knew him," she wrote in her diary. "Bogart was at least straightforward and devoid of prima donna behavior, something that cannot be said about Henreid."

Wallis's first choice to play freedom fighter Victor Laszlo was Philip Dorn, but he had a scheduling conflict. Paul Henreid was his second choice, but, Henreid recalled, "I saw the script and I turned it down. I thought it was a ridiculous fairy tale." The actor was coming off the romantic lead in *Now,*

Voyager and wanted top-banana roles. Lew Wasserman, Henreid's agent, convinced the actor that, due to his Austrian background, he would do well to keep his head down and keep working.

Looking back, Henreid had little good to say about *Casablanca* or his coworkers: "Mr. Bogie was nobody. Before *Casablanca* he was nobody. He was a mediocre actor. He was so sorry for himself in *Casablanca*. Unfortunately, Michael Curtiz was not a director of actors; he was a director of effects. He was first rate at that, but he could not tell Bogart he should not play like a crybaby. It was embarrassing, I thought, when I looked at the rushes."

Bergman's daughter, Pia Lindstrom, by contrast depicted Henreid as petty. "He grumbled that he 'hated his white suit . . .' He said, 'Why would a man who escaped from a concentration camp, who's hiding, be parading around in a white suit?'"

Roles in *Casablanca* were filled with strong contract players including Claude Rains, Sydney Greenstreet, and Peter Lorre. For Sam, the piano player, Wallis was eager to cast a woman. He checked the availability of both Lena Horne and Hazel Scott then, again, changed his mind. The role finally went to Dooley Wilson, a drummer who could act, but couldn't play the piano.

Even after the cameras started rolling, script pages kept coming in. Wallis brought in Casey Robinson to write the flashback of Rick and Ilsa in Paris, one of the few pieces of exposition in the film. Koch hated it, but Curtiz insisted that it should stay in.

Bergman's big problem with the script was that she couldn't figure out whether her character loved Bogart or Henreid. Curtiz had no patience with her questions, complaining, "Actors! Actors! They want to know everything!" He advised her to "play it in-between." It turned out to be good advice.

Bogart several times invited Koch to his dressing room to discuss an ending. Says Koch, "He was always nonchalant. It was 'Come in and have a drink.' Most of the talk centered around the lack of an ending. That was mostly what Bogart was concerned about."

In the play, Rick sends Ilsa off with her husband and Rick is in turn arrested, but Wallis didn't want to make a movie in which the Gestapo seemed to triumph. Koch was told to stop the themes of duty and resistance to tyranny.

On the other hand, it would seem perverse for Ilsa to leave her freedom-fighting husband, just for her own personal happiness. Further, the Production Code wouldn't allow a married woman to experience such a "happy ending" with her lover. Victor Laszlo could be killed, but, again, the world situation would make that ending too downbeat.

Julius Epstein claims he and his twin were driving to the lot when they simultaneously exclaimed, "Round up the usual suspects!" That was their solution. Rick would kill the Nazi, Strasser; Renault would protect him by pretending it was a mysterious death. Koch's alternate ending had Rick pulling a gun on Renault so that Laszlo could escape to America and join Ilsa. The movie would end with Rick and Renault sitting down to a chess game and Renault saying, "Ricky, I was right. You are a sentimentalist."

They decided to shoot two endings. But after shooting the first, they called it a wrap—but not due to creative satisfaction, according to Lindstrom. "They were on a tight budget, so they shot one ending and it was good enough, so they said, 'That's it, let's not worry'."

Like most films of that era, *Casablanca* was ruled by the dictates of the budget. The airport in the final scene was constructed on a soundstage. Assistant director Lee Katz insisted that the airplane, a cutout, looked pretty shoddy. Fog was pumped in to mask the low-budget look. Katz then came up with the notion that midgets should play the mechanics to give the scene the illusion of depth and dimension.

Warner Bros. was known for being stingy, but there was an excuse in this case. Metal and lumber were needed for war-related construction, not for "frivolous" movies. In 1942, the War Production Board had placed a $5,000 limit on building sets, which usually cost up to $20,000. The Board later revised its decree, saying studios could spend more if they spread costs over several films. *Casablanca* hence used the railroad station from *Now, Voyager* and the generic French street from *The Desert Song*, a musical starring Dennis Morgan. The set's total cost was $18,000. The final cost of the film was $1,039,000.

Looking at the film from today's perspective, it's hard to imagine *Casablanca* facing censorship problems, but the film came under close scrutiny. Joseph Breen, who now headed the Production Code, complained to Jack Warner on May 19, 1942, that several lines in the script were too "sex suggestive," such as "Of course, a beautiful young girl for Messieurs Renault, the Prefect of Police" and "It used to take a villa at Cannes, or the very least, a string of pearls—now all I ask is an exit visa."

Breen wrote: "Specifically, we cannot approve the present suggestion that Capt. Renault makes a practice of seducing the women to whom he grants visas. Any such reference to illicit sex could not be approved in the finished picture." He continued, "The suggestion that Ilsa was married all the time she was having her love affair with Rick in Paris seems unacceptable, and could not be approved in the finished picture. Hence, we request the deletion of Ilsa's line 'Even when I knew you in Paris.'"

All this came at a sensitive time for Warner Bros. Early in 1941, Harry Warner had been called before a Senate subcommittee investigating "war mongering" in Hollywood films. If *Casablanca* had been released earlier, it clearly would have been called into question. But now that America had entered the war, the politics in *Casablanca* were welcome.

Amid all the infighting about the code, the ending, and its political fallout, no one at the time seemed to realize that the score would emerge as the hidden star—at least one immortal song. Contrary to widespread belief, the song did not even originate with *Casablanca*.

In the play *Everybody Comes to Rick's*, co-playwright Burnett had specified that he wanted "As Time Goes By" used in the show. It was a tune composed by Herman Hupfeld for an obscure 1931 Broadway show, *Everybody's Welcome*. Wallis respected Burnett's proposal, but when Max Steiner was brought in to score *Casablanca*, he decided to cut the song and use one of his own compositions. He'd just enjoyed a big hit, "It Can't Be Wrong," based on a theme he wrote for *Now, Voyager*. Steiner soon realized, however, that he was stuck with the song because Bergman had already been filmed asking Sam to play "As Time Goes By." Reshoots were impossible, since Bergman's hair had by now been severely cropped for *For Whom the Bell Tolls*.

Steiner had to resign himself to the other musical set piece as well—the scene when patrons of Rick's Cafe sing "La Marseillaise" to counter the German singing "Die Wacht am Rhein." Further, during the singing of "La Marseillaise" half the cast was crying. The reason: They were all true refugees. On-screen and off, *Casablanca* represented one of Hollywood's first truly international films. The cast included seventy-five actors in bit parts, almost all of them immigrants representing thirty-four nationalities. Eight of the ten actors who get top billing were born outside the United States: Bergman, Rains, Henreid, Conrad Veidt, Lorre, Greenstreet, S. Z. Sakall, and Madeleine LeBeau. In addition, Curtiz and many of the crew were born abroad, as were two of the four Warner brothers.

When the Allies landed in North Africa in November 1942, Jack Warner moved up the release by seven months. He exhorted his marketing team that the "entire industry envies us for having *Casablanca* ready for release. We should take advantage of this great scoop. Naturally, the longer we wait, the less important the title will be."

The Warner publicity department and the folks assembling the trailer were suitably responsive. The only doubters seemed to be those who'd written the film. Julius Epstein recalls, "When we previewed it for the first time, I thought it was a flop. We wrote a note to Hal Wallis telling him so. Thereafter, he kept that memo in his desk. Whenever we had an argument with him about anything, he would take out that memo and give it to us."

The movie was released on November 26, 1942, Thanksgiving Day, at the Hollywood Theater in New York, in what was called a "pre-release engagement." The studio publicity machine trumpeted its timeliness. At the premiere, supporters of the Free French forces of General Charles de Gaulle marched down Fifth Avenue, sang "La Marseillaise," and unfurled the Free French flag at the theater. One poster for the film bragged, "The Army's Got Casablanca—AND SO HAVE WARNER BROTHERS!"

Some reviewers were nonetheless unimpressed. In the *Nation*, James Agee wrote: "Apparently, *Casablanca*, which I must say I liked, is working up a rather serious reputation as a fine melodrama. Why? It is obviously an improvement on one of the world's worst plays; but it is not such an improvement that that is not obvious."

The *New Yorker* was more blasé: "The Casablanca on the screen is the old Casablanca of three or four weeks ago . . . but there is probably enough topical truth left in the picture to suit the topical-minded. Not to speak of the eternal truths always to be found in the better screenplays . . . It's as good a tune ("As Time Goes By") as any to attach sentiment to, and a good one to attach to this picture, which, although not quite up to *Across the Pacific*, Bogart's last spyfest, is nevertheless pretty tolerable and deserves attractive accessories."

The liberal New York paper *PM* called it "an exciting film built around an exciting new idea . . . that leaders of Europe's anti-Fascist underground are terribly important people these days, rating priorities ahead of even millionaires and playboys in such traditional specialties of old Casablanca as stolen passports."

The *New York Times'* Bosley Crowther wrote that Casablanca is a "picture that makes the spine tingle and the heart take a leap."

Variety wrote:

By a curious quirk of fortune, history-making caught up to this picture set against a background of French Morocco, and its timeliness assures big box-office reception. . . . Warner's, and especially Hal Wallis, are to be commended. Every role, every bit has been cast with care, and the writers have made every part essential to the plot.

Casablanca played at one theater in New York for ten weeks to a gross of $225,827. It opened in the rest of the country in January 1943 and brought the studio $3,015,000 during its first release in the United States.

Overall ticket sales were $3.7 million, yielding the seventh highest gross of 1943. The leader was Paramount's *For Whom the Bell Tolls*, which sold nearly $11 million in tickets. Twentieth Century Fox's *Song of Bernadette* was second, making $7 million. "As Time Goes By," meanwhile, stayed number one on the Hit Parade for four weeks in spring of 1943.

Since *Casablanca* didn't open in Los Angeles until 1943, the Academy of Motion Picture Arts and Sciences mandated that it would be eligible for that year's Oscars. That was another stroke of good timing for the film; if it had opened in L.A. in 1942, it would have competed with *Mrs. Miniver*, another smartly crafted Hollywood film about the urgency of involvement in the war. As it turned out, *Casablanca* received eight Academy Award nominations in the race of 1943, cited for best picture, director, actor (Bogart's first nomination), supporting actor (Rains), screenplay, cinematography, editing, and music. Warner's earned more nominations than any other studio that year, with twenty-eight—eight for *Casablanca* and four apiece for *Watch on the Rhine* and *Air Force*.

The ceremonies were held March 2, 1944, at Grauman's Chinese Theater, the first year at that venue. After fifteen years of banquets (the last nine years at the Ambassador Hotel's Coconut Grove or the Biltmore Hotel's Biltmore Bowl), the Oscars needed more room. And with food in short supply, it seemed insensitive to stage a lavish banquet. The Academy invited men and women from the armed forces to attend the evening with Jack Benny as the host.

When *Casablanca* won the first of its three awards, for screenplay, Koch accepted the trophy for the Epsteins, who were in New York working on a play. These were pretelevision days, so the Epsteins didn't realize they'd won for nearly twenty-four hours. Julius Epstein recalled: "One of the wire services made a mistake and concluded *The Song of Bernadette* had won. It had won everything else." The Epsteins sent a congratulatory telegram to that film's writer, George Seaton.

Meanwhile, Curtiz had prepared speeches the previous two years when he'd been nominated, but didn't prepare one this time. When he won, he blurted, "So many times I have a speech ready but no dice. Always a bridesmaid, never a mother."

When film producer Sidney Franklin announced the best picture winner, the audience gasped, then heartily applauded the unexpected result. Hal Wallis was taken by surprise not only by the upset (*Song of Bernadette* was the clear favorite) but also when he saw who was rushing to accept it. Wallis recalled in his autobiography, "I started up the aisle to receive my award. To my astonishment, Jack Warner had leapt to his feet, ran to the stage, and received it ahead of me. Almost forty years later, I still haven't recovered from the shock." Most observers agreed that Wallis, as the producer and driving force, deserved the trophy, but Warner wasn't out of line. At that time, the best picture trophy was given to the studio; not until 1951 were individual producers listed (the first was Arthur Freed for *An American in Paris*).

Wallis's indignation was ameliorated to a degree by the fact that he was awarded the Thalberg Award "for the most consistent high quality of production by an individual producer." Nonetheless, after the ceremonies, he sent his secretary to Warner to demand the Oscar. She was turned away. And when Wallis was told he would not even be photographed near the statuette, Wallis told his publicist to spread the word. In the next morning's *Los Angeles Times*, Edwin Schallert, the film critic, wrote, "The question is being vigorously raised in Hollywood whether J. L. Warner or Hal B. Wallis should have accepted the award tendered for *Casablanca* as the outstanding production at the big Academy shindig."

The studio demanded a retraction. Warner's even drafted a letter of apology for Wallis to send to the *Times*, but Wallis refused, denying that he had planted the story. The egomaniacal Warner reiterated his demand and Wallis, realizing who and what he was up against, capitulated, sending a letter stating, "I have been with Warner Bros. for twenty years and during this time it has been customary here as elsewhere for the studio head to accept the Academy Award for the best production. Naturally I was glad to see Jack Warner accept the award for *Casablanca* as he did for *The Life of Emile Zola*."

But the damage was done. In 1944, one month after the ceremonies, Warner's cancelled Wallis's contract on a technicality, citing the supposedly insufficient number of films he had worked on that year. The studio also sent out a press release emphasizing that Wallis's success had stemmed from the fact that the studio had given him the "choicest assignments, including numerous best sellers and Broadway hits."

After *Casablanca*, Bogart replaced Erroll Flynn

as Warner's top box-office star. Bergman won her first of three Oscars for the 1944 *Gaslight*. She then created a scandal by leaving her husband, Peter Lindstrom, for Italian director Roberto Rossellini and having his baby out of wedlock. She was persona non grata in Hollywood for years and denounced on the Senate floor; she made a triumphant comeback in the 1956 *Anastasia*, winning a second Oscar.

Hal Wallis, meanwhile, having burnt his bridges at Warner Bros., made his move to Paramount, where, throughout the '50s, he turned out solid studio fare with adaptations of mainstream plays such as *Come Back, Little Sheba* and *Becket*. All performed respectably but unspectacularly. Clearly the movie audience was changing, and the aging Wallis did not have a handle on the nature of this change. He tried some Dean Martin–Jerry Lewis comedies, such as *Hollywood or Bust*, and then focused his attention on Elvis Presley, with such films as *Easy Come, Easy Go, King Creole*, and *Blue Hawaii*.

While his subsequent experience on *True Grit* was a gratifying one, Wallis knew he had few, if any, friends at Paramount. He resented the fact that he'd not been involved in *The Godfather*, but had shown little interest in the property or its director, Francis Coppola.

Fortunately for Wallis, one studio had remained firmly under the control of the sort of traditional mogul he understood. That was Universal, whose austere boss, Lew Wasserman, presided over his empire from his Black Tower. Wasserman still wore black suits and preferred to deal with old-line producers like Wallis (his efforts to cope with the younger set, such as George Lucas, had been traumatic). Ensconced at his new studio, Wallis produced *Mary, Queen of Scots* and *Anne of the Thousand Days*, eminently respectable films that represented all the values of a bygone studio era. As his swan song, he turned out the creaky sequel to *True Grit*, titled *Rooster Cogburn*. That was in 1975 and it was to be his final film.

Given his predilections, it seems appropriate that Hal Wallis is remembered as the driving force behind *Casablanca*, a perfectly realized studio picture. Of all Warner Bros. wartime movies, only two topped *Casablanca* at the international box office—*This Is the Army* and *Shine On, Harvest Moon*. But only *Casablanca* infiltrated the pop culture. Not only are its ratings still consistently high when it plays on television, but a few theaters around the country, like the Brattle in Cambridge, Massachusetts play it regularly. Fans keep coming in trench coats, reciting lines of dialogue ("Play it once, Sam, for old times sake . . ."; "Of all the gin joints in all the towns in the world, she walks into mine . . ."; "Round up the usual suspects"). Of course Woody Allen's superb film, *Play It Again, Sam* in 1972, further enhanced its mythology. There were even a few lame attempts at re-creating *Casablanca* as a TV series—David Soul starred as Rick in seven episodes in 1983, with Scatman Crothers as Sam.

In 2001, the American Film Institute conducted a survey of filmmakers and educators asking them to choose their favorite love story. *Casablanca* won, over *Gone with the Wind*—yet another reminder of the affection that individuals both inside and outside the industry hold for Hal Wallis's remarkable film.

21 Family Time
Life with Father (1939)

On the face of it, there was nothing instantly captivating about the idea of doing *Life with Father* on Broadway. The property consisted of a series of magazine pieces about an affluent New York family circa the 1880s—it was an upper crust *All in the Family*. The sitcom was built around the familiar persona of a domineering, if good-spirited, parental figure.

Written by a stockbroker named Clarence Day Jr., who was bedridden by severe arthritis, the magazine pieces had been published as a modestly successful book titled *God and My Father*. Rights to the property were controlled by his widow, and other heirs following Day's death in 1935, and the family was suspicious of promoters eager to exploit the work. Two distinguished Broadway producers, Antoinette Perry and Brock Pemberton, had tried to secure the stage rights, but without success. An aggressive talent scout named Oscar Serlin, who had once been an aide to David O. Selznick, also tried and even hired a screenwriter to turn the stories into a vehicle for a W. C. Fields comedy. While Fields liked the script, however, the heirs to the Day estate disdained it. Perhaps out of pity, Day's widow agreed to let Serlin try again to develop it as a play—provided he could summon up a big-name playwright and come up with an acceptable script. Then she might consider an option.

In the face of these obstacles, most neophyte producers would have bowed out, but Serlin, a tall man who habitually wore a beret, had invested too much financially and emotionally to give it up.

Knowing he had to come up with an acceptable "name," Serlin approached Howard Lindsay, who seemed to share the property's upper-crust sensibility. Lindsay had made a name for himself writing *She Loves Me Not*, a 1933 hit about preppies set at Princeton University, he then collaborated with a crusty ex-newsman named Russel Crouse on a hit, *Anything Goes*. It turns out Lindsay had been a fan of the original Clarence Day Jr. stories, and had faithfully read them to his wife, actress Dorothy Stickney, who suffered from chronic vision trouble.

Crouse, too, needed no persuasion. Having written three books with Victorian American settings, he was an authority on the period and it was one which he relished. Without any written permission from Mrs. Day, he and Lindsay set to work. Together they hammered out a forty-page scenario, which Lindsay read to the Day family in New Haven as Serlin and Crouse waited nearby. There was no discernable response to the reading, and the trio from Broadway returned downcast to New York. Then came the word— Mrs. Day had thought the outline charming. Lindsay and Crouse were now authorized to settle down to the writing of the play.

Accounts differ of how Lindsay and Crouse became writing partners. In 1934, producer Vinton Freedley had found himself with a Cole Porter score and a book by Guy Bolton and P. G. Wodehouse that needed reworking. Set aboard a Europe-bound ocean liner, the plot of *Anything Goes* culminated in a farcical wreck at sea. Freedley knew it didn't work, and its prospects became even dimmer on September 8, 1934, when the USS *Morro Castle*, returning from a cruise to Havana, sank in flames off New Jersey, with the loss of more than one hundred lives. Obviously such a situation would no longer play as comedy.

Lindsay had already been hired to direct the show, and Ethel Merman had signed to head the cast. Lindsay realized he had to rewrite it entirely if the show was to be salvaged. "Who the hell can we get to work on it with you," his producer demanded. An agent dropped the name of Russel Crouse, who was then working as a press agent for the Theater Guild.

Crouse's background was in journalism, rather than theater. The son of a newspaperman, Crouse grew up in Toledo, Ohio, and Enid, Oklahoma, moving with the ups and downs of his father's newspaper career. Crouse later spent several years as a night reporter on the *Kansas City Star* before joining the Navy during World War I. After receiving an honorable discharge, Crouse couldn't find a job when he returned to Kansas City, so he moved to

New York, landing a spot on the *New York Globe*. There he met his first wife, fellow writer Alison Smith, who ran with the Algonquin Round Table crowd. They wed in 1923.

The *Globe* folded, sending Crouse to the *New York Post*, during which time he also wrote for the *New Yorker*, particularly its "Talk of the Town" section. His career as a playwright began with *The Gang's All Here*, written in collaboration with Morrie Ryskind and Oscar Hammerstein II. It was, as Crouse put it, "one of the most colossal flops in the history of the theater." It opened February 18, 1931, and ran for two weeks.

Working days as a press agent for the Theater Guild, he set about writing his second musical, *Hold Your Horses*, a collaboration with Corey Ford. During tryouts in Boston, its producers, the Shuberts, made major changes. It was another flop.

Crouse, hence, was open to taking on a new partner—Lindsay, on *Anything Goes*. It was a rush job—there was a two-week deadline—and Crouse was still working days at the Theater Guild. However, both men were fiercely ambitious and durable, and somehow the show got written.

Anything Goes ran for 420 performances. The collaborators found they worked amicably together and Lindsay suggested that they form a partnership. Crouse was hesitant. While his salary as press agent at the Theater Guild totaled $150 a week, it was at least steady income.

Lindsay went off to work with Damon Runyon on a play, *A Slight Case of Murder*, but in 1936 Lindsay and Crouse were reunited with Freedley and Porter on *Red, Hot and Blue*, again starring Merman alongside Jimmy Durante and newcomer Bob Hope. It opened October 29, 1936, at the Alvin Theater, to mixed notices, but managed to run for some five months. Another musical, *Hooray for What!*, produced by the Shuberts and starring Ed Wynn, managed 200 performances at the Winter Garden.

A brief stint in Hollywood was not especially satisfying. Lindsay and Crouse wrote a picture for W. C. Fields, *The Big Broadcast of 1938*, but the final product bore no resemblance to anything they'd written.

Fortunately, Day's *Life with Father* beckoned.

After weeks of conversation and deliberation about character and structure, they hammered out the play in seventeen days. Lindsay, the actor, articulated the dialogue as he paced back and forth; Crouse, the onetime newsman, retained his perch at the typewriter, mixing his own flourishes with Lindsay's theatrics.

The work proceeded well until tensions arose over issues of casting. Lindsay let it be known that he saw himself as the lead—he was the perfect

Father. Oscar Serlin, who had fostered the project this far, had earlier approached Alfred Lunt and Lynn Fontanne as the leads—they were, after all, the superstars of their era—but the Lunts turned it down. Always the opportunist, Lindsay and his wife, Dorothy Stickney, presented themselves to costar at a tryout at Skowhegan, Maine.

Variety's review of the tryout was felicitous. "The common acceptance of Howard Lindsay as a playwright was increased in its scope when he undertook the role of Clarence's father, with Dorothy Stickney (Mrs. Lindsay) handling the part of the mother. Both turn in excellent performances." The reviewer added, "Play needs some re-writing, but it suggests Broadway possibilities. Oscar Serlin has an option on the play and plans to present it on Broadway this fall."

And a review of the tryout in the *New York Times* called it "a simple nostalgic comedy," in which "the authors have adhered to the spirit of Mr. Day's stories of life in his own family, adding only enough plot to give them continuity and a slender but appealing love story for Clarence himself." The review noted that the play drew the largest audiences of the summer season at Skowhegan.

The authors sharpened the script after the tryout and engaged the theatrically-named Bretaigne Windust to direct it for Broadway, with Lindsay now secure as the lead.

Lindsay played the blustering Father Day, a rigid Wall Streeter whose chief concern is that everything in his comfortable 1880s Victorian household be done the way he wants it. Stickney played his patient wife, Vinnie, whose inability to stay within her household budget drives Father crazy, one of many things that cause him to bellow, "Oh, God!" with regularity. They have four redheaded sons and assorted domestic servants, including a devoted cook and, almost daily, a new maid (since Father scares them away on a regular basis). Father spends most of the play fending off the turmoil intruding into his life, particularly visits from country relative Cousin Cora (Ruth Hammond) and a young friend she brings along to the big city, Mary Skinner (played originally by Teresa Wright). The eldest son, Clarence Jr. (John Drew Devereaux) promptly falls in love with Mary, compounding Father's frustrations.

Despite his frequent "Oh, God!" exclamations, it turns out that Father has never been baptized—a revelation of some consequence to the family. Mother thus determines in her own inept way to remedy this situation, a mission fervently opposed by her husband. His opposition melts, however, when Mother becomes seriously ill, and Father promises he will do whatever it takes if she is cured. When she recovers, she holds him to his word. The play ends with Father heading off to church, attired in his Sunday best, bellowing, "I'm going to be baptized, damn it!"

Despite its creaky plot, the show struck a major chord with its audience. "*Life with Father* is Broadway's newest hit," proclaimed *Variety* on November 15, 1939. "Laugh show opened mid-week at the Empire and drew rave notices, following with standee attendance. It may reach the $19,000 class, which would be among the straight-show toppers."

In the same issue of *Variety*, a review read: "Another click has come to town. This one originated in the sticks, having been regarded the leading Broadway possibility in the rural show shops during the past summer. Period or dated comedies rarely grace the boards successfully, but here is the exception."

Walter Winchell, in a *Daily Mirror* review, wrote, "Happy Days Are Here In *Life With Father*. The *Mirror*'s man made a positive fool of himself almost throughout the show, chuckling, giggling, tee-heeing or laughing right out loud . . . For *Life with Father* is indeed charming entertainment when it is not provoking robust laughter."

Richard Lockridge, in the *New York Sun*, said, "They have captured all the life which bubbled in the stories, and all the richness of character of the man who became simply *Father* to thousands, and all the comedy which was so tender and at the same time so vigorous. You would never have dreamed any one could do so beautiful a job of translation . . . by all odds the most engaging, happiest play in town."

Dorothy Dunbar Brown, writing in the *New York Post*, put her finger on one reason for the play's success: "The book-into-play *Life with Father* will tax your risibilities, being the portrait of a rugged individualist of the 1880s who does not know how funny he is . . . Coming after *The Little Foxes*, which is not exactly a celebration of American family life, and after the headlines from Europe, which put your sense of humor into cold storage, *Life with Father* was just the play New Yorkers needed as an anchor to wholesome reality."

And reviewing for the *New York Times*, Brooks Atkinson was prophetic: "Sooner or later everyone will have to see *Life with Father*, which opened at the Empire last evening. For the late Clarence Day's vastly amusing sketches of his despotic parent have now been translated into a perfect comedy by Howard Lindsay and Russel Crouse and must be reckoned an authentic part of our American folklore."

The lone dissenting voice was that of the critic for the American Communist Party's newspaper, the *Daily Worker*. The review, signed only with initials N. C., says: "*Life with Father* in spite of having been almost hysterically welcomed by an audience of Father's peers—is a play which is completely unrewarding. Father is a stuffed shirt who never condescends to a lovable moment of human uncertainty. And Mother, who is so terribly concerned about getting him into heaven, has nothing to say when a servant girl has a bad fall down a long flight of stairs except, 'Why couldn't she have finished clearing the breakfast table!'"

However, Atkinson was proved right. The show ran a record 3,224 performances on Broadway—a record that still stands—and as it chugged along, investors started to get their money back. Oscar Serlin, who produced *Father*, computed the grosses of the original company on Broadway in its first year as $972,734; second year, $859,456; third year, $631,479; fourth year, $707,251. There were five companies on tour grossing a total of $3,228,164, so that the show's total in and out-of-town was $6,399,084.

By November 1946, on the play's seventh anniversary, the *New York Daily Mirror* reported, "To date *Life with Father* has been seen by over 6,000,000 customers, who have paid approximately $9,500,000 for their ducats."

Lindsay and Stickney continued to play the roles of Father and Mother Day for the first five years of the Broadway run. They returned for a special two-week engagement, starting June 14, 1947, to mark a special milestone: *Life with Father* had taken the title of longest-running play on Broadway from *Tobacco Road*. By then it had moved to the Bijou Theater, then to the Alvin, where, as Ward Morehouse put it, "It may continue for another hundred years." But even with lower ticket prices at the Alvin, its stay there was less than a month, and it played its final performance July 12, 1947.

A page-one story in *Variety*'s November 15, 1939 edition listed some of the show's lucky backers. Among them were "wealthy socialite and sportsman" John Hay "Jock" Whitney, "who almost seasonally is a silent partner in one or more attractions." Also among the dozen owners of the show was Whitney's sister, Mrs. Charles Payson, and a then young Canadian actor, Hume Cronyn.

Lindsay and Crouse used some of their royalties from the show to buy a theater, the Hudson, where they produced the comedy hits *Arsenic and Old Lace*, and *The Voice of the Turtle*, and a revival of Shaw's *Man and Superman*.

The inevitable sequel to *Life with Father*, titled *Life with Mother*, again produced by Serlin and written by Lindsay and Crouse, opened October 20, 1948, at the Empire Theater. Lindsay and Stickney, returning as Father and Mother Day, were rejoined by many of the original players. Because they felt that the play's cache was considerable, the new venture's simple advertisement in the New York papers said simply:

Mr. and Mrs. Clarence Day
At Home
On Wednesday evening, October twentieth
from eight until eleven o'clock
at Fourteen hundred and thirty Broadway
Entertainment

Brooks Atkinson growled, "It is more laboriously contrived. It is thinner, and there are moments when it barely hangs together as a drama. The comedy is neither as hilarious nor as nostalgic as its eminent predecessor, but it is a pleasant elongation of a drama which became very much a part of American life." In the sequel, Mother demands of Father the engagement ring he never gave her. Things heat up when Mother learns Father had a fiancée before her, Bessie, who did receive a ring and has never taken it off. The still-flirtatious Bessie returns to the action, but of course Mother wins the day and the ring. *Life with Mother* ran for 265 performances, a respectable run, but still lost its investors $40,000.

While *Life with Father* brought great wealth and celebrity to all its players and backers, Oscar Serlin—the man who had stubbornly stuck by it—remained a fringe player in Hollywood and on Broadway. Growing up in Chicago, the Polish-born Serlin had felt himself an outsider because of his strong accent. He told friends that as a young man he had spent hours before a mirror repeating phrases in an attempt to mask his accent, but without success.

Serlin had been desperate to make a name for himself in show business, but with marginal success. At one point he even returned to Europe and observed Max Reinhardt's productions in Salzburg and Munich, studying stagecraft. Back in the United States he began to line up work as a stage manager and finally connected with David O. Selznick, who hired him in a series of minor positions. In the early '30s, Paramount put Serlin to work as a talent scout in the East, and he later boasted of having "discovered" Cary Grant. This helped get him a ticket back to Hollywood, where he served as an assistant producer on some of Selznick's films.

Life with Father, however, was Serlin's entrée to the glamour and success of mainstream show business, and while he wallowed in it, efforts to replicate its success proved unsuccessful. His later Broadway productions included John Steinbeck's play *The Moon Is Down*, in 1942 and Victor Wolfson's short-lived *The Family* a year later. Always impeccably dressed and very European in style and manner, Serlin continued to appear on the fringes of Broadway for some years. He died in obscurity in 1971.

Serlin's basic franchise, however, remains one of the remarkable anomalies of pop culture. Here was a play that touched a vast audience of playgoers, spanning ages and classes, yet it was resolutely upper crust in its setting and characters. On one level, *Life with Father* tapped into a rich vein that was later exploited by the TV hit, *All in the Family*. Both focused on a family tyrant whose view of the world was hopelessly anachronistic. Both characters were at once hilarious and empathetic. And both families, though inaccessible in differing ways, were intent on retaining their bonds, dining together every night despite the raging arguments and intrigues—behavior that was as reassuring on Broadway as it later proved to be on television.

22 Walt's Folly

Snow White and the Seven Dwarfs (1937)

This was, I was told, a seminal moment in the history of the Walt Disney Company. I was seated in a screening room in the animation building at the studio. A publicity man was on my left, and on my right was the then head of animation, Peter Schneider. As editor-in-chief of *Variety*, I was about to be granted a private glimpse of a $200 million movie called *Dinosaur*, which was to be released a year later, in 2000. *Dinosaur*, I was advised, represented a giant leap forward in the history of animated filmmaking. The creatures depicted were utterly realistic in every detail, their movements vivid down to darting eyeballs and rippling fur.

Further, what had been achieved here was a remarkable photorealistic placement of computer generated creatures within the framework of real-world settings. The landscapes were real; the animals were not, but they seemed real, down to the details of their muscle movement and shadows—even their point-of-view shots.

The room went dark and the movie began to roll. For the next few minutes I was riveted by the artistry. This was not an ordinary exercise in animation. The dinosaurs and other creatures dancing before my eyes were brilliantly alive and I was delighted to be in their company. Surely, had Walt Disney himself still been here, he would have been in awe of this spectacle.

As the minutes passed, however, it was becoming clear that while the creatures were superbly realized, their personalities were not particularly interesting. Their actions were stunning but their dialogue was flat. The incidents were fascinating, but the story wasn't going anywhere.

I began to stir uneasily in my seat; my companions in the screening room peered at me anxiously. I knew I'd be facing questions when the footage ended and I steeled myself for the onslaught. I'd be polite, I told myself. I would heap praise on the work—after all, I was an editor, not a film critic. I would tell them that old Walt would have been proud.

No, I would not say that. Walt Disney was a quirky man, and these animated characters were not quirky. He was a storyteller who liked to spin his narratives for adults, not just for children, and the *Dinosaur* story wouldn't have pleased him.

My reservations turned out to be valid. *Dinosaur* was a very expensive flop for the Disney Company. Peter Schneider would leave the studio months later. Indeed, the entire Disney animation program was effectively disbanded, and a process of re-invention was initiated. In the increasingly bountiful animation business, the leaders would be companies like Pixar, which Disney acquired for $7.5 billion in 2006, and DreamWorks (headed by Disney alumnus Jeffrey Katzenberg) absorbed by Viacom, also in 2006, and the entity that old Walt had founded eighty years earlier would become a has-been, its own animation unit marginalized.

No one hated failure more than Walt Disney. A boldly innovative man, he disdained the constraints of the numbers men (including his brother, Roy) who tried to inhibit his forays. His instincts, both in art and commerce, were brilliant, and he completely trusted them. He was uninterested in figuring out what "the people" wanted; he pursued what *he* wanted. And he wouldn't have wanted *Dinosaur*.

As one of the true pioneers of the motion picture industry, Walt Disney posed a sharp contrast to his fellow moguls. Louis B. Mayer, Harry Cohn, and Jack Warner: they were obsessed with glamour and glitz. Disney, who came to Hollywood from Illinois in 1923, just wanted to draw *Mickey Mouse* and *Lucky Rabbit*, and *Silly Symphony* animated shorts. The other moguls yearned to work with big stars. Yet when Mary Pickford approached Walt about doing *Alice in Wonderland* (she would play the title role surrounded by his animated characters), Disney rejected the project.

Mayer and the others were rough guys who yelled a lot. Disney possessed a quiet charisma; his manner was distanced, not confrontational. The moguls (except for Darryl F. Zanuck) were Jewish guys whose manner and tastes were still tied to their Eastern European roots. Disney remained something of a hick from the Midwest who thought of Jews as accountants and merchants. I once made the mistake of asking Walt a question that had business implications (we were having lunch in the Disney commissary at the time) and he replied by saying, "Let me check that with my Jew." He started to summon a financial aide nearby, but I quickly changed the subject.

The first time I visited Disneyland (I was a young reporter for the *New York Times* then), I was delighted that Walt actually decided to meet me there. As he showed me around, several things became clear: First, it was the design and engineering of the rides that still intrigued him, not the business side or the merchandising. Second, he had invented this theme park for adults—indeed for himself—not as a playground for children. It was not that he disliked children—he paused once or twice to smile at some kids and pat heads—but he, obviously, was not especially interested in their response to his creation. This was the House of Walt, not a kiddie park.

And, yes, I discovered that I really liked Walt. He was a curious man, the classic maverick. He wasn't particularly engaging and had none of the CEO's ingratiatingly sociopathic traits. He was indeed more akin to his animated characters, impulsive and intrinsically amusing. It was as though he understood that the sum total of his experience defied all reasonable expectations. He had created an empire unlike that of any other innovator—one that was totally the product of his imagination.

Snow White and the Seven Dwarfs, the movie he produced between 1934 and 1937, was the ultimate product of Walt Disney's idiosyncratic creativity. It was a film that seemed at first to be out of synch with the times, and counterintuitive on a business level. It was the wrong project at the wrong time, and everyone around Walt essentially told him so with relentless persistence. But it was something Walt felt he had to do. It was not so much a product as a compulsion. There was no business plan; there was simply a creative drive.

At that time, the mid '30s, there was little to be optimistic about. Though the national economy had shown a spark of life by 1937, thanks to the programs of President Franklin D. Roosevelt, unemployment was again on the rise, hovering around 20 percent by the end of the year and efforts to revive the economy seemed fruitless. What had been the Hoover Depression was now being called the Roosevelt Depression, but it was a Depression nonetheless.

To be sure, Hollywood was thriving as a provider of a wide range of escapist fare. The hits of the moment ranged from *The Life of Emile Zola* starring Paul Muni to Laurel and Hardy's *Way Out West*, from *Camille* with Greta Garbo to *The Awful Truth* starring Cary Grant.

And the Disney studio itself had seen hefty profits from its animated shorts. Audiences were delighted with Walt's cast of characters ranging from Goofy to Pluto to Donald Duck. But by the '30s, theater owners were increasingly booking double features as an added inducement to filmgoers and the demand for cartoons was declining. To Walt, the writing was on the wall: It was time to move into the great unknown. Shorts were yesterday's news. Animated features were the future.

Walt's brother, Roy, his financial mentor, was stunned by this decision. With profits in decline, Walt wanted to budget as much as $250,000 for a new venture (it would ultimately escalate to $1.7 million), yet the resources were not there to support it.

Walt, however, was focused on another type of resource. He had surrounded himself with a uniquely skilled band of animators, many of them Midwesterners like himself, and they were as loyal as they were talented. They would rally to his side, he told himself.

Veteran Disney art director Ken Anderson recalls, "One night in 1934, we came back to the studio to work after dinner, and Walt called forty of us onto a small recording stage. We all sat in folding chairs, the lights went down, and Walt spent the next four hours telling us the story of *Snow White and the Seven Dwarfs*. He didn't just tell the story, he acted out each character, and when he got to the end he told us that this was going to be our first feature. It was a shock to all of us because we knew how hard it was to do a cartoon short. He was doing something no other studio had ever attempted, but his excitement over *Snow White* inspired us all."

Says animator Ollie Johnston, who also was present that evening, "It took guts to do what Walt did. The story is based on the idea that the Queen is going to murder this girl. That's one drawing killing another drawing. Walt convinced us that this could be done so that it would be credible and we all believed him."

E. Cardon "Card" Walker, a camera operator on *Snow White* (and subsequently president of Disney), said of Walt: "He absolutely scared us all to death by betting the entire company's future on a full-length, animated film. Nobody, but nobody, thought people would sit still for a full-length cartoon. There almost wasn't enough money to finish it. In fact, Walt said the bankers were losing more sleep than he was."

Walt recalled years later: "You should have heard the howls when we started making a full-length cartoon. It was prophesied that nobody would sit through such a thing, but there was only one way we could do it and that was to plunge ahead and go for broke. There could be no compromising on money, talent, or time. The whole country was in the midst of a crippling Depression. . . . I admit that as the cost climbed higher and higher I, too, began to have some doubts. I wondered if we could ever get our investment back."

Disney's doubters focused not only on the economics of the project but also on the story. The notion of doing *Snow White* had first occurred to Walt when he was a newsboy in Kansas City and caught a silent film version of the Grimm's fairy tale, starring Marguerite Clark. Walt's idea was to draw Snow White and Prince Charming realistically, while the real stars of the show, the Seven Dwarfs would be caricatured characters in the manner of his short cartoons. The serious elements of the story would be unfolded in a credible enough manner to grab the adult audience while the dwarfs provided comic and musical hijinks to keep the kids happy.

As Roger Ebert described the process, "If Walt Disney's *Snow White* had been primarily about Snow White, it might have been forgotten soon after its 1937 premiere. But *Snow White* is really about the Seven Dwarfs, and the evil Queen and the countless creatures of the forest and skies, from a bluebird that blushes to a turtle who takes forever to climb a flight of stairs. . . . Disney's inspiration was not in creating *Snow White*, but creating her world. When he decided to make a full-length feature, he instinctively knew that the film would have to grow not only in length, but in depth."

Walt's key aim was to give his supporting cast a variety of distinctive personalities. When *Snow White* first comes across the cottage of the dwarfs, she goes upstairs and sees their nameplates: "Sleepy," "Grumpy," "Dopey," and so on. The dwarfs and other creatures are immensely entertaining, and yet much of the surrounding material is darkly Grimmish—the Queen's fall to her death, etc. For all the rump-butting of the animals, there also were dark reminders that this was, after all, a true Grimm fairy tale.

Walt Disney persevered in his ambitious plan, though the production process was excruciating in every detail. The task of making the dwarfs lovable was given priority by the corps of animators. Walt had decreed, for example, that each of the dwarfs was to be utterly individualistic; each would even snore in a different sound, thus creating what he called "a symphony of snores."

The scene in which the dwarfs march home from the jewel mine singing "Heigh-ho" itself took almost six months to create, requiring some 2,000 drawings. It was drawn principally by an artist named Shamus Culhane, who was acutely mindful of the shortage of money and time. One day his assistant dropped cigarette ashes onto his stack of drawings and flames erupted. Culhane realized that the "Heigh-ho" sequence was no more; there were surely no funds available to redraw the scene. After a careful examination, however, he decided the drawings weren't so badly damaged that they could not be photographed. The sequence lived on.

A training program for the artists was started informally at animator Art Babbitt's home and later moved to the studio. Don Graham, an instructor from Chouinard Art Institute, was brought in to help in the animators' training. He taught them how to make simple and direct statements, his "action analysis" classes with live models proved helpful and, as a result, *Snow White* was able to overcome the stiffness and awkward motions that had earlier plagued Disney's female characters.

Production costs still spiraled from the initial $250,000 budget to $1.7 million. For the three years the film was on the drawing boards (1934–1937), Walt Disney and his brother Roy put up everything they owned as collateral. Hollywood tagged the production "Disney's Folly."

Walt later admitted: "We had no idea how long it would take. The undertaking had no precedent. No one had ever tackled a similar job and after we started we just went on shooting and experimenting until the thing was finished. And it took almost three years. The process of making a full-length dramatic feature in color called for new photographic equipment. Most of the conventional machinery used for making animated motion pictures had to be scrapped and new devices invented. An entirely new kind of story-telling technique had to be developed."

Walt's exasperation was heightened when he was compelled to show his still-unfinished film to bankers and key exhibitors. He looked on in terror as W. G. Van Schmus, the august general manager of the Radio City Music Hall, then the biggest and most important theater in the nation, saw bits and pieces of *Snow White*. Before even leaving the screening room, Van Schmus booked the movie into his giant theater, providing Walt and his colleagues an enormous psychological—and financial—boost.

Shortly thereafter, Walt ran the same material for Joe Rosenberg, the taciturn vice president of the Bank of America, from whom Walt needed a $250,000 leap of faith. Rosenberg did not give any indication of his reaction as he left the screening room and headed toward his car. Finally, he turned to an anxious Walt and said, "That thing is going to make a potfull of money." The line of credit was secure.

Meanwhile, Walt faced a conflict with his long-term distributor, United Artists. The sales gurus at United Artists insisted that *Snow White* be marketed as a romance, because its central story involved a prince and princess. Walt wanted the film sold as a fairy tale because, as he put it with his customary bluntness, "That's the way it is." There was another wrinkle as well. Though their deal with United Artists had yet another year to run, Walt and Roy insisted that the contract be revised to give them control of future television rights—an amazing insight into future technology. United Artists balked and Walt and Roy moved their deal to RKO.

Amid these intrigues, the film continued to expand, now encompassing more than two million drawings and sketches assembled by a staff of some 750. In addition, an orchestra of more than eighty musicians was hired to score the movie. As Ken Anderson recalled, "We worked nights, weekends, until all hours. But we loved it; we were totally involved with the story Walt had told us and caught up in the challenge of making it happen."

The biggest problem facing the animators, ironically, related not to the comic creatures but to animating Snow White and her prince. The characters resisted caricature because they had to meet the standard criteria of beauty. In desperation, the decision was made to have their movements Rotoscoped, a process which Walt declined ever to discuss. Rotoscoping involved photographing live action against a blank background and integrating these shots with animated sequences by tracing them frame by frame onto the film and painting the photographed figures so they looked animated. As Richard Schickel pointed out, the figures never looked entirely in synch in the context of an animated film; "their movements are jerky and hesitant." Sheepish about the process, Disney publicists claimed that photographing live models had been done only for "study" and not to appear in the final product.

The studio was more garrulous, however, in describing other technical innovations, such as the multiplane camera, which was developed for *Snow White* to endow animated scenes with a 3–D quality by photographing the cartoon characters within painted backgrounds on several levels or on planes of glass. Each plane was lighted separately for effect and moved at different speeds. The picture overcame the flatness of previous animation.

Disney animators also worked feverishly to find final hues to be used in the backgrounds to suit the needs of Technicolor film. The fear was that the traditional hues used in cartoons would be too bright for an audience in a feature-length film, so the palette was softened.

If Walt was obsessive about his colors, he was even more attentive to the voices of the characters he had created. Prior to *Snow White*, the studio had never required natural voices for its cartoon characters, but now Walt insisted his princess should have a "universal voice." More than 150 actresses auditioned. They were identified only by number as Walt listened to them sing and speak. (He sat behind a screen; he preferred not to watch them, feeling that their physical appearance might influence his judgment.) One hopeful was Deanna Durbin—this was just prior to her successful screen career as a teenage star at Universal. She was passed over because her voice sounded too old.

In the end, Adriana Caselotti, a singer of some experience, was chosen to be the voice of Snow White. Caselotti later recalled, "All the dialogue and musical portions were done in a short period of time. I probably didn't work at the studio more than a week or two."

Of her voice, she said, "It's not my normal voice, of course. I had to push it up to get that never-never land quality Mr. Disney was looking for. It was easy for me to do because of my early operatic training." Caselotti later revealed that voicing *Snow White* was the highlight of her career, but she was unhappy that Walt left her name off the credits because he wanted to maintain a sense of mystery. Caselotti also said that she was paid only $14,000 for her work on the film and for public appearances.

She recalled: "Walt drove me home twice in his little old Essex. It was the middle of the Depression, and sometimes I didn't have the money for carfare. One day he took me to lunch across the street from the studio. I remember him saying, 'Adriana, see what a nice dinner we're having? It's fifty cents each. You can always come in here and eat.' What he didn't know was that I didn't have fifty cents. Until I started getting paid for each day I worked, sometimes I'd only have ten or fifteen cents."

Of the *Snow White* premiere: "I went with Harry Stockwell (voice of the Prince). We went to the door and the girl said, 'May I have your tickets?' I said, 'I'm 'Snow White' and this is 'Prince Charming.' The girl said, 'I don't care if you're the witch. You're not going in if you don't have a ticket.' When she wasn't looking, we sneaked in."

Snow White opened on December 21, 1937 at the Carthay Circle in Los Angeles. The film had been rushed in order to open during the Christmas holiday. Ken Anderson recalls: "As the date for the premiere of *Snow White* grew closer, we were running out of money and time. Everyone was putting in overtime to get the picture finished. The print from Technicolor arrived at the theater only a few hours before show time."

In attendance at the glittering premiere were Hollywood's royalty: Charlie Chaplin (he was prepping his controversial *The Great Dictator*), a young Judy Garland, Douglas Fairbanks, Carole Lombard, John Barrymore, Charles Laughton, Marlene Dietrich, *Amos 'n Andy* stars Freeman Gosden and Charles Correll, tennis champ Fred Perry, Louella Parsons, and Ed Sullivan.

"The audience was so taken by the magic of what they had seen that they applauded after individual sequences, just as though they were watching a stage play—I've never seen anything quite like it since," observed "Woolie" Reitherman, a Disney animator.

Walt was so unnerved at the event that, when asked by an interviewer to talk about the dwarfs, Walt Disney could only remember the names of "Doc," "Happy," "Grumpy," and "Dopey." "I can't remember them all tonight," he chuckled.

In the background, an orchestra played tunes from the film and Caselotti sang. Real dwarfs, dressed in costumes, frolicked about the cottage and diamond mine the studio had built on Wilshire Blvd.

The critics' reaction was ecstatic. Said *Variety*: "There never has been anything in the theatre quite like Walt Disney's *Snow White and the Seven Dwarfs*, seven reels of animated cartoon in Technicolor, unfolding an absorbingly interesting and, at times, thrilling entertainment. So perfect is the illusion, so tender the romance and fantasy, so emotional are certain portions when the acting of the characters strikes a depth comparative to the sincerity of human players that the film approaches real greatness. It is an inspired and inspiring work, the commercial success of which will be notable."

The *New York Times'* Frank S. Nugent declared, "Let your fears be quieted at once: Mr. Disney and his amazing technical crew have outdone themselves. The picture more than matches expectations. It is a classic, as important cinematically as *The Birth of a Nation* or the birth of *Mickey Mouse*. Nothing quite like it has been done before; and already we have grown impolite enough to clamor for an encore. Another helping, please!"

Some reviewers were more critical. Otis Ferguson wrote in the *New Republic* that when the queen transformed into a crone she bore an uncomfortable resemblance to Lionel Barrymore. He was also disappointed in the comedy—things kept running into doors and trees.

A few critics expressed concern that the film was too violent and frightening for children—a charge that occasionally was leveled at Disney movies in later years. Dr. Benjamin Spock later wrote that the seats in Radio City Music Hall had been wet so often by frightened children that they had to be reupholstered. The most controversial moments of *Snow White* were when the Queen transformed herself into a crone and when the huntsman's knife seemed to flash down on the girl, leaving it unclear whether he'd killed her.

Nonetheless, over the first three months more than 20 million people came out to see *Snow White*, a box office record that was held until *Gone with the Wind* was released in 1939. The run at the Radio City theater was the longest on record surpassing *Top Hat*, *Cavalcade*, and *Little Women*, thus paying off the faith of its general manager, Van Schmus.

Walt Disney himself was astonished and daunted by the rapturous reception. Praise came from unexpected sources: Sergei Eisenstein, the great Russian filmmaker, called it "the greatest movie ever made." Other artists joined in praising Walt's courage as well as his artistic achievement. In the face of all this, Walt seemed to duck for cover. He attended the Academy Awards on February 23, 1939, however, where he received a special award of a golden Oscar inscribed, "To Walt Disney for *Snow White and the Seven Dwarfs*, recognized as a significant screen innovation which has charmed millions and pioneered a great new entertainment field for the motion picture cartoon." The award was presented by a nine-year-old Shirley Temple.

But Walt's primary aim was to get back to work. His colleague, "Woolie" Reitherman, visited Walt at the studio the morning after the premiere and remembered: "Instead of talking about how he could now take a little rest after all the tensions of the past four years, he began talking about his next animated feature and how he wanted to get started right away and all the new things we were going to do at the studio. That was Walt."

In part, Walt's instinct was one of self-preservation. He did not think of himself as a great artist; he was a guy who drew cartoons and whose tastes happened to be in synch with those of the general public. He was also a man with large dreams. He envisioned building a vast model community of homes. He saw his studio expanding in important new directions.

What he never envisioned was the giant empire that Michael Eisner was to perpetuate in his name, spanning television, theme parks, cruise lines, and $100 million tentpole pictures that were to open in multiple big-city premieres around the world. It was to be the crowning paradox of Eisner's reign that the one sector he could not sustain was animation—the seedbed of the company he inherited. Eisner managed to build a multi-billion-dollar mega-company, but Walt's unique vision eluded him.

The Disney empire had become all about money; the quirks were gone and so was the art.

Hence, following Eisner's forced retirement in 2005, one of the first steps taken by his successor, Bob Iger, was to outsource animation—at least that's what it essentially came down to. The focus of animation would be, not the Disney studio where Walt had long labored, but rather Pixar's studio in Emeryville, California. The chief of newly acquired Pixar, Steve Jobs, reminded Disney old-timers of old Walt in some ways—his independence, passion, and reliance on his "gut" to determine company products. Walt Disney would not have been pleased to see the torch being handed to someone outside his studio, but at least it would be passed to another maverick, not some anonymous corporate bureaucrat.

23 Fadeout for the Little Tramp
Modern Times (1936)

As the actor, he was the lovable loser, the short, dorky little vagabond with the ridiculous, pointy footed walk, who was always messing up the job, losing the girl, and getting swept away by the forces of power and privilege. As a filmmaker, he crafted his stories so that he was the champion of the little man oppressed by bosses, by cops, and by big business.

And when he jauntily waddled into the distance at the end of *Modern Times*, Paulette Goddard finally at his side, the violins wafting "Smile" in the background, who could resist a tear? Charlie Chaplin was the ultimate movie icon. How could it be that his public, indeed his industry, ultimately turned against him?

Chaplin started production on *Modern Times* in 1932, twenty years before he was effectively forced into exile. Still the clouds were beginning to loom even as he started on the film. Following the release of his hit, *City Lights*, Chaplin had embarked on an eighteen-month trip to Europe in which he sought out the company of those he regarded as the seminal thinkers of his time, ranging from George Bernard Shaw to Winston Churchill to Mahatma Gandhi. Appalled by the worldwide economic depression and the rise of fascism, Chaplin steeped himself in books on economics and politics.

And he also realized that his own still youthful industry was rushing past him. The era of silent pictures was over, yet Chaplin's Little Tramp was a creature of the silent era who had delighted his audience in *The Gold Rush*, *The Circus*, and *The Kid*. Chaplin realized, too, that the cost of making films was on the rise and he could no longer subsist, as *Variety* pointed out at the time, on "a hit-and-miss schedule . . . according to his moods." Chaplin's moods were, indeed, operatic—as was his personal life, which was periodically disrupted by his recurring fascination with extremely young women.

One of those women, Paulette Goddard, was to become an important force in *Modern Times*. Chaplin met her on the yacht owned by Joseph Schenck, the imperious mogul who was president of United Artists and would found Twentieth Century Pictures (later Twentieth Century Fox) in concert with Darryl F. Zanuck. The ravishing Goddard, born Pauline Levy in 1911, had been a Ziegfeld girl at fourteen, married and divorced by the age of sixteen and, by twenty-one, was ready to take on the mercurial Chaplin. Though a bit over age by Chaplin's standards, Goddard inspired Chaplin to create the part of the "Gamine," a teenage orphan and street urchin who would be his co-star in *Modern Times*.

After his long layoff, Chaplin seemed ready to attack the subject with a special passion, but also a certain ambivalence. He was enormously wealthy by this time, a Brahmin of the new film elite who received the world's celebrities and self-styled great thinkers at his Beverly Hills mansion. But he'd climbed far to get to Beverly Hills, growing up in 1890s London, often going hungry as a child. It was this early poverty that led him to return to themes of class differences, oppression, and hunger even while hovering in the privileged stratosphere of a superstar.

Born to music hall performers, Chaplin came to the United States on tour with a vaudeville troupe and stayed on when William Morris got him a gig in the New York theater. After moving to Hollywood, he stumbled upon the Little Tramp character while playfully experimenting with costumes at Mack Sennett's Keystone Films. Restless and pugnacious, he began directing and starring in a series of pioneering short films starting in 1914, scraping together enough money to build his own studio at La Brea and Sunset in 1918. By 1931, *City Lights* was already a semi-anachronism, since most films, including that year's Oscar winner, *Grand Hotel*, were made with synch sound. Chaplin, however, was still at home with the Little Tramp, and in his mind it was clear that the character should not speak. Implicit in this stubborn notion was the reality that his signature character's days were numbered.

Chaplin had returned on June 10, 1932 from his eighteen-month world tour, but no longer felt comfortable in Hollywood. He was in no mood to battle the talkies. Briefly he talked about retiring, but, still in his early forties, he was too restless to turn his back on the business he loved.

Besides, he sensed he still had his fan base. He told *Film Pictorial* magazine in December 1934 that the reason he didn't work more often was that he didn't want his public to tire of him—a deft rationalization. "Particularly since the influx of the talkies, Chaplin believes that even one silent film a year would be a bigger dose than filmgoers would swallow," the magazine said. "He thinks the films should be so far apart that they will be genuine novelties, something for which the public will be waiting. There is no way of telling whether Charlie's star has dimmed until his new film is put on the market."

In July 1932, Chaplin had his fateful encounter with Goddard on Schenck's yacht. Goddard had played bit parts in several films and had been the family breadwinner since childhood. Chaplin identified with all this; he was also vulnerable to a new romantic linkup.

At the time, he was beset by tax problems and was even instructed by his lawyers to destroy the negative of Josef von Sternberg's *Sea Gulls*, which he helped produce, to prove that the losses taken on the 1926 film were justified. His own company, United Artists, was also having problems. UA had been founded in 1919 by Chaplin and his friends Mary Pickford, Douglas Fairbanks, and D. W. Griffith. Their aim at the time was to protect their interests as an independent against the oligopoly posed by a recent series of mergers in exhibition and distribution. Chaplin also was preoccupied with writing the memoir of his European adventure for *Woman's Home Companion* for a fee of $50,000. His brother, Sidney, was prodding him to get to work on another film, which would prove far more lucrative than writing for ladies' magazines, (although $50,000 was no small payday at the time).

Still uncertain and unfocused, Chaplin acquired his own yacht called *The Panacea* in the spring of 1933, and after a few pleasure trips, took advantage of the seclusion to work on the scenario that was to become *Modern Times*. There would clearly be a major part for his companion, Goddard.

At this time, Chaplin also was beginning to come under fire for speaking out on politics, arguing that high unemployment would ultimately undermine the free-market myth. He'd even decided to sell off his own portfolio of stocks.

In 1932, Franklin D. Roosevelt had been elected to his second term, the Spanish Civil War had begun, unemployment had passed 17 percent, and much of Middle America had become the Dust Bowl. By the time Chaplin was shooting *Modern Times*, Roosevelt's New Deal was beginning to grapple with the Great Depression, but so-called "Hoovervilles"—tin-and-tarpaper shacks for the homeless—still surrounded major cities.

Chaplin was preoccupied by these conditions as he prepared his script, which at first was titled "Commonwealth," and later "The Masses." He gave an interview to Flora Merrill of the *New York World*, in which he commented, "Machinery should benefit mankind. It should not spell tragedy and throw people out of work. Labor-saving devices and other modern inventions were not really invented for profit, but to help humanity in the pursuit of happiness."

Though enthusiastic about Roosevelt and the New Deal, Chaplin was wary of inserting social commentary in his films. "I am always suspicious of a picture with a message," he told Merrill.

Yet the scenes invading his imagination all reflected a distinct point of view: The Little Tramp posing as a steam shovel operator; the Gamine being punished for eating surplus eggs; even an alternate ending in which the disillusioned Gamine becomes a nun. Following a trip to Detroit, Chaplin also was obsessed with the image of the assembly line. To him, man's production in industry had become a dehumanizing force.

Chaplin never completed a full-length script of *Modern Times*. Still, dialogue scenes were written in the eventuality that he might decide to shoot with sound. He even brought on Carter De Haven as a general assistant to pursue this possibility and in November 1933, he sent an outline of dialogue scenes to chief censor, Will H. Hays, so that he might elicit early warm-up of code violations.

Production designer Danny Hall leased four acres of land in the port town of Wilmington to build a street set and factory. The customary open-air, silent film-style stage was covered with a roof to allow for possible sound shooting. Chaplin clearly understood that the rising cost of labor and of location shots on the San Pedro docks made a leisurely production pace impossible.

Shooting on *Production no. 5*, as it was designated, started October 11, 1932. The production manager, Alf Reeves, who had been with Chaplin since his vaudeville days, assured everyone that Chaplin expected to have the picture finished by January 1935. As it happened, final shooting was not completed until August 30, 1935.

Throughout the production, Chaplin still wavered about using sound. He and Goddard did sound tests and both reportedly had pleasant voices that recorded well. Substantial dialogue was prepared for the department store sequence, for example, but the dialogue struck Chaplin as redundant, and he reverted to pantomime except for sound effects and the Tramp's final song, which was recorded in famous gibberish.

As if to emphasize his complete autonomy, Chaplin persisted in the expensive practice of cutting each sequence as it was finished, keeping the entire production crew on payroll through the process. *Variety* observed at the time, "*Modern Times* is as 100 percent a one-man picture as is possible. Produced, starring, authored, composed (special music) and directed by Chaplin, the pantomimist stands or falls by his two years' work as it unreels."

The ending still caused the auteur special anxiety. The original climax saw Charlie landing in the hospital with a breakdown. He is visited by the Gamine, who has now become a nun, and they part with sad smiles. Two months after shooting the scene, he decided it was a mistake. In a new, more optimistic ending, the Tramp and the Gamine would walk off into the sunset and the title card reads, "We'll get along."

During the extended shoot, Chaplin pushed himself to the limit, putting in eighteen-hour workdays, sleeping on a cot at the studio. He resisted delegating tasks to others, even producing the sound effects and, of course, the score.

Alfred Newman, who had worked with him on *City Lights*, was brought back as musical director and Edward Powell was to be orchestrator. Powell hired a young composer named David Raksin to work with him. Although only twenty-three years old, Raksin had already accumulated several important credits. Chaplin proceeded to convey the basic themes to Raksin, who created the score. In return, the young Raksin was liberal with his suggestions.

"When I think of it now, it strikes me as appallingly arrogant to have argued with a man like Chaplin about the appropriateness of the thematic material," Raksin later wrote. "In the area of music, the influence of the English music hall on him was very strong. I felt that nothing but the best would do for this remarkable film, so I thought his approach was a bit vulgar. I would say, 'I think we can do better than that.'" Chaplin, not surprisingly, fired Raksin, but Newman and Reeves persuaded him to take Raksin back.

Chaplin was particularly obsessive about his filmic set pieces which, he correctly anticipated, would achieve a certain immortality: There was the giant automated feeding device for workers designed to increase productivity; the shot of a worker stuck in the giant cogs of an automated machine; the department store roller-skating stunt with a blindfolded Chaplin blissfully circumnavigating the abyss; and the singing waiter scene where Chaplin's voice is finally heard. All of them became classic scenes of cinema comedy.

When Chaplin finally finished his edit and previewed *Modern Times* in San Francisco, audiences loudly applauded at the end. He still decided to make many additional changes.

In New York, *Modern Times* finally made its world premiere February 5, 1936 at the Rivoli Theatre, opening to solid business but mixed reviews. Responding to the knocks, when *Modern Times* opened at Grauman's Chinese Theatre in Hollywood a week later, Chaplin surprised the audience by appearing on stage to defend his film. His peroration lasted for twelve minutes.

He even lampooned the head of Fox West Coast Theatres, Charles Skouras, who had complained that for a $5.50 premiere price, Chaplin would have to give the audience much more than just a silent movie.

Chaplin later told Jean Cocteau, "I worked too long on *Modern Times*. When I had worked a scene up to perfection, it seemed to fall from the tree. I shook the branches and sacrificed the best episodes. They existed in their own right. I could show them separately, one by one, like my early two-reelers."

Chaplin's self-doubt was exacerbated after the film opened. "When we arrived home in Beverly Hills, news from the studio was encouraging. *Modern Times* was a success," Chaplin wrote. Yet he had difficulty in accepting the fact that the film did not reach the heights of ticket sales or financial success of his earlier pictures.

Chaplin hence decided to remove himself from the whole process. "Nothing is more nerve-wracking than to receive bulletins informing that the first week's attendance broke all records and that the second week fell off slightly," he complained. "Therefore, my one desire is to get as far away as possible from any news of the picture. I decided to go to Honolulu, taking Paulette and her mother with me and leaving instructions with the office not to send messages of any kind."

His fears were justified. *Modern Times* was Chaplin's first film that didn't achieve blockbuster status. The onslaught of heavy rain in Los Angeles didn't help. "Days on end of heavy downpour played havoc with grosses all around, with few spared," said *Variety*'s Los Angeles box office report on February 18, 1936, "Record week loomed for Charlie Chaplin's *Modern Times*, but J. Pluvious decreed otherwise and farmers are counting the profits instead of house managers."

Yet an ad in *Variety* read "Warning! No house record in the world is safe . . . either for cash or attendance . . . because Charlie Chaplin's *Modern Times* has already smashed every house record in the following cities! New York-Montreal-Boston-Philadelphia-Los Angeles-Miami-London."

Given this hoopla, none of the critics seemed ready to toll the death knell for silent films. The *New York Sun* reviewer called the movie "Somewhat old-fashioned, but boasting some grand slapstick." The *New York Times* said, "This morning there is good news. Chaplin is back again. Time has not changed his genius."

Despite these supportive notices, *Daily Variety* summed up critical opinion as "tepid." A February 6, 1936 story reported, "Notices were good, but not sensational. Reviewers for some reason were only mildly enthusiastic. Some sounded as if they remembered Chaplin from their kid days."

A week later, *Variety* excerpted the rave review from the *New York Journal*'s John Anderson, in which he lambasted the critics for not swooning enough: "The critics . . . somehow didn't bother to capture the delirium of the picture, or to indicate what seemed to me a highly exciting event of the theatre."

Audiences, too, indicated a certain hesitation. *Modern Times* grossed $1.4 million domestically, at least a half-million dollars less than each of Chaplin's previous films. Box office results did not even cover production costs until it went into foreign distribution, something highly unusual for a Chaplin film at the time.

Fortunately, Chaplin was one of the few Hollywood stars whose films were more popular overseas than at home, and although the film was banned in Italy and Germany, it was a hit in Chaplin's native England as well as Hong Kong, Japan, and other territories. A report from United Artists related: "Despite bad weather and a rickshaw strike, *Modern Times* had a brilliant premiere in Nanking's Metropol theatres also creating new record gross for Shanghai breaking previous record held by *City Lights*."

Despite the fanfare, *Modern Times* wasn't nominated for a single Academy Award in 1936. *The Great Ziegfeld* with William Powell and Myrna Loy won best picture while other Oscar-nominated films that year included Frank Capra's *Mr. Deeds Goes to Town*, Gregory LaCava's *My Man Godfrey*, and William Wyler's *Dodsworth*. It wasn't until Chaplin's later sound pictures, *The Great Dictator* (1940) and *Monsieur Verdoux* (1947), that his films received Oscar nominations, though still no wins, other than a 1973 music Oscar for the delayed release of *Limelight*.

Although *Modern Times* proved Chaplin could still please the public, his politics were proving to be increasingly troublesome. During the summer of 1935, a top emissary from the Soviet film industry, Boris Z. Shumiatsky, visited Chaplin's studio and screened a rough cut of the picture. Shumiatsky told *Pravda* upon his return that Chaplin had been receptive to his suggestions, that the pessimistic nun ending was a mistake, and that he thought a new ending would show Chaplin's awareness that it was important "to fight for a better life for all humanity with a conviction of the necessity for active struggle." The interview was reprinted in the *New York Times*, causing Chaplin uncomfortable moments.

Further, news that Chaplin had even considered "The Masses" as a possible title for *Modern Times* exacerbated the "communist sympathizer" charges. Catholic groups, too, learning that the "nun" ending had been dropped, also were weighing their response warily.

When Chaplin learned that the film had been banned by Benito Mussolini and Adolf Hitler, he told a United Press reporter "Dictators seem to believe the picture is Communistic. In view of recent happenings, I am not surprised by the ban. But our only purpose was to amuse. I have no political aims whatsoever as an actor. And anything Communistic would be quickly stamped out in the United States."

Indeed, Chaplin seemed to want to have it both ways. On the one hand, he was a businessman who faced recurring financial crises and, as such, was prepared to cut scenes that violated the Production Code or offended other enemies. Then there was the politically conscious Chaplin, who with Goddard, joined the Hollywood Anti-Fascist League, a left-leaning group whose ostensible purpose was to battle the mounting Nazi intimidation of the film industry.

When the film was released, leftist critics were confused by its mixed messages. One praised the film for showing how a capitalist factory had driven the Little Tramp mad, while another lectured Chaplin that "machines were not the enemy, they were necessary to raise the living standards of the working class."

After a trip to Asia, Chaplin cast about for his next project, working sporadically on a story on the life of Napoleon, which he had been considering for several years. He also worked on a script, which would eventually become the basis for *A Countess from Hong Kong.*

But first, he settled on his first all-sound picture, the self-financed *The Great Dictator*, which riveted world opinion makers as Hollywood's first statement against the Nazi dictatorship and the persecution of Jews. Its opening in 1940 was immensely successful. Yet Chaplin was never to regain the kind of mass-market success he enjoyed in the silent era of the '20s.

Chaplin's friendship with Orson Welles led to a collaboration on the story for *Monsieur Verdoux*, but the pair's participation in a 1942 Carnegie Hall political meeting led to another anti-Communist outcry. Suddenly, Chaplin's re-entry permit was revoked by Attorney General James P. McGranery because of "public charges" associated with Communism and other "grave moral" issues. While he could have legally challenged the ban, Chaplin had grown tired of running the political gauntlet. He decided on voluntary exile to Switzerland.

In 1972, several top Hollywood players stepped up pressure for the Academy of Motion Pictures Arts and Sciences to finally recognize the Little Tramp and his creator. They let it be known that the eighty-two-year-old Chaplin might be willing to return to the United States for the first time in twenty years to receive an honorary Oscar. In the end, Chaplin gratefully accepted his belated kudos and was accorded what may have been the loudest and longest ovation in the Academy Awards history.

Chaplin died of natural causes six years later, in 1977, leaving eight children from his marriage to Oona Chaplin and one surviving son from his early marriage to Lita Grey. But Chaplin's art lives on, thanks to the dawn of videocassettes, laserdiscs, and DVDs, all of which have provided a bonanza for students of cinema and created new generations of Chaplin lovers. A 1992 Fox Video/Image Entertainment laserdisc was the first *Modern Times* release to include supplemental material, such as an interview with composer David Raksin, who died in 2004. In 2003, Warner Home Video released a DVD of *Modern Times*, the transfer made from a new print restored by Cineteca Bologna, the Chaplin archive in Italy. The restored version was screened as the closing film at the Cannes Film Festival May 25, 2003, and played theatrically in several countries including the United States and France.

Writing in the *New York Observer* May 10, 2004, Andrew Sarris noted:

Charles Chaplin's *Modern Times* was hailed or reviled in its time as the first Chaplin film to tackle a theme of social significance with any degree of ideological consistency. Yet its alleged topicality was always the least of its charms . . . Chaplin hated machinery for reasons more aesthetic than ecological—an attitude more Luddite than Leninist . . . Chaplin himself remains the supreme cinematic performer of all time.

24 Studio Gorilla Tactics
King Kong (1933)

There are a handful of timeless images that immediately conjure up Hollywood movie magic: Charlie Chaplin as the Little Tramp, Humphrey Bogart in a trench coat, Marilyn Monroe with her skirt billowing over a subway grate, and a giant gorilla poised menacingly atop the Empire State Building.

While all of the stars are recognizable, the film titles may not be. (Is that the Bogie of *Maltese Falcon* or *Casablanca*?) Yet everyone knows the name of the mythic gorilla movie.

When it opened in 1933, RKO was on the brink of bankruptcy. If *King Kong* had tanked, it surely would have marked the end of the studio. Would the public accept a scary love story involving a five-foot blonde and an eighteen-foot gorilla?

As it turned out, *Kong* was a sensation, providing escapism of a grand scale for a nation that had sunk into a desperate economic sinkhole. Dwindling movie admissions instantly recovered as film scholars and psychoanalysts were left to scramble for explanations of the film's extraordinary appeal. Some said it was a metaphor for the immigrant experience—after all, African Americans were brought to our shores in chains, like Kong. Others more expansively cited Kong as the embodiment of Depression-era rage against the failed promise of capitalism. Still others suggested that the movie represented the ultimate sex fantasy—witness *Kong* removing Fay Wray's dress and then delicately sniffing his hand (a scene which censors

King Kong

277

later were to remove). Under this theory, *Kong* was the perfect precursor to the "size matters" school of horror flick.

When asked whether the Empire State Building was intended as the ultimate phallic symbol, Merian C. Cooper, the film's creator, scoffed. He was exasperated at "all these super-intellectual ideas." He had intended the movie as "escapist entertainment pure and simple."

King Kong was released on March 2, 1933, a few days before Franklin D. Roosevelt's inauguration as President. It was the low point of the Depression. That month, Roosevelt declared a moratorium and closed banks. Yet *King Kong* set records at Radio City Music Hall. That opening weekend saw an estimated 50,000 tickets sold.

A singular driving force is usually present behind every film project of *Kong*'s magnitude, and Merian C. Cooper, a self-styled playboy–adventurer, was clearly the propellant behind the great gorilla saga. Cooper loved travel and adventure, and he also understood that adventure could be packaged as a business. *Kong* represented the classic realization of that vision. Cooper codirected and coproduced the film as well as cowrote the script. He recruited pivotal backers and investors along the way—even David O. Selznick, then a honcho at RKO, became a believer. It was Cooper who had the vision and persevered despite the many obstacles.

Cooper was a rich man's son; a prep school graduate who got bounced out of Annapolis in his senior year for excessive partying. Perhaps it was this experience that prompted a life-long compulsion to prove his machismo. He became a combat pilot in World War I and was shot down in a dogfight over France. This led to two years in a German prison camp. Not long after the war Cooper turned up in Poland fighting the Bolsheviks, an experience (real or imagined) which led him to become a lifetime anti-Communist crusader. In 1921, he joined the *New York Times* as a reporter then became a correspondent for *Asia* magazine.

As a certified global adventurer, Cooper was eager to join the documentary film craze that had been kicked off by Robert Flaherty's 1922 *Nanook of the North*. That documentary chronicled a year in the life of an Inuit tribesman and his family in the Arctic. *Nanook* whetted audience appetite for more films about primitives who were far removed from normal society. Big-game hunters, such as Frank Buck, who acquired the nickname "Bring 'em Back Alive," stirred the imagination of Depression-era folk.

Unlike other hunters who brought back animal skins or heads, Buck returned to the United States with exotic animals from Africa, South America, Borneo, and New Guinea. He sold many of these animals to zoos and circuses, wrote first-person accounts, and also produced several motion pictures, including three adapted from his books: *Bring 'em Back Alive* (1932, the year before *Kong*), *Wild Cargo* (1934), and *Fang and Claw* (1935).

Cooper and his friend Ernest B. Schoedsack, a cameraman, wanted to be part of these adventures. After filming documentary footage of Ethiopia, the two traveled to the Persian Gulf, where they shot the 1925 documentary *Grass*, about the Bakhtiari tribe that makes an annual migration over a perilous mountain range.

Two years later, they again collaborated on *Chang*, chronicling their fourteen months in the jungles of Siam. Like *Nanook*, it concerned a family's struggles to survive against nature. It was a success, despite grumbles that the producers had staged sequences and manipulated real-life events for dramatic effect.

The nadir of pseudo-documentaries was the 1931 *Ingagi*—not one of Cooper's. In one scene, several "African" women, who are conveniently topless, are chased by a gorilla. The women, in fact, were Californians and the "gorilla" was an actor in an ape suit. The film boasted a "virgin sacrifice" which also was staged in Southern California.

After *Chang*, Cooper and Schoedsack were hired to shoot footage for *Four Feathers* in Africa, an experience that evoked Cooper's own fascination with gorillas. Fueling his imagination were tales of his friend, Douglas Burden of the American Museum of Natural History, who had just returned from the Dutch East Indies with a pair of Komodo dragons or, as they were then called, "dragon lizards."

Inspired by these tales, Cooper hoped to shoot footage of a gorilla in the Congo, then go to Komodo Island and film the dragons, and tie the footage together. His plan was to "giantize" the gorilla and personalize his traits and mannerisms. Cooper also had the idea to pair his gigantic gorilla with a gigantic building. As it turns out, the tallest building in the world was under construction in Manhattan: the Empire State building, completed in 1931.

On June 12, 1964, Cooper wrote a letter to Burden, recalling their earlier talks: "Your description of Komodo Island fulfilled my dramatic 3–D's—Distance, Difficulty, Danger . . ." Burden wrote back to encourage him, recalling how Cooper had contacted him before at the museum seeking information about gorillas. "Your invention of the name *Kong* had stuck in his mind," Burden wrote.

Cooper decided to write a screenplay and, in 1931, went to Hollywood to pitch the project to the studios. None were interested in his story, but they were interested in him.

Cooper later wrote that he'd found RKO in turmoil. David O. Selznick was taking hold with a firm hand and asked Cooper to work for him. Cooper reiterated that he was focused only on producing *King Kong*, but nobody in Hollywood was willing to commit the considerable money. Hence Cooper ended up taking the Selznick job anyway.

Like other industries, the studios were hit hard by the Depression. The payroll of the major companies had tumbled to $50 million from $156 million two years earlier. "Screen tests and interviews with players at studios have been called off because of uncertainty of future production," *Variety* reported. Facing bankruptcy, David O. Selznick had put all productions on hold. Cooper's job was to evaluate projects left over from the previous administration to see if they were still viable.

One such project was *Creation*, a film dealing with prehistoric animals. Cooper wrote a memo to Selznick dated December 19, 1931 stating, "The present story construction and the use of the animals is entirely wrong. The whole secret of successful productions of this type is to create a sense of sensation. But that sensation must have character. Animals can be made into sensational characters, as well as people. My idea is to take them out of their present character of just big beasts running around, and make them into a ferocious menace. The most important thing is that one animal should have a really big character part in the picture. I suggest a prehistoric Giant Gorilla, fifty times as strong as a man—a creature of nightmare horror and drama."

Despite this sort of persistent prodding, Selznick was still not enthusiastic about Cooper's gorilla film. "He didn't have the slightest idea what I was doing. Still, he said that while Schoedsack and I had only made three films they had all been smashes, so he'd back me. And he did, too. He never interfered, never tried to tell me what to do," Cooper wrote.

RKO assigned British adventure–mystery writer Edgar Wallace to flesh out the *Kong* screenplay; Cooper agreed to share screen credit. Wallace promptly died of pneumonia after finishing a draft. Ruth Rose, who was married to Schoedsack, then took his place. The studio later insisted on restoring Wallace's credit, since he was a household name and would supposedly give weight to the project. Wallace had written 175 books in his relatively brief lifetime. At one point, his publisher claimed that 25 percent of all books purchased in the country had been written by Wallace.

In working on *Creation*, Cooper was impressed by Willis O'Brien, who had pioneered the process of stop-motion. Cooper didn't like *Creation*, but liked O'Brien's work. Stop-motion uses miniature models that were pliable, the artists painstakingly move the model, shooting frame-by-frame, to create the illusion of movement. Cooper wanted to steal both the man and the process for *Kong*.

Since RKO executives continued to fret about risking so much on *Kong*, Cooper decided to create one reel to demonstrate his vision, and recruited O'Brien to help.

Cooper filmed a scene where several men were poised on a log that served as a bridge over a deep chasm. An angry Kong shakes the log until they all fall to their death. Reception to the reel was enthusiastic; despite all the alarm that Cooper kept inventing new rules as he went along, the production money started flowing.

Soon O'Brien, too, started to worry about Cooper's brash rules. Kong was supposed to be eighteen feet tall, for example, and O'Brien and his team fought for consistency. But Cooper was a showman, and he didn't care if Kong's height varied: In some scenes, he seemed eighteen feet tall, in others, closer to sixty. To Cooper, this wasn't relevant.

Cooper said, "I felt confident that if the scenes moved with excitement and beauty, the audience would accept any height that fit into the scene. If Kong had been eighteen feet high on top of the Empire State Building, he would have been lost, like a little bug. So I continually shifted his height to fit the settings and illusions. He was different in practically every shot."

The RKO publicity department, meanwhile, continued to publicize *Kong* as a fifty-foot gorilla. The *King Kong* cast and crew even sent Cooper a Christmas card in 1932 in which Cooper is shown in the caricature yelling, "Make it bigger! Make it bigger!"

Though skeptical, O'Brien and his team labored on, making effective use of glass shots and rear projection, both crucial cost-saving devices. On glass shots, artists painted scenery on a plate of glass, which was placed in front of the camera. A portion of the glass was left blank, to capture actors' movements, so actors moved on a jungle setting that was carefully lined up with the glass. The rest of the jungle—the tall trees, the cliffs in the distance—had been painted on the upper portion of the glass.

Equally stubborn in casting, Cooper was adamant that the character of Ann Darrow be played by a blonde. At one point, the filmmaker hoped to land Jean Harlow, who was already an established name thanks to Howard Hughes's *Hell's Angels* (1930) and *The Public Enemy* (1931). Harlow was aloof to Cooper's entreaties, however. To her, it just seemed like another job. She had been turning out as many as twelve films a year and despite Cooper's hard sell, didn't think this one would be especially distinctive.

Then someone suggested Fay Wray. Cooper had Wray spend one full day practicing her scream, shrieking up and down the scale until she hit the perfect note of terror. Based on her scream and blonde good looks, Cooper decided she would have the part.

The real star of the film was, of course, Kong himself, and he didn't even appear on camera until halfway through. Though the don't-show-the-monster idea is almost universally applied in contemporary scary movies, Cooper's approach was especially scary to RKO. When he was shooting *Jaws,* some four decades later, Steven Spielberg didn't reveal his deadly shark until well into the movie because he couldn't get the damned contraption to work. It wasn't a question of building suspense. Cooper was also fretful about his giant ape, but, more important, he felt it was vital to do a "long build," tossing in many suspense-building hints along the way. Early in the film, for example, as the crew of adventurers makes their way to Kong's island, one of the crew members turns to another and asks ominously, "What does he think he's going to see?" RKO executives, however, fearful that their company was going down the drain, wanted immediate thrills and chills.

Cooper fought his battles throughout the film's excruciatingly long fifty-five-week schedule. Along the way the cost-cutting pressure was incessant. The RKO production chief, B. B. Kahane, even asked Max Steiner, head of the music department, to eliminate the music score (some films at the time simply appropriated themes from Tchaikovsky or other composers for their main themes). RKO executives thought the gorilla looked phony, but Cooper ordered Steiner to get to work, offering to pay him himself. The score was a landmark.

Despite Selznick's survival strategy, in January 1933, RKO went into receivership. In February 1933, a month before *Kong* opened, Selznick himself resigned, moving over to MGM. Cooper assumed the role of production head at RKO, and one of his first battles predictably was over his gorilla movie. RKO's marketing team thought the title *King Kong* sounded like a movie about a Chinese general. Cooper irately disagreed. And now he was positioned to win this sort of argument: He was the boss.

When *King Kong* finally previewed in San Bernardino in January 1933, audiences didn't worry about the title. They were caught up in the film—almost too intensely. In the scene where the sailors are eaten by giant insects, the audience screams were deafening. Patrons were chattering about the scene for the rest of the film.

"It stopped the picture cold," Cooper said, "so the next day back at the studio, I took it out myself. O'Brien was heartbroken: He thought it was the best work he'd done, and it was, but it worked against the picture so out it came."

The final negative cost of *King Kong* ranged from $430,000 to $513,242, depending on the source. Either way, the studio had bet big; *Variety* estimated RKO's ad campaign for *King Kong* at $25,000, a big number for the time—spent primarily in newspapers.

Top Hollywood publicist Russell Swanson wrote of *King Kong*, "If ever there was a show sired by the spirit of P. T. Barnum, it's the mastodonic miracle of the movies!"

RKO created a 1930s equivalent of an infomercial for radio. On February 10, 1933, the National Broadcasting Company aired a thirty-minute radio show about the film, a scripted work with realistic sound effects. The studio also created trailers that showed, not the monster, but shadow: "This is only the shadow of King Kong. See the greatest sight that your eyes have ever beheld at this theater—beginning this Sunday," the announcer proclaimed.

On February 28, before the film's Gotham premiere, *Variety* ran a two-page ad: "The only picture big enough to play the world's two greatest theaters at the same time. *King Kong* opens Thursday, March 2. Radio City Music Hall and Roxy Theatre 10,000 seats . . . 10 shows daily!"

Ads in the *New York Times* showed Kong holding Fay Wray atop the Empire State Building. The ad copy read: "KONG—THE MONSTER. Huge as a skyscraper . . . crashes into our city. See him atop the Empire State Tower, battling planes for the woman in his ponderous paw. King Kong out leaps the maddest imagination."

The Hollywood premiere was held March 24 at Grauman's Chinese Theatre. Owner Sid Grauman arranged for a seventeen-act musical show for the gala. The theater's forecourt displayed the bust of Kong that was used in filming his close-ups.

Variety's March 7 review was at once laudatory and bemused. "Highly imaginative and super-goofy, yarn is mostly about a 50-foot ape that goes for a five-foot blonde. . . . So purely an exhibition of studio and camera technology—and it isn't much more than that—*Kong* surpasses anything of its type which has gone before it in commercial filmmaking."

The review cited some of the film's shortcomings, such as the "machine-like movements" of its animals and the fact that the "story background is constantly implausible." Yet it went on to applaud the film's technical innovation.

Like *Variety*, Mordaunt Hall, in the *New York Times* on March 3, compared it to *The Lost World*. His review read: "Through multiple exposures, processed 'shots,' and a variety of angles of camera wizardry, the producers set forth an adequate story and furnish enough thrills for any devotee of such tales."

When it opened in other cities, the enthusiasm seemed contagious.

On March 27, *Variety* ran a story that stated, "Everything's *King Kong* this week. Everybody else is doing average business, but the ape man is aiming at a house record for Keith's."

Thanks to the hoopla and word of mouth, *King Kong* ended up grossing $2 million—more than four times its cost. The box office seems paltry now, but it was impressive in the middle of the Great Depression, when a loaf of bread cost a nickel and a movie ticket averaged thirty-five cents. Full-page ads for *Kong* ran in, *Variety* crowing "The Answer to Every Showman's Prayer! Give me a picture I can advertise and then BANK ON!"

RKO had banked on *King Kong* in a big way. Long before Universal released two *Back to the Futures* within a year, *King Kong* was so revered that RKO rushed out a sequel that *same* year. *Son of Kong* was more whimsical, with a more lovable giant ape. The Schoedsack-directed film, has a script again by Rose.

Many theories have been advanced as to why *King Kong* made such a formidable impact on cinema and culture. First, of course, was its bizarre love story, which had one of the most famous closing lines in movie history: "It wasn't the airplanes. It was beauty that killed the beast." The film opens with an "Arabian proverb" that states "And the prophet said: 'And lo, the beast looked upon the face of beauty. And it stayed its hand from killing. And from that day, it was as one dead." Cooper says he wrote that proverb; others attribute it to scripter Ruth Rose.

It wasn't just the love story that enthralled audiences. They also relished the destruction. Like *Lost World* before it, *Kong* showed civilization being laid to waste by primitive forces. After *Kong*, several films borrowed that theme, such as RKO's *The Last Days of Pompeii* (1935), *San Francisco* (1936), and *Hurricane* (1937).

With the onset of World War II, audiences lost their appetite for disaster movies. The image of destruction was all too real in newsreels. It wasn't until the 1950s when radiation and atomic testing were in the headlines that movie audiences again embraced the *Kong* genre. They welcomed *Godzilla* from Japan as well as giant bugs (*Them!*, *Tarantula*) or even proto-humans (*Attack of the 50-Foot Woman*). While the 1930s views of destruction were set in the past or in exotic locales, the 1970s disaster movies were vividly contemporary: *Airport*, *The Poseidon Adventure*, *Earthquake*, and *The Towering Inferno*. Producers seemed determined to reimagine the "real" into the "unreal."

In the decades since its premiere, *King Kong* has become an imposing brand name, spawning sequels, remakes and sequels to the remakes. In 1976, Dino De Laurentiis produced a version that featured Rick Baker, himself a makeup artist, in a monkey suit and Jessica Lange, in her film debut, sitting in Kong's palm as he climbed the World Trade Center towers. A decade later, De Laurentiis tried yet again with *King Kong Lives*, in which the giant ape survives the fall off the World Trade Center and is paired with a giant female ape.

And, of course, there is Peter Jackson's $208 million remake, which is set in Gotham in the 1930s and uses computer generated effects to create Kong.

In the meantime, there were homages such as *Mighty Joe Young* and the 1960 Brit film *Kong* as well as a slew of B-picture projects that traded off the name, such as the 1962 Japanese *King Kong vs. Godzilla*, the 1967 *King Kong Escapes*, and the 1968 *King of Kong Island*. Perhaps the strangest was *The Mighty Kong*, a 1998 animated musical version featuring Dudley Moore as the voice of both Carl Denham and Kong, with songs by the Richard and Robert Sherman (who wrote the tunes for *Mary Poppins*)!

Videogame players, of course, became fans of the game in which the heroine, Paula, must be saved from the giant gorilla with the odd name of Donkey Kong.

Kong itself was also reissued several times. In 1952, a censored version hit theaters. Cut from the rerelease were scenes showing the rampaging Kong eating one villager and stepping on another; the gorilla peeling away Fay Wray's dress and then sniffing his fingers; and Kong, in New York, picking up a blonde woman and then casually tossing her to her death when he realizes it's not Ann Darrow. Still, *Kong* clearly achieved his own unique immortality, his "lustful embraces" largely intact.

His creator, Merian C. Cooper, however, remained an all-but-forgotten figure in the industry. Post *Kong*, Cooper married actress Dorothy Jordan, and struggled to keep RKO aloft, but was more at ease as a promoter than as a corporate "suit." His RKO stint brought him a minor heart attack. After recuperation, he formed a venture in the mid '30s that brought forth a few Technicolor films, which Cooper rightly thought to be the trend of the future. The upshot was *Becky Sharp*, which didn't do much business, but won an Oscar nomination for Miriam Hopkins. A year later, he merged his company with that of David O. Selznick, but that partnership ended in acrimony. Their final quarrel was over the casting of *Stagecoach*; Selznick wanted to sign Gary Cooper and Marlene Dietrich, while Cooper favored John Wayne and Claire Trevor.

The advent of World War II finally provided Cooper with a stage that he could relate to. The old adventurer, now in his mid-forties, joined the United States Air Force and served as a combat pilot in the Far East, winning a Distinguished Service Medal. After the war, he was involved in producing a few John Wayne films like *Fort Apache* and *Rio Grande*. An ardent anti-Communist, he rallied to the support of Senator Joe McCarthy during his red-baiting crusade.

In discussing his John Wayne movies, Cooper explained: "The whole trick is to do something beautiful and American that will arouse the emotions of the audience . . . If they are ever recognized as a subtle kind of American propaganda, then I will have failed."

Always scouting for the next breakthrough, Cooper became smitten with Cinerama in the '50s, serving as a vice president and a board member of the company that pioneered the widescreen format. His aim, he said, was to make movies that "celebrated American history and the outdoors." The company closed after only a few productions. He was finally awarded an honorary Oscar in 1953 and died of cancer in 1973.

Cooper was the classic dreamer who, early in his life, achieved his "Big Dream" and, like his friend, Selznick, spent much of the rest of his life trying unsuccessfully to top it. Like Kong, he kept climbing and, like the character he invented, he couldn't manage to keep his footing when he reached the top.

The image of King Kong as a long-standing symbol of the Hollywood megapicture—the sure-fire hit—was clearly one that would endure through many generations of filmmakers. Yet Peter Jackson's version in 2005 did not turn out to be the money machine that the director or his studio, Universal, had envisioned. While the film generated a projected $550 million in film grosses around the world, the "take" was not sufficient to turn a profit on Universal's $208 million production budget plus another $100 million in worldwide advertising costs. Most surprisingly, though Jackson was the darling of the Oscars for his *Lord of the Rings* trilogy, Kong stirred little excitement among Academy voters, eliciting just four nominations.

Some of the charisma clearly had rubbed off of *King Kong*. Until, that is, the next generation of filmmakers decides to turn its attention to the creature.

25 Rule of the Rustics

Tobacco Road/Abie's Irish Rose
(1933/1922)

In most compilations of theater greats, Anne Nichols and Jack Kirkland do not exactly rank up there with Eugene O'Neill and Arthur Miller. Yet these two playwrights can rightly stake their claim to an important place in Broadway history.

Nichols and Kirkland created the two most popular theatrical hits of the '20s and '30s—shows with sharply contrasting settings and characters, but also with stunning similarities. Both plays were dismissed by critics as vulgar sideshows, yet both tapped into narratives that found wide appeal with the mass audience. And, most remarkably, both shows owed their success to the almost messianic dedication of their playwrights—unknown writers at the time, who believed so deeply in their work that they ended up cofinancing and coproducing them.

Abie's Irish Rose by Anne Nichols, which opened on May 23, 1922, was a *Romeo and Juliet* comedy about two families' efforts to stop the marriage of a Jewish boy to a Catholic girl. When it finally closed on October 11, 1927, it was the longest running show in Broadway history, and it still ranks as the third longest running nonmusical.

Tobacco Road by Jack Kirkland opened on December 4, 1933, and ended its amazing run eight years later, only to return to Broadway three more times. Meanwhile, touring companies were performing all over the United States (stirring up bad reviews and intense censorship campaigns) along with twenty-one countries abroad ultimately pulling in well over $5 million.

Both shows accomplished a feat that surely would be impossible on Broadway today, given the higher costs and the audience's shortened attention span. Opening to blistering reviews and tepid box office, they managed to sustain themselves long enough to build a word-of-mouth cult following.

Robert Benchley in *Life* magazine called *Abie's Irish Rose* "something awful" and the *New York Post* said "it seems that all the stock lines which were ever put into the mouths of the Jewish and Irish were heard once again." This critique may have had some validity, since Georgia-born Anne Nichols had no firsthand knowledge of the ethnic groups she was writing about. She'd hammered out her play in three days based on stories related to her by a friend. Yet, when the play was struggling, Nichols borrowed money from her lawyer, sold her sparse jewelry collection, and even elicited $30,000 from the mobster Arnold Rothstein to keep the show running.

Abie's reception was warm compared with that accorded *Tobacco Road*. Not only was Kirkland's play itself slammed, but the critics even mocked its audience. Said the *New York Herald Tribune*, "At the theater these nights are sailors arm-in-arm with gum-chewing blondes, truck drivers in wind breakers and rodeo bronco-busters who utter Indian war cries . . . Many of them have never seen a play before."

Traditional theatergoers were appalled not only by the language ("by God" and "by Jesus" were considered shocking phrases), but also by the *Tobacco Road* characters: Sister Bessie, the forty-year-old itinerant preacher who marries sixteen-year-old Dude because she can't keep her hands off of him; the farmer, Jeeter Lester, who married Ada when she was eleven and cheerfully admits he has no idea where his seventeen offspring live or even if they're still alive; one daughter, Pearl, fourteen, who won't sleep with her husband on general principles.

As the play opened around the country, local officials reacted like Mayor Edward J. Kelly of Chicago, who revoked the license of its theater to halt a "mass of filth and degeneracy." As word of the "filth" spread, the audience kept swelling in city after city.

Still, Kirkland had to sink his own money into the Broadway production to keep it from folding, and actors agreed to cut their pay to the forty dollar a week minimum until it found its legs.

Kirkland was drawn to the tale because, like Jeeter and his kin, the Kirklands were a large family of poor Southern dreamers. Unlike the fictional Lester clan, though, the Kirklands were of genteel Southern stock. Jack Kirkland was born in St. Louis, Missouri, the youngest of nine children. He began work at sixteen at the *St. Louis Post-Dispatch*, and worked at a variety of newspapers. His clips were good enough to earn him a scholarship to the Columbia School of Journalism. While he soon landed a job at the *Daily News* in New York, he became enamored of theater when he met actress Nancy Carroll, whom he married in 1925.

His first play, *Frankie and Johnnie*, set in a waterfront saloon, opened in September 1930. After the third performance, the police arrested the writer, ten actors, and four others at Brandt's Carlton Theater in Jamaica, New York, charging them with indecent behavior. Two years later, the State Court of Appeals overturned the convictions, stating, "the fact that Frankie and Johnnie and their companions were not nice people does not in itself make the play obscene."

Kirkland and Carroll shortly moved to Hollywood, where she appeared in *The Devil's Holiday*. Meanwhile, Kirkland picked up random screenwriting jobs, working on such films as *Now and Forever*, starring the unlikely combo of Shirley Temple, Gary Cooper, and Carole Lombard.

In spring 1932, an agent gave Kirkland a copy of *Tobacco Road* by Erskine Caldwell, figuring that, as a Southerner, he would enjoy the new novel. Kirkland not only liked it, he felt it was a play. He decided to hide out in Majorca for three months to adapt it to the stage. "I'd made a few bucks on the Shirley Temple movie," he said. "You might say Shirley was really responsible for *Tobacco Road*."

Tobacco Road seemed an astonishing leap of faith to experienced theater folk. Broadway had never been particularly hospitable to the problems of poor farmers. Further, as raw as it was, *Tobacco Road* was not quite comedy and not quite *Grapes of Wrath* drama. The book was not yet a best seller, so Caldwell agreed to Kirkland's request for a free option, doubtless assuming that nothing would ever come of this effort. In exchange, Kirkland agreed to split any profits fifty-fifty with Caldwell.

Caldwell, a missionary's son born on an isolated farm deep in the red clay hills of Coweta Country, Georgia, was just achieving some recognition for his writings. In 1932, he was already at work on what would become an equally famous work, *God's Little Acre*.

The literary establishment did not quite know how to respond to Caldwell's work, which depicted the hardscrabble life of poor rustics. The fact that his books were selling so well was also off-putting to critics, who preferred to "discover" a new writer and make him a star.

Caldwell, a big imposing man of considerable gravitas, was becoming a star on his own, however, and despite the raw language and frank sex in his book, he was clearly a serious writer who wanted to explore social justices, race, and class.

Over time, Caldwell's books would come to penetrate a new sector of publishing; they were huge best sellers in Signet and Gold Medal paperback editions. By the end of the 1940s, he had written twenty-five novels and twelve books of nonfiction that sold roughly 80 million copies. He also had married a famed photographer, Margaret Bourke-White, with whom he collaborated on a remarkable book called *You Have Seen Their Faces*, an unsparing look at the nation's poor.

At the time Kirkland "discovered" Caldwell, however, he was still a relatively obscure Southern novelist. When Kirkland completed his script for the play, he submitted it to a neophyte producer named Anthony Brown, who couldn't even come up with funding for an out-of-town tryout. Kirkland managed to scrounge up $6,000 and opened a Broadway production cold, without previews or publicity. A supportive editorial in the *Daily News*—done out of loyalty to its ex-staff member—was the lone promotion.

The opening at the Masques Theater on Forty-eighth Street on December 4, 1933, caused culture shock but scant praise. Brooks Atkinson, the distinguished and normally empathetic critic for the *New York Times*, said the play as a whole represented "one of the grossest episodes ever put on the stage." *Variety* warned the show contained "too much dirt," and described its characters as "too distasteful for stage fare."

Yet, underneath the supposedly sensational material were serious themes that Depression audiences could relate to. In the play, when a banker from Augusta comes to reclaim the farm and suggests the family relocate to a city and work in a mill, Jeeter has an outburst: "It's the rich folks in Augusta that's doing it. They don't work none, but they get all the money us farmers make . . . By God, that ain't right. I tell you. God won't stand for such cheating much longer. He ain't so liking of the rich people as they think He is. God, He likes the poor." Later, Jeeter says sadly, "I was born here on the land and by God and by Jesus, that's where I'll die."

Week after week Kirkland kept the play going with his own money. "I had to get drunk every Thursday for five weeks to find the courage to write the checks to keep the show alive. The critics loathed the play," he wrote in an unpublished autobiography. The turning point came at the end of those five weeks, with a good notice in the *Daily News* praising the performance of Henry Hull.

Now the monthlies came out: George Jean Nathan, Robert Benchley, and Dorothy Parker all came out for it. The play was praised for dealing with poverty. When the play moved in 1934 to the Forrest Theater on Forty-ninth Street (now the Eugene O'Neill Theater), it began to attract larger and more sophisticated audiences. As the theater anthologist Stanley Richards noted,

"While it may have attracted curiosity and thrill seekers for a while, it also drew regular patrons, for no production could survive for that length of time on the merely curious."

Though Atkinson's *New York Times* review had been negative, he now acknowledged that while the play "reels around the stage like a drunken stranger to the theater . . . it has spasmodic moments of merciless power when the truth is flung in your face with all the slime that truth contains."

Kirkland, meanwhile, had become a hands-on producer, overseeing casting changes, publicity, and every other aspect of the show. It was also making him $10,000 per week, a good payday, to put it mildly, at the height of the Depression.

As the Broadway production developed legs, censors increasingly tended to pounce when the show expanded on the road. The first ban came in Chicago in October 1935 the Mayor proclaimed "Liberalism does not condone filth . . . It is an insult to decent people." After a series of legal hearings, the ban was upheld. Two weeks later a Detroit court closed the show. A federal judge upheld a ban in St. Paul, but theatergoers jumped across the river to neighboring Minneapolis to catch the play there. Tulsa, Albuquerque, and Raleigh followed with their own bans soon after.

In 1937, one of the touring companies booked an old riverboat, *The Dixiana*, with plans to perform at various Great Lakes ports. But days before the first performance in Michigan City, Indiana, *The Dixiana* sank under mysterious circumstances. After repairs, the company performed for a month on the boat, but then it was rammed by the United States Naval Reserve boat *Hawk*, ending the Great Lakes tour.

In a 1952 introduction to the play, Caldwell says that, for the twelve years that it toured, "Attorneys for the management often appeared at court hearings on a schedule as closely timed as the train schedules that enabled the cast and scenery to be transported overnight from one one-night-stand to the next." There were frequent threats to throw the actors in jail. "Neither Jack Kirkland nor I wished to be the cause of actors going to jail, but at the same time we knew it was unwise, economically, to cancel performances and refund money."

Sometimes the producers compromised with the government. In November 1937, New Orleans officials banned the play but then changed their minds after policemen and clergymen saw a private preview in a hotel room and chose which parts to delete. When the touring show hit Cleveland, the Hanna Theatre refused to book the play, so it played the Masonic Hall instead. In March 1936 in Albany, the company manager, Irving Becker, was arrested and spent the night in jail on charges of indecency. The case was eventually thrown out.

In his memoir, Kirkland wrote with pride that the play dealt a blow to New York censorship and that "actors no longer are arrested for appearing in a Broadway production, no matter its content."

Meanwhile, Kirkland kept an eye on the various performances of the play, while also writing new scripts, including an adaptation of John Steinbeck's *Tortilla Flat*, which debuted in 1938. The same year, the writer created a stir at the Artists & Writers Club in New York when he slugged *Herald Tribune* critic Richard Watts, who had made a disparaging remark about one of the actors in *Tortilla*.

Soon after, *Tobacco Road*'s longtime press agent, Michael Goldreyer, cooked up a big celebration: The play would be breaking the record of *Abie's Irish Rose* as Broadway's longest-running show. Goldreyer consulted Burns Mantle's annual volume of best plays, which listed *Abie's* as having played 2,532 performances between 1922 and 1927. He determined *Tobacco Road* would break the record on November 18, 1939.

Goldreyer denied the *New York Times*' claim that the play was operating at a loss during summer 1939 and the producers only kept the show on the boards in order to beat *Abie's* record.

On November 4, two weeks before the scheduled celebration, Goldreyer received some mortifying news: When *Abie's* had closed in 1927, most press accounts disagreed with the Burns Mantle figure, declaring that *Abie's* total was 2,327 performances. This meant that *Tobacco Road* had actually broken the record back in May. Goldreyer, who had been mounting a publicity campaign in anticipation of the November 18 performance, decided to hold the celebration that day anyway.

Tobacco finally ended its Broadway run on May 31, 1941. In an article announcing the play's closing the day after, the *New York Herald Tribune* pegged *Tobacco Road*'s total Broadway gross at $1.82 million and its touring gross to date at $2,482,040. *Newsweek*'s estimates were much higher, estimating the play's total worldwide take at more than $5 million, with 2.5 million ticket buyers on Broadway alone.

Tobacco returned to Broadway three times: September 1942 (starring Barton), September 1943, and March 1950. The show ran for, respectively, thirty-four, sixty-six and seven performances.

As things turned out, Kirkland achieved a lot out of *Tobacco Road*—including $1 million and two wives. After divorcing actress Carroll in 1930, he had two quick marriages, to actresses Jayne Shadduck and Julia Laird. Then in 1938, he married wife number four, Haila Stoddard, who was playing Pearl in *Tobacco Road*. Soon after their 1947 divorce, he was married for a fifth time, to Nancy Hoadley—who was also playing Pearl.

Despite all the scandals caused by his plays—particularly over their language—Kirkland maintained his guise as a Southern gentleman, insisting that his children have impeccable table manners, never chew gum, and never use foul language. (No "by God!" or even "by gum!" for them . . .)

In all, he had six offspring: Pat (from Carroll), Christopher and Robin (from Stoddard), and Johanna, Gelsey, and Marshall (from Hoadley).

Kirkland's prize was a farm that he bought in Buck's County, Pennsylvania, in the late 1930s. It was a "gentleman's farm" with a lake, willow trees, horses, and a huge house (fully staffed with servants) on 250 acres of rolling land.

He continued to write, often producing and directing shows, but none was as successful as *Tobacco*. In 1945, he and Haila Stoddard adapted another Caldwell book *Georgia Boy*; in 1956, he adapted *Man with the Golden Arm*, the Nelson Algren novel.

But the upkeep of the farm and Kirkland's habit of investing in his failed plays took their toll. In 1956, he was forced to put his farm on the auction block. It was a case of art cruelly imitating life. Kirkland had found his greatest success by writing about a Southern man who lost his farm. And, twenty years later, like an elegant version of Jeeter Lester, Kirkland ended up losing his spread.

As daughter Johanna recalls, "The farm was him. That was my father. It meant everything to him." In the 1950s, Kirkland moved Nancy and the family to Paris, where he would still write scripts for films, never getting on-screen credit. Kirkland died February 22, 1969, of a heart ailment at Roosevelt Hospital, New York. He was sixty-six.

In 1941, when the play ended its initial Broadway stint, Twentieth Century Fox released a film version. Fox had beat out RKO for the screen rights, paying a reported $100,000. On paper, it looked like a winner, since it reunited director John Ford, screenwriter Nunnally Johnson, and producer Darryl Zanuck, who had collaborated a year earlier on *The Grapes of Wrath*.

Lightning did not strike twice. The *Variety* review noted that "the sensational elements of the play—the dialog and low-life manners of its people—have been deleted, altered, or attenuated to the point of dullness." And, in an apparent attempt at a happy Hollywood ending, family matriarch Ada Lester, who dies in the play, was allowed to live in the film.

Caldwell was happier with the 1958 United Artists release of *God's Little Acre*, because it was done independent of studio control. United Artists released the film, directed by Anthony Mann, with the tagline: "It's on the screen! The explosive, lusty story that 20 million readers said never could be made!" The film concerns another dirt-poor farmer, Ty Ty Walden (played by Robert Ryan), who's obsessed with finding buried gold on his land. There's also a sexy relationship between Aldo Ray and Tina Louise.

Caldwell died in Paradise Valley, Arizona, on April 11, 1987.

West Side Story was almost about Jews and

Catholics. In January 1949, Jerome Robbins approached Arthur Laurents about the idea of writing a contemporary musical version of *Romeo and Juliet* using that particular religious divide. So Laurents jotted out an outline of a show he tentatively called *East Side Story*, but for some reason the story felt a bit too familiar. Then he remembered why: *Abie's Irish Rose*.

"Familiar" is the word that perhaps best describes *Abie's Irish Rose* and it's a description that, ultimately, was a double-edged sword. The day after it opened on May 23, 1922, critics lambasted the play for its stock characters and ethnic stereotypes, so much so that it was in danger of closing in its opening week because no one was showing up. But this very conventional comedy about a Jewish boy and a Catholic girl who want to marry each other against the wishes of their reactionary fathers struck a nerve. It eventually ran for 2,327 Broadway performances.

Its unlikely author, Anne Nichols, was born in the tiny town of Dale's Mill, Georgia, and grew up there until her family moved to the Philadelphia area when she was ten. She later ran away from home and moved to New York to become an actress, and eventually began writing vaudeville sketches, and then plays. At a dinner party, her frequent collaborator, Fiske O'Hara, a popular Irish tenor and comic actor, told her the story of a friend of his, the son of an Orthodox Jew, who had fallen in love with an Irish Catholic woman but was afraid to marry her for fear of what his father would say. Nichols wasn't even aware of the nuances of ethnicity until she was a grown woman, but she'd become familiar with Jewish humor from acting at resorts on the Borscht Belt and exploring the Lower East Side.

Nichols wrote her play in a mere three days. Producers were also quick to turn it down. Finally, Nichols showed it to producer Oliver Morosco, who didn't think much of it, but agreed to produce the play in Los Angeles provided Nichols foot the entire $4,000 capitalization if it failed. In return she'd get 10 percent of the receipts.

In March 1922, *Abie's Irish Rose* began a run in Los Angeles that would eventually last forty-four weeks. Nichols was delighted, but still wanted a

Broadway run, and Morosco wasn't helping. She returned to New York and decided to produce the play herself, mortgaging her home in Queens to raise the $5,000 necessary.

Reviews were not encouraging. *Variety* gave the play one of the more generous notices, writing, "The humor is not of particularly high order, but the play will measure up to the standard of warm weather entertainment." William B. Chase's review in the *New York Times* reported that the audience "took the little comedy very heartily," thus damning with faint praise.

But Benchley and the *New York Post* hated the show. Heywood Broun in the *New York World* called it "a synthetic farce," and slammed, "There is not so much as a single line of honest writing."

Later, when the play had succeeded, Nichols laughed off those critiques. "I sent them birthday cakes when *Abie* was a year old," she said. "Heywood Broun wouldn't eat his, said I put cyanide in it." At one point Nichols ran into Benchley at the Algonquin Hotel. Seeing his arm in a sling, she recalled, "I told him God had punished him. We were fast friends after that. I think he really enjoyed my play."

In its first few months, when the play was struggling financially, it looked as if the naysayers had prophesized correctly, but Nichols insisted on keeping it going. The actors took a pay cut, and tickets were sold at reduced rates. She begged her lawyer to lend her money. He begged her to close the show, but eventually consented. She also borrowed $30,000 from gangster Arnold Rothstein's organization.

In desperation, Nichols offered producer Augustus Pitou 50 percent of the show for a $5,000 investment. Pitou and his wife went to see a Saturday matinee, and during the second intermission his wife told him, "Gus, if you put $5,000 into this terrible play, don't ever dare to say no to me when I want a new fur coat for the rest of my life." During this period, Morosco sued Nichols for $57,000, claiming that she'd stolen the play from him by producing it on Broadway. He wanted $50,000 in damages plus $4,000 for the scenery he said she took from him.

Remarkably the Broadway production soon caught on. By its closing date of October 1, 1927, there were productions running in Seattle, Cleveland, Philadelphia, and Brooklyn, plus one company touring England, another in Vienna, and another in Australia.

As Nichols explained at the time, "If anyone else had put money into the production, *Abie's* would have been dead inside of a week. But I owned it absolutely. I staked everything I possessed on my faith in the play."

Her ownership became an obsession. She felt the need to monitor all its various productions. In 1962, she told the *New York Times*, "Invariably, I'd find that the minute my back was turned the actors would start distorting the play and ad-libbing for laughs. I had to travel back and forth the country to keep them in check. I hardly found time to write anymore."

The obsession took other forms. In 1926, she sued Universal Pictures, producer of *The Cohens and the Kellys*, for $3 million, claiming that the movie stole the plot from *Abie's Irish Rose*. The court ruled that the story of young lovers torn apart by their families had been used so often—in *Romeo and Juliet*, for instance—that it was in the public domain.

Still, Nichols considered filing lawsuits against a variety of corporations, organizations, and individuals on the grounds that she felt "a continuing conspiracy" to restrain the *Abie's Irish Rose* franchise. Among the groups she named was the Anti-Defamation League, which she blamed for the cancellation of a radio series based on the play. She also named the American Communist Party and its newspaper, the *Daily Worker*, which once called the play "an insult to the Jewish and Irish community."

Returning to her typewriter, Nichols sought to update the play for a 1954 revival, but it closed after only twenty performances. As the critic Walter Kerr wrote about the production, "Of course, it's terrible. But apart from that it isn't so bad." In a 1975 *New York* magazine review of a production in upstate New York, Alan Rich wrote, "*Abie* hangs on in our history as the most popular turkey in American theater."

So why did it succeed to begin with? Did some greater message ring true?

Nichols said the play encouraged "the spirit of tolerance." It was also timely, coming at the end of a wave of immigration that brought many Jews and Irish Catholics together into the American melting pot. The audience would applaud when the Rabbi and Father Whalen gave speeches that preached mutual understanding between the religions. Still, many found it too lowbrow to be taken seriously. The *New York Post* wrote, "This might have been made into something entertaining if Miss Nichols had the sincerity of some purpose beyond provoking laughter at any cost."

Taken together, *Tobacco Road* and *Abie's Irish Rose* represent rare examples of the egalitarian strand in the American theater. Both were "people" shows; audiences coveted them even as critics proclaimed their disdain. Both tapped into a vein in public tastes that later was to manifest itself in television sitcoms. The resurgence of blue collar TV comedy in 2004–05 reflected the lexicon and settings of Erskine Caldwell. Norman Lear tapped into the *Abie's* milieu with sitcoms like *All in the Family*.

If these were "people shows," they also vastly enriched two playwrights who were distantly removed from the Broadway mainstream. Anne Nichols and Jack Kirkland briefly became the Neil Simons of their day. In due course, they were to disappear, not only from memory but even from most histories of the Broadway theater. Only their legacy lives on, echoing in the populist entertainment of the day.

26 Hollywood in the Trenches
The Big Parade (1925)

It was a conversation that easily could have taken place in contemporary Hollywood. Irving Thalberg, at twenty-five, the boyish head of production at Metro-Goldwyn-Mayer, was enmeshed in an intense meeting with one of his smart young directors, King Vidor, age twenty-eight. Thalberg had been on the job for only a year. MGM had only recently been formed under the aegis of his boss, the fierce and aggressive Louis B. Mayer. Indeed Hollywood as a whole still seemed like a playpen. The town was all but bursting with entrepreneurial energy. Eager young filmmakers were invading the studios, passionate about their own new ideas (albeit their films were still silent; the idea of sound was considered anathema). Charlie Chaplin was shooting *The Gold Rush*. Harold Lloyd was working on *The Freshman* and, in quite a different vein, Eric von Stroheim was prepping *The Merry Widow*. Also in production were projects as disparate as *The Phantom of the Opera* and the first *Ben-Hur*.

The Texas-born Vidor was both exhilarated and discouraged by this burst of activity. So many films were being churned out that many were playing for only a week and then quickly forgotten. Radio was broadcasting more and more drama and comedies that were stealing potential customers from Hollywood's releases. Since Thalberg already was being gossiped about as a "boy wonder," Vidor hoped to propose a few projects to test his resolve; how courageous would this studio chief really turn out to be?

Thalberg opened the meeting with words that would resonate well at today's film studios. He said he wanted to make big pictures on big subjects—movies that would linger at theaters for months, not weeks. He said he also wanted star vehicles.

And that was all the opening Vidor needed. The young filmmaker declared that he would like to shoot a film about war, but not war as Hollywood had been presenting it. This would not be a sanitized, glamorized view of war, like *The Girl Who Stayed Home* (1919) or *Shootin' for Love* (1923). This would not be about handsome officers in sparkling uniforms and polished boots. It would be a tough glimpse at the trench warfare of World War I, with blood dripping down soldiers' faces and legs shot off. There would be star roles, but the actors would have to steel themselves for a tough shoot. Further, there would be no heroic roles. The protagonist would be an ordinary guy doing his job—a passive hero, not a charismatic patriot.

The way Vidor pitched it, the movie was a silent precursor of *Saving Private Ryan*. And it would, upon its release, build Vidor into a director of Spielberg-like prestige.

Thalberg liked the idea. He promised to back Vidor all the way, even if it meant shocking both his boss, Mayer, and the audience. It turned out to be an inspired decision. *The Big Parade*, as it was ultimately called, became MGM's biggest hit—that is until *Gone with the Wind* came along. It grossed a record $11 million.

The triumph was short-lived, however: within only two years, talkies were to push silent movies like *The Big Parade* to the sidelines; Thalberg was to die at age thirty-seven. The two stars of *The Big Parade* were to become silent film relics—John Gilbert drank himself to death at age thirty-six and Karl Dane shot himself.

At this highly energized and exuberant moment in the mid-twenties, however, there could be no awareness of these dark clouds. Not only was Hollywood enjoying its most fruitful era to date, but the nation as a whole was experiencing a period of prosperity and optimism. The horrors of World War I had faded from the public consciousness, but there were sporadic reminders. In 1924, the play *What Price Glory*, written by Laurent Stallings and Maxwell Anderson, was a hit on Broadway. Thalberg had even bought a script called *Plumes* that dealt with the war, and was pondering how to put it together. Given his respect for Stallings and the interest of Vidor in the subject, Thalberg decided to join the two.

Vidor and the movies were born around the same time. His birthplace was Galveston, Texas; and the date was February 8, 1894. No one else in Galveston was much interested in motion pictures. "You just couldn't go around town and buy a motion picture camera in those days, even if you wanted to. You had to send to New York or Chicago to have the film developed," he told screenwriter Nancy Dowd in a series of 1970s interviews.

As a six-year-old in Texas, Vidor witnessed the 1900 hurricane and flood that killed 10,000 people—more than one-third of the Galveston population. He still remembered that event and its aftermath; when another huge Gulf Coast hurricane arrived in 1913, the nineteen-year-old Vidor and Roy Clough (who had built his own camera) recorded the storm and sold their footage. "From then on, I was a newsreel cameraman," he later told associates.

But Vidor settled for a job in a theater, taking tickets and filling in as projectionist during breaks. It was a dicey job, since films were printed of flammable nitrate stock and even the slightest spark would send the whole thing up in flames (as we saw in *Cinema Paradiso*).

In 1915, Vidor married Florence Arto and decided to take his bride to California, "where the action was." They made a $25 down payment on a Ford and filmed the car trip, with the Ford Motor Company agreeing to buy the results for sixty cents a foot.

Florence Vidor started landing small parts in films, and King tried out as extra, actor, prop man, assistant director, and even writer, selling one script for $30. Though Universal had sixty directors under contract making short films, Vidor was initially unable to get a job with a studio.

Finally, he signed a contract to make several shorts for First National Exhibitors. For the first, the 1920 *Jack-Knife Man*, he was given a budget of $75,000. He spent only $62,000; the executives weren't happy. Vidor recalls, "I didn't understand then, they wanted bigger pictures, and they wanted me to spend all of the $75,000. I didn't know at the time that their main interest was getting the pictures as big as they could be. There was no other source, nobody to talk to, no school to go to, nothing. Everything had to be discovered."

After making *Family Honor* for First National, Vidor built his own ministudio. His father moved to Hollywood and together they bought one square block of land for $15,000 on Santa Monica Boulevard.

In 1922, he directed *Peg o' My Heart*, in which Laurette Taylor repeated her starring role in the 1912 stage hit. Though playing an eighteen-year-old (Taylor was thirty-eight at the time of filming), audiences seemed willing to suspend disbelief. The film was a modest success and attracted the attention of MGM. Thalberg offered Vidor a contract at $2,500 a week, plus a 25 percent interest in *The Big Parade* provided he agree to an independent deal to run his own ministudio. "I didn't want the responsibility of a studio operation, watching the box office results, advertising, all of that," Vidor later explained.

Upon meeting Vidor, Laurent Stallings, the playwright, was surprised that this young Hollywood director wanted the movie to be gritty and realistic. Stallings himself had lost a leg in the war and, prompted by this, Vidor now wanted the hero in *The Big Parade* to come home without a leg. He told Stallings to cut out "all the bunk, all the fantasies" connected with combat.

At the same time Vidor understood the realities of Hollywood. He felt the script should be structured to seduce the audience with initial scenes of comedy and romance. The story line he hammered out with Stallings unfolded as follows:

Pressured by his pals and girlfriend to enlist in 1917, rich kid Jim Apperson (John Gilbert) is shipped off to France. The film follows Jim and his two pals, the rough and lovable Bull (Tom O'Brien) and the rubber-faced, tobacco-chawing Slim (Karl Dane) as they brawl with the MPs, shovel manure, and romance the local girls. But at the halfway point, the movie switches tone. When the troop is suddenly transferred, Vidor stages a bravura scene in which Jim and his newfound French girlfriend Melisande (Renée Adorée) try to find each other to say goodbye amid the chaos of the troop movement. From then on the film is quite dark, with epic scenes on the battlefield, the three friends stuck in a foxhole amid the nightmare of combat.

Though Stallings helped shape the story and propel the film forward, Vidor and Thalberg ultimately set the pattern for later film development, bringing in a succession of writers. Stallings received story credit, with the script attributed to Harry Behn, a twenty-seven-year-old Harvard graduate who was shortly to leave Hollywood to return to poetry and children's books.

Despite his lack of experience, Vidor had always been confident that he could deliver a script that would satisfy Thalberg. But he also knew he had to deliver in another department: He needed a star.

He set his sights on John Gilbert. Gilbert, it was well known, drank too much. He also was identified with soft romantic roles—but this could work to his advantage. Casting a romantic star in a gritty war picture could be an attention-getter for filmgoers. It also would please Thalberg. Further, Gilbert was available—stars of that era moved ceaselessly from picture to picture as though fearful their careers could end at any moment.

Vidor sent his script to Gilbert. The star signed on for the role, admitting later that he'd never read the material. To Vidor, this was just as well; he didn't want script suggestions from his actor, he just wanted his trust, and this he got. "The stars of silent film," Vidor later wrote, "were much more pliable insofar as their directors were concerned. They knew you had a way of transferring emotion to them. It's like a love affair; you just can't describe it. I actually remember moments when I didn't say a thing. I'd just have a quick thought and Gilbert would react to it."

Aside from that telepathic connection there was another mood-setter for the actors: "We had music on the set, which was very helpful to get the mood. John Gilbert liked to listen to 'Moonlight and Roses'," Vidor wrote in his book, *A Tree is a Tree*.

Even on location, the orchestra came along. Vidor said the "orchestra" often consisted of a portable organ and a violin. During the ten-week shooting schedule, Vidor relied on what he called "silent music," using a metronome to direct scenes. He had studied D. W. Griffith's theories on how to build excitement and concluded that "the most important thing about motion picture directing was tempo." So he made each scene in the film progressively faster, following the beat of a metronome.

In one suspenseful scene, the squadron is marching through the woods, knowing that there are German snipers lurking in the vicinity. During filming, the actors marched to the beat of a drum. "We had no loudspeakers and we had no synchronized music to go by, (so) we used this big bass drum so everyone could hear the metronome," Vidor said.

Every movement was timed to the beat as Gilbert and his friends tried to conceal their fear, comrades falling one by one to snipers, with even the falling actors timing their movement to the drumbeat.

Though the film has an epic look, it was filmed on a modest budget of $205,000, with foxhole scenes lensed on the back lot in Culver City. The finale, in which Renée Adorée is tilling a field, was shot in what is now downtown Westwood, which, at the time, was mostly barley fields. To add scope, Vidor used a few scenes that the Signal Corps had shot, which portrayed battle scenes and troop movements; Vidor studied the footage before choreographing his scenes and even incorporated footage of a biplane being shot and exploding midair.

The director also wanted a scene with 200 trucks, jammed with 4,000 men, traveling in a straight line, so that it would seem like servicemen stretched into infinity. He arranged to shoot the scene in Texas. His military adviser, however, countered that such a troop movement would actually be formed in a zigzag, not a straight line, so that's how Vidor shot it. After seeing the footage, however, he changed his mind; the U.S. Army again redeployed 4,000 recruits to meet Vidor's revised demands.

The Big Parade, to be sure, also had its memorable, intimate moments. In one scene, Gilbert sits on a bench and teaches the French farm girl, Adorée, how to chew gum—no movement, no cutaways, just two people sitting on a bench. "To let a shot run three hundred feet was an absolute innovation in motion picture making then," he told Dowd. "This was the perfect excuse for all of the pantomime that you could want. I thought at this time that I would have people in all of my pictures who couldn't speak the same language."

Renée Adorée and Karl Dane ironically were both immigrants who flourished in silent Hollywood. She was born Jeanne de la Fonte in Lille, France, the child of performers who performed stunts in the circus. The Danish-born Rasmus Karl Gottlieb was part of a comedy team called Arthur & Dane. In the two years after *Parade*, Dane was cast in other films, but when talkies came in, his thick accent tolled the end of his career.

When Thalberg saw a rough cut of *The Big Parade*, his response was immediate. He demanded more. He wanted an epic war movie, and ordered up a climactic night battle with hundreds of actors. Vidor smoldered. He liked Thalberg and appreciated his support, but decades later he bristled at the myth that Thalberg had "saved" his film with his suggestions. "It's just one of those things that happens in filmmaking," he said. "Thalberg got a lot of credit for doing certain things to add to the bigness of *The Big Parade*. One of them was a night battle. The ironic thing is that the pages I had written for the beginning and end were initially rejected. So all I had to do was pull out the original pages I had written, but then I had to hear for years and years how the film was 'saved' and how other people added to it. . . . Not many people know about that, but that's how films are made," Vidor said.

The added cost was $45,000.

While Thalberg was touting his creative decisions, Louis B. Mayer was in charge of the financial ones, but he fretted about the final scenes featuring John Gilbert as an amputee. Mayer was afraid that scenes of a crippled

Gilbert would offend his fans, who thought of him as a romantic lead, and insisted that Vidor reshoot the scenes with Gilbert limping on a wounded leg.

Vidor shot the material but told the assistant cameraman not to print it—the scenes were merely to be a safeguard in case Mayer proved insistent. As it turns out, Mayer gave in, and Vidor's ending was the one that was used. According to a 1925 *New York Times* story, "So powerful were the climactic scenes between Gilbert and his parents, that not one preview audience ever demanded that the alternate ending be shown."

Mayer was also concerned about Vidor's portrayal of Germans. MGM, unlike other majors, still catered to its German audience. But Vidor again didn't want to compromise. Just as Jim remained a passive hero, the Germans remained, for the most part, faceless.

There was one notable exception. During the night battle, Slim dies and Jim cries out, "They got him! They got him! God damn their souls!" Jim pursues Slim's killer into a foxhole and prepares to slit his throat. Without a word, Gilbert is transformed from murderous rage to shock as he realizes that his enemy is just a kid—and a kid with a serious wound. Gilbert stares at him for a long time, eventually giving his last cigarette to the boy, who takes a few puffs and dies. Jim finishes the cigarette. It's a moment of sublime acting that captured the glory of silent-film storytelling.

The film opened November 5, 1925, at the Egyptian on Hollywood Boulevard, on a reserved-seat basis. On November 19, 1925, it opened at two New York venues, the Capitol and Astor. Vidor, who had wanted his films to play longer than one week, got his wish: *Parade* played six months at the Egyptian and an astonishing ninety-six weeks at the Astor, grossing $1 million at that site alone.

The film grossed $11 million overall. By comparison, *Ben-Hur* grossed $9 million, and its production cost was significantly higher (an estimated $4 million).

On November 25, 1925, *Variety* reported that in one week, *Big Parade* took in $21,000 in Los Angeles, with tickets ranging from 50 cents to $1.50. The article stated, "There has been much talk that folks did not care to see pictures with war themes; with the result that trade was not as brisk as it should be. However, those who did see it, liked it and are now carrying on a mouth-to-mouth exploitation campaign." In New York, the following week, the paper reported $20,000 in its first full week; in addition, there was an advance sale of $5,000 for the next two weeks. "The reason that the advance is not greater is because the box office at the Astor is so small, only two weeks' tickets can be racked at one time."

One element promoting box office at the major theaters stemmed from the elaborate sound effects provided. At the Egyptian, a crew of eighteen was posted backstage with bugles and iron hammers making noise like real battle sounds. Ten-foot metal drums would augment the big explosions. "The theatre would shake," Vidor recalled.

The December 2, 1925, review in *Variety* favorably compared the "backstage effects" to those used in *The Birth of a Nation,* and added that "the musical score, perhaps, outranks anything of its kind since that Griffith masterpiece." The score by Dr. William Axt and David Mendoza utilized World War I songs and variations, along with original themes. At the 4,000-seat Roxy Theater in New York, a seventy-piece orchestra played two shows a day.

The success of *The Big Parade* helped establish MGM as one of Hollywood's premier studios. Over the next decade, the studio held true to its formula of combining big stars with big stories. And Thalberg continued to micromanage shooting, frequently sending directors back to the soundstage for reshoots.

While the film was a major career boost for all of those involved, the success was short-lived because of the advent of sound. In 1926, Warner Bros. had released *Don Juan* with synchronized sound. It was a popular picture, but some observers thought it was a onetime novelty. Then the following year, *The Jazz Singer* opened the floodgates when it bowed on October 6, 1927, with scenes of synchronized dialogue and singing.

The transition to sound was traumatic for many in the industry. For the first time, technicians were calling the shots. Sound men dictated where the microphone could be placed, which in turn dictated how scenes could be shot and even how sets could be built. The cameras made so much noise that at first they were put in a soundproof room, which restricted camera movements.

Just starting his career as a director, Howard Hawks was asked if he'd directed dialogue scenes. When he said no (he'd earlier made such silent films as *The Road to Glory* and *The Cradle Snatchers*), he was immediately branded as a director who couldn't handle talking actors and he was out of work for more than a year.

In January 1928, there were 20,000 movie theaters. Only 157 were equipped for sound. Two years later, that number jumped to 8,741. The public had passed its decree: Talkies had won the day.

In the 1952 *Singin' in the Rain,* Gene Kelly plays a matinee idol who is hooted when he has to recite lines like "I love you, I love you, I love you." The character is partly based on John Gilbert, whose career collapsed despite the success of *The Big Parade.* At the time, some said his voice was too high.

"That was not true at all," countered Vidor, years later. "He had a good voice, but his image was that of the passionate lover, like Valentino. And you can't put that into words. In silent films," Vidor said, "the facial expressions conveyed his romantic yearnings and the audience could supply its own words of endearment."

A second theory holds that in Gilbert's 1929 talkie, *His Glorious Night*, the MGM sound department turned up the treble and forgot to turn up the bass, resulting in a squeaky voice. The mistake may not have been an accident. Gilbert's daughter, Leatrice Gilbert Fountain, claimed that Louis B. Mayer was fed up with Gilbert's high salary ($1.5 million a year) and that the two had squabbled for several years. Hence Mayer had ordered the bad sound mix and then spread the rumor of Gilbert's bad voice, she claimed. Whatever the cause, the actor's career hit the skids; he drank heavily and died at age thirty-six in 1936. The cause of death was attributed to heart failure.

His costars met similarly dark ends. Only five years after *Parade* opened, Adorée at age thirty-two contracted tuberculosis and died three years later. Dane was another victim of talkies. Thanks to his thick Danish accent, roles in talking films quickly dried up. By 1934, he was selling wieners in front of the gate at MGM, where he had once been a star. One evening after work he went home to his apartment in L.A.'s Fairfax district and put a bullet through his head. He was forty-seven.

F. Scott Fitzgerald had based the character Monroe Stahr in *The Last Tycoon* on Thalberg. Fitzgerald based another of his fictional characters on King Vidor. In the '70s, Vidor proudly showed biographer, Richard Schickel, an autographed copy of short stories by Fitzgerald, stating that the film director in the story "Crazy Sunday" was based on Vidor. In the inscription, Fitzgerald said Vidor had the only "interesting temperament" among American directors.

Unlike some of his *Parade* colleagues, Vidor thrived in the years of the talkies. After finishing principal photography on *Big Parade*, he immediately started work on the 1926 *La Bohème*, a bizarre example of Hollywood's eagerness to shoot silent versions of musicals and operas. Vidor had two hits in 1928, *The Crowd* and *Show People* starring Marion Davies, a deft comedienne who is probably best remembered as the mistress of William Randolph Hearst. In 1929, Vidor directed *Hallelujah*, an all-black film, which was revolutionary for that era, followed by *Street Scene*, in 1931 and *Our Daily Bread*, in 1934.

In 1939, Vidor directed some of his most famous footage, for which he is uncredited: The farm sequences in *The Wizard of Oz*. After George Cukor was fired as director of *Gone with the Wind*, David O. Selznick asked Vidor to step in, but he declined, because he lacked enough preparation time. So Victor Fleming was then called in to take over. But Fleming hadn't yet finished shooting *The Wizard of Oz*. Thus Vidor ultimately was summoned to shoot only the black and white Kansas sequences, including Judy Garland's singing of "Over the Rainbow."

In his biography of Vidor, Richard Schickel terms him "the most sophisticated American-born master of silent film," and that he was. Remarkably, he also went on to become perhaps the most durable filmmaker in the history of American cinema, his career spanning sixty-seven years. The explanation for that longevity can be traced to *The Big Parade*. Vidor knew when to be stubborn and when to be political. While he masterminded the shoot, he also shrewdly managed Thalberg and Mayer, both of them egomaniacs. He ended up with the movie he wanted, but made his bosses feel that they, too, had a pivotal role in its creation.

Clearly these gifts displayed at age twenty-eight remained with him throughout his remarkable career. As the ultimate survivor, Vidor had demonstrated the Hollywood reality that it's not enough to master filmmaking; one also has to master dealmaking.

27 Jump-Starting the Epic
The Birth of a Nation (1915)

The giant multinational companies that own the Hollywood studios today regularly convene conferences and summon marketing gurus to analyze the magic recipes for making blockbusters. Over the past decades, however, a few brilliantly instinctual showmen seem to have known those recipes by heart—from Cecil B. DeMille to Samuel Goldwyn to Steven Spielberg. Perhaps the very first of this breed was D. W. Griffith.

Give the audience something it's never seen before, Griffith believed. Deliver epic scenes with raging battles and rousing rescues. Tell your story with sweeping camera movement interspersed with intense closeups. Promote the hell out of it, hailing your film as "the greatest of all motion pictures"—modesty is not a proper motivator for a filmmaker. And finally, stir up controversy, even if you have to offend as many as you attract.

These were the dicta Griffith adhered to on *The Birth of a Nation*, which was released in 1915. He bragged that he'd spent a then astonishing $500,000 to produce it and hired 25,000 extras to serve as soldiers (the number kept growing in every piece of promotion). In reality, his budget was probably $100,000, but even that was sufficient to make his investors catatonic. To pacify them, Griffith threw mammoth premieres, even hiring actors to dress as white-sheeted Ku Klux Klansmen riding through the streets of

Manhattan. He demanded a top ticket price of $2 at a time when the usual price was between twenty and thirty cents, on the grounds that his film ran three hours compared to the customary thirty minutes.

Griffith was a man who clearly would stop at nothing. His showmanship paid off. *Birth of a Nation* pulled in an estimated $60 million at the box office. Adjusted to today's economy, that surely would beat even *Titanic*. It drew in people who had never gone to a movie before and thus built an audience for future filmmakers. It also struck many as an appalling example of racism, but that did not diminish box office returns.

The premiere of *Birth of a Nation* came at a midway point between the end of the Civil War and the inception of Civil Rights legislation. If the film's production values were cutting-edge at the time, its sensibility was clearly nineteenth century. The film showed the Ku Klux Klan riding to the rescue of white people who are being victimized by greedy and violent black men. One Caucasian heroine jumps to her death from a cliff rather than submit to a lecherous black man. And the film's solution to post-Civil War racial problems? "Negroes" should be sent to Liberia. This was presented as if it were Lincoln's intention.

In 1915, the misgivings about the film were drowned out by a chorus of enthusiasm. Politicians, teachers, clergymen, critics, and moviegoers across the country were rapturous. When the film was screened at the White House and before members of Congress there was not a word about the tacit racism. But as recently as 2004, when the Los Angeles Silent Movie Theater announced a showing of *Birth of a Nation*, the owner received death threats. He canceled the screening.

D. W. Griffith became, in his own words, "the man who invented Hollywood," though it's a dubious claim. Griffith certainly pioneered many filmmaking techniques, but he borrowed just as many from American and foreign filmmakers. His most unique contribution was to put them together in a way that awakened a new audience and made movie-going a part of daily life.

In the nineteenth century, magic-lantern shows and zoetropes gave the illusion of movement. When inventors such as Thomas Edison began filming in the 1890s, they recorded fleeting moments: a woman dancing, or a wave crashing on the shore. The most famous example was Auguste Lumière's 1895 footage at La Ciotat station in Paris, shooting a train coming directly at the camera. Audiences screamed and jumped out of the way when they viewed the footage. Edison's film of a couple kissing was considered shocking.

Then someone decided to add storytelling. In France, Georges Méliès's 1902 *Le Voyage dans la Lune* was one of the first special-effects films, a comical look at a rocket ship to the moon. In America, Edwin S. Porter shot *New York Harbor Police Boat Patrol Capturing Pirates* in 1903, the same year he directed the wildly popular *The Great Train Robbery*.

As with any startup industry, the film business saw a rush of innovation within a short time. In his elegiac book about the silent era, *The Parade's Gone By*, film historian Kevin Brownlow writes that by 1912, every cinema storytelling device had been established: Close-ups, tracking shots, flashbacks, inserts, fades, dissolves—everything. "But it was as though the steam train had been assembled and no one knew how to light the boiler," he adds. "For while all the components of the narrative film had been devised, no one was fully exploiting them. The first match was struck by Griffith and it led to an explosion, the effects of which the industry is still feeling."

Still, these early movies were blue-collar commodities, not for the middle class, who remained focused on vaudeville and "legitimate" theater when they sought entertainment. Movies were for the poor and for immigrants, who couldn't follow the language-heavy plays and couldn't afford the price of vaudeville tickets. They learned about their new country by going to the movies. "Theater owners protested that their houses were clean and free from vermin; they had sprayed the disinfectant themselves. Somehow, the middle classes remained unconvinced," writes Brownlow. Movie houses were like pool halls in the '20s. They weren't disreputable, but if you were "nice," you probably didn't want to spend much time there.

A native of Crestwood, Kentucky, David Wark Griffith was one of seven children born to Jacob Griffith, a surgeon who had become an army colonel fighting for the Confederacy. While never able to provide a stable, comfortable home for David and his six siblings, Jacob was a lively storyteller and irrepressible braggart. In his autobiography, *The Man Who Invented Hollywood*, edited by James Hart, Griffith wrote: "The stories told by my father, and about him, particularly by veterans who had fought under his command, were burned right into my memory." *Birth of a Nation* was but an echo of the stories told of the gallant soldiers who fought one of the most brilliant wars known to history. . . . I think that picture owes more to my father than it does to me."

Griffith aspired to become a playwright, and he dismissed the first films he saw as "silly and tiresome." Anyone who enjoyed going to the movies, he said, "should be shot at sunrise."

Griffith started working as an actor to advance his playwriting ambitions. He traveled the country, picking up gigs wherever he could. When he was thirty-two he wrote a play called *The Fool and the Girl*, which was staged in

Baltimore and Washington, D.C., in 1907. It was far from a hit, but it led to offers of film work, which he grudgingly accepted.

Griffith succeeded in Hollywood almost inadvertently. He began working as an film actor at the American Mutoscope and Biograph Company in 1908. A few months later, the company's only full-time director fell ill, so Griffith agreed to take on the job, with the proviso that he could return to acting if the directing gig didn't work out.

Once he got a shot at directing, the Civil War came to the fore as his subject matter. Between 1908 and 1913 Griffith turned out twelve Civil War-related shorts, including *The Guerrilla* (1908), *In Old Kentucky* (1909), *The Honor of His Family* (1910), *The House With Closed Shutters* (1910), *The Fugitive* (1910), *Swords and Hearts* (1911), *The Battle* (1911), and *The Informer* (1912).

He depicted the Klan in very different postures. In *The White Caps*, Klansmen heroically tar and feather a man for beating his wife. But in Griffith's 1911 short, *The Rose of Kentucky*, Klansmen attack a white plantation owner who refuses to join them.

In 1910, Griffith directed *His Trust* and *His Trust Fulfilled*, which together tell the story of a slave who uses his meager income to take care of the plantation owner's orphaned daughter and send her to a nice school. The message of the films, articulated by a white attorney, is that perhaps blacks are not to be distrusted after all.

Griffith's filmography thus reflects a willingness to cast "Negroes" and Klansmen as heroes or villains—whatever suited the needs of the plot. Racial subtext did not seem to matter to Griffith as much as sweep, spectacle, and audience involvement.

Filmmakers of the period were still influenced primarily by the stage: A camera was placed at a distance, to catch all the movement of the actors, with rare cuts to a close-up to register reactions. But Griffith soon began experimenting. He mounted the camera on a rolling platform and began using shorter takes. *The Guerrilla* in 1908 had forty-plus shots packed into roughly ten minutes. Most important was his use of crosscutting between two and even three different planes of action to build tension in chase scenes. When one Biograph worker asked him if that would be confusing for audiences, he replied, "Well, doesn't Dickens write that way?"

By 1912, Griffith decided he wanted to make longer pictures, because he had bigger themes to explore. His ambitions were fueled by two Italian Biblical spectacles, *Quo Vadis* and *Cabiria*. Though they featured elaborate costumes and scenery, he felt the spectacles lacked vitality. Griffith was sure he could outdo them.

His first attempt in 1913 was *Judith of Bethulia*, a four-reel Biblical epic that he shot without the permission of the Biograph's managers. They were so angry that they refused to release the film. They finally opened it in March 1914, but by then, Griffith had left the company. Biograph soon began producing feature-length legit adaptations, yet refused to let Griffith direct.

"They procured real stage-play directors. Since I was only a movie man, they would let me supervise, but not direct any more," Griffith wrote in his autobiography (which was never completed). "*Judith* had double-crossed me. She had cost too much money and the company was reaching for the ax."

Still, Griffith had become a "hot item" in this new industry and he understood it. Griffith, never shy, took a full-page ad in the *New York Dramatic Mirror* announcing the resignation of "D. W. Griffith, Producer of all great Biograph successes, revolutionizing Motion Picture drama and founding the modern technique of the art."

Having already turned down a $500,000 salary from mogul-in-the-making Adolph Zukor, Griffith became supervisor of production for Harry E. Aitken, who headed both the Reliance and Majestic studios and the Mutual Company a distribution company. Griffith completed four features for Mutual before resolving to create what he described as a motion picture so long and so powerful that people would stop wondering whether movies could ever be as good as live drama.

Griffith's friend, Frank Woods, had told him about the novel *The Clansman*, written by Rev. Thomas Dixon, who had also adapted it into a stage play. In his autobiography, Griffith wrote, "I skipped quickly through the book until I got to the part about the Klansmen, who, according to no less than Woodrow Wilson, ran to the rescue of the downtrodden South after the Civil War. I could just see these Klansmen in a movie with their white robes flying."

Griffith seemed oblivious to the implications of Dixon's novel. "I think Griffith just wanted a goddamn good story," says Arthur Lenning, a film historian and University of Albany professor. Dixon, indeed, had an agenda. He was a white supremacist who was particularly intolerant of miscegenation. "Dixon was an ideologue. He had a mission, he had a purpose," Lenning says. Dixon's work ridiculed the idea of Negro civil rights. He ignored violent acts of the Klan and focused instead on several postwar incidents in which blacks staged uprisings against white Southerners. It was the Klan who always rode to the rescue.

Working from a scenario by Woods, Griffith sought to broaden the narrative. Rather than focusing on the Reconstruction era, the film started earlier, depicting the lives of two families caught up in the excitement and sweep of Civil War battles. Black roles were cast with white actors, as was the tradition of the time. (Even in the traveling 'minstrel shows,' most of the performers were whites in blackface.)

Dixon wanted $10,000 upfront for his novel, dismissing Griffith's offer of 25 percent of the profits. His stage play based on *The Clansman* had been a flop, and as Dixon himself said, "I've heard something about movie royalties. They sound nice, but nobody ever gets them." Nonetheless, he eventually settled for $2,000 cash plus 25 percent of the profits. Harry Aitken wrote the $2,000 check, even as he and his brother, Roy, were struggling to raise capital in New York. But Griffith had already started rehearsing and was busily spending money on sets, costumes, and props.

The Aitkens managed to raise $25,000 for the movie by pledging percentages of their salaries and stock to various businessmen. But Griffith was still $15,000 short. Cast and crew members chipped in, including $300 from actresses Lillian and Dorothy Gish (it was all the money they had).

In the end, Griffith didn't use much of his script; he and his cast mused over every scene and then new dialogue emerged. There was one last-minute change in the cast. Griffith had originally planned to cast Blanche Sweet as heroine Elsie Stoneman, daughter of the abolitionist Sen. Austin Stoneman. But Sweet was absent during a rehearsal of a crucial scene, in which mulatto politician Silas Lynch tries to force Elsie to marry him and ends up chasing her around the room. So Griffith settled on Lillian Gish, whose "fluttery, child-like gestures" made her an ideal fit for the part, wrote Griffith.

Because of Griffith's idiosyncratic technique, the production went substantially over schedule. Still, he was by now an experienced filmmaker. He got the movie he wanted.

At the end of filming, sneak previews were arranged at the Loring Opera House in Riverside, California, on January 1, 1915. There were few, if any, blacks in the audience, nor were there any critics. A reporter for the *Riverside Daily Press* declared that Griffith "has treated his subject fairly." The audience's enthusiasm confirmed Griffith's belief that he had made a potential smash. From the beginning, he had vowed to sell the film as something special—not just a movie but an extravaganza, to be "exhibited in only the best theaters and to the most educated and refined people of the United States."

The film's premiere was scheduled for February 8 in the Los Angeles Auditorium. W. H. Clune, its owner, had himself invested $15,000 in the production on the promise that his auditorium could screen the picture.

Learning about the film, the fledgling National Association for the Advancement of Colored People, sought an injunction from the Los Angeles

City Board of Censors. The censors, however, quickly approved the film, with a few very minor cuts, so the NAACP took a new approach: To convince the City Council to order the chief of police to suppress the film, on the grounds that it might heighten racial tensions and cause riots. In an odd compromise, the chief decided to ban the opening-day matinee of the film, with no mention of the evening premiere or any subsequent screening. *Los Angeles Times* film reviewer Grace Kingsley wrote, "And now . . . comes the protest of the darkies and the interference of the police."

So the premiere went forward on the evening of February 8 as planned, with seventeen policemen stationed at the doors. A huge crowd gathered outside the 2,500-seat theater. Inside, usherettes wore 1860s garb and passed out petitions urging that the L.A. City Council not to ban the film; many signed.

When the film ended, the reaction was even more positive than in Riverside. The *Los Angeles Times* proclaimed the film "the greatest picture that was ever made and the biggest drama ever filmed."

The controversy itself fueled public interest. *Variety* reported on February 10 that "the film is packing the huge auditorium where lines, starting early at 7 o'clock for an afternoon showing, are formed." Meanwhile, the title of the film, originally called *The Klansman*, was officially changed to *The Birth of a Nation*. After its Riverside showing, Dixon, who wrote the original novel, had suggested the new, grander title as a nod to *History of the American People*, written by President Woodrow Wilson. Wilson had written that America had been "an aggregation of jangling, discordant, antagonistic sections" until the Civil War, which brought it together as a united nation.

It was a lofty idea, one that disguised Dixon's real motives. In a letter to presidential secretary Joseph P. Tumulty, Dixon wrote: "I didn't dare allow the president to know the real big purpose back of my film—which was a presentation of history that would transform every man who comes out of our theaters into a Southern partisan for life." Clearly, Dixon—if not Griffith—was becoming aware of the "propagandistic power" of cinema. He was persuaded that a screening for the president, and his tacit approval, would short-circuit any protests that might arise.

Because Woodrow Wilson was mourning his recently deceased wife, however, he was unavailable to attend a public screening—and thus *The Birth of a Nation* became the first film ever screened at the White House.

Wilson's response seemed one of approval. He was quoted as saying "It is like writing history with lightning. . . . My only regret is that it is all too true." Tumulty, later advised him to distance himself from the film. Tumulty wrote to Congressman Thomas C. Thatcher of Massachusetts that the President had seen the film, but "at no time expressed his approbation of it." The screening, Tumulty said, "was a courtesy extended to an old acquaintance."

Dixon also set up a screening at the National Press Club, where the audience of 500, including Supreme Court justices and members of the Senate, the House of Representatives, and the diplomatic corps applauded enthusiastically.

Another "official" premiere was then scheduled March 3 at the Liberty Theater in New York. Though the NAACP's West Coast campaign hadn't been successful, the group stepped up its efforts in the East; demonstrators turned out to protest the movie and its message.

Griffith and his investors, to be sure, relished the protests. Future mogul Louis B. Mayer even called to offer $50,000 if he could distribute the film in his Boston theater. At the premiere, wrote Griffith, "The opposition was out in full force. . . . It became a contest. The booers tried to drown out the applauders and vice versa." He also claimed a lot of eggs were thrown at the screen. One ended up hitting a bass violinist in the orchestra, "smelly eggs cascading down his bald head." Despite the hecklers, there was repeated applause during the battle scenes.

And the reviews the morning after the premiere were rhapsodic. In a typical paean, the *Evening Globe* declared, "Beyond question the most extraordinary picture that has been made—or seen—in America so far."

In the *Evening Journal*, C. F. Zittel intoned: "Children must be sent to see this masterpiece. Any parent who neglects this advice is committing an educational offense, for no film has ever produced more educational points than Griffith's latest achievement." *Variety*'s March 12 edition ran a news item describing the film as the "sensation of the picture trade" that would likely "draw not less than $14,000 this week."

As Richard Schickel relates in his excellent book, *D. W. Griffith: An American Life*, in subsequent weeks, a ritual process of protest and quasi-judicial proceedings greeted *Birth of a Nation*. In Boston, Mayor James Michael Curley told black protestors that he was powerless to ban it. Griffith and Dixon took out newspaper ads advocating freedom of speech. When the film opened, the *Boston American* reported that Griffith "was so moved by the sympathy of its audience that he could hardly speak."

In response to continued pressure from the NAACP, the National Board of Censorship on March 13 finally ordered the excision of a scene depicting the deportation of blacks back to Liberia. The Board also mandated a unique opening disclaimer: "This is an historic presentation of the Civil War and Reconstruction period and is not meant to reflect in any way upon any race or people of today."

This led Griffith to add his own preface to the film entitled, "A Plea For the Art of the Motion Picture." It declared: "We do not fear censorship, for we have no wish to offend with improprieties or obscenities, but we do demand, as a right, the liberty to show the dark side of wrong that we may illuminate the bright side of virtue—the same liberty that is conceded to the art of the written word—that art to which we owe the Bible and the works of Shakespeare."

While delivering himself of this hyperbole, Griffith also agreed to cut a love scene between Senator Stoneman and his mulatto mistress as well as a fight scene between a black and a white. And he later consented to send a cameraman to a Negro college to shoot "the progress of the colored people." The piece was tacked on the end of the print, after the scene showing the Klansmen's victorious parade. He did this, he said, because "in all fairness, the advancement of the race since that time should be shown."

The movie played for eleven months at the Liberty in New York. Some 825,000 people saw the film in its various New York area engagements. In its twenty-two weeks at the Los Angeles Auditorium, 350,000 paid to see it. In Boston, despite a few demonstrations and a handful of arrests, the film played for nearly seven months.

On March 5, 1915, *Variety* reported that tickets in New York were priced at $2 tops. In fact, $2 was only the maximum; tickets were still available for 25¢ to $1 to $1.50 for the front of the balcony. Thus, exhibitors were using a Broadway-type pricing structure for seats.

Rev. Dixon, who'd been skeptical of percentages, nonetheless reaped $1 million from the picture. The Aitken brothers, who'd originally invested $25,000, earned $5 million for their gamble. Griffith said that William Clune, the Los Angeles Auditorium owner who'd invested $15,000, "made hundreds of thousands out of it."

Paradoxically, while virtually every film school now deals with Griffith's work, his epic is rarely shown publicly. It is a mythic movie, but one that has essentially disappeared from the public consciousness.

Griffith's subsequent filmmaking ventures did not enhance his reputation. Following the success of *Birth of a Nation*, Griffith, as an act of supreme hubris, shot a three-hour saga with the bizarre title of *Intolerance: Love's Struggle Through the Ages*. The film intercuts four stories set in various historic periods: ancient Babylon; Jerusalem in the time of Jesus Christ; France circa 1572; and the United States in a then contemporary setting. In each story, religious rivalries condemn the principals to ugly fates.

Given Griffith's approach to his craft, this improbable movie was shot as a series of epics with hundreds of extras. Stars such as Lillian Gish, Mae Marsh, and Constance Talmadge were cast in key roles. Griffith's assistant directors included King Vidor, who went on to make *The Big Parade*, Allan Dwan, who made *Sands of Iwo Jima*, and Victor Fleming, who went on to direct *Gone with the Wind*.

Despite the spectacle and the big names, audiences showed complete disdain for *Intolerance*. It bombed. Griffith went on to make other films, such as *Broken Blossoms* and *Way Down East*, but he never regained his stride. In the '30s he even tried his hand at some "talkies," such as *The Struggle* in 1931, but none proved a success. Griffith died of a cerebral hemorrhage in July 1948, after some sixteen years of inactivity.

Viewed from today's perspective, Griffith remains a fascinating anomaly. He was at once a visionary who fully grasped the potential of his medium, yet he could not shake off the attitudes of his upbringing. His sensibilities were at once free-flowing, yet hopelessly imprisoned.

Hence he was to achieve an ambiguous immortality—a liberator and a bigot, an innovator and still the voice of a dark past. In the historic fraternity of filmmakers, he is at once revered, yet forgotten—a truly great artist whose work no one wants to grapple with.

A Conclusion

So what are we to make of this cavalcade of mythic hits? What are the common denominators? Pundits relish analyzing the reasons for failure, but less so with success. Especially blockbuster successes that seemed to defy conventional wisdom.

Scrutinize the entries in this book and certain through-lines suggest themselves:

- A substantial proportion of the plays, films, or TV shows reflect a singularity of vision. Whether it's Lucas or Lucy, the "voice" makes itself heard. It's loud and idiosyncratic, and it prevails, despite all the committees and interfering bureaucrats who tried to intrude.
- In the same vein, a strong point of view—a sensibility, rather than ideology—guided many of these mythic shows, from the antiwar euphoria of *Hair*, to the antique racism of *Birth of a Nation*, to the anti-industrial parodies of *Modern Times*. Despite Sam Goldwyn's admonition that messages are best sent through Western Union, strong attitudes reflected themselves in many of our major blockbusters.
- An emotional tug, real or synthesized, runs through most of these shows, ranging from the mawkish contrivances of *Sound of Music*, to the romantic ambiguities of *Casablanca*, to the paternal rantings of *All in the Family*. And then, of course, there's Oprah—that totally

TV creature who demanded tears, not truisms, from her myriad guests.

- Last and most important, many of the mega-hits of show business were just that—pure show business. They all but drowned in their own theatricality, whether the cameras were focused on charging chariots, heroic hobbits, singing felines, or even a giant gorilla groping a screaming blonde. This was about alchemy, not story, and it grabbed the audiences.

To be sure, it was this basic appetite for theatricality that has always stirred the great divide between the critics and the ticket-buyers. Each generation of filmgoers has rallied to the mythic King Kong because of the thrills. Its various incarnations are not so much films as theme park rides: They represent pure show business.

And critics, over the generations, have tended to disdain both the show and the business. What the public may see as spectacle, they see as contrivance. Of course their disdain, time and again, has proven irrelevant. Somehow the "buzz" has always overwhelmed the disdain. Even in the days of *Birth of a Nation,* word somehow spread across the vast land that this was not so much a movie as an experience—one that was magical and eye-opening, even down to its bogus subtext.

This phenomenon still exists, but the pace has exponentially quickened. Whether in film, TV, or theater, the phenomenon of public recognition has become instantaneous. A film like *Bonnie and Clyde* in 1969 might have opened in a few theaters (or even regionally) and there would be time for the word to spread in invisible cognitive waves. Today a film may open on 4,000 or more screens and, by nightfall of its opening date, its fate will be sealed.

If the shelf life of a new film is limited, so too is the life span of its DVD at the WalMarts and Best Buys. The returns will be dispatched to distributors within six weeks of its arrival. On Broadway, the price tag of most plays is such that the chances of surviving bad buzz are also remote. A survival story like that of *Tobacco Road* would be unlikely today.

Given the fact that the global monoliths that supply "content" to the marketplace are essentially distributors rather than production entities, they are ideally positioned to capitalize on the phenomenon of the instant hit. They are, after all, obsessed with the pipelines, not the product. They are in a global battle for "eyeballs," as they appropriately put it (the minds are clearly detached from the eyeballs). Their concern is to disseminate their content to screens, stages, cell phones, DVDs, portable digital devices, and computers as swiftly and cost-efficiently as possible. If those eyeballs prefer to focus on

Desperate Housewives on hand-held devices on the way to work Monday rather than on their TV screen on Sunday, that reality will be engineered into the system. By weeks end, however, that particular product will disappear into cyberspace, to be regurgitated and repurposed at a later date in some new fiscally-felicitous environment.

The grand design of these companies therefore is to design product that will instantly arouse appetites or trigger recognition. Product is predesigned to be perishable. Decisions are prompted by a marketing sensibility rather than any semblance of a creative one. The weight is always on the side of sales, not production.

To be sure, the Hollywood studios of old were also corporate entities, but they were curiously chaotic and undercapitalized, and movies were their only product. The Brahmins of the studio system were an oddly idiosyncratic band of entrepreneurs, many from immigrant backgrounds.

When MGM's founder, Louis B. Mayer, would prepare a speech, or even write a personal note, aides would rush to correct his spelling and grammar, and his aesthetic sensibilities often scandalized associates. But the studio system could function only if he could marshal the energies of talented filmmakers who had their own personal aims and ambitions. Moreover, Mayer and his confreres, by dint of their own educational shortcomings, yearned for a degree of cultural acceptance. Inevitably, therefore, some fortuitous "mistakes" would slip between the cracks. Producing *The Best Years of Our Lives* placated William Wyler, the director and made Samuel Goldwyn feel respected.

Today's media and entertainment corporations are vastly more sophisticated and imperial than the studios of old Hollywood. The men who control them—Rupert Murdoch of News Corporation (Fox) or Sumner Redstone of Viacom—have no sense of cultural inferiority and are utterly disinterested in imposing any personal predilections of tastes or sophistication. Their only mantra is stockholder value, which translated, means personal aggrandizement. Their top executives sign on with that understanding. Hence the corporate objective is, not to engage public tastes, but rather to re-shape them. When the $100 million campaign for a new blockbuster blasts off world wide, the aim is to infiltrate every vein and artery of the popular culture. The mass marketers don't need to detect an appetite for their particular project; they feel they can create that appetite.

It is this sort of cultural arrogance that is responsible for the decline not only in the quality of product but also for the decline in the aspirations of those creating that product. If filmmakers once complained about the tyranny of the Hollywood studio chief, that was nothing compared with the tyranny of the marketing mavens. Under the "ancient regime," those fortuitous "accidents" could penetrate the system; under the new world order, they are few and far between.

Those "voices" that ignited the great hits of the past are now, more than ever, voices in the wilderness.

Bibliography

Andrew, Geoff. *Stranger Than Paradise*. New York: Limelight Editions, 1999.

Andrews, Bart. *Lucy & Ricky & Fred & Ethel*. New York: Dutton Publishing, 1977.

Barabas, Suzanne, and Gabor Barabas. *Gunsmoke: A Complete History*. Jefferson, NC: McFarland & Company, 1990.

Becker, Edith, and Kevin Burns. "Empire of Dreams: The Story of the Star Wars Trilogy"; Documentary. *Star Wars* Trilogy Boxset DVD (1977–1983), 2004.

Berg, Scott. *Goldwyn, a Biography*. New York: Riverhead Books, 1993.

Bianculli, David. *Dictionary of Teleliteracy*. Continuum Publishing Co, 1996.

Biskind, Peter. *Easy Riders, Raging Bulls*. New York: Touchstone Books, 1998.

Bonann, Gregory J., and Brad Alan Lewis. *Baywatch: Rescued From Prime Time*. California: New Millennium Entertainment, 2000.

Brooks, Tim, and Earle Marsh. *The Complete Directory to Prime Time Network and Cable TV Shows: 1946–Present*, 8th ed. New York: Ballantine Books, 2003.

Brownlow, Kevin. *The Parade's Gone By*. New York: Random House, 1976.

Cagle, Jess. "Lure of the Rings." *Time*, December 2, 2002.

Caldwell, Erskine. *Conversations With Erskine Caldwell*. Jackson: University Press of Mississippi, 1988.

Caldwell, Erskine. *Erskine Caldwell: Selected Letters, 1929–1955*. Jefferson, NC: McFarland & Company, 1999.

Caldwell, Erskine. *Tobacco Road*. Lightyear Press, 1981.

Doughan, David. *A Biographical Sketch*. tolkiensociety.org

Dowd, Nancy, and David Shepard. *King Vidor*. Lanham, MD: Scarecrow Press, 1988.

Fingeroth, Danny, and Stan Lee (Foreword). *Superman on the Couch: What Superheroes Really Tell Us About Ourselves and Our Society*. New York: Continuum International Publishing Group, 2004.

Fonda, Peter. *Don't Tell Dad: A Memoir*. New York: Hyperion Books, 1998.

Griffith, D. W. *The Man Who Invented Hollywood: The Autobiography of D. W. Griffith.* James Hart, ed. Louisville, KY: Touchstone Publishing Co., 1972.

Hanson, John Stag. "The Man Who Killed King Kong." In *Movies International,* 1, no. 2 (1966).

Harmetz, Aljean. *Round Up the Usual Suspects.* New York: Hyperion, 1992.

Herman, Jan. *A Talent for Trouble: The Life of Hollywood's Most Acclaimed Director, William Wyler.* New York: Da Capo Books, 1997.

Haver, Ronald. "Commentary." *King Kong,* Criterion Collection DVD.

Hirsch, Julia Antopol. *The Sound of Music: The Making of America's Favorite Movie.* New York: McGraw-Hill, 1965.

Holson, Laura M. "Process: A Franchise Fantasy." *New York Times Magazine,* November 3, 2003.

Johnson, Hillary, and Nancy Rommelmann. *The Real Real World.* New York: MTV Books, 1995.

Koch, Howard. *Casablanca: Script and Legend.* New York: Overlook Press, 1992.

Krohn, Katherine E. *Oprah Winfrey (A&E Biography).* Minneapolis, MN: Lerner Publications, 2001.

Lang, Robert, ed. *The Birth of a Nation.* New Brunswick, NJ: Rutgers University Press, 1994.

Lenning, Arthur. "Myth and Fact: The Reception of *The Birth of a Nation.*" *Film History: An International Journal,* June 2004.

MacQueen, Scott. "Old King Kong Gets a Face Lift." *American Cinematographer,* January 1989.

Martin, Mick, and Marsha Porter. *DVD & Video Guide 2005.* New York: Ballantine, 2005.

McClay, Michael, and Deanna Gaffner-McClay. *I Love Lucy: The Complete Picture History of the Most Popular TV Show Ever.* New York: Warner Books, 1995.

Oppenheimer, Jess, and Gregg Oppenheimer. *Laughs, Luck . . . and Lucy: How I Came to Create the Most Popular Sitcom of All Time.* Syracuse, NY: Syracuse University Press, 1996.

Peel, John. *Gunsmoke Years.* Las Vegas, NV: Pioneer Books, Inc., 1989.

Sanders, Coyne Steven, and Tom Gilbert. *Desilu: The Story of Lucille Ball and Desi Arnaz.* New York: William Morrow & Co., 1993.

Schickel, Richard. *The Disney Version.* New York: Simon & Schuster, 1985.

Schickel, Richard. *D.W. Griffith: An American Life.* New York: Simon & Schuster, 1984.

Schickel, Richard, and Ivan R. Dee. *The Men Who Made the Movies.* Chicago: Value Publishing, 1976.

Shapiro, Marc. *Baywatch: The Official Scrapbook.* California: Boulevard, 1996.

Sibley, Brian. *The Making of the Movie Trilogy.* New York: Houghton Mifflin, 2002.

Sklar, Robert. *Movie-Made America: A Cultural History of American Movies:* New York: Vintage Books, 1994

Thomson, David. *The New Biographical Dictionary of Film.* New York: Knopf, 2004.

Vidal, Gore. *Palimpsest: A Memoir.* New York: Random House, 1995.

Vidor, King. *A Tree is a Tree.* New York: Samuel French Books, 1953.

Wallace, Lew. *Lew Wallace: An Autobiography.* New York: Harper & Brothers, 1906.